NEW YORK STATE

GHOSTS

Volume Two

David Pitkin

Also by David Pitkin

Ghosts of the Northeast

Haunted Saratoga County

Spiritual Numerology: Caring for Number One

New York State Ghosts Volume 1

AURORA PUBLICATIONS
E-MAIL ADDRESS:
pitkinaurora@aol.com

NEW YORK STATE

GHOSTS

Volume Two

David J. Pitkin

Aurora Publications
Chestertown, New York

NEW YORK STATE GHOSTS
Copyright © September 2008
by David J. Pitkin

Aurora Publications
P.O. Box 690
Chestertown, NY 12817

E-Mail: pitkinaurora@aol.com
URL: www.afterworld.info

PUBLICATION DATA

Pitkin, David J. 1939-
New York State Ghosts, Volume 2
ISBN 978-0-9663925-6-2
Published September 2008

1. Ghosts   2. New York State   3. Haunted Houses
4. Folklore   5. History

Library of Congress Control Number: 2006904143

Cover Photo: *The Old Walloon Church*
Huguenot Street Historic Site, New Paltz, NY

Table of Contents

Preface

A haunted house. Forty years ago, that term seemed silly to me, likely referring to a child's object of entertainment or a fantasy. Then I had my first experience: not a sighting but rather a hearing of feet walking on a hayloft floor that no longer existed. Learning soon afterward that the loft had been the scene of a decades-ago suicide by hanging, I felt compelled to decide whether the sounds of footsteps that I heard really were foolish or imagined. If genuine, was I brave enough to follow where my curiosity led? Could it be that ghosts were possible? The quest for that answer had no discernible goal except to expand my own understanding. Today, I'm glad that I chose to pursue that provocation, as it has affected my entire understanding of life.

Since 1968 I have walked through spirits and have had them walk or drift through me. I have been physically touched by invisible beings and have heard conversations, sometimes ambient and sometimes addressed to me. I sometimes catch smells sent to me by identifiable deceased loved ones, and several times have seen individuals who were there one minute and vanished in the next. I even gave a ride to a hitchhiker who vanished in an instant after leaving my car. There have been a number of dreams of deceased friends and relatives—experiences so vivid or profound that I'm sure they were not the product of my imagination or repressed desires to maintain contact beyond the veil of death. In spite of all these experiences, I do not consider myself any more gifted or different from those who read my books or who supply me with story leads.

In these past four decades, my understanding of ghosts has expanded to encompass quite an exciting prospect, namely that death is only the dropping of our hardware (in computer jargon), while our software and programming continue on into what can only be called other planes of existence. It seems certain that death has what might be termed "a therapeutic value" for our souls or spirits. Though many educated people believe that they comprehend the fullness of life, others (visionaries or adept seekers) claim to have penetrated much farther into the "Summerland" of continuing life.

So, then, if we are to fully comprehend death, I believe we must understand the profundity of the life experience. Researching ghost stories has prompted me to dig more deeply into the potential meaning of our brief span of life and whether or not it can truly end. Since our life energy is a form of matter, and because science tells us that matter can neither be created nor destroyed but only transformed, the sting of death may not be that bad at all. And, as I have just hinted, bodily death may indeed be necessary for our growth as eternal beings; in a dimension, time, or place where our consciousness can be re-formed and re-evaluated. Research in Western parapsychology asserts that the death of the body likely is not the end of our consciousness—a theme promoted for millennia in Eastern cultures.

The continuity of life in some form has traditionally been the province of the world's religions, each seeking to inspire and connect (or re-connect) humanity to the Source of All Life, commonly known as God. Nevertheless, science (which many religious folk once felt was opposed to the concept of a deity) is providing much research on subtle energies and on the nature of consciousness, dreams, bioelectric fields and even on the essence of time.

Stories that once were ignored by Western media and tossed in the newsroom waste basket now often become syndicated feature stories, spread around the world. Consider this incident from 1992.

On April 10th of that year, on U.S. Route 95 outside Needles, California, singer, actor and performer Sam Kinison's Pontiac Firebird was struck head-on by the pickup truck of a young man who had been drinking. Why Kinison took that route instead of his usual shortcut through Laughlin, Nevada, was never determined. Kinison and his new wife, Malika Souiri, were being tailed by two of Kinison's friends, Carl LaBove and J. J. Wall, in a van.

In the minutes after witnessing the collision, the friends quickly turned onto the shoulder of the road and jumped out, where they saw Kinison struggling from the wreck. LaBove rushed to his friend's side and propped up Kinison, who didn't seem to be seriously injured. The actor appeared to be staring down the highway in the direction from which he had just come, then suddenly spoke to someone, though LaBove knew it wasn't him, "No, not now," Kinison said laughing. Then in another minute, he chuckled again and said, "No, not yet," almost in a pleading tone. He laughed once more, then sagged perceptibly and said, "Okay, okay," whereupon he died immediately in his friend's arms. What forces were at work there, invisible to the two friends and Kinison's injured wife? It is my guess, based on dozens of interviews with near-death experiencers, that the welcoming committee from the other side appeared to Sam, as they will for us all. I do not believe that anyone dies alone.

It is these numerous strange encounters with death that many are reported to have in the United States, in Iraq or Afghanistan, or in regions covered by foreign news sources which keep me fascinated with peoples' end-of-life experiences. There no longer is any question for me about the vital part of us surviving the cessation of our body's operations. I believe that, eventually, we are given a succession of bodies in which we can develop personalities with which to understand the essential one-ness of the universe and finally accept our being in that.

There appears to be a loneliness or desperation in many departed spirits, some uncompleted task, some unhappy relationship still to be made right, some victory still to be won. All of these are only apparent tasks as, lacking bodies with which to finish those jobs, the present game is over and the conscious being must leave the physical world in order to review its past, learning from a debriefing done with the aid of angels, spirit guides or enlightened individuals. I have come to believe that there is an analysis (a last judgment for each personality) in which the deceased must participate. When all the work of each persona has gone as far as it might, the old body is laid down, a review of the experiences is completed, and then we pass into light once more for reassignment.

Though the manner of death might be repulsive, the beauty of our opportunities remains. For that reason, treat others in the world of spirit as you would treat your living loved ones. Offer a hand (even to the point of telling them they are dead and must now move on) where and when you can. If these are difficult spirits, not anxious to leave, get someone with power to send them on their way. There is no need to fear the remains of someone's life. Compassion on earth and in spirit is the only way out for both the living and the dead.

David J. Pitkin
Chestertown, New York
August 2008

CHAPTER 1

HAUNTED HOUSES

A BAD LUCK HOUSE
A BUSY PLACE
A HOUSE, NOT A HOME
A LIFETIME OF EXPERIENCES
A STITCH IN TIME
A WORKING MAN'S HOUSE
CARRYING ON
FAMILY TIES
HIGH STREET IN GOSHEN
HOLDOVERS
IN A NEW HOUSE
JESSIE BELLE
JOHN
LINGERING
MAE
OLD FARMER
STILL ACTIVE
THE JUDGE
THE VISITORS
THE WETMORE-SMITH HOUSE
THINGS WERE POPPING
WATCHING JONATHAN

Bad Luck House

Laurel House

This is one of the hardest luck stories I've ever interviewed, not that I believe the world is governed by luck. But, I don't know how to account for the goings-on there. If these events were happening today, I would bring several investigators into the place to see what could be sensed in regard to ambient energies. Surely the following events must result from what one can only call negative energy. But whose? And from where?

Carrie Anderson once lived in a nice bungalow on Birch Drive in Laurel, a modest community on Long Island's North Fork. It is a pretty area and my trips to the area lead me to believe that North Forkers are among the most blessed in the state when it comes to natural beauty. However, what took place in Carrie's house was anything but beautiful. These events would require any resident to search relentlessly for a philosophy that can encompass it all.

"My parents bought the house when I was three years old, and we lived there for seven years," she remembered. "So, I saw and heard all these events from a child's perspective, but the memories remain powerful to this day. My dad's father had died in a truck accident shortly before we moved in, so I guess our family was still grieving at the time, but I don't think that fact can explain why a series of seeming disasters began in and around the house.

"Not long after my sister was born, three years later, I became ill with a hernia and then an appendectomy. As I was recovering, I remember Mom putting baby Cindy in her little baby chair on the kitchen counter, and as soon as Mom turned away for a second, the entire chair moved across the shelf and off, dumping my sister on the floor. Cindy wasn't seriously hurt, but I was mystified as to how such a thing could happen. A few years later, Chet, Jr. was born, but I remember that he was always ill with some problem."

Shortly after that, Carrie's dad, a trucker, was severely burned on his leg while gassing up a tractor. "Soon after that," she recalled, "I was riding my scooter on the sidewalk and tumbled into a pit, where I received serious cuts and bruises. I still can't understand how that happened.

"We had a little dog that all of us kids loved. One day, the puppy disappeared and we found it a short time later, hung up in a tree that bordered our neighbor's property. We had no question but that he had killed our pet and then displayed it terribly, just to provoke us. We took the little dog down and buried him. Not long after that, however, I heard a dog howling in the night and, you know how people know their pet's sounds? That was the howl of our dead dog, which stunned me, because I didn't know that some part of an animal can survive death. Later, I had to speculate whether or not the same was true for people.

"Not only were members of my family continually sick, but it also seems that anyone who came near our house on Birch Drive, suffered in some way too. Dad had gotten ahold of an old iron pump and painted it up, then merged it into our front yard lamp post. A neighborhood kid, riding a bicycle, came down the street and ran into it, resulting in a broken leg. You see what I mean? These are all so way out of the ordinary things!

Another event was the day that we saw a car drive slowly down our street, which was a dead end. He wasn't anyone we knew, so it seemed clear that he'd taken a wrong turn or some such thing, and sure enough, as I watched from the living room window, I saw him turn around, but then come roaring back up the street, up over the curb and onto our front lawn, directly at the picture window. We feared that he would crash through the wall. Stunned and unable to move, I saw the car get closer and closer, to the point where I could see the driver's very red face. He looked like a devil to me. Sliding to a stop on our ripped-up lawn, he circled and then sped off. We never got his license number. Who would do such an uncaring thing? Why?

"And snakes! There was a pond out back which must have attracted them, as they would be all over our front yard and got into Dad's lawn sprinkler pipes. Why so many snakes? Why all the time?" she puzzled.

Carrie's mother had had enough and, being of Italian heritage, she called the parish priest to come bless their house and yard, as it surely must be under a curse of some type. No one yet used "the g word," however. The ceremony didn't seem to help, and the family's drug store bills continued to mount.

"I remember, with all the continuing problems, that things came to a head shortly after the blessing. [It should be noted here, that a blessing of the house isn't guaranteed to make everything wonderful again. If a house is infested with unhappy or mean spirits, they can take offense at the attempt to spiritually evict them, and strike out even more forcefully at those who threaten to send them into the cosmos. Nevertheless, families must try blessings as a necessary first step inreclaiming their lives.]

"I never liked sleeping upstairs in the house, either," Carrie continued. When Cindy was small, she usually slept there because she was only two or three at the time, but she was able to sleep all night. Some part of me seems to have stayed awake, though," Carrie continued, "as, when I had to sleep upstairs one night, I was so edgy and fretful that Mom had to come into the bedroom and lay down beside me. I was comforted by her presence and drifted off to sleep. I woke suddenly, though, when I heard loud scratching on the back of the bed's headboard. It was impossible for anyone to get back there and scratch because the headboard was up against the wall. Mom was right there beside me, but her eyes were closed—apparently she was asleep, so I woke her and told her of the scary sounds, but she couldn't hear anything. The scratching was so loud and ominous, how could she not hear it? Nevertheless, I don't think she doubted me. In any case, our family moved soon afterward, and I was able to leave all that turmoil and fear behind me. What a childhood!" she exclaimed with humor. Still, I could see how powerfully she is affected forty years later.

"I tried to keep in touch with what was going on at our old house," she told me. "Sometimes I feared that so many of these things had just been coincidences or that I'd imagined them. Secretly, I think I was also afraid that the ghost or spirit might move with us, though it didn't. Then I heard about the people who bought the house from my parents. The husband died soon after they moved in, and I have always wondered if it was from fright, or was it just another of those "accidents" that seemed to plague the house.

A Busy Place

"Even today, looking back, I can't believe it all happened in just over a year," Pat Burget told me. She referred to her brief residence at 191 Harrison Avenue in Kenmore, part of Greater Buffalo. "My father remarried a few years after my mother died, and they bought that house on Harrison Avenue. Dad died in 1970, so it soon became my husband's and my house. We slept in my parents' old bedroom downstairs, and my husband made the upstairs into two bedrooms.

"We had a little boy three years of age at the time, and one evening he came down to our bedroom, saying, 'Mom, that man in my bedroom scared me.' So we let him sleep in a sleeping bag on our bedroom rug. There couldn't have been a man upstairs, because my husband slept right beside me, so we chalked it up to our son's restlessness or imagination." But that didn't suffice for long.

Gradually, Pat and her sister, Cheryl, who lived in the house, began to suspect that someone else resided in that house, especially after the party. "My sister threw a party for her friends at our house, and in the course of the evening, one of the girls became sleepy and went into our bedroom to catch just a wink of sleep on our bed. Not too long afterward, she came out the bedroom door with a strange, part terrified and part puzzled look on her face. She kept looking back into the open bedroom door. Then she told us an almost unbelievable story.

"She had just gotten comfy on the bed when she felt another presence in the room, and felt someone enter and lay down on the bed behind her. She brushed the person away and asked to be left alone, but nothing or nobody moved. She rose up on an elbow and looked at the other side of the bed, only to find it empty. There was, however, an indentation in the bedspread, as if someone had just been there. But it was none of us. More and more, we began to think we had a ghost.

"So, it came as no surprise," she told me, "when relatives came to visit and were given that bedroom. Later, they told us of closing and locking the bedroom door, but being awakened in the night by the sound of footsteps in the room. It was too dark to see, but the footsteps continued, not even pausing to open the door, but they could hear them continue, without a break in stride, on the outside of the door!"

Her sister had the larger of the bedrooms upstairs, but that chamber was also plagued by former residents who wouldn't admit or didn't suspect that their tenure had ended. Cheryl usually locked the door (not that a genuine ghost is ever bothered by such things) when she went to sleep, but usually found the door chain either disconnected and loose, or broken and on the floor in the morning. Some ghosts are determined to keep up their former life. As they tend to operate mainly in their own reality, they often don't seem to see or acknowledge the living. Perhaps, whatever reality they are in, they often get puzzled by who keeps locking the door. Do you think they bawl one another out because of that?

Cheryl allowed one of her friends to use the room when she was away on a trip. The friend came downstairs to ask Pat why there was no ashtray in the room. Pat assured the woman that there was one there, and even went upstairs to show her where it was. However, once in the room, it became clear that the ashtray was missing. Where might Cheryl have put it? "We looked all over," Pat laughed, "and then we found it, smashed to pieces, behind a vanity. Cheryl wouldn't have done that and our guest hadn't, so was some former owner of the house against smoking?"

"One of the most frequent experiences that I had in our year there was in the kitchen. I'd feel an energy suddenly enter the room behind me and I would turn, though nobody ever was there. Maybe the scariest incident was the night that something woke me. I was a pretty light sleeper then, and especially if it was the noise of our kids, I'd be sure to hear it. Nevertheless, when I opened my eyes, or tried to, there was nothing to see. It was pitch-black and cold in the bedroom. It was as if my eyes just wouldn't work right. Then I heard a gravely voice say, 'Can you eat?' I wasn't hungry. I didn't need to eat. My husband hadn't said it, and I just didn't know what it meant. I still don't. I woke my husband, but he denied anything strange was going on, and went back to sleep. He didn't hear or see a thing."

Cheryl recalled feeling so anxious that she feared she was having a heart attack. "I prayed like I never prayed before. Who or what was there? Why couldn't my eyes work right? Why wouldn't my husband agree that something very odd was going on? After I had prayed a while, suddenly the feeling of the presence ended and everything was normal again, and the cold vanished.

"One other witness to the oddities in that house was my younger sister, who, along with me, heard a man cough in our family room, though there was no man there.

"Not too long afterward, due to changes in our life, we sold the house and moved. Was it all in our imagination, as my husband thought? Or had we peered into some other world, where former owners never die, but just keep doing what they always did? I've never heard any other stories from that house in the thirty years that we've been gone."

I believe this story illustrates how determined to "carry on as usual" it can be for specters who aren't sure they have died. They need someone to tell them directly that their body has died, though that is not all there is to life. Willingness to surrender to a higher power or reality seems to have its own beauty and peace.

5

A House, Not a Home

"The house was a typical residence on the west side of Binghamton," Tammy remembers, "and it was home to my new friend, Arlene, when we met in fourth grade in 1985 after her family had come from Texas. It was a strange place, and whenever I visited there I was never fully comfortable with the thick drapes and clutter that reminded me so much of a funeral home. For me, there was an oppressive feeling at all times. Then I was invited for a sleep over. It wasn't the normal sleepover that young girls have because the interior was creepy—there was a sense that something oppressive was there, and I couldn't sleep.

"Five years later, when we were fourteen, a group of us friends, more daring now, decided to use a Ouija board to contact whatever spirits were moving things around inside the house. I had been given the board as a game, and we were curious. Arlene once had witnessed a kitchen knife flip from the counter onto the floor all by itself. She picked it up and put it back, she told us, but found it on the floor again just a few minutes later."

Tammy was surprised by the actions, or non-actions, to be exact, of Arlene's parents, who were devout Catholics. "They had many statues of Jesus, Mary and the saints on shelves and on the walls, which were also adorned with rosaries. Sometimes her family members would enter a room and find all the statues piled in the center of the floor; nobody would admit to doing it. On another occasion, Arlene's father witnessed the icons falling from their shelves, yet these didn't break upon hitting the floor. Sometimes the father would return the fallen statues to their spots, only to witness them tumbling a short time afterward. Yet, the parents never sought the cause of these strange events and seldom even mentioned them." Curious, too, that they never felt empowered to deal with what clearly was abnormal. The new residence saw her parents increasingly cranky and cantankerous with one another.

The big old farmhouse at 2 Seminary Avenue had originally been a single-family home, in the center of a great farm during the 1800s. Over the years since, however, it had been divided into upstairs and downstairs apartments. Arlene's grandmother owned the property and lived upstairs when Arlene's family migrated there from Texas in 1985, at which point, the grandmother rented the ground floor to the new arrivals. Even grandmother had her experiences with the ghosts, however. Her deceased husband had been a cigar smoker, and she sometimes could smell cigar smoke upstairs. It didn't bother her that much, as she just assumed it was her dead husband. But could the grandfather have been the cause of all the moving objects? And why did Arlene's parents fight all the time? They had never done so in Texas.

"One night, Arlene and her sister moved upstairs with Grandma, and slept in the front bedroom there," Tammy continued, "but Arlene was roused from a deep sleep by the sound of someone calling her name. Her sudden movement woke her sister. The two girls sat up in bed to see a tall, dark figure standing at the end of their bed. While it didn't move or threaten them, they knew it wasn't Grandma, so they ran from the room. With Grandma in tow, they came back to the bedroom a few minutes later, only to find the figure gone. Figuring it was an intruder, Arlene's father and grandfather made a careful search of the entire building, but without any result.

"Years afterward, when Arlene and I discussed those incidents, I could see why it seemed plausible that we could game our way to a better understanding the situation twenty years before, though the Ouija board gave us no visible results. Nevertheless, after that Ouija session I seldom felt comfortable inside that house, and usually waited on the porch for Arlene to come outside.

"At that time I didn't know that Arlene's parents had asked a Catholic priest to do a house blessing, which he did, though it never curbed those odd happenings," she told me.

By the early 1990s, the house's condition had deteriorated, as had the health of Arlene's parents who were severely ill and in need of an assisted living residence. Grandmother and Grandfather had died and Arlene's sister had returned to Texas. Arlene had moved to New York City and sought tenants for the old house, which she now owned. As the neighborhood had deteriorated, someone was needed to keep an eye on the property and do light maintenance, so that workmen who Arlene planned to hire could initially renovate the first floor, then the second. "I was a single mother in need of a cheap apartment, and Arlene immediately thought of me," said Tammy.

"Yet, the minute that I moved in, I recognized that something was very strange, though it was rent-free. In spite of my childhood discomfort in that house, something seemed more actively wrong, and I knew I'd never call it home, and when I could afford to, I'd leave Seminary Avenue. With an empty downstairs, my seven-year-old and I moved into the upstairs. My son had never had difficulty sleeping, but right away, he chose to not sleep in his bedroom; often I'd find him on the living room couch in the morning. When I asked him about the situation, he said that someone was watching him in that bedroom. It was a large room and had three windows, so I thought maybe he was seeing shadows cast by passing traffic. The room had once been a kitchen and still had cupboards and a counter, as well as a washing machine, though the other appliances had been removed. I tried to get him to return and sleep in his room, but he refused.

"One evening, as I sat on the couch, watching television, I spotted one of my cats sitting on the landing that led downstairs to the lower apartment and the front door. I had discouraged the cats from going down there, as I feared they might get into that apartment and then might flee to the outdoors through one of those broken windows. I glanced down to ponder how I should handle it, but only a few seconds later, when I looked up again, the cat wasn't there. I have three kitties, and knew one of them had been there. Yet, I looked around the room and found two cats curled up together, asleep in the rocking chair. It had to be the third one then, I decided, but I found him asleep behind me on top of the couch. It wasn't any of them! But it was somebody's cat. Could we have a ghost cat living with us? I never figured it out, though I was certain I had seen a cat coming up those stairs.

"A few months later, Jason, my fiancé moved in with us. We had been friends for years and always got along fine, yet almost as soon as he began to live there, we started quarreling—over little things. It seemed as if we couldn't agree on anything, and the two of us sat down to try understanding it. What had gotten into us? All we could do is write it off as adjustment problems, which we expected to work out. One day, he was in the basement looking for a tool, though he was unable to find it. He was getting ready to explode when he heard a quiet voice tell him to turn around and look, and there he found the tool. He knew it wasn't me whispering, and came up out of that cellar like a shot. He never went back down as long as we lived there," Tammy said during our interview in May 2008.

"Unknown to us at the time," Tammy continued, "Arlene had contacted several parapsychology groups in the Triple Cities area, to see if they would come and investigate the phenomena. But none of them would come without seeing and hearing a videotape or tape recording of the strange events. She told me in later years that she had feared to videotape or audio tape any of the goings-on herself, for fear of retribution by the spirit or spirits."

Arlene, taking stock of what would rent well in Binghamton, decided to convert the old house into student quarters, which were badly needed in the city, so she hired a contractor to do the conversion. The man worked downstairs during the daytime, tearing out the kitchen cabinets and counter on the first floor and removing the old ceilings there. "Strangely, once the downstairs work began, I noticed many odd events in my upstairs apartment," Tammy continued. "Often, I'd hear someone call my name from another room, but when I entered, whoever was there told me it hadn't been them! Years later, Arlene told me that members of her family had experienced the same type of event. Then I began to find bats in the apartment every week; at the same time I had a lot of light bulbs blowing out. What on earth was up? Then I'd find my locked doors unlocked in the mornings. Only years afterward, when we talked about these experiences did I learn that Arlene's family had encountered such things. She just hadn't told me when these were going on. Her family had changed the locks several times, thinking they were faulty."

She told me of a short period in which she feared to drop off to sleep in her bedroom, and had to go out to the couch in order to get any sleep. Her son, by this time, had vacated the couch and was sleeping in a sleeping bag on her bedroom floor. "I discovered that the room that my fiancé and I slept in had been the room where Arlene and her sister had seen the dark figure," Tammy told me. It was with a sense of relief for her that the contractor finished the downstairs and, by her agreement with Arlene, Tammy, Jason and her son now had to find other quarters. "We found a nice house that I could afford to rent and we moved out at the same time as the big flood in Binghamton. Eventually, when the owner put that house on the market, we moved to our new home," she added.

"Though we now had a new place to rent, the water tank and other plumbing had to be replaced before we could use the shower there. So, we'd drive over to Arlene's house to take showers, we decided. On the first day, when Jason went alone, he came back quickly to complain how creepy it was to be all alone at the Seminary Avenue house. 'Next time I go, I'm taking the dog with me for company,' he said. This struck me as strange, causing me to remember that I'd hung a crucifix on the apartment wall on the day we left, instructing Jason not to remove it until we were finally and officially gone. In retrospect, I don't know what made me say or do those things because I'm not strictly religious.

"The next day, I went over to the old house to shower alone. While the shower was running, I had just rinsed my face and turned around, when I saw a dark figure that appeared to be a young adult man wearing an old style wide-brimmed hat, like that of the Shakers or Amish," she grimaced. "He was peeking into the shower at me! I ran out the other side of the shower and into the next room, where I turned to confront the man. Nobody was there. Then I paused to evaluate what I had just seen. It had been a dark shadow, but it had no features. Yet, in some way, I knew it had been looking at me. Though the shadowy man had made no effort to hurt me, I was never able to shower there again."

Jason did return one last time, taking their dog with him for company. When he returned to their new house, he carried the small crucifix and told her there was no reason to ever return to 2 Seminary Avenue. "I asked him if something had happened, but he evaded me just by saying that he'd rather go a week without showering than ever venture into that house again. Even the dog had been upset there and had stayed very close to her fiancé. "From then on, my son slept very well in his own room, Jason and I almost never had a disagreement after that, and we had a new baby. Life is good," she smiled.

It turned out that life wasn't that good for Arlene, however. Tammy said that the construction costs began to exceed Arlene's budget, and she put the house on the market, not knowing or understanding what Tammy and Jason had experienced there. The one time that Arlene did come up to Binghamton and entered the Seminary Avenue house, she was overcome with feelings of sickness and dread. She spent her remaining time in the city with her parents at their new assisted living residence.

That old house needed a blessing, Arlene quickly decided, and she found a Catholic priest who agreed to come and bless the house. However, when the cleric got to the front porch, he declined to enter any further and went away, saying that, as a man of God, he couldn't enter and complete the task. She then asked her old Greek Orthodox parish priest from Binghamton to do the work, but when the two entered the building, they found much graffiti on the upstairs walls, not just names and slogans but satanic symbols painted in bright red. Nevertheless, the priest completed his assignment happily.

It was all too much for Arlene and, as she had no desire to return to the house, she put it on the real estate market for sale "as is." It sold within the week to a property dealer, who likely knew a bargain when he saw it. Whatever happened, however, the house still sits, again deteriorating slowly, with no occupants, and it appears to be abandoned.

My analysis is that, while there may have been ambient spirits in the house when Arlene's grandmother bought it, nobody ever dealt with them from the beginning. Perhaps the grandmother or grandfather eventually joined the throng, but again, no one ever knew how to send these souls into the light. Nobody needs to entertain ghosts. They are not a cute atmospheric adornment for a house, and all residents and family members, deserve to live in untroubled peace. The accumulated negativity there made an easy access for mindless and anarchic Satanists.

I continue my mission of urging ghost hosts to seek professional help when needed, and to send unwelcome spirits away, back to their source. Once a building gets a reputation for ghosts, uneducated and uncaring individuals (most of whom stand a good chance of becoming miserable ghosts themselves when they pass) will enter and make the situation even worse. Ghosts aren't playthings. If you truly love the human race and the Creator, send them away into light. Number Two Seminary Avenue was a situation which continued to get worse because nobody knew what to do.

The long-ago use of the Ouija, which the naïve teens thought was a game, may actually have attracted more low-vibration entities into the house than were already present. With Ouija, one opens a door to "whoever." Does anyone ever tell the board users that a door must be closed at the end of such sessions? Would you leave your front door open all night? Young people, not seeing the entry of a discarnate (or a horde of them) assume that nothing happens. Ask Arlene.

A Lifetime of Experiences

"I have lived in three different houses with spirits," Richard told me. "I grew up in Elmira and encountered the first one when I lived on Ovid Street, not far from Woodlawn Cemetery. It was a place that my wife and I rented for eight years, and the ghost was so regular that I could almost set my watch by him."

In our interview, he admitted that he had had a number of premonitions, such as the tsunami that struck Indonesia, the likelihood of the racehorse Barbaro breaking his leg, knowing when family members died, and when women relatives were pregnant. Others have told him that he is psychic, but his response to that is matter-of-fact. He knows what he has experienced, and calmly accepts it.

"In the Ovid Street house, we often heard the screen door slam. Now, we had a screen door, but not a wooden one, which is what I heard banging away almost every night. Then there were the footsteps, which traveled through the living room, dining room and kitchen and down the basement stairs. Sometimes we would hear the steps coming back up, but then they would stop for the night. I had known the family who lived in that house when I was a kid, and ran into one of their sons at a church festival. I don't think he was surprised when I told him about the footsteps. He told me that a man in his family had hanged himself near the top of those cellar stairs. I guess he's a candidate for ghost, right?" Richard asked.

We talked a bit about suicide ghosts, and the fact that it is hard for a suicide not to engage in ghostly activity. Maybe, after death, they get to see their potential future, and that things would have turned around for them if they hadn't killed themselves. So, we can expect guilt to be a part of their energy field when they return to the old house and try to re-enact the suicide and maybe change the outcome. But, they can't. What is done is done. All the living can do for these individuals is pray for their release into the light, or find "house cleaners" or exorcists who can send the soul on its way.

"Now, after a divorce, the second place I lived, on Grove Street, was also a rental, and we only stayed there for about two months," he told me. Both my girlfriend and I felt watched by someone we couldn't see. When my son would visit us on weekends, he also claimed that someone was staring at him, and it made him nervous that he couldn't see anyone.

Some researchers who investigate body energies claim that our focused eyesight, when directed against another person, animal or object, actually exerts a subtle force, so maybe it isn't that much out of line that we can feel such an energy. Notice how pets often show discomfort when you stare at them.

Richard and his girlfriend didn't have very long to experience this entity because his landlady gave them sixty days notice, and they had to begin planning to move. "But the night she gave us notice, something very unnerving happened," Richard continued. "In the middle of the night we were awakened by a loud banging on the bedroom dresser's top. I heard the small stack of coins that I had there fall on the floor. Needless to say, we didn't sleep very well the rest of that night!" He wasn't a bit unhappy to be looking for a new apartment.

"It was always ice cold when we'd get out of the shower there," he told me, "even though the bathroom was warm, we'd run into a frigid spot just outside the bathtub. We asked the landlady if there was a ghost there, but she claimed that she knew nothing about it. Whether or not that was the truth, we never found out.

"Then, instead of renting, I found a new place—my deceased grandmother's house on Sunset Terrace in Elmira Heights. I believe that a Mrs. Whitmore had owned it first, as it wasn't that old of a house, probably built in the 1950s. Then, Grandma had lived in the house over ten years before dying there. My mother also lived there another twenty years, though she didn't die there, but in the hospital. Nevertheless, both of them were family, so I thought I'd finally found a house without a ghost," he laughed. "My girlfriend and I moved in during 2002, and I began to do some cleaning in the basement, an area that we turned into a recreation and television room.

"With the redecoration done, I sat watching TV one night and idly glanced up at the wall. I couldn't believe what I saw—it appeared to be a silhouette of a pointy-hat witch riding a broom. I called my girlfriend and, trying not to influence her, asked what she could see in that spot. 'Well, it sure looks like a witch on a broom,' she replied. When we looked again, however, the image was gone. So we went back upstairs, but had to keep returning to the basement because the TV kept turning itself on when we switched it off.

"We slept in the bedroom where Grandma had died, and on at least one occasion, I saw a dark figure standing by the bed. It didn't threaten us, but I knew it wasn't anything of this earth. Once, someone or something knocked my shot glass collection off the shelf. I think it had to be that spirit or ghost or whatever it was," he said. "Remember on Star Trek, when Scotty used the transporter, and the individuals that were coming or going were in mid-trip? That semi-person, part here and part not, was how that figure looked."

His experiences and descriptions seemed quite traditional, though not many people talk about their ghostly experiences, so how could Richard have understood all the phenomena? Perhaps people die and take a period of time to acclimate themselves to not having a body. Some remain on this plane of existence for quite a while, trying to work out some problem. Many times, their main obstacle is that they can't seem to get the living to see them or recognize that they still exist; only their body has died. When that is the reason that the spirit remains earthbound, it sure can enliven (pun intended) our lives. "I say amen to that!" Richard added.

A Stitch in Time

Gerry McDyre is a first generation Irish lady living in Scotia, New York. I had heard she was a sensitive and had some experiences with ghosts, so, on St. Patrick's Day in 2006, I interviewed her in her home on Third Street. "Yes, it's true," she said. "My father came from Donegal and my cousin from County Cork, and maybe my sensitivity comes from that bit of Ireland in me. But, of course, their idea of Heaven is clouds and harps, and that's a long way from my experiences with the other world," she laughed.

"When our family first moved into this house, my father-in-law had a heart attack and went to the hospital. We had set up a crib for the baby here, but there wasn't much other furniture. However, we felt a strong presence in the house that night. It could have been my father-in-law, getting ready to depart, because his energy is still a quiet presence here even today."

13

Gerry told me that when her older son was six he had many illnesses. In his bedroom one evening, she sensed someone in the doorway of the room and turned. "Hi, my name is Doc," a voice said, though her son didn't hear it. That was the beginning of her life in a so-called haunted house, she told me. "I never dared to tell my husband of the presence at that time. From time to time, I'd sense Doc in the upstairs, though he never came down.

"One day a friend came to visit, and upon entering, asked, 'Are you burning candles? Is it flowers? I smell something very sweet.' Off-handedly, I responded, 'Oh, that's probably just Doc.' The woman asked me who Doc was, so I told her. Boy, she broke all records in fleeing my house! The scent lingered for another two years, and then stopped. But, you know, my son rapidly got better and went for many years without any illness or injury.

"From time to time, I'd see a shadow of a large man upstairs, but I was never afraid. It was like having my own in-house physician, I figured. Then, one of my relatives in Brooklyn was hit by a truck and killed. I went there for the funeral, but when I returned, Doc was gone. He's never been back, but I'm so grateful he was here to help my son."

As time passed, Gerry realized she was sensitive to the spirit world and often agreed to help friends who had spirits in their houses. One day, her reputation got her invited to an old farmhouse up in Charlton, north of Schenectady. "It was on a back road, and I can't remember the address any more, but it was a typical old farmhouse with small windows under the eaves. We went in, and the lady of the house complained that a ghost kept upsetting her knitting, leaving yarn, needles and thread strewn all over the living room floor. She asked if I could locate the lady ghost causing the upset. I told her I'd try, but wondered why she insisted it was a lady."

First, Gerry said, she had to inform the woman that she had immediately gotten an image of two young men fighting at the foot of the stairway to the second floor. "Oh, that's my son and his friend. They do that all the time!" Gerry then understood that she could pick up on the energy of ongoing events from this plane too. "I turned toward the stairs because I could feel someone watching us from the second floor, and I went up. In a small room, I noticed three spirit women in old-fashioned dress doing the work of over a century ago. They seemed to be in their thirties and were pressing linens, making the beds, cleaning and other such chores. Among them was a child, a little girl of about age six. The adults seemed to be annoyed with the girl, as she always seemed to be underfoot.

"I had the impression that the child, whose name I couldn't get, was bored and maybe a bit mischievous. It was the little girl who was responsible

14

for throwing the knitting around downstairs. Her only relief was to go into the backyard, where a handyman named Charlie, who lived in an outbuilding, would appreciate her and chat. He was the only man around, and it seemed that the women's husbands had gone off to a war. Two of the wives were childless and the third was the little girl's mother. I saw that the child became ill and was put to bed in that small upstairs room, where she died, probably of a fever. She never left the house, and maybe doesn't even know she has died."

Back downstairs, Gerry told the homeowner about the girl, but the lady seemed quite dissatisfied, claiming that the ghost had to be an adult woman. It is possible that the owner was more attuned to one of the women spirits on the second floor, if they were actual spirits and not just "house memories." But, nevertheless, Gerry was certain that the tantrum in the sewing room was the little girl's fault. "Make a little rag doll for her," Gerry urged. "When the child is seeking something to play with, she will have a toy. I think the little girl is buried quite near this house. The women from this building's past are just doing what they can with what they have in their lives. There were wartime shortages in their time, you know? So, let's work with what you have here—make her a doll."

As in the case of so many hauntings, Gerry asked the owner if she wanted the ghost child sent away. "Oh, no!" the lady replied, in the manner of many homeowners who have grown emotionally attached to their unseen guests. Many homeowners like to complain of a presence, but then seem reluctant to send an "old friend" on his or her way.

"A few weeks later, I asked how the situation in the sewing room was going," Gerry said, "and I learned that the ruckus had stopped. In fact, the object that was now moving was the little rag doll. Every few weeks, it was found in a new location. The homeowner finally seemed happy to be able to help. And, as far as I know, the little girl is still there, playing happily with her toy and in no hurry to move on into the world of bright light," Gerry concluded with a big smile.

A Working Man's House

"I once lived in Olean," Lorrene told me, "at 417 North 7th Street. Years before it had been a working man's house, and today I suspect that he still comes to visit. I wasn't a great believer in ghosts back in 1981, though I didn't rule them out. Little did I know, however, that this house was going to make me a confirmed believer," she smiled.

15

"It was an old, two-story, single-family house that was being converted into upstairs and downstairs apartments. My roommate and I lived downstairs where the renovations had already been done, though nobody lived upstairs, as the work still had to be completed up there. Soon after moving in, at about 10:00 p.m., I was getting ready for my job on the third shift and stood in front of my closet, picking out an outfit. Suddenly, from upstairs I heard a crooning sound, a muffled singing or humming, plus the sound of a rocking chair moving back and forth. That's impossible, I said to myself, nobody lives up there! Yet, if I didn't know better, I could have sworn that a mother was rocking her baby to sleep upstairs. I immediately got goose bumps and the hair on my neck began to rise, yet I stood my ground, determined to make sense out of it. What could the explanation be? After a few minutes the sounds ceased."

Lorrene Adams told me that she spent the first few months in that apartment trying to rationalize sounds emanating from a clearly empty apartment, but to no avail. Then came the night when the roommates had retired and the downstairs apartment was quiet. From overhead came the sound of a broom falling on the floor. "It's a sound that you know from years of exposure to various noises, but I couldn't accept that someone had just dropped or thrown a broom—after all, that apartment needed lots of work and I knew it was empty. Nevertheless, in the morning I went up the stairs and opened the door. The apartment was totally empty, no broom or any other object on the floor.

"Another time, when I was in that bedroom, I heard heavy footsteps climbing the stairs on the other side of my bedroom wall. Must be the landlord coming to do some work, I surmised, and I have some questions for him anyway, so I'll catch him before he gets to work." She told me that she hurried up the back stairs to intercept the man in the overhead rooms, but when she got there, the apartment was empty. Nor was there anyone on the front stairs.

She described how her apartment in the front of the house had been modernized by the installation of a drop-ceiling, with foam panels set into a metal frame, making a neat, patterned ceiling. "In order to get to the bathroom at the rear of our apartment, however, one had to go out of the bedroom, through the living room, and then through the kitchen," she said. "One morning, though this also happened several times afterward, just as I was awakening, all the ceiling tiles over my bed fluttered, then dropped back into place. I tried to rationalize that, but found no windows or doors open. There was no air moving in the apartment and no fans turned on. Without a breeze, it would have been impossible to make those tiles move, I knew.

"Then, one day when neither my roommate nor I were cooking, we were treated to the smell of a wonderful pasta sauce. The windows weren't open and the upstairs was still unfinished—no tenant up there yet. The odor had to come from somewhere, and though it smelled like it was cooking right there on our stove, the burners were off. The next smell that I couldn't explain was that of pipe smoke. Neither of us in that apartment smoked. If I dared to let the thought coalesce, however, the easiest and probably the only possible explanation was that it was the smell of some long-ago resident's pipe. But that would mean we had a ghost! With the smell of the sauce and the heavy footsteps, I visualized an Italian guy and created the name Dom (short for Dominick) to explain the ghost person to myself. I opened the door and went into our living room and saw that room's ceiling tiles do the same progressive fluttering as I moved along."

Her sister came to visit and Lorrene didn't tell her sibling of her previous mysterious experiences. In fact, she hoped the girl didn't encounter anything at all weird, but no such luck. The girl blurted out that when she had awakened, she felt someone watching her. In fact, she either intuited or visualized the individual—a man. "From the description that my sister gave me, I realized she was describing the image of a man whose photo I had seen in an old box of accumulated junk upstairs.

"By the end of the second month, I was starting to get used to the occasional icy cold breeze blowing across my neck," she continued. "It's funny that I could pretty much tell when 'he' was going to manifest in my apartment; some days I just knew he was there, and other times I knew he was gone. But to where?

"Sometime later, I accidentally locked myself out of the apartment, but figured I could get into the upstairs apartment and then come down the back stairs and into my apartment. I went up the front stairs that ran along outside the downstairs apartment, and at the top was a small landing made from the heavy boards of an old packing crate. As I stood there trying to open that door, I noticed writing on the wood, and bent down to be sure what I was reading: Dominick Dimarco, 417 North 7th Street, Olean, NY. How had his name come to me? I tried to find out more about him, but was unable to do so, but now I seemed sure who my spirit man was," she laughed.

This is one of the questions that so many ghost encounters prompt: Who is it? Then, where do they go when they aren't in my house or apartment? My thoughts on this matter are complicated, but (if Einstein was correct and there is no time, the spirit's consciousness has simply focused in another plane of existence or some other location in what was their life. The personality of that deceased individual, I believe, still hasn't dissolved, and there seems to be a rumination that we all must experience once we have stopped being "us." It seems to be a cosmic "debriefing," where our souls re-hash all that we did and aspired to do in the just-ended life, and, likely the nature of our motivations for the actions that we took. Probably, in cosmos time, the process takes but a second. But, on our level of understanding, which we call "reality," there needs to be a linear thinking-through of cause and effect. How else can we make better choices next time?

Lorrene moved on to a new home and occupation, but she can never forget that first encounter with the uncanny world. "It sure made me realize that if ghosts are real, then I don't understand very much at all about our world," she laughed.

On my research trip, I hoped to photograph the old house and chat with neighbors or current residents, but all to no avail. The building and its neighbor had fallen into bad shape after Lorrene moved on, and they were torn down, to be replaced by a large garage. None of the current neighbors knew of the ghostly past there. Now, the working man and his legacy remain, if only as active memories in Lorrene's mind.

Carrying On

It is estimated that the average American will move at least five times in their adult life. We rent and buy our living spaces with an eye on practicality, closeness to work or schools, purchase price, etc. Nevertheless, most of us never consider the lifestyle or experiences of those who lived in this space before us, and what happiness or troubles accompanied that tenure. There are several instructive stories in this book which should make the average buyer ponder such concerns, though. Other peoples' belongings, such as antiques or heirlooms, can retain their memories or energies, forces that can occasionally manifest in ghostly activity. We leave our imprint on our living spaces as they, in turn, shape our lives. Here is a fairly uncomplicated story from Greece, New York, a Rochester suburb.

"I bought a house on Menard Street with one of my buddies in 1981, then bought him out two years later, about the time I met my future wife, Sue," Marc told me. "It was a nice little Cape Cod with about 1100 square feet—a nice 'starter home' in 1983 when my new wife, Sue, joined me." As he works in a physically demanding occupation, Marc enjoys staying in good shape and schedules regular workouts. "I had a workout space in the cellar and was exercising one evening when I heard Sue call my name from upstairs. Knocking off my activity, I hurried upstairs to ask what she wanted. 'What do I want?' she asked, 'You are the one that just called me! What was it that you wanted?' Nothing like that had ever happened before, so we chalked it up to 'house sounds' or maybe traffic noises outside, though Menard Street was a quiet thoroughfare. But that event repeated itself many more times than I can count," he laughed.

There are enough difficulties for young-marrieds adjusting to living as a couple, and this pair didn't need the added stress of ghosts in their home, though it didn't immediately occur to them that there were others there. When his tools began to disappear, seemingly never more to be found, Marc attributed that phenomenon to his forgetfulness—after all, he ran a big company and might have become absent-minded at times with business details. Still, he began to remember that when he and his buddy, Tom, lived there earlier, Tom often spotted Marc's dog, Angel, following something around the room with her eyes.

"The big eye-opener came one night when Sue and I awoke to sounds of someone noisily opening and closing our kitchen drawers. Figuring we had a break-in, I grabbed my pistol and ran stark naked down the stairs to catch the intruder. But when I got to the kitchen, everything was quiet and undisturbed, just as we had left it at bedtime. When I got back to the bedroom, Sue was fully awake and, as we discussed it, we determined that we had to have a ghost. She was more of a believer than I was, as she had an aunt who did automatic writing, what some call 'spirit writing,'" he said. "All we knew of the previous owners was that they were an older couple that divorced, placing the house on the market for us to buy."

Doors in the kitchen occasionally opened and closed themselves and the metal kitchen drawers did likewise. Then there were the voices calling out from upstairs when Marc worked out in the cellar. But the caller was never Sue. She told Marc about her aunt, who performed automatic writing, and who pronounced that there were two spirits. For a short period, the aunt maintained contact with one of them, an entity who claimed to be a farmer from Iowa. The being drew a crude picture of an old-fashioned bicycle with the large front wheel and smaller rear tire. The meaning of the bicycle, as a symbol, was never made clear; neither was the connection with Iowa, though spirits often drift to "open" people in the disembodied life, attempting to communicate some material that is very meaningful to them, or was. After the aunt's death, both Sue and her mother, having learned the communication technique, used to communicate with Auntie by automatic writing. Sue taught the method to Marc, though he never did the writing by himself.

"The second spirit," Marc said, "seemed to be a little boy. And, as little boys will, the child spirit seemed to be a prankster. When Sue and I moved out prior to selling the house, we found most of my missing tools beneath the washer and dryer, a place almost impossible for any living being to reach! After we got used to the strange house sounds, we were never bothered by the activity going on around us, and as we moved out, we even invited the ghosts to come along with us to our new house," he smiled. Such invitations are more likely to lead to trouble, I noted, because you never know who is going to come along or whether they will change their behavior.

Some years later, Marc ran into one of his former neighbors, who told him that the new owners, after him and Sue, stayed in the house for only a year after they purchased it, then put the building up for sale. Some people can live with ghosts, especially if they are tolerant and realize that most ghosts are not dangerous, just troublesome. Some people, however, believing that all spirits are demonic, just can't abide the phenomenon. "That sure was an interesting time in our life, but the ghosts didn't accompany us to our new house," Marc chuckled.

Family Ties?

"My father-in-law grew up in this 150-year-old house," Lee Briggs told me, "and he lived in the Saratoga County towns of Waterford and Halfmoon most of his life. In the 1980s he converted what had been a single family home into three apartments. I have lived in all three of those at one time or another, and today I tell you that there is something or someone invisible here."

I visited Lee at the old home on a well-traveled road in the Town of Halfmoon, just east of Clifton Park. "What goes on here, and how did you first notice that it was unusual?" I asked him.

"In 2002," he replied, "my wife, Diana, said that she kept noticing movements out of the corner of her eye, yet when she looked at those spots directly, there was nothing unusual to be seen. Maybe it was just a shadow, she suggested. Then, when we repainted our downstairs apartment and I was alone with my paint pan and roller, and heard a creaking sound out in the hallway. Was someone coming? I looked out into the hallway, but all I could see out of place was a spotlight that used to point down onto the stairs. However, now it was pointed straight upward, though nobody could have reached it and gotten away so quickly. I returned to my painting, convinced that I was just hearing things. A few minutes later, two things happened simultaneously: I heard a loud crash in the stairwell and the extension cord running out to the spotlight suddenly popped out of its plug behind me, sped past my legs and out the door. I looked out and saw that the spotlight had crashed to the floor below. How?

"When I got past my nervousness over something that 'couldn't happen,' I returned to my painting. At another time in that apartment's kitchen I heard something metallic hit the floor, and instantly, I knew the sound—it was a metal cookie sheet. I wondered how it had gotten out of a closed cupboard and walked out to the kitchen to see. But there was nothing on the floor! Nothing—cookie sheet or whatever—nothing was out of place! I opened the cupboard door and all the cookie sheets were standing where they should be. Now, this was getting serious and mysterious," he smiled.

"Activities seemed to increase, as my wife and I both noted that when we showered alone, we'd see shadows moving outside the bathtub curtain, but if we pulled the curtain aside, nobody was there. While we were trying to figure all that stuff out, a pack of muffins flew off the top of the refrigerator—it couldn't happen, but it did. On another occasion, a few months later, the freezer door on the fridge suddenly opened and a frozen roast of beef flew out and hit the floor."

Most people, when they realize that something uncanny is taking place, do one of two things: either they attempt to analyze the situation or else go into denial. Lee chose the former. He and his wife began asking questions. One lead they turned up is that a former tenant was alleged to have committed suicide in that apartment. Then his father-in-law told the pair that, when he had finished painting for the night, he heard a knock on the upstairs window (in the room that Lee had been painting when the light fell). Looking up, the father-in-law saw that the light was on in the room that he'd just left. Going upstairs, mumbling to himself because he knew he'd already shut the light off, he once more clicked the light switch and exited the house. When he looked up, the light was now off, but the man spotted a dark figure closing the curtain of that room. That was enough for one night—he kept walking away.

A visitor told them that she had once seen a woman fly out an upstairs window, as if propelled by an unseen force, though there was no historical accident record of such an activity. Other former tenants or family friends were queried and many of them had odd tales to tell, stories that they had remained mum about until now. One little boy told of seeing a man in a military uniform (though he couldn't be specific about its design or age) in the upstairs apartment when his family had lived there. "My grandfather had been in the military, though he was still alive at the time of the incident. Who was the unknown soldier?" Lee said. This was the same room that he had been painting when the spotlight fell.

And a handicapped girl who once visited the upstairs apartment had complained "The man won't leave me alone!" When asked for details and where "the man" was located, she pointed to a corner that seemed vacant to those in the room. Finally, Lee heard a rumor that the old house, or perhaps a former one on the site, had been a stop on the Underground Railroad, though no proof has yet appeared.

"It just keeps on," Lee told me, "though it's nothing that we can't handle. Not long ago, my wife, first child and I were in the back apartment (which room has now become the children's bedroom) seated on the couch. A ball slowly rolled across the space from the dining room on our left and into the living room. Yet, nobody had been there to start it rolling.

"Then, not long ago, an experience gave me a clue as to who one of our ghosts might be. My mother lives in one of the upstairs apartments and I usually go up to say goodnight. One particular evening, taking my son along, I climbed the stairs and knocked at her door. As it swung open, I was hit with a strange, strong cooking odor. And, instantly, I was taken back in memory to the smell I associated with mom's father and mother. Certain cooking smells mixed with their cigarette smoke characterized their kitchen in another place. But my Mom doesn't smoke, and she was cooking chicken and vegetables that night. That first scent lingered just a moment, and then it was gone.

"I began to think about all the phenomena. Many revolved around the kitchen (cookie sheets, refrigerator, etc.). My mom's father, my grandfather, died in 2001, and one time, as I pondered the mysteries of those smells, his face suddenly came into my mind. Those were the smells that he associated with a kitchen, though it was now long gone. Could he somehow have brought his familiar smells along, perhaps to show us who was visiting Mom's apartment? Maybe, even, to show her that he still loves her, is close by, and will help her when it's time for her transition into the next world?

My Grandmother never lived here, so even though those are her kitchen smells too, we're pretty sure one of the spirits is my grandfather. He worked in the construction industry and, in his spare time, as a hobby, Grandpa made model ships. I've heard that ghosts can linger with things they possessed in life, and right there in my mom's apartment is one of Grandpa's ship models. What do you think?"

When we deal with things that can't happen, we have to decide how to deal with the matter. I think that Lee is onto something with his theories.

Though more research may yet be done, it is a comfort to know that the love of one's ancestors is stronger than the bonds of death.

High Street in Goshen

"My late grandmother's house on High Street in Goshen, Orange County, New York, was haunted by a man in 1800s dress, who would, on occasion, rise from the old brass bed in the spare bedroom, take a tour of the upstairs through the walls, return to the bedroom, lie down again on the bed, and disappear," Judith told me.

"From the time I was four years old until I turned eleven, I both saw him in the afternoon and felt him when I slept there at night. I was the only member of the family who could sleep in that bed, even though I only did it six or seven times during those years. The first time I stayed there, I looked into that room and saw a man lying on the bed. He then rose and began walking. 'Mommy, who's that man?' I asked. Mom said nothing, thinking I was scared."

Judith saw the man walk through solid walls, across the openings to stairways, through railings, and closed doors. Then he'd lie back down on the bed after his ambling and simply disappear. Another time, she said, she was sleeping on a mattress on the floor while her mom slept on the bed. During the night, Judith awoke and saw a man sleeping alongside her mom…the ghost man! "When I was nine, I was big enough to sleep in that bed. One night, I felt a movement next to me. I turned and saw an old man in old-fashioned clothes on my bed! Then he just disappeared.

"Grandmother and I were the only ones not afraid of him when he made his appearances. She encouraged me to use my intuition to try and see the man and pay attention to what he did. Nobody knew who the ghost was, and he never seemed to notice us or hurt anyone. We assumed he was the builder of the house during Victorian times, but nobody could remember his name anymore. My grandmother, before she died in 1972, told me that the stairways and walls had been restructured several times since the house was built, perhaps accounting for the ghost walking on floors that no longer existed.

"In those days when I stayed with Grandmother, the house looked different from when my mother had grown up there in the '30s and '40s. I don't know what, if anything, had been on the property before Grandmother's house was built, but the cellar always felt older than the rest of the house to me, so maybe her house replaced a previous house."

Judith also heard many tales of others' experiences in the house. Her Uncle Bobby, who became an Air Force general, also saw the man when he was growing up. Bobby wasn't afraid of the ghost; he was more puzzled than anything else. As a kid, when he saw the ghost man, he tried to play with him. One time, young Bobby almost fell down the stairs when he tried to follow the man through empty air over the open stairway.

"Now, older aunts live there," Judith told me. "I never hear tales of the ghost man now. Maybe they don't have the ability to see him. How unfortunate," she sighed.

Holdovers

Westfield House

I have traveled the New York State (Thomas E. Dewey) Thruway for years, always enjoying the neatly sculptured vineyards along the Lake Erie shores of southwestern New York. Little did I suspect that I'd find a nice story from an old farmhouse there, not far from Route 20 outside Westfield.

David wrote to me that the few strange and ghostly experiences of his life took place there in the early 1970s. If one asked him whether or not he is psychic, I'm sure he would deny it, but a number of factors seem to have taken place during a three-year period from 1971-1974 when he and his wife, Doreen, rented an old farmhouse amid the plantings of what he called "a grape farm." And the spirits made themselves known.

"Once we settled in, I asked a neighbor about a strange light-colored rectangle on the lawn," he began. "Whether it rained or not, something seemed to keep that spot from becoming a lush green. The man told me of a legend that, many years before, a vagrant man tramping the roads of southwestern

Chautauqua County took shelter for the night behind the woodpile on that old farm. A youngster in the house, spotting the apparently furry hide of a woodchuck behind his woodpile, took up his .22 and fired, hitting the man in the head. The victim leaped up, swore, danced around, then dropped dead there. Was that enough to put a mini-curse on the lawn? We could never know, though I'm sure my neighbor believed the story."

David and his wife had three small boys then, and the couple began to hear footsteps in the upstairs hallway during naps and at night. "I could look out our bedroom door and down the hall, but could never see anyone in the hall," he told me. "Doreen was sure it was our boys, but she could never catch them out of bed either. When it first occurred, she went into the hall and stood. The footsteps approached her, but nobody was there." I asked him if the footfalls sounded like children, and he had to admit, no, more like an adult. But who else was there to walk around? he puzzled.

Eventually the two parents shared the strange events with another couple, who suddenly got knowing looks on their faces. They introduced David and Doreen to John and Jenelle, who had been previous tenants of the house. "I asked them if anything strange ever occurred during their tenancy," David said, "and they asked, 'Like what?' I responded, 'You tell me!' She looked at John who responded, 'Well, there were those strange footsteps….' Bingo. So, now I knew we weren't just imagining things.

"But then, Jenelle hadn't finished. As we talked, she informed us that her grandfather's ghost had visited them when they lived in the old farmhouse, and in fact, he took up residence with them. 'But if you are hearing footsteps, we know it isn't Grandpa, because, when we moved, he came with us to our new home.'" Isn't that neat, I cogitated—ghosts from two different places and periods! An old-timer and a short-timer. I wonder whether or not the walker ever met Grandpa, and if so, did he wonder where the old fellow went after John and Jenelle moved out?

"As it is over thirty years past, I can't quite remember how or why we chose to use a Ouija board, but I suppose that we might have wanted to contact the footstep maker," David laughed. "Doreen and a friend, Tom, got pretty good at getting the pointer to move. I usually kept track of the message being spelled out, writing down each letter or number, but reached a point where I thought the communications were so unbelievable that I had the two close their eyes while working the planchette pointer. But even then, many of the messages were coherent. I'm not sure we ever got in touch with our house ghost, but sometimes we got spirits of foreigners, such as one guy from Germany.

"In another case, I had just replaced a sprocket on a motorcycle, and neither Tom nor Doreen knew the specifics of that part. I asked the Ouija how many teeth there were on that sprocket, and it immediately announced 28, a fact that neither of them could have known—and I wasn't even touching the planchette. On another occasion, though, the entity communicating with us claimed to be the Devil. And almost immediately, we got another message, where the pointer moved at a frantic speed: 'This is Grandmother,' it said. 'If you keep up this Ouija stuff, you are in danger,' the message said. We stopped right then and never again tried to contact the spirits."

As I note in every book, use of the Ouija may be entertaining, but it can be like leaving one's front door open for twenty-four hours a day. One can never tell who is going to come through it. And there are some really bad characters out there in spirit land—individuals who died in a less-than-spiritual frame of mind. Cutthroats, swindlers, manipulators, obsessed entities and others that you'd never want to entertain in your living room can come through. And you are permitting them free access to your mind. Unfortunately, some weak-minded or unprincipled users seeking cosmic thrills can become possessed or obsessed by such entities. My father used to say, "Before you start the car, you had better know how to operate the brake." I do not recommend use of the Ouija board to anyone. Often, when storytelling to teens, I find that over half of the group has played with it as a harmless entertainment. It isn't harmless.

"Our pets seldom would stay in the room when we were working the Ouija," David continued. "Once, our cat was lying on top of the couch when we began a session. It stared intently past us, as if seeing something we couldn't see, and then shot out of the room. That should have been a warning, I guess. Another curious thing that I noticed is that most or all of those who came through to us in those Ouija sessions seem to have died violent deaths, though I'm not sure what to make of that," he concluded.

So, who was the walker? Might it have been the tramp who died behind the woodpile, assuming that legend was correct? Might it have been a former owner or the builder of the house? How we use our physical and mental energies while we have bodies seems to play a big part in what we experience after death. Maybe, in this case, David and his family experienced some former resident who was still dealing with his or her "sour grapes."

Having left the house in 1974, David has been ghost-free for over thirty years. However, in a side story, he told me of visiting the famous World War II destroyer, USS The Sullivans, at the Naval & Servicemen's Park in Buffalo a few years ago. "I was uneasy from the first minute I set foot aboard. It was a quiet day and I couldn't see anyone else there, so I decided to see what being on the ship's bridge was like. When I got up there, I couldn't stay. I was jumpy and nervous and actually fled from the ship. At the time, I knew nothing about the big old relic, but just three months later, while surfing on the television, I saw the ship featured in a story. And the program turned out to be 'America's Most Haunted Places.' That ship was haunted and I hadn't even known!"

In a New House?

When I began researching new New York State ghost stories for this book, I encountered Pat Orcutt in Penn Yan. Before long, I had more stories than I ever expected—all from just one person. Though born in Elmira, Pat grew up in a "busy" ghost house on West Lake Road south of Penn Yan, and then, after her marriage, moved into another active dwelling in Wisconsin. She and her husband, Bill, finally returned in 2005 to build a new log home on East Bluff Drive, not far from her childhood house. Maybe now, the encounters with the unseen could stop, she thought, not that the previous ones had been especially terrifying, but a retired woman should expect some peace and the opportunity to deal just with the visible and material things of life.

In our initial contact, Pat told me of the puzzling experiences that she has had and is having in this new house. Shouldn't a new place be free of spirits? Readers know, however, that prior occupants of the land might remain in spirit. Oftentimes, when such events cannot be rationally explained, someone hypothesizes that the dwelling might be built on an "old Indian burial ground." Even if true, though, not all the world's ghost stories can be explained in this way; probably not even one percent. Historians don't know of any Indian burials on East Bluff Drive.

Here are her current experiences: "One evening while we were watching 'Ghost Hunters' on television, two porcelain birds flew off their shadow box display case on the living room wall and landed on the love seat. They did not fall, and there was no vibration in the house. They literally flew across the room.

"An earring disappeared and we searched under every piece of furniture and on dresser tops. Even our cat, Mokie, was enlisted in the search, as she had found dropped or lost earrings before. Two days later, the earring appeared in an isolated spot on my desk.

"A large round paperweight that had been on a shelf was found halfway across the dining room. I think I heard it fall during the night, but Mokie was on my bed—not her fault, and besides, she never normally went near those shelves. Likewise, a small iron frying pan flew across the room.

"I was in the front of the house when I heard a crash. Running into the kitchen, I found our antique oak clock lying on its back on the kitchen counter. It had been flush against the wall, so even if the cat had knocked it down, there is no way it could have landed on its back.

"I was dusting and cleaning upstairs, where the bedroom doors had been closed all summer and nobody had been in the rooms but me. I found the quilt on the guest room blanket chest to be half off the chest and partly on the floor. A small ironstone cup of dried flowers was tipped on its side on the desk in the hall.

"I had been wearing Grandmother Smith's wedding band on the little finger of my right hand, and found it missing when we returned from a parade and pizza one night. We thoroughly searched the sidewalk, the car and the pizza place—no ring! A week later I was inventorying some antique jewelry in a safe and opened an old envelope marked 'gold rings.' There was Grandma's ring!

"The door to our library continues to open on its own, though we had our construction man, Mark, work on the problem, and I make sure to latch the door when I exit.

"Bill and I both have observed ghost cats. Occasionally I feel one jump on the bed at night and, when I reach to pet it, my hand passes right through. Bill has seen these cats on the hallway floor, and when he tries to push them out of the way with his cane, it passes right through them. There are two or three of them, semi-transparent, but they seem to have no distinctive color. If we try to pet them, our hands pass right through!" Pat refers to Mokie as "our living cat."

"Then there were all the problems with the phones in the house. We have two lines, and some jacks on a line will work while others don't. We have spent so much time replacing jacks and other fixtures, but they all seemed to have a mind of their own. Finally, I'd had it! I spoke out loud and firmly told 'whatever is messing around with the phones' to stop. And that was it—not a problem since," she laughed.

Recently, Pat turned her computer on, only to have it not boot up. Checking all the power connections, she found everything in order, except that her little lamp and computer were inoperative. Checking the surge protector, into which these items were plugged, she found it connected to the wall plug, but the toggle switch on the device was turned off. "That is a rather heavy switch, and it's located on the back of the surge protector where it couldn't have been inadvertently hit by us or our cats. Do you think it's one of the spirits?" she asked me. I responded in the affirmative.

This is just a smattering of the incidents that Pat has carefully recorded in less than three years. She has been around ghosts almost all of her life, now. There have been countless other incidents in this new house, often exasperating ones. So, Pat's first question to me involved how (Indian graves aside) this could happen. Because I have collected so many similar stories, I asked if she had any antiques in the house.

"Oh my goodness, I never thought of that!" she responded. "Yes, our house is almost entirely furnished with antiques from both sides of our family. In fact, when we lived in Wisconsin, I had a problem with a photo of both sets of my grandparents. The framed picture was hung on the wall, but I always found it face down on a dresser in one of the bedrooms. So, I kept re-hanging it, using larger and larger nails each time, but soon, I'd find that photo face down on the dresser. I mentioned it to my mother and she reminded me that her mother (in the photo) didn't like photos of herself to be displayed. That frame is here in our new house, but it has stayed put so far.

"I remember when we brought our first-born home from the hospital, and, as I sat holding the baby, Grandma's ghost appeared in the room, probably a visit to see her first great-grandchild. I called Bill quietly, but she disappeared the minute he walked through the doorway. Bill is a skeptic, as I've told you, and he remarked that I must have been dreaming, which I hadn't been. Hardly had those words escaped his lips, when all four window shades rolled up with a loud 'brrruuup!' Grandma had a great sense of humor, so maybe that was her response to Bill," Pat laughed. Maybe Grandma still visits with the Orcutts from time to time, we agreed.

If you encounter unexplained ghostly events in your home or office, no matter the age of the building, consider the objects that you have inside. An old friend and I used to joke that we were going to write a book called "What Are You Bringing Home?" which would probably deal a death blow to the garage sale, tag sale, and barn sale industry, and probably scare people out of antique shops all over the world. In *Ghosts of the Northeast*, I wrote ("The Clock") of the amazing adventures of a man in Clifton Park, who had been gifted with an ancient grandfather's clock from Scotland.

We know from studies done with psychometry (where a physical object is held by a sensitive person, and insights, often accurate, can be given about the owner or prime user) that human beings impart some of their energy to their possessions. How and why this energy, which may be a part of the deceased or living individual's personality, "sticks" can't yet be explained. I suspect that wherever we direct our energy (consciousness, love, anger, hate) some of it remains. This can be good news or bad for readers. Most of the gifted psychometrists that I have known could have a field day at an antique sale, although validation for their insights might be difficult if not impossible to achieve.

Nevertheless, do consider that the objects in your home and workplace right now are absorbing energies, bits of your consciousness, which will remain with those things long after you have gone. Maybe someday, part of you will appear to a psychic or unsuspecting homeowner who found "something pretty" at an estate sale.

Jessie Belle

Noonan's

Whenever I'm looking to have an historical photo improved and made presentable for my books, I usually give the assignment to Michael Noonan, whose studio is in the Old Chocolate Factory in Ballston Spa. We have shared many strange tales and photo stories over the years, since he first told me of his ghost experiences at 1 Phila Street in Saratoga Springs, the former George Bolster Studio.

Mike and his wife, Maeve, moved to the neighboring village of Ballston Spa and bought a cozy cottage there in order to be closer to his new place of business. And wouldn't you know it? The place, at 7 Charles Street, has a ghost.

"When we first visited the house, we found '1857' carved into one of the large tree trunk posts in the cellar. Those supports still have their original bark and were probably cut here atop this hill," Mike told me. "The previous owners were Norman and Nancy Hammond, but they never seem to have experienced the phenomena that have, since we bought it, become normal in the house. Actually, Nancy sold us the house in 1998, as Norman had died in the living room after shoveling too much snow during a storm. One might expect Norman to have remained here, but we have never encountered him.

"We began renovating in 2000 and discovered, by investigating the various building materials we found, that the original small cottage had been added onto at least four times in one hundred and fifty years. So, the issues of 'who' and 'when' became important when Maeve first spotted a woman's reflection moving in a mirror's reflection." Mike continued that both of them had vague visions out of the corner of their eyes though, for some time, neither talked about these to the other. But in 2005, they had a more substantial experience.

"I walked through our narrow hallway one day and side stepped to let a woman pass. I was deep in my thoughts and assumed it was Maeve passing through. A second later, I realized it wasn't her and turned, just in time to see a woman with shoulder-length black hair and wearing a long white dress walking away from me. Then she vanished. I noticed that the ghost was slender and much taller than Maeve. I told my wife about it later and we figured we did, indeed, have a ghost."

One day, Mike noticed a driver passing their corner lot very slowly and asked the young driver if he needed directions. The young man said, no, he was just interested in seeing the place, as his grandmother, Jessie Belle Guido, once owned it and had died there. "I often wonder whether or not she would show up if somebody did a séance here," the young man said. Mike countered with, "Don't bother. She's here, because we see her from time to time." He then gave the driver a description of the spirit woman he had seen. "That's her," the passerby said, "you've described her to a tee, except that she had white hair when I knew her!" So now the Noonans knew the identity of their boarder. They learned that she had died in a hospital bed in what is now their living room, though the Noonans have reconfigured the house's interior.

In early 2007, Maeve, descending the stairs, had to walk around Jessie. "Things were a little messy that day," she told me, "and Jessie gets very perturbed when the house isn't picked up and neat."

Later that year, the Noonans sat watching television and Mike saw Jessie lean out the library doorway and look directly at him. Was the spirit checking on the couple? After Mike announced Jessie's presence, Maeve spoke up and informed the spirit that everything was okay and that she could relax. "Jessie shows up approximately every two weeks, so she is still actively participating in the house management," Mike laughed. "When we find objects moved to unaccustomed places, we just jokingly blame Jessie."

Mike told me that his observations are increasingly more visual in recent years. "While my earlier sightings were wispy, now I see more solid images, especially of Jessie, and today she appears to me like a figure in an old 1800s photo." His wife tends more to receive feelings, which she then translates for him, but they both agree on the substance of these apparitions.

The Noonans sometimes hear or feel people passing by or walking through their fenced yard, though they are not living people. "There seems to be different ones at different times," Mike told me. "I've tried to get pictures of them and have taken many nighttime exposures, with some resulting in images of drifting energies, which I call 'plasma.'" None of those figures have enough detail to be identified, unfortunately. Clement Street meets Palmer Street at the Noonans' corner, and Mike senses that many of the spirit travelers come from the early 1900s, when the neighborhood wasn't as densely populated.

So, here is another old historic village like many in the Empire State, with both old and new homes coexisting. Maybe, with his expertise in old Saratoga County photographic prints, Mike finds it easier than many to compose modern vintage photos in his mind of those who have chosen to stay behind.

John

An 1878 Victorian house stands at 105 Sea Cliff Avenue in Glen Cove. Originally a fine single-family house, at some time in the 1950s the owners converted the upstairs into an apartment. "That's the way I found it when I bought the building from my grandmother's estate in 1999. I had spent much time there when Grandma, Helen Harvey, was alive and I enjoyed roaming upstairs and down," Mike Trunkes told me. "Grandpa Henry Harvey was a maker of gravestones and monuments. As far as I could discover, the Harveys were only the second family to live there."

Henry and Helen Harvey had purchased the house in the early 1960s from the Wilson family, Mike said. Mrs. Wilson had purchased it from her grandmother, Kate Darby Wilson. However, Kate and her husband, John, a carpenter, had never lived in the house, but merely renovated it and then sold it to Mike's grandparents. Seldom had I so quickly been presented with such a complete domicile pedigree when researching a suspected haunted house. When

I asked Mike about that, in the light of their experiences there, he responded that he and his new wife, Petra, felt it was vital to discover all those who had lived there before them, in hopes that such information could identify the spirit entity which remained.

"When Michael closed on the house, he took me first through the upstairs, and I saw a nice little apartment," Petra recalled, "but as soon as we went into the downstairs section, I got awfully bad feelings. 'I don't think I can stay here,' I told him." But Michael, though intuitive, had experienced nothing negative on the first floor and the couple planned a renovation of their own, which might remove the odd feelings. The pair decided to first modernize the kitchen.

Cabinets were removed and the walls were made ready for repainting. "Long ago, some resident had walled in an area under the stairs, and we felt that area could be opened up and made into a nice space, so I got my wrecking bar and hammer and went to work demolishing the partition," Michael said. "Once that wall was down, however, I felt a strong chill there, which was hard to understand. If I walked a few feet away I'd be warm because the whole house was toasty, but not that spot under the stairs. We later discovered that a big old coal furnace had once been directly below it in the cellar, though it no longer was operative and there was no longer a heating grate in the floor there. For the first time in my life," he said, "I felt watched by someone I couldn't see. And what was that cold spot all about?"

One evening, Mike was working on a project in their new house and took a break to call Petra. In the middle of their conversation, the line went dead; it had never done so before and never did again. Was that a spirit interruption? Michael continued his projects: plumbing, electrical work and painting. He told me that he'd always been an easy sleeper, but since beginning work in the Sea Cliff Avenue house, his sleep had regularly been punctuated with nightmares. There seemed to be no reason for those, unless there was some energy in the house.

Petra remembers, "We worked hard to get the kitchen finished and, one night around 1:30 a.m., I took a break from painting and sat on the floor. And a ghost walked by me—just like that! A man I'd never seen before: tall, lean and stoop-shouldered, just strolled past. And as he did so, I felt overwhelmed with his feelings of resignation or defeat. I knew he was a ghost, but didn't know who, and I 'sent a thought to him' that I was there to help him, so why be downcast? When Mike returned to the room, I told him about the incident which sure was puzzling."

A few days later, puzzled by a plumbing problem, Michael took a section of the piping to the R & G Plumbing shop on Glen Cove Avenue, hoping the Coyle brothers, the owners, could advise him. "One of the men looked at the piece of pipe and said, "This came from the Harvey house, didn't it?" How could he know that? The owner responded that he and his brother had done the first modernization of the Harvey house during the 1950s. Michael then told him of the ghost man and, without batting an eye, Bob, the plumber, said that it certainly matched the description of John Darby, one of the former owners. How could Bob be so certain? He told Michael that John Darby was his uncle. Talk about coincidences—or was it really?

John Harvey had been an artisan of sorts, both carpenter and plumber, a trade that still continues in the Coyle family. If the tall ghost was the energy remains of John Harvey, why might he remain on the premises? A long life of hard and dedicated work might be a logical response. By retirement time, many of us become resigned to the outcome of plans and projects in our lives that didn't turn out as we hoped. John Harvey also may have had some financial problems, of a nature that seemed a burden. There may have been disappointments in family members or even in himself. Many ghosts seem to retain guilt or an inability to forgive themselves for perceived failures, and this self-grudge can keep them earthbound. Any or all of these things may have kept John there, though he never again troubled the Trunkes family. Sometime later, they sold the house and moved to the quiet of the Catskill Mountains, leaving the ghosts of the past behind.

Lingering

Haakon and Inga Engelsen bought a very small, rundown house in the Long Island village of Lake Grove in 1982. The price was right and it was a structure that could be remodeled and expanded, thereby enhancing the property's value if it was necessary to sell. Nevertheless, they hoped to make it a home for many years. As Haakon stood outdoors discussing expansion plans with his wife one evening, neighbor John Holden walked up, anxious to meet the new residents at 49 Pond Path. "This place has quite a history," he began. "It used to be a trailer park of some kind in the old days," he continued without giving specific details. "Then an elderly couple moved into the main building. The old guy was an exterminator, but got exterminated. It seems that his wife was quite a drinker and, for whatever reason, she put some of his poison in the man's soup! Not too long after that, with a snoot full of booze, she went out to waltz in traffic, where she was struck by a car and killed."

Eventually, the property passed to Greenpoint Savings Bank, the mortgage holder, and two years later, to the Engelsens. With Holden's horrible tale soon forgotten, the Engelsens set about renovations and expansion. Maybe Holden had just been trying to entertain them, they thought. In any case, of good Norwegian stock, Haakon and Inga weren't great believers in the likelihood of bad vibes continuing. Things were different for their daughter Laura, however. "My parents never experienced anything out of the ordinary," she told me, "or, if they did, they never talked about it.

"I didn't grow up there, but often went to visit my parents in their pretty new home. They had kept the original shack part and built around it. [Ghost story lovers here should immediately say, 'Oh, oh! You kept intact the physical scene of a murder?'] Whenever I had the chance to stay overnight with my parents, I just couldn't sleep," she pursed her lips. "I was always uneasy, but it was hard to describe why. When my two sons came along with me to visit, they felt the ominous atmosphere too. And my sister slept over on the downstairs couch one evening, with her gentle dog dozing on the rug at her feet. In a dream, my sister heard a loud moan, accompanied by her dog barking loudly in waking life. It didn't make sense because the dog just wasn't a barker! She never discovered how or why the two of them had roused at the same instant. And whose moan had she heard?

"About ten years later my dad died of cancer and we had relatives staying with us during the time of the wake. Dad's sister slept on the downstairs couch in the living room. There was a fireplace there with wall lights on either side. Those seemed to be leftovers from previous owners and never worked, but my parents kept them there because they looked nice. My aunt told us that those lights suddenly turned on in the middle of the night, waking her. Not understanding that these were inoperative lights, she got up to find the wall switch that controlled them, but never discovered it. In fact, my parents didn't know where it was either, as the lights had never worked. Groggy and unable to turn the lights off, she shuffled back to the couch and dropped off to sleep. In the morning, however, she told us in wonder about finding them off when she awoke. Nobody in our family had done the deed. We then flipped every switch that we could find in the room, but were never able to get those lights back on. Well, that was mysterious, but it didn't automatically indicate a ghostly presence," she grinned.

The kitchen had a cathedral ceiling as part of the renovations, she told me, and on one of the thirteen-foot-high walls there was a small door into the crawl space overhead. One would need a ladder to reach it, so nobody ever tried. "One night when I slept over on the couch I was awakened by a strange noise from the kitchen. At first, I couldn't identify it, but then I realized it was the sound of an animal gnawing on something, perhaps the roof rafters. It wasn't a wimpy little mouse sound, but it sounded like something huge—maybe a raccoon? I stayed awake as long as I could, expecting that something might suddenly chew a hole in the wall, but that never happened, so somewhere in the night I dropped off to sleep again. In the morning, everything was quiet and calm. That neighborhood was wooded in those days, so it was always possible that some wandering animal had gotten into the crawl space, though this event never happened again, as far as I know, and if that was the only strange event there, I'd probably have forgotten it all by the time I read your ad in the newspaper," she told me.

"But then things got a bit scary. I had a little female cockapoo dog who lived most of her life indoors, and who didn't like the outdoors, venturing outside just to go to the bathroom. One afternoon I went to visit and left the dog inside while my family and I went away together for the rest of the day. When we came home, everything seemed fine. We said our goodbyes and my son held the dog in the back seat as we drove to our home. Suddenly, my son exclaimed that, underneath the dog's curly hair, there were many small, bleeding wounds—almost like bites, he thought. What was this? We took her immediately to the vet.

"The veterinarian verified that these were indeed animal bites. He asked if the dog had been outdoors, but we denied it. 'She must have tangled with a rat or big rodent of some kind,' he observed, but how was that possible? When she went to the bathroom outside, I always watched her, knowing that she would want to hurry inside when done. There was no sign of rodent damage anywhere in my parents' house and, even if the dog had gotten into a fight with some animal, she would have been traumatized and shaking. But such was not the case. How did she get those wounds? Just going to the groomer, the poor little dog would shake and shake for hours afterward, so if she had gotten into a fight (and if so, with what? where? when?) she would have been anxious. Yet, here she was looking and acting just fine. It didn't make sense. My son and I agreed that whatever had happened to her must have taken place inside my parent's house, as he had played with the dog on the way over there, and she had been fine."

The other strange event that Laura remembered from Pond Path was during the aftermath of her father's death. Inga lived on alone in the house for another year after Haakon's death, but she told Laura that her washing machine often turned itself on without being touched. When Mrs. Engelsen inquired about a potential cause, the utility company gave her an unsatisfactory technical explanation about the power entry to her house being "downhill," thus flowing a power surge into the machine. But why only the washing machine? the family wondered. Why not the television? Why not the house lights? Perhaps, I suggested, because every housewife has an ear for her washing machine, for when it finishes its cycles. Maybe that is where a husband now in spirit might begin to communicate the assurance of his survival of death.

Though Laura visited her mother every weekend after Haakon's death, there were no more anomalies, and Inga sold the house in 1996. Laura told me that she didn't consider this all a serious ghost story, but I think she had a real adventure in spirit contact.

Mae

Fred H. Cluett came from the Arrow shirt-making family in Troy, N.Y., but chose to have his own business instead. Cluett and Sons who sold pianos and organs in their large music store at Broadway and Second Street in that city. The family had a nice home in Troy, but as the business prospered, Fred decided to build a summer house at the Methodist Church summer camp in the Saratoga County hamlet of Round Lake.

In 1903, Fred completed the spacious home on Janes Avenue which faces the Albany-Saratoga Road and the lake itself. Quite late in life, Fred suddenly married Mae, his attractive young secretary, though he died a few weeks after the honeymoon, leaving the house to Mae, then to the Church after her death.

In time, Mae married two other husbands but never became a mother. Her second marriage was to a doctor, and then, after his death, Mae married Roy Simmons, who had worked at the old Cluett Music Store. Until Mae's death, Roy spent much time in maintaining the once-beautiful grounds. Upon her death, the contents and the home itself were auctioned off, with Roy remaining just a bit longer. Then, in a strange turnabout, Roy married his secretary at work, and the couple lived happily elsewhere in Round Lake, taking an active role in community affairs.

There were a few short-term owners of the Cluett house, and then, for six years, the house was on the market. The real estate agent explained to prospective buyer Tina Harris that all purchase offers had fallen through. "So, the house was there waiting for us," she smiled. "Jeff and I were expecting our first baby, and I was thrilled with the view, the large lawns, and the neat interior details of the house," Tina told me. "Maybe it was our aim of having a happy family life there that instigated the ghostly events that followed."

They recognized that the house needed some modernizing, so the couple continued living in their Guilderland condo while those changes were made. Then, Jeff took a job (hopefully just a short-term one) in Nebraska soon after the closing, and Tina supervised the movers in unloading and placing the numerous boxes in the Round Lake house. After finishing the move, Tina's next task was to make sure the heating system was in tip-top shape before she took up full-time residence, and she hired a repairman to look over the furnace and pipes. As he finished his tasks in the cellar, the man told her that he hoped never to come back. She asked what he meant, and the man (who had never been in the main part of the house) said he kept hearing an organ playing upstairs while he worked.

After relating these anecdotes, Tina took me to the living room and showed me the Cluett's Estey pipe organ from the early 20th Century. "I'm sure the furnace man didn't know this organ was here, but what is mysterious is that there's no way this organ can play—part of its workings are inoperative!"

Weeks and then months went by, and Jeff remained in Nebraska. It looked as if he'd never be able to leave there in order to live in their new Saratoga County house. The couple discussed the matter, and it appeared prudent for Tina to repack all the belongings and move to Nebraska, so they could start their family life together. Once more, she searched for large cardboard boxes, hired a moving company and a real estate salesman, and after listing the house, planned the move to Nebraska. The movers came again. "Taking a break from the job, the men sat with me, having a cool drink. One of them said, rather apologetically, that he was a sensitive, and that he sensed the strong presence of a woman in the house with us. 'That lady has been standing and watching us all day,' he said, but I couldn't verify that." Tina smiled, "Nevertheless, I didn't automatically disbelieve him."

During their time in Nebraska, a son was born. Back in Saratoga County, there were offers to buy the Round Lake house but each of those fell through. Tina began to wonder if the house itself, or something in it, was sabotaging the sales in order to have Jeff, herself, and the new baby return. She also considered that Round Lake might retain an ambience of Methodist spirituality, a very important feature of the Harris family's life, dating from those long-ago days of summer camp meetings that had been attended by thousands. Maybe that energy kept her small family connected to the old Cluett house.

Then came a change in Jeff's job, and it became possible for the Harris family to come back to New York State. Tina once more moved their belongings and baby back to the large Janes Avenue house in Round Lake. Again, one of the new movers appeared to be sensitive. Returning from the attic after depositing boxes there, he told her of his strong sense that someone invisible was watching him throughout the task, and stated that he didn't want to go back up there again.

Finally moved in, and with another baby to care for, Tina found her own senses sharpening and noted that she was distinctly uncomfortable on the back servant's stairway—nothing that she could identify—just a strong dislike of making that turn on the stairs. She also began to sense a friendly female presence, though she saw nothing. Shortly thereafter, as she passed through the foyer and living room, she experienced a "mist" that puzzled her. At first, she tried to wipe her eyes, thinking that vision was the problem. But the haze remained, puzzling her.

When her son was three, he sat in front of the television watching a PBS children's program and Tina, working in the kitchen, heard the word "ghost." The narrator said that ghosts could sometimes appear as a mist! That quickly made connections for the young mother, and she seriously began to consider that there was a spirit there.

These events prompted Tina Harris to research the history of the house and the Cluett family in particular. She learned that Mae had no children, and then overheard a neighbor's suggestion that Mae and her husband weren't happily married. Could that be true? And was Mae, now in spirit, perhaps drawn to the energy of a young and happy family?

In 2003, Tina was seeking some stored object in the attic; turning around, she found an old check lying at her feet. It was dated 1933 and signed by Mae herself. As Tina described the find, we considered that the check, made out to the telephone company, dealt with the issue of communication. "I think Mae wanted me to find the check and let me know she was there with me and had our family's best interests at heart. Shortly after that I would talk to her during the day, like a companion, and I put the check in the family Bible for safekeeping.

"Lots of little strange things kept occurring," she told me. "For example, we bought and installed a brand new dishwasher in the kitchen. Long after it finished its cleaning cycle, during the night it would suddenly start a brand new cycle, so we had the control panel replaced. Then another one. And then, a third one! Finally, that unscheduled activity stopped. A short time later, I sat reading the children a bedtime story and was so tired that I kept drifting off to sleep myself. My daughter had to keep correcting me on the parts I missed. Suddenly, our security alarm went off. Jeff wasn't home, and I was startled awake. Had someone forced their way in? I quickly called the alarm company, and they reported that their system showed our front door open.

"Cautiously, I went down. Nobody was around. The front door was closed and locked. I tip-toed through the rest of the house and found all the doors were locked and just the kids and I were inside. I looked outside to see if there were footprints in the snow, but there were none. The next day, I had the connector terminal for the front door replaced, but wondered why it went off while I was so sleepy. Was Mae worried about me? It has never sounded again."

A month later, Tina heard her son say, "Oh, oh!" and the toddler came into the kitchen. "I broke this Mommy," he said. The child held two ripped sections of Mae's check. Tina forgave the boy, but secretly wondered what effect the tearing of the check might have. "I've not been aware of Mae's presence since that day," she told me.

The old Cluett house has been rather quiet, except for occasional noises in the upstairs. "Once or twice, I've heard a voice call my name, and thinking it was one of the kids, I'd go see what they wanted, but they always denied calling me," she said with a big grin. It seemed to me that Tina was missing her old friend, Mae. She smiled again when I voiced that concern. "Well, now there's something else. From time to time I've begun to sense a more masculine presence. And then, sometimes a movement outside on the lawn will catch my eye, but when I turn to look fully at it, there is nothing there." Tina left it to me to hypothesize that, with Mae fading into the background and maybe even finally passed over into The Beyond, her husband thought it was a good idea to occasionally manifest in his role as groundskeeper.

Several times in 2006, her son balked at entering several rooms, complaining that "the ghost is there." To date, the boy hasn't been very forthcoming with a description, but that may change. As readers know, most children under age seven are quite sensitive to the denizens of that Other World.

Meantime, Tina and Jeff continue to take part in the cultural events in Round Lake Village, where she recently stepped down from the presidency of the Woman's Round Lake Improvement Society. And why not? She has already improved the village's atmosphere, helping one former dweller to exit to Paradise.

Old Farmer

Gerling's barn

Not far from Lake Ontario, in the Orleans County village of Lyndon-ville, lies the house and barn of David Gerling's family. On what was once a commercial poultry farm, the Gerlings now raise rabbits in the old L-shaped barn. "We purchased this property in August of 1994," son David told me. "It hadn't been used for animals in quite some time, but we got it back into shape, using the old brooder rooms for our rabbit cages. In the middle of those rooms is an old foyer space that has a door to the outside, and it's a door that we still use for entry. And that is where my sister first saw him," David said very seriously.

"One day, as she looked toward the barn, my sister, Sue, saw an old man trudge across the yard and walk up to that door, open it, and enter the barn. She wondered aloud who it could be, so we checked the entire interior of the building, only to come up puzzled—there was nobody inside!" he told me in amazement. "It took us a while to conclude that it might be a ghost—maybe the spirit of the old guy who ran the poultry farm. Sue is the only member of our family to actually see the ghost. What is important is that, when we went to inspect the barn, we found that access door locked, so nobody could have entered the door."

When I asked if anything has happened in the decade and a half since that sighting, David smiled. "Well, in the autumn of the year, especially, I often hear somebody whistling when I'm working out there. It's not a specific song, but kind of a mindless tune that has no real structure. It's as if an invisible worker is doing his job and just making some music to fend off his isolation.

At other times, I hear someone moving around and walking upstairs. For quite some time I used to go up to see who's there, but I don't do that any more, because no one is ever there," he told me.

The house itself seems almost ghost-free, except that the windows facing North Lyndonville Road sometimes are found raised, requiring some family member to shut them. Those windows seem to open on a random schedule, never predictable. "It is as if the spirit of the invisible person is more focused on working in his barn," David told me. I shared with him how common it is for the spirit of the deceased to continue working at tasks from their life—activities that were once meaningful. If one does not, or cannot, acknowledge his or her death, then they keep doing what gave them their identity and sense of accomplishment when alive. Having grown up with chicken-raising, I know that there is always some type of feeding or cleaning to do until the birds are bedded down for the night. So, it's not surprising that the old gentleman stays busy.

I asked David if he was ever scared when working in the barn. He grinned and said, "Well, I'd just as soon not go out there at night, if you know what I mean. But once, during the day, while I was working in the brooder room, I was hit in the back of my leg by a brush that I had placed on a table behind me. I didn't knock it off, because it struck me, though not hard. It was almost as if someone just tossed it at my back." He gave another grin as he warmed up to the interview.

"One of the best things you can do for people who are unmindful or in denial of their body death," I told him, "is to talk to the being, telling them that they are dead and can finally let go of their labors."

"I do talk to whoever it is," David responded, "and once, I asked him to tell me who he is and what's troubling him. Then I left a pencil and paper out there so he might respond, but all I found the next morning was that the pencil was moved. Maybe he couldn't quite pick it up," David smiled, "or maybe he thought it was just foolishness. After all, in his mind, he probably still owns the place.

"Once in a while," he told me, "I find a rabbit cage opened when I enter the barn in the morning. And sometimes I note that the rabbits are jumping around and quite upset. Maybe the old man's spirit upsets them, and on occasion, our dog, whose kennel is just outside the barn."

I told David that he had a nice story of a spirit still at work. "So, that's all that goes on, right?" I asked.

He grinned again, as if taking my measure. Lots of people who provide stories to me do this, just as they are about to reveal something that they find incredible and figure that I might not believe them. "One day last fall, as I walked through the yard, I noticed a leaf in mid-air behind me," David told me. "Okay, leaves fall every autumn, I decided, and kept walking. A minute later, I turned to find the leaf still there—moving at chest height. Now, I'm over six feet tall, so that leaf had to do some real dancing to maintain that altitude, and, even so, it kept changing direction with me! It continued to pursue me wherever I went for over ten minutes! I don't know if that was made possible by the old man or some other ghost. The Law of Gravity wasn't suspended for me, so how could the leaf remain floating? There were thousands of leaves on the ground or falling in the air that day—how could a single leaf escape the laws of nature and chase me around?"

Here is another adventure with the unseen, one that plays itself out in David's back yard from time to time. Maybe it all does follow laws of nature, ones that we don't yet understand.

Still Active

The City of Glens Falls is an active and rapidly growing community, but retains its quiet, tree-lined neighborhoods, parks and playgrounds. Still, quiet neighborhoods can have very active ghosts, and here is such a story.

"We came to our house on Lincoln Avenue in 1988," Terry Kelly told me, "and it didn't take long for our experiences to start, but at first, we never thought about a ghost. I remember putting groceries in the fridge one day in December of that year and, as I was bent over, I felt a pat on my fanny. I stood up to joke about it with my husband, Bob, but discovered he was way across the room. Let me anticipate your next question," she said with a smile, "it was the left cheek!

"Soon after we moved in, I was cleaning the glass on my husband's bookcase doors and I needed my bottle of Windex from the kitchen, but found it gone when I looked," she said. "That just couldn't be—I had an upstairs bottle and one downstairs, and window washing wasn't Bob's job, so I could not believe he'd moved it. I went upstairs, got that bottle, and did my work, but when Bob returned home at day's end, I asked him where he'd moved the spray to. At first, he didn't know what I was talking about, and denied even knowing I had a downstairs bottle. Okay, I'm forgetful, I told myself, and dropped the matter, but when I found that spray bottle on a cellar shelf two weeks later, in a place where I'd never have taken it, I got goose bumps. I ran upstairs to tell Bob and reassure myself that he had moved it, though he again denied it. Was it possible that someone invisible was living with us? And if so, were they just trying to get my attention, or was it something else?

"We eventually discovered that whenever changes take place in our house, the spirit activity seems to be more frequent. Just before our baby, Jimmy, was born, I stood upstairs in the doorway of the nursery, which was painted and decorated for the upcoming birth. Suddenly, right behind me, across the hallway, the door to the attic began to rattle and shake on its hinges, and the doorknob turned, as if someone wanted to go upstairs or come down. I nervously looked, but nobody was there. I had no way to understand or explain that," she said.

Eight months after Jimmy's birth, Terry got up one night to change the baby's diaper. Finishing, she returned to bed, noting that it was almost 3:00 a.m. In the nursery, Jimmy's little rattle, having slid down into the space between a dresser and the wall, began to rattle, as if shaken by an unseen hand. Then Bob and Terry could hear a small musical toy on the dresser begin to play its song. "I got up quickly, picked up Jimmy, and put him into bed with us that night. Such activities had never happened before and I was too tired to figure out the complicated mechanics of it all. But, in the morning, I stood in front of the dresser. Now, with a clearer head, it dawned on me that the toy needed to be wound up in order to play, but nobody had wound it the previous night. Sometimes, when all run down, such toys do play a few notes if you shake them hard, but this was a rendition of 'Twinkle, Twinkle, Little Star' that lasted for several minutes! Fortunately, that activity never happened again," she said with a relieved look on her face.

Then, Terry's mother arrived and told me that she had her own experiences, too. "I just won't stay here overnight any more," Ginny told me. Both mother and daughter laughed before Ginny sat down to tell of her experiences. "In the summer of 2006, while Bob, Terry and Jimmy were up at camp, I volunteered to walk and feed their dog. As it was late at night, I decided to sleep on Terry's bed, but not for long.

"In the middle of the night, I felt I wasn't alone and roused from my sleep. There was a man in the room and I didn't know who he was. He stood not far from the bed, with his back to me as he stared at the closet. Surely, he must be a burglar, but what should I do? Maybe he hadn't seen me, but if I moved, I might be in danger. Nevertheless, I felt I should grab the bedside phone and call the police. I was scared and almost paralyzed. I studied the stranger and noted that he wore a short-sleeved print shirt, dark pants and very dark hair. How could he have gotten in, because the dog hadn't made a sound? Then, as I watched the man, he stepped toward the closet and disappeared! Had he gone through the closet doors and inside? I looked, but nobody was there."

That made Terry's mother remember another strange experience from Jimmy's youth. When her son was 2½ and sat on Terry's lap admiring the Christmas tree, he suddenly said, "Mommy, who's that man? It's not Daddy?" Terry scanned the room and told her boy that there wasn't any man there, but the youngster was adamant and pointed to the figure, though he couldn't give much of a detailed description at that age.

Also, about that time, Bob returned home to notice the round globe of a hanging lamp sitting on the couch. He asked Terry why she had taken it off the light fixture, but Terry not only hadn't removed it, she hadn't even noticed it was off until her husband commented on it. These things are sometimes easily explained by the supposition that one or the other parent had been "forgetful," though Jimmy sure hadn't removed the globe.

"Then there is the perfume smell upstairs," Terry said. "It is definitely a woman's perfume, though Jimmy and, more recently Mom, had seen a man here. Maybe we have two ghosts, though they have never seemed bad to us," she said. "Recently, Jimmy, who is a teenager now, returned home from school and asked, as he entered the house, 'Who's been smoking cherry-flavored cigars in here?' Certainly it wasn't Bob or me. Even when Bob was a smoker, he did all his puffing outdoors, but that was long ago. So, is it likely that we have a perfumed woman and a cigar-smoking man here?"

This is an interesting case, as it has elements of physical movement (e.g., the door, toy and rattle) as well as visualization (two sightings of the man) and smell. How to solve the mystery?

Knowing that the Kellys had bought the property from another Kelly named Ed, though no relation, I learned that he'd been a teacher in nearby Hudson Falls. I contacted the school office to see if one of Ed's old colleagues was still around, and they referred me to Bob Dingman, who had been a fellow Social Studies teacher, and who had lived right behind Ed's Lincoln Avenue house.

My first question for Bob was whether or not Ed had been a smoker. "Certainly not cigarettes, that I remember," he responded. Later, however, he recalled Ed occasionally smoking a pipe, so we decided the cherry-scented smoke could have been from a pipe, as Jimmy isn't a connoisseur of smoke. Bob was familiar with the interior of Ed's house and remembered that Ed's home office is the room now used as Terry and Bob's home office. The interview with Bob went along without any strong "hits," however, until I asked if Ed was a "hands-on" guy. Bob broke up in laughter. "That's your ghost, for sure." Ed was a toucher in school, and some of the women teachers used to joke that they crossed the hall when they saw him coming. "Left cheek, eh?" he asked, and broke up laughing again. It turned out that Ed Kelly had died in 1980, just a year before Terry and Bob moved in. A year is many times too short a time for a spirit who loved the physical life to depart from his beloved home.

Ed Kelly, from all evidence, loved teaching and was dedicated to his students, retaining old yearbooks and class photos long after his students had grown up, married and moved on. Reminiscing with Bob, we agreed that those of Ed's files that remained should be preserved. When I passed on Bob's physical description of Ed Kelly, Ginny laughed, certain that she now knew who she had seen in the bedroom.

For readers just becoming interested in ghost stories, such revelations can seem amazing. For old timers and investigators, however, the events of Ed Kelly's house cause us to nod, "Yes, that's a good one." It is always interesting to see proof that personality continues on after one's death. One can sometimes almost catch the twinkle in the spirit's eye.

The Judge?

Judge Hodson's

With World War II in its early years, Pat Orcutt's father moved the family to a majestic Queen Anne house at 239 West Lake Road, near Penn Yan. At age eleven, she was overjoyed at the grandeur of the building and the acres of woods and orchard, plus a private beach on the lakefront. A wealthy person must have built this place, she concluded. What most attracted her was the tower, a vantage point from which she could look out onto Keuka Lake and surrounding countryside—it all promised adventure.

Gradually, her parents restored the interior, banishing the dingy wall-paper and scuffed floors. For the first time in its existence, electric power was installed in the house, and Pat was excited at choosing the new glass and brass light fixtures. Her mom exulted in the fertility of the soil and planted beautiful flower gardens.

Pat also enjoyed life at her new school, and the recreation of roaming the woods and nearby fields during her free time. A tree house that she built in the orchard was the perfect place to munch the abundant local fruits while she read adventure stories. Little did she know that she was soon to experience all the excitement that a youngster could wish for.

"Dad worked in the city and came home on weekends," she remembers, "and I can't recall how long we lived there before another he began to manifest. Sometimes, in my bedroom, I'd hear footsteps in the attic overhead. Assuming that it was my mother, I was often astonished to find her working in her garden when I went downstairs; she denied being in the attic that day.

"Then came the night," she grinned. "Just as I was about to drop off into sleep, I knew I wasn't alone and popped my eyes open. An ominous figure dressed all in black (a cape or cloak held over his lower face) and wearing a black top hat stood at the foot of my bed. In the dim light, I could see his dark, sunken eyes above his high and hollow cheekbones. The figure just stood and glared at me, and I screamed for my father as loudly as I could," she said. The apparition vanished as her father swung open the bedroom door, leaving Pat a bit embarrassed. That was the first night of many, however.

"The manifestation became more visible and more clearly defined during succeeding nights, frightening me. When the weather was pleasant, I'd take my pillow and blanket outside my window, where I'd bed down on the little mop porch outside the bedroom window," she told me. "With Dad gone on weeknights, I'd often feign being cold and could sleep with Mom. On weekends, if the ghost appeared, I'd just scream for Dad. The spirit never appeared in any other room, though I'd hear him walking heavily in the attic, especially if I was alone in the house. Eventually, I made it a practice not to be alone in the house at night until one of my parents came home. Sometimes I'd just sit and do homework on the neighbor's porch."

In 1948, Pat went away to college, but still had to contend with the dark visitor when she returned home for weekends or vacations, though she no longer cried out for her father when the dark man visited at night. Nevertheless, on "those nights" of his visits, it was almost impossible to return to sleep unless she could sleep on her porch outside.

Pat married in 1957, but visits home allowed the young couple to sleep in another bedroom, so the ghost no longer troubled her. Nevertheless, wherever the newlyweds went, during one longtime stay in Wisconsin, for example, she had mild experiences with "the other world." These were enough to pique her curiosity and she did extensive reading about the paranormal. One year, her parents visited Pat and her husband, Bill, in their new home, and the foursome sat looking through photos in an old album. One of these was of their old Penn Yan home.

A face?

Suddenly, there in an upstairs window image of the old place, Pat spotted a face—the very gaunt visage of her nocturnal childhood tormentor! Two other pictures taken on that same long-ago day, however, showed only empty windows. Her mom postulated that the facial image was just a reflection in the glass. Pat took the photo to a local photographer, who made an enlarged copy for her but was quite skittish when she returned to pick it up.

"I made you the one copy, but please don't ever bring this photo in for a reprint. I felt very spooky all the while I worked with the original," the man told her.

Later, questioning her mother, Pat learned that her mother had known the house had a "reputation" when they bought it in 1942, but hadn't told Pat because the girl was "quite nervous as a child." Finally, her mom remembered that the ghost was alleged to be that of a judge who, it was rumored, had killed himself in the home years before they bought the place. Pat immediately connected the black robe of a judge with the black garments that she had seen on the specter. Then, there was the renovation of his old home that her parents had done; structural or decorative changes often bring out dormant ghosts on a property. From her studies later in life, Pat also realized that a teenager in a house often can help ghosts find the energy to manifest.

Who was the judge, and why might his consciousness or energy have remained attached to the house? It is well known that suicides seem overcome with guilt at their deed, and cannot forgive themselves enough to permit a more complete passage into the world of spirit.

Pat began research on the property's past and discovered that the house was likely built in 1888 by a member of the prominent Purdy family, who owned much land along Keuka Lake. In 1922, the property passed to Judge Devoe P. Hodson, a jurist from Buffalo whose childhood was spent in Yates County. Fifteen years later, Hodson's widow, Marietta, sold the house, and it passed through a succession of owners before Pat's parents bought it. Marietta Hodson apparently was a Spiritualist, and may have remained in contact with the judge after his suicide, but likely was unable to send him on his way. My own research suggests that Judge Hodson had developed an incurable illness and, despondent, took his own life rather than face prolonged suffering.

When she and Bill retired back to the Penn Yan area, Pat Orcutt hoped that her scary old home might be for sale. Maybe the judge had vacated. Instead, she found the house was in bad physical shape, with the old orchard gone and the gardens long overgrown. Doing a bit of research, she discovered that, while several successive families had bought the old house, none were able to capitalize on their dreams. More recent owners had acted strangely, the neighbors said, and the house was now abandoned, no longer able to provide shelter and happiness for the living.

"Bill and I built a new house only a few miles away. Though no one lives in my old house today," Pat wrote me recently, "I believe I can see movements behind the curtains when I drive by. Neighbors say that, occasionally, the house is ablaze with lights, though no car is ever seen in the weed-covered driveway.

"I wish Bill and I had been able to buy the old place in 1996 because I think I have learned enough about spirits since my childhood that I might have been able to communicate with the judge. He never did me any harm except to stare at me. Probably he couldn't figure out who I was and why I was in his bedroom," she mused.

The Visitors

Dutchess County in the Hudson Valley is one of the oldest settled areas of the state, a place where, long ago, people from western Europe succeeded the Native Americans as farmers, fishermen and traders. Many of the old farms are still thriving, producing bountiful crops from the rich soils. One of these is a 64-acre operation just outside Hyde Park, a farm that was in one family's ownership for over one hundred years before coming into the possession of a non-profit organization in the late 1900s.

Melinda Riggs and her family live in a fairly new home on that old farm. She seems accustomed to the ghostly visitors who frequent the home, but wishes that she could identify them—one of the most difficult things for historians to achieve.

Her husband, who died there at the young age of forty-one, might be one of the spirits, as many of his possessions are still present in the house for his spirit to cling to. There are other energies, however, which are not readily identifiable. Melinda first became aware of the resident entities when her smoke alarms began to trigger without any identifiable cause. Electricians could not find a cause because the alarms are battery operated and not wired into the house system.

In 2006, she began to notice movements in her peripheral vision, where most people first spot ghostly entities. When Melinda looked directly at those spots, however, nothing out of the ordinary was visible. Then, her daughter, Morgan, a young teen, reported that she had awoken the previous night to see a little girl standing in her bedroom. "She had long dark hair and wore a blue suit," the girl said. Clearly, this was not a living being, though at first, the child ghost didn't daunt Morgan. She just looked, rolled over, and went back to sleep. The child's spirit continued to appear in early 2007 and Morgan initiated a conversation with her new-found friend. "The little girl told me her name was Loretta," Morgan said. So far, the child has not disclosed the purposes for her nighttime visits, or whether she ever lived in that house.

"Now, I have seen another visitor," Melinda told me. "One day recently my daughter told me there is now a man visiting her room at night. Not wanting my daughter to be fearful, I went into the bedroom the next day and spoke to the man. I accept that ghosts can be real, so I spoke to him, acknowledging his presence. He responded to me by turning the room's lights off. Then I asked him not to startle or scare my daughter any more. 'You're welcome to stay if you want, as long as you don't scare anyone,' I said. 'I'm going downstairs now.' With that, the lights came back on. I am not imagining his presence, because I could hear the wall switch click just before the lights came on or off, so I know the spirit can manipulate physical objects. Another thing," she added, "One night, my son's heavy dresser fell over with a loud bang during the night. There is just no way in which that could happen normally."

50

Melinda and her daughter often discuss their ethereal guests, and Morgan recently told her mother that she now thinks the ghost girl died in a house fire set by an uncle. Unfortunately, Morgan doesn't know how she knows this, but suspects that she got the information telepathically from her little visitor. Psychic friends of Melinda have sat quietly in the house and several have received the information that the man has returned to the house to contact Loretta and then lead her across the divide between this world and the next. "Something like a rescue mission, I guess," Melinda said. Could this man be the girl's father? Might it be a part of the uncle's unfinished work and perhaps part of his making amends?

This story is ongoing, as both Melinda and I search historic records from the county and through on-line genealogy sites.

The Wetmore-Smith House

The Wetmore-Smith house

The old brick house has stood atop the bluffs on Riverview Road in Rexford, N.Y., since 1756, though the first known residents were not likely the builders. History records that Theodore Smith and his wife, Martha Wetmore Smith, lived there in the 1860s, and Martha, or "Mattie," was the matriarch, organizing and running the household with a firm hand.

The Smith's daughter, Virginia, is the subject of this tale. Her childhood was not much different from that of other well-to-do women of her time, and she had the best of educations in nearby private schools. She was attractive, having blue eyes and distinctive auburn hair, and when she came of age, her beauty attracted men's attention. It was merchant Albert Brown II from Schenectady who won her hand, and they wed in 1895. In a few short years, the happy couple had three healthy children, but then a fourth, a boy, died soon after birth. Virginia, who had gained the nickname of "Nina," slipped into a post-partum depression.

While the nations of the world waged war in Europe during World War I, Nina fought an inner battle against depression, struggling to maintain a normal life for her husband and children. She often crossed Riverview Road to sit pensively in her wrought-iron garden gazebo overlooking the Mohawk River to the south. Here, she communed with nature, at times overcome with the natural beauty of the rural neighborhood. She wrote many poems expressing her love of nature and life, and one can see in her aggressive cursive writing style the desperation with which she sought to maintain a hold on her world.

In one of these verses, *August*, from March 10, 1905, she wrote,

A love in its springtime is love to test; But love in summer is love at its best.

Though surrounded with the love of her family, she was continually tested, becoming increasingly anxious and depressed while attempting to maintain an untroubled exterior for her loved ones. Finally, unable to control her fragile emotions any longer, she sought psychiatric help. Failing to heal her deepening neurosis, however, the doctor finally committed her to the Rochester State Hospital. The prognosis for recovery was extremely poor, and Nina spent the remainder of her life confined in a gloomy mental ward, unable (on the advice of doctors) to see her children. Readers should be aware that there were few medications at that time which could assuage her symptoms.

She died at age thirty, and her body was returned to Vale Cemetery in Schenectady for burial. The death certificate gave the cause of death as tuberculosis and dementia praecox with a duration of three or more years. Nevertheless, Nina's friend Jennie had visited the hospital during her confinement and later wrote that she felt Nina was always lucid, coherent, and "wrongly put away." Nina's illness also took its toll on her surviving children. Her daughter, Elizabeth, later remembered the fear that she and her brothers experienced—that they, too, would become ill and die young. Therefore, any discussion of their mother's death was taboo. Only in later life did they come to understand Virginia's love for them.

In time, the Brown family moved from Riverview Road, and the old house gained new tenants—less-dignified ones. From its position high above the Mohawk River, the house was an ideal place to locate a speakeasy during Prohibition, as access to the building could continually be monitored, and it would be near impossible for law enforcement officers to sneak up on the operation. After the end of Prohibition in 1933, the bootleggers moved on and the old house sheltered a new family, but it became run-down over time, and the decaying old porch was torn off.

Then, in 1972, Mr. Reed brought his family to live on the old estate, determined to restore some of the former beauty. Youngsters Cara and Marty enjoyed the spacious lawns and surrounding forest and walked through the overgrown fields. "However, I'd hear footsteps at night when everyone was in bed, and I remember being afraid to get up in the middle of the night if I had to go into the hall," Cara told me. "I hated going into the basement, too, because strange things that I'd never experienced before seemed to happen at our new home. Then, one night, I had an intense dream—Mattie came to visit. She was friendly and calming and wanted to share her world, to put me at ease. It worked, and I felt protected after that, not scared but very respectful."

During their first week in the new home, Marty and his brother, Roger, slept in the keeping room. At night, they soon noticed that the door to the room would not stay closed, and another door in the kitchen also refused to stay closed, even when securely latched. One day, as Marty scrubbed the door, there came a force pushing it, as if someone actually had entered, and he heard footsteps walking through the house. Though he called out, nobody answered. Rising, he explored the building, seeking to view the man whose heavy footfalls he could hear just ahead of him, but the boy found no one else in the building. At other times footsteps were heard in the upstairs when no one was there, and even more mysteriously, they were heard on the roof.

On another occasion Marty, sleeping in the room with Roger, awakened with the feeling they were suddenly not alone. Just as he spotted Roger asleep in his bed, someone or something lifted a pillow and whacked Marty in the face with it. Turning on the bedroom light, he saw no one else there.

In March 1980, when she was thirteen, Cara had a vivid dream which led her to explore the house's history and mystery. She recorded that her dream began with the sensation of someone besides family being in the house. She saw herself rising from her bed and going downstairs. As she descended, the girl saw a short woman with what appeared to be strawberry blonde hair pulled back standing before the china cabinet, perusing the contents. The stranger, dressed in a creamy golden-colored, high-necked, full-length satin dress with puffed top sleeves and a lace bodice, picked up a china teacup and examined it closely, then smiled at Cara as if they were old friends. Though the rest of her family appeared to also be downstairs, the woman began to chat exclusively with the dreaming Cara. Black and white photographs of the girl's childhood years in the house suddenly appeared and became animated. She saw herself swinging in the backyard, and then observed a small boy sitting with her on the same swing.

Accompanied by the mystery woman, Cara walked out of the house in her dream nightgown, and the teenager turned to look back at her home. It looked radically different now, with a new-looking wrap-around porch and railings, lots of glass décor and French doors. She had the sense of a happy and active household inside the house as her dreaming self walked back to the barn, seeking a favorite horse called Ambralight, who was about to foal. The spirit woman who accompanied her said that when she had lived there she also had a bay horse like Cara's, and then commented that on the following day Ambralight would have a foal prettier than her dam.

The pair continued walking toward the rear of the property, then crawled through a hole in the fence, where they spied a vast open field with one large barn. The dream woman informed Cara that there used to be a carriage house there, where she herself had played with a little boy, perhaps referring to her brother. Soon after that, the dream ended.

The next day, the teenager was excited because, just as the lady had predicted, Ambralight gave birth to a foal with the same coloring and markings, a beautiful horse that they named Lillian's Vision. In further confirmation weeks later, an old veterinarian visiting the family told of a large barn and a carriage house once standing in the back fields that now had other owners. Here is the woman in a sketch that Cara drew the morning after her dream.

Cara's sketch

Thus began a series of events that defy explanation. A year after the dream the Reeds held a dinner party for relatives; Cara remembers thirteen people at the table. In the middle of the meal, there came a terrible crash, sounding as if a chandelier had crashed to the floor. Everyone arose to seek the source of the sound, though nothing was found out of place. Strangely though, Cara did find part of a crystal goblet near the fireplace in the keeping room, but oddly, the glassware was in a pattern that her family didn't own. The remainder of the goblet was never found.

Some months later, a contractor named Jeff began renovation of the living room and often complained of bumping into an invisible "something or someone" blocking his path. He had to remove eight layers of wallpaper from the walls, and his efforts at repapering were also frustrating as, though he carefully measured his lengths, once the paper was put up, it was always a bit short.

Another unfathomable phenomenon involved roses. The garden behind the house produced beautiful red roses, though when these were cut and brought into the house, they turned brown or black within an hour. At the same time, family members visiting the cellar often remarked about the strong odor of roses there, though none had ever been present. Other varieties of roses kept well inside the house, so what was the mystery of the red roses? The Reeds never found an acceptable answer.

In 1982, around Christmastime, Cara walked into the dark front hall and heard Christmas tree ornaments tinkling, as though someone had just brushed against a decorated tree, or as if an open door had created a draft that moved ornaments on a tree—yet there was no tree in the hall. Then she remembered that during the first Christmas her family had spent in the house, there had been a tree there. Were these sounds emanating from an earlier holiday in her or her predecessors' house?

On several occasions, Mr. Reed awakened at night to hear revelry downstairs and, assuming that his teens were having a party, descended the stairs to rebuke them for their noise. But the downstairs was dark, and the teens were found asleep in their beds. On another occasion, Cara's friend Lori visited the Reed home during Christmastime. She came down to breakfast one morning with a strange dream to tell. During the night, she had seen herself in a rose garden behind the house, as a woman dressed in white led her through long arbors of bright red roses. The woman walked just out of Lori's reach. Though she felt the mystery woman, whose face she couldn't see, welcomed her, Lori was unable to catch up, and at one point, it seemed as if the rose bushes extended on forever into the distance. After she told the dream, Cara recounted her own dream of meeting such a woman, as Lori had never known of the ghostly presence.

On another visit, the friend had her own experience of Nina's presence. Rising from in front of a warm fireplace one evening, Lori walked through the living room and into a very chilly spot. The girls didn't understand how that frigid experience could happen so close to a warm fire.

So during the Reed family's ownership of the old estate, the unusual became usual. The most common thought now is that Virginia, perhaps the woman of the roses, and an unknown male still lived in or visited the old house as spirits. Nancy Reed, Cara's mother, several times dreamed of driving up to the house and finding it overgrown and uninhabited. One wonders if that was a projection of Virginia's fears for her former home. Or perhaps that was her experience in the spirit world, that she couldn't fully inhabit the house any longer.

After the Reeds sold the house and moved on, Rob Cole, who lived across the road, discussed some childhood memories with his mother, Doris Cole, noted Rexford artist. "Mom, did I ever tell you about the time I was on a ledge down along the bluffs, drinking beer with some friends? We looked out onto the Mohawk River and saw a woman in a long white dress walking toward us, across the river's surface. I never said anything about it at the time, considering the beer and its effects, but now after hearing all the stories from people who lived and visited in the old Wetmore-Smith house, I wonder. I really do wonder!"

Several families have owned the old house since the Reeds left, and much interior renovation has been done. Apparently, Mattie and Nina, if they still remain attached to the dwelling, have chosen to withhold their memories and visions of its former beauty. Perhaps the new people have their own vision to promote and aren't interested in listening.

Things Were Popping

"Islip Terrace, in the Town of Islip, was a cozy neighborhood and my husband and I thought it would be a peaceful retreat from our work life. We moved into our house in 1994, and our first years there were happy and uneventful. In March 2000, we had boy/girl twins, and the children were a blessing—we couldn't have been happier. It was soon after their birth that we first discovered our ghost," Cherie told me.

"On a June night, when the twins were three months old, we hired a babysitter for them. After she got the kids to bed, the sitter entertained herself by making a big bowl of popcorn and seems to have spilled half of it inside the house. Though she cleaned up some, there was plenty still around when my husband and I returned home," Cherie continued. "We had a mess of popcorn all over and couldn't find our TV remote. Though we searched high and low for it, even overturning all the furniture and searching through the cushions, the remote couldn't be found. No matter how I cleaned, I kept finding pieces of popcorn everywhere," Cherie continued, "but, eventually, I became sure I had it all swept up. We also figured the sitter had absconded with our TV remote control, as we searched high and low for it, even turning over all the furniture and searching through the cushions, but it was nowhere to be found. Still, I kept putting off a call to the sitter, hoping not to embarrass her with the question, and hoping we'd find the remote somewhere.

"Well, six months went by and Christmas was coming and, one night, my husband fell asleep on the couch while watching television, in the spot where the sitter had sat, back in June. He awoke in the middle of the night to find the remote control laying on his chest and surrounded by whole pieces of popcorn! He ran up the stairs in a cold sweat, waking me from a nice dream, to yell at me for playing one of my pranks on him. We were the only two people in the house at that time, so who could have done this? The incident sure made a believer of him! Well, we had our remote back, but we were then treated to something more.

"We began to find lights turned on when we were certain that we'd turned them off," she said. "Likewise, lights would be turned off when they had been on a minute earlier. This activity started a month or two before Christmas and continued until after the holiday. Who was our phantom electrician? I pondered. Then objects, usually little things, would disappear, only to reappear later among our Christmas ornaments and decorations. What was this Christmastime mischief? What was it about the holiday season that put her into motion?" Cherie asked.

I told Cherie of several instances that I knew of where ghosts became suddenly energized at holiday times. That really is no surprise, I said, because holiday events and get-togethers are often some of the happiest memories that we take with us at the end of life; also, the saddest at other times. And either emotion, joy or regret, if it is powerful enough, can serve as a restraint for the soul which should have left the earth plane. Some entities want to keep experiencing what may have been one of the few happy memories of the just-ended life. Others cannot get over some type of unhappiness, perhaps wishing they or their loved ones had behaved differently.

"Then I began to notice shapes or movements out of the corner of my eye, though if I looked directly, nothing was there. My son came down one morning to tell me he had seen a woman in his bedroom during the previous night. 'Mommy, she pulled my nose and I smacked her,' he said, and four years later, he continues to tell the same story. This house was only about thirty years old, and probably had only one previous owner. I had met the family one or twice, and knew they had raised all their children here, and I knew that the woman had later passed away. What I also knew is that she had to go. So, one quiet day, I stood in the living room and simply explained to her that she had died, that she no longer owned the house, so she had to go onward to what comes next. I then watched my twins, who were then four years old, turn their heads toward the stairs as they followed something or someone up the stairs and out the door. . Then they turned to me and said they had just seen a woman fly up from downstairs and out the door and up to the sky. And that was it. We never lost objects again, never had lights turn on or off, and never again saw figures."

I confirmed to Cherie that she did everything just right. Most of the beings who remain in the houses we buy or buildings where we work are not evil or mean. Most are simply confused or hoping they can get a second chance at physical life. Understandably, they don't want to leave what seems to be their only life, but most can be convinced.

Less than ten percent of ghosts, by my estimation, resist and give a homeowner trouble. Most of those, however, if you are persistent, will go; must go. One cannot be of two minds about the matter, however. Don't be wishy-washy—be firm and insist that they move on. If you are religious, send them on their way in the name of God or The Creator or Jesus, or whomever you hold most high. It is best for them and you that they go.

Watching Jonathan

"Not long after we bought the big old house on Gifford Street in Lakewood, almost twenty years ago, I learned that I was pregnant," Pam told me. "It was a time of delight, with a new home and a new baby on the way. The house was over one hundred years old and had previously been owned by a Baptist minister, Reverend W.G. Gerthe, and his wife. All he told us when we inspected the house was that it had been remodeled, and we were pleased with the interior appearance, so we made a purchase offer.

"Expecting a child, I cut back my hours at work and spent more time at home, and maybe that fact can explain how I became aware of the presence," she said. "Sometimes, when I was in the shower, the lights would turn off and I'd be in pitch darkness. In a windowless bathroom, that really frightened me, and after little Jonathan was born, I used to bring his bassinet into the bathroom with me just in case he cried, so I could locate and tend to him. One of our relatives is an electrician, so we had him check out all our wiring, and he found it hard to believe there was any malfunction, because the wiring was all up to code.

"There was something a bit eerie in that house, and I was upset that I couldn't see or hear anything, though my senses told me that someone or something was there. So, many days, I would take the baby to the mall and we did a lot of walking," she smiled, giving me to know that she preferred not to stay home and be scared.

"When Jonathan was a year old I observed that he would chatter away, apparently talking to someone near his seat or bed. When I'd look in on him, however, there was nobody else there. But I was content that he was happy."

Their house on Gifford Street had been designed as a 3-family dwelling, but an earlier owner had merged one apartment into the other, leaving them with a large upstairs apartment that they could rent out. But that upstairs apartment didn't extend over the kitchen, which was a single-story later addition. "So, you can see how I was at first puzzled, then troubled, when I'd hear footsteps overhead when I worked in the kitchen. There were only rafters in that space, I was sure, and when I told my husband, he attributed the sounds to outdoor noises. So, there I was in a new home, with strange noises in a place where they shouldn't be, bathroom lights that extinguished themselves, though the wiring was all fine, and a husband who was in denial. Well, he didn't have to stay home and listen to the commotion all day!" she feigned upset and then smiled.

As her son grew older, he loved to play with toys on the living room floor in front of the television, and Pam often took photographs of the boy for their album and to send to relatives. "One day, when some developed pictures came back, I noted something strange on the television screen. The set was turned off, I'm certain of that, yet the photo showed a large man's face in close-up on the screen—with his eyes at the top of the screen and his upper lip at the bottom. And all across the top of the screen was a series of numbers that were meaningless to me.

"Fortunately, the spiritualist center at Lily Dale is not far from the south end of Chautauqua Lake where we lived, so I called up to get some reassurance. The woman who answered my call told me that as long as the face was behind Jonathan, it wasn't anything bad. 'It is almost as if the being is guarding or watching over your son,' she told me. 'If his image blotted out your son in the photo, the spirit might be trying to take over the boy—then you'd have trouble. But, it is okay—the entity seems protective.' And I found that to be true. Whoever our spirit was, he only did a little mischief from time to time, to let us know he was there.

"Eventually, our circumstances changed and we got out of the landlord business and moved to our present home. We allowed the new buyers to move in even before the closing. On the first night after they moved in, I got a call from the woman, who informed me that most of the water pipes had broken somewhere upstairs, and that many things were ruined. What could I say? Broken pipes wasn't part of our ghost's act up to that time, so how could I attribute it to him? And, after all, not all problems had to be his fault. We didn't know if the buyers would experience the same events that I did, so we didn't say there was a ghost. In any case, the new owner was relieved that her homeowner's insurance policy was already in place and all the damage would be repaired."

Pam told me, however, that the repairmen who then came to the Gifford Street house had to rip out some old carpeting, partitions, and timbers in the upstairs, and uncovered a small room over the kitchen that she had suspected was there, though her husband pooh-poohed the idea. Perhaps most important, the newlyexposed beams were scorched from some long-ago fire. Maybe that was why old Reverend Gerthe had "remodeled!" So, who was the spirit? Might some member of his family have perished in that fire? Or did the burns come from a fire during someone else's occupancy? "We have been unable to track down the minister, so we'll never know. We're in a nice house now, and John is graduating from high school, so he grew up well. And maybe that was because of his guard or guide."

The Gifford Street house sat abandoned for ten years, perhaps waiting for a new occupant to annoy. Or maybe the spirit left. The Village of Lakewood finally auctioned off the property. Many times, once a house's "secret" has been exposed to daylight, the spirit can relinquish its hold on its former world and begin acclimating to the next one.

During my research, I located Rev. Gerthe in Minnesota, where he lives in retirement. He told me that he and Mrs. Gerthe never had any haunting experiences and theorized that the ready presence of a Bible would have kept such annoyances away. For whatever reason, however, the entity was ready and waiting for Pam's family. I attempted to contact the present resident of the house but received no reply to my query.

NEW YORK STATE GHOSTS

CHAPTER 2

HISTORICAL GHOSTS

A Museum of Time

Old Stone Fort

Attempting to discern the Iroquois meaning of the name "Schoharie" yields two prominent themes: "drift" and "to cross over." Both ideas seem relevant to the Old Stone Fort Museum in the Village of Schoharie, originally built by the first settlers as a church, a structure in which some energies or consciousnesses may continue to drift, not yet crossed over.

By 1713, immigrant German farmers began to populate the Schoharie Valley, and as the fields yielded increasing bounty, work began on a large stone church. Yet, in the sixty years of settlement along the Schoharie Creek, conditions had changed. Originally, the Germans and later the Dutch got along well with local Mohawk tribes, but in six decades, the Indians began to notice that they were losing or selling more and more of their ancestral lands, and it was becoming more difficult to find game in the forests. Also, the fractious colonials were resisting British rule.

When the Reformed Church was completed in 1772, it was, as Luther might have termed it, "a mighty fortress." Its architecture indicated the strength of God, but shortly thereafter, as the Revolution began, the pews were removed, a perimeter stockade was built, strong window shutters with loopholes for musket fire were constructed, and the old stone church became an earthly stronghold to which threatened farm folk could flee when Indians raided. The Six Nations of the Iroquois, minus the Oneidas, remained loyal to Great Britain throughout the war, and sought to exterminate the settlers. Raiding parties aside, there was no serious military challenge to the old fort itself until 1780, when Sir John Johnson and his Tory army invaded. The old fort was not conquered, though a cannon shot pierced the roof gable, a structural wound that can be seen even today.

Over the years after the war, this "lower fort" (one of three in the valley) reverted to its original function of worship, but in 1844, the congregation moved out, having constructed a finer brick church in the village. Maintaining ownership of the old church, however, the Reformed Church continued its use for Sunday School classes and funerals for old timers until 1857, at which time New York State purchased the edifice for use as an armory.

Local residents kept alive the stories of legendary local Revolutionary War soldier Timothy Murphy, whose keen eye and sharpshooter rifle killed British General Simon Fraser at three hundred yards during the Battle of Saratoga in 1777. Schoharie Valley residents have justly been proud of their history and, after the state closed the armory, the local historical society began to gather artifacts at the old stone building for a museum in 1888.

Today there is a grouping of seven buildings in the museum complex, permitting both school children and adults to learn of colonial and early American life in the valley. Though I had visited the museum long ago, I had never heard tales of ghosts there. But then, in 2005, I got my first report, from a visitor who had "strange feelings" when visiting the exhibits. Then came another story; this one of a former historian and curator who often heard footsteps crossing what he knew to be an unoccupied upstairs gallery. It seemed the right time to visit the Old Stone Fort Museum again.

In May of 2007, joined by my professional dowser friend, Bill Getz from nearby Gallupville, I visited the old building. As it is a living museum of valley history, today one can find little indication of it having been a church, though the outer form of the building, minus its ancient steeple, is that of a house of worship. Inside, I visited the historical society's research library, one of the finest I've ever been in, where I sought in vain for mention of ghosts in old newspapers stored there. Meanwhile, Bill searched the building's interior with his dowsing L-rods. He later returned to tell the librarian and me of his findings.

Downstairs, he got a strong reading of a presence near the Timothy Murphy artifacts display case. Beneath its glass can be found Murphy's powder horn and pocket watch. Bill found his rods reacting strongly with a piece of paper in the cabinet, but his bi-focal glasses didn't give him a clear image of the writing. He asked the rods a series of yes-and-no questions beginning with, "Is there a spirit here?" When he received a positive response, he commenced an inner dialogue with his source, which revealed a young black woman who called his attention to the contents of the case. When I heard this, I walked over to the display and clearly read a document of sale (Timothy Murphy to Jacob

Mann) of a young Negro woman. I read the paper to Bill, who was happy with the result. He'd received a valid "hit."

On the way to the upstairs, I asked staffer Laura if she had ever heard footsteps overhead, and she affirmed that such footfalls had been heard when the gallery was unoccupied—at times when she knew she was alone in the building. Another guide, Martha, had heard the footsteps and felt a cold chill, which she tried very hard to convince herself was the air conditioner. Kristeen, another staff member, had heard stories of others who had such experiences, though she herself had none.

On the second story are display cases of countless Indian artifacts (flint knives, arrowheads, spear points, etc.), many of which pre-date the coming of the Europeans. Other display cabinets hold silver and household china from Schoharie Valley settlers in the 1700s, some passed down in Murphy's family. On the second floor, Bill's dowsing rods focused on an invisible woman standing near an arrowhead collection, though the wraith or spirit consciousness didn't interact with him. We later discovered that that particular collection was donated by a woman, so was it the donor, still proud of her contribution? That was pretty much the result of our day there. While footsteps had been heard and vague presences had been indicated through dowsing, I felt or saw no particular spirits. Was it possible, we wondered, that the emanations came just from the artifacts?

Bill and I discussed the matter for quite a while, and we then learned of a local woman, Corbie Mittlied, who is sensitive to spirit energies, and who has done psychic readings throughout America and Canada—might she help us? I phoned and made an appointment for her to meet us at the Old Stone Fort Museum in mid-July. We found her a most engaging and high-energy lady, who couldn't wait to begin her scans of the interior.

My intuition works mainly in my head and senses. Bill's functions through the dowsing rods. Corbie operated in an entirely different way, using an object that she calls her "talking stick," which appears inspired by American Indian design. Its pointer end is a large Danburite crystal, which many believe can both receive and project energies. After sensitizing herself, she moved directly to an old large child's rocking horse on the first floor, and after asking questions of the spirits there, stated that it dated from the 1840s or early 1850s. She sensed that it had been owned by a boy whose father was a soldier who had died in battle. "So, the boy grew up hearing stories of his father's bravery and, when Fort Sumter was fired on in 1861, he enlisted in the Army." Bill leaned into the exhibit and discovered a museum tag indicating that the horse dated from the 1840s. As it wasn't known who originally owned the large toy, we had to take that as a partial "hit."

Upstairs, Corbie was drawn to a large 1700s porcelain plate, donated by a descendent of Tim Murphy. "This was a valuable wedding present to the woman who later donated it to the museum," she said. "It was a 'big gift,' meant to impress the bride's family." Carle Kopecky, the museum director, informed us that it was "luster chinaware," likely made in England for export trade to America. We were unable to determine whose energy remained around the plate: the donor's or the bride's?

Perhaps the strongest energy in the room for Corbie was a Civil War uniform in a display case. "There is a lot of energy here, perhaps the man's spirit visits on occasion, saying, 'A good soldier never leaves his post.'" I read the history of the uniform and accoutrements that belonged to Col. Simon Hosack Mix of the 3rd N.Y. Cavalry. The owner had migrated to the valley in 1838 and became a publisher, working with famed Horace Greeley for a few years. "To him, this is still an armory or fort," Corbie interjected. The tag said that Mix immediately enlisted in the Union Army at the start of the conflict, and he disappeared at the long battle at Petersburg, Virginia. His body was never found, though the museum's uniform was a "spare," donated by family. There were huge explosions at the Battle of Petersburg and many soldiers were buried alive. One wonders if Mix is still sorting out where his duty lies, as the battle seems on hold in some strange way.

We then moved to Bill's "woman near display case" section. Without telling Corbie what he'd picked up, he asked her to take a reading and use her intuition to decipher the result. The seer didn't find a donor woman there, and in fact, provided a response that puzzled us all, including the museum director. Corbie got the sensation of a white woman begging for her life, "but this was long before the European settlers," she told us. It appeared to come from a time long before the Europeans were in America, in fact. "This woman wasn't well," Corbie told us (perhaps referring to hunger or illness) and she watched the Indians kill her child, then lunged at them with something sharp, some kind of kitchen utensil. Her captors ended her life quickly, almost as a mercy killing," our psychic concluded.

Suddenly, I remembered psychic information provided to me in the late 1970s, when working with the noted psychic Millie Coutant from Lake George. Millie, when asked if Vikings ever came to upper New York State, told of "watching" a Viking long ship ascend the Hudson and a party (did it include women? I can't remember) of that group then moved westward on the Mohawk River and then south, where they encountered the Schoharie Creek. "They settled in lean-tos there, but were eventually all killed by the Indians," she had told us. By some longshot chance, might the female ghost presence be one of those Scandinavians? As I have often said, chasing ghost stories often provides more puzzles and questions than answers.

Both ventures to Schoharie were illuminating, as each of the three of us researchers sought information in a different way. So it wasn't really a surprise that each of us received different information. In summary, it seems that energies come and go at any reputedly haunted site. Perhaps the spirits of the deceased focus (in incorporeal consciousness) on an object or location for only a period of time, and then move elsewhere in eternity, though they may revisit objects that were once important to them. Eternity seems to be about growth, learning, and movement, and surely there are schools "over there" that help the deceased sort out the eternal meaning of the life that has ended.

So, are there ghosts at The Old Stone Fort Museum? Apparently, sometimes. For brief periods. The objects preserved there help inform both the living and the dead as to the profound meanings of life, especially in this garden spot of Schoharie County.

A Burr-den Laid Down

Burr house

In the early morning mists on July 11, 1804, two rowboats at a distance from one another crossed the Hudson River from Manhattan, headed for the Heights at Weehawken on the New Jersey shore. Two longtime political adversaries, one the sitting Vice President of the United States, and the other a former Secretary of the Treasury, with their seconds, took up positions on the popular dueling ground. The New Jersey site was made necessary by New York

State's recent ban on dueling. Friends of the pair had made ineffectual efforts at compromise, and as the pistols were loaded and primed, no other avenue seemed open to the pair. Alexander Hamilton shot first, raising his pistol well above Aaron Burr and the bullet struck a tree limb overhead. Burr, however, shot to kill, striking Hamilton a mortal wound in the right abdomen. Returning to New York City, Burr dined on eggs and toast. Hamilton died the following day and was buried in Trinity Churchyard in the city.

Murder charges were then leveled at Burr in both New Jersey and New York, though in the end, neither case went to trial. Where did Burr go while under indictment? It is known that he was in South Carolina, living with his daughter in early 1805, but is it possible that (between July and January) he had a hideout in the village of Lansingburgh, just north of Troy, until he could make that journey southward? And, if so, did Burr's ghost return there after death?

During the late 1800s, Anthony Augustus Peebles and his wife, Mary Louisa, owned a house at the southeast corner of Third Avenue and 114th Street in Lansingburgh. For a number of years, they noted, curious throngs came to stand on 114th Street at night, looking upward at the wooden building's attic windows. At intervals, illuminated by the glow from a gas lamp on the corner below, a white-shrouded figure would appear in the windows. For a number of reasons, locals interpreted the apparition as being Aaron Burr's ghost.

At the time of the 1804 duel, the house was occupied by Cadwallader Colden, nephew of New York State Governor Morgan Lewis, a close friend of Burr. Old timers, as well as her husband, informed Mrs. Peebles that strong wooden shutters had always been closed over those windows during Colden's tenure there, and the back door to the house had been barred. In 1862, Mr. Peebles' half-sister told Mary Louisa that she knew Burr had resided there for a time, though if he ever ventured outdoors, it must have been at night. Members of the Peebles family showed her asparagus and rose plants which Burr had allegedly sent to the Colden family from France, so the Colden-Burr relationship must have been close. Additionally, Mary Louisa discovered that her in-laws, upon hearing footsteps upstairs when the rooms were unoccupied, would whisper, "Shhh—that's Aaron!" The experience seemed not to be a joke played for the sake of the new wife.

It is common ghost lore that the departed spirit often returns to places (and times) of intensely emotional events in the just-ended life. After the 1804 duel, Burr learned with a certainty that Hamilton (on the night before the duel) had written that he intended to waste his first shot and not fire at his opponent. Why had no one in Hamilton's party disclosed that fact to Burr? Is it possible that, following his death, Vice President Burr came to understand that he had needlessly killed Hamilton when honor had been salvaged? Hamilton was the son-in-law of the powerful Philip Schuyler family in Albany. In fear of retribution, Burr must have feared for his political, if not his physical life? Might some residue of that fear have lingered in the upstairs of the old Colden house, where the angst was re-created from time to time?

By the early 1920s the old structure had aged so badly that it wasn't worth restoring, and the property was sold to a neighbor who tore it down. Curiously, a jar of gold coins was found in the wreckage. When he died in 1836, Aaron Burr was penniless, divorced and disgraced. His life might have taken a turn toward greatness in the Election of 1800, when he and Thomas Jefferson received the same number of electoral votes, but Hamilton had worked tirelessly to elect Jefferson. Such anger and resentment on Burr's part certainly would be a hard burden to lay aside after death.

Remains

Knickerbocker Mansion

When Col. Johannes Knickerbacker and his wife, Elizabeth, came to build on the plain along the Hoosic River in northern Rensselaer County in 1770, the land had been in the family's possession since before 1709. At least two family homes had existed there since old Herman Jansen Knickerbacker bought the land from the Mohawks. Before the coming of the white men the area had been an ancient hunting ground, as well as a battlefield, for the Mohawks and Mohicans. In a conciliatory move, the area tribes met where the Knickerbacker's house now stands and, in 1676, planted a peace tree, known to whites as the Witenagemot Oak. Some part of that tree survived until the giant tree fell over in a Hoosic River flood in 1949; it has subsequently fully died. A cement mold of the fallen tree can still be seen in the back yard.

The Knickerbackers built in the old Flemish or Dutch brick style on fields where, just four years later, the 14th Albany County Militia would muster before crossing the Hudson to fight Burgoyne's army at Bemis Heights and Saratoga. It was an old site, where earlier family members had trapped, traded and farmed, and Native Americans had fished and farmed for centuries before that. The Knickerbackers were farmers who kept open lines of communication to Albany, the most genteel of area communities. From that city came many of America's notables to visit an elderly Johannes Knickerbacker and his family, and one of those was Washington Irving, who wrote about the "Knickerbockers" in his 1809 work, *A History of New York*, using the pen name of Diedrich Knickerbocker. This book launched Irving's career. Likely because of Irving's misspelling, the now-famous family dropped the a and converted it to an o.

As an aside, the Irving book had a cover illustration of two Dutch boys in knee-length pants. Prior to its publication, most folks called such trousers "breeches," a term that quickly was replaced with "knickerbockers," which then became "knickers," later adopted by the British as a euphemism for ladies' underpants.

For almost two centuries, the large farm with huge barns was worked, but by the 1950s, the mansion was showing its age. Though the Knickerbockers ceased living there before 1920, the property and house were sold only in 1946. Later tenants were unable to afford the necessary maintenance and the structure fell into disrepair. "The front wall had pretty well collapsed and vandals were further destroying what had once been a proud homestead," Leslie Allen told me. The local historical society has made the preservation and restoration of the old home their priority, she told me. At the time of my visit, accompanied by my sidekick, Susan, who has accompanied me to many eerie sites, Leslie was our guide. We talked about the annual Harvest Festival and Haunted House tours conducted every fall. "Is there a ghost or two here?" I asked.

Noting that there was no history of horror about the place, she did say that various guides or reenactors have had unique experiences there, and welcomed Sue's and my visit to the building, to see what we might turn up, and how any of that information might square with others' tales. Sue and I split up once inside, as we usually do, to receive whatever inspirations we could. To me, it simply looked like another old house on the verge of expiration, though I could see that important restoration had been done. Shutters were closed against the bright sun, but also to keep out vandals who have little appreciation of the house's history and uniqueness, as few such old Dutch homesteads survive today.

I wandered into the front left parlor, which was dim, dusty and empty. I was surprised to turn and note a black man with curly white hair, just lighting a fire in the large fireplace. I looked at him and knew him to be a house memory rather than a frightful ghost. Yet, we communicated, with me mentally asking what he was doing with his lit, rolled-up newspaper. "Got to warm up this room for visitors," was the reply that I perceived. His livery seemed to be a pale violet with a starched white collar, and he looked quite spiffy for a hired man or slave. I had to readjust my thinking to slavery, to remind myself that New York State did permit slavery up into the 1820s. Then he was gone and I was alone again. I felt the room had once been a library or retreat for the master of the house, though there are no bookshelves there today.

Strolling to the front foyer, I noted the large, old front door, which seemed original. Then, I strolled into a partially restored bright parlor with a beautiful old fireplace. When Sue and I had first arrived, as we stood in front of the mansion, I had "heard" loud piano music from inside the old house, something that our guide said no one had ever commented on before. Now, inside the front right parlor, I decided that this was the room from which the long-ago sound had emanated. Not much else here, I felt, so up the stairs I went.

In the large, front right bedroom, my insight focused on a woman dressed in a yellow, high-waist dress and she was just tying the bow of a bonnet beneath her chin, seemingly unaware of me. I guessed from the clothing style that this was a scene from the 1820s or 1830s. In the large, front left bedroom, I imagined several men in 1840s or 1850s dress, several with knee-high boots and beaver top hats lounging about. One carried a riding crop. Then, in a right rear bedroom, I spotted two girls, about eighteen, sitting on beds and chatting. In a small, center-rear room I spied a misty copper bath tub, and wondered if that had, indeed, been a bathing room. All that is found in that room today are pieces of exterior eaves moulding, stored and awaiting restoration.

In the back left bedroom, I found a cheery scene. A curly, white-haired dowager sat propped up in her bed, covered with a comforter and surrounded by younger folk who seemed to enjoy waiting on her. A servant boy was just removing a basin of water from the room. Then, out that door, I trudged up the steep and narrow stairs to the attic. As I passed the attic floor level, still on the ascent, I saw and heard a thin black woman, a slave whose name seemed to be Tulia. I knew her to be a trusted and competent young woman. Later, outdoors, I felt that a large iron cooking or rendering cauldron had been buried at one time, though later, Leslie said she'd never heard of such an event. Intuitives never can be quite sure about such impressions, but we have to at least speak them.

When we came inside from outdoors, we joined up with Sue, who was just descending from the upstairs, and Leslie invited us to visit the cellar. Down a narrow passageway, we entered the dirt-floored cellar. Our guide urged Sue to walk into the far reaches of the dim space, to see what she might pick up intuitively. Sue told us that she heard a spirit sound similar to metal being hammered, and she wondered if an anvil had once been located there—maybe blacksmithing? Then she took some photos with her digital camera, or I should say, tried to take some. She snapped a few, but her flash wouldn't work. "That's because I know there is energy over there," she grinned. "I could feel it and tried to get a picture." Surely, it must be her camera's malfunction, I thought, but when I tried, my flash was also inoperative. The few pictures that did come out showed nothing. Leslie told us that her sister, Stana, had tried three times with various cameras to get pictures in the house, without any luck. "Her cameras were later found to be broken," Leslie smiled.

Sue had better luck getting photos in other parts of the cellar, but when she stepped back into the "anvil space," the camera again wouldn't work. This second venture into that space gave Sue a jolt, and she told us, "I just saw a large black man in front of me, and realized that he doesn't want us to take pictures here." Leslie smiled and told us that Knickerbocker slaves had lived in that area at one time, and she pointed out ancient wall fastenings for chains.

Sue sensed the smell of baking bread and Leslie told us that this part of the cellar was once the site of a cellar oven, where bread was made daily by servants, while other family cooking was done there in the evening.

When we returned upstairs, it was time for Sue and I to present our other sensations for Leslie to either confirm or deny from her studies of the Knickerbockers. First, Leslie smiled when I asked for details of black slaves in the house's history. "We have written records on only one of them, though there certainly were others. In Johannes' will, he mentions a 'Tom,' as a Knickerbocker servant, who used to enjoy telling ghost stories up in the attic to children of his time." I wondered if that was the aging gentleman who I'd met lighting a fire in the front room.

"Where you saw the old lady in bed," Leslie continued, "various visiting psychics often pick up sounds of children playing upstairs." Sue smiled and said, "Yep! That's what I got in the attic—children playing, and I sensed that these were the family's children and not those of servants or slaves." Did we hit upon different times in history, making us both correct? Or were both of us in error?

Fortunately, Sue had verification of her insights from the other sensitives. Leslie told us that some members of the historical society, while strolling outside, have seen an old lady looking out that upstairs room's window.

Our guide then took us out front, and we knew she was testing us to see if we'd pick up a verification of scenes that others had gotten there. "Yesterday, before we came here," Susan told us, "I got German or Dutch words, something like *strudel* and *schnitzel.*" She noted that she also had "seen" images of the Knickerbocker Mansion. At one time, I could keep it a secret from her as to where we were going, and she never knew our destination until we pulled up outside. Now, however, she is getting better and better, often knowing in advance where we'll be working the next day or week, and often receiving images. She told us of sensing an American Indian spirit before we came that day, and that the figure had given her the word "Seneca" and telling her that he would be at the mansion for a special gathering. Was it a modern or historical event? Sue wondered.

Leslie urged Sue to walk to what appeared to be an old wood pile behind the house. At that spot, Sue felt a lot of Indian energy and felt herself in the 1600s, and said she heard the word "blockhouse." Later, Leslie told us that the cement and rotting wood was all that remained of the old Witenagemot Oak, and that early settlers had some type of "fortification" there, though records don't say whether or not it was an actual blockhouse.

At that point, we three stood on the ground near the front entrance to the house and Sue again felt an Indian presence and the word "massacre." When questioned, she felt this related to an event perhaps a mile to the north. "So, why am I picking that up here, getting images of people being chased down?" She told us of having experienced the image of a Seneca Indian when she had meditated a day or so before coming to Schagticoke. That sounded like a clear error, as the Seneca Indians lived in western New York State. After a minute or two, however, Leslie spoke of a man who regularly teaches at festivities at the Knickerbocker Mansion and who is a reenactor of Mohican Indian life during the Harvest Festival held there. "He is part Seneca," she smiled. So, Sue was picking up both historical and present-day information.

Leslie continued, telling us that an Indian interpreter, Paul Stillman, often stays overnight upstairs during the festivals and, one misty morning, awoke and looked out eastward into the fields. There, he beheld a small village of Iroquois longhouses situated between the mansion and the Hoosic River, though the scene suddenly vanished. She continued, "My son, who dresses as a colonial soldier for our celebrations here, sometimes stays overnight and sleeps in that same upstairs bedroom. He told me that once, in the middle of the night, he heard a noise and woke to see Paul, probably still asleep, pushing a ghost off his body." "Gee, I did see some militia-uniformed men up in the attic, too," Sue responded. "I wonder if that was Paul and his friends or someone from long, long ago."

For my part, I saw men maneuvering a coffin down from a front porch shaped differently from that of today; different in shape even, from those shown in historic etchings or photos. Most wakes were conducted inside the deceased's home in yesteryear, and dead Knickerbockers would have been taken around the western side of the house and across the road to the large family cemetery there.

We went inside again, and Leslie admitted that she once had seen a man looking out the front parlor window, his hands pressed against the glass. "While we're here in this front room (the fireplace room)," she continued, "let me tell you about a painter we hired to finish the walls in this room on the day before Mother's Day a year ago. As he hurriedly painted to make the room ready for the next day's open house, he heard a rather noisy, chatty group of people coming into the foyer and hallway. Who could it be, he wondered, and stopped his work to investigate. The hallway was empty. Another time, a society member heard noises in an upstairs bedroom and went up to see who it was. But all the rooms were dark and empty. In this present living room, which probably was where they entertained their quality guests, camera flashes often malfunction. This is one spot where my sister's camera broke."

Sue then asked about that front parlor, feeling that it once had been the ballroom. Again, Leslie smiled and responded that the ballroom had been the one across the hall, as there are extra supports underneath it in the cellar. Sue was unhappy to be one room off on that one, but all three of us, I think, were happy that so many of our insights were 'hitting.' "Politicians from Albany often came up to this farm with John and Elizabeth," Leslie told us, "to get the wheat rent, and they partied here during their overnight stays. Who is to say the events weren't centered over in that room?"

In the upstairs room that I had suspected of being a former bathroom, Sue had touched some old exterior trim cornices being stored there. "These weren't part of the original house," she told us, "because I get 1834." Again, Leslie smiled and stated that Sue was correct. "We believe they were added sometime in the mid-1800s." Sue laughed and said, "I'll take it—close enough!" In a few parts of the house, the original wallpaper has been preserved, and the historical society had the exact pattern custom-made for the front parlor. But, perhaps, those few original swatches retain some of the ancient vibrations created in that space over the centuries. Maybe yesteryear's sounds or scenes replay themselves from time to time.

Sue asked Leslie about the rear dining room, because she'd spotted a lady in Victorian dress there, one who was not a servant. "In all likelihood, that was a kitchen in the original house," Leslie said. "One more oddity, ghostly or not," our guide said, pointing, "see that shutter on the front window? No matter how careful we are to latch it when we leave and turn on the burglar alarms, many times we find it unlatched when we return."

It is well that the historical society now protects the treasured building electronically. Too many young vandals, seeking a cheap thrill, and having no appreciation for how irreplaceable the house is, can, and have in the past, broken in. Leslie told me that the society had once paid to have exact replicas made for the spindles on the stairway, only to return a few days after installation to find them all shattered.

Physical preservation of historic sites is a must in today's world. For those of us who visit places of reputed hauntings, there is the additional bonus of sometimes interacting with those deemed long dead. But, what good times and good people both Sue and I had a chance to interact with at Schagticoke! In the native tongue, Schagticoke means "the meeting place of the waters." In symbology, water often represents the souls or spirits that endure for eternity.

Nick of Time

Union Hall, Johnstown

Large numbers of settlers moved both north and south of the Mohawk Valley once the Revolutionary War ended in 1783. In what became Fulton County, animosity toward the Iroquois (who had sided with Great Britain) slowly subsided, and Indian traders became frequent visitors to Fulton County towns such as Johnstown because a plentiful supply of Adirondack furs were still desired by local white traders. Many times, the Native Americans stopped at a local tavern after selling their furs. And one favorite watering hole after 1798 was Capt. Vaumane FonClaire's Fon Claire Inn.

An outdoor stairway descended to the cellar barroom, keeping rowdy drinkers separated from the more genteel upstairs inn which, by 1824, was known as the Union Hall Inn. Somewhere around that time, a local roughneck, Nick Stoner, killed an Indian in that taproom. There are many legends about Stoner, who had at various times been a Revolutionary soldier, musician, hunter, trapper and farmer, so the precise year of the murder is difficult to discern.

In any case, Stoner had heard the Indian (overfilled with local brew) bragging about killing white men in the old days, and had seen him showing the scalp of Stoner's father. Enraged by the mix of the Indian's swagger and, perhaps, emboldened by his own overconsumption, Stoner is said to have grabbed a red-hot andiron from the fireplace and hit the Indian, instantly killing the man. Stoner himself suffered burns. Because of his Revolutionary War service, the local veterans kept Stoner from facing trial. This is the only major act of violence recorded at Union Hall, which still stands at the junction of East State and East Main streets.

Since the early 1820s, the inn has had many owners, including the Balch, Williams, DeWitt, Zendzian, Desidoro, Smith, and Rose families. There have also been many renovations over the centuries, though the northwest dining room (sometimes called "the Presidents' Room," as it used to have portraits of all U.S. presidents) seems near to its original configuration. Perhaps that touch with the past explains why that dining room and the foyer outside are the most frequent haunts of ghosts.

"There was more than one," Peter Zendzian wrote in 2002. "I had seen an image in a dress—very small, could have been a child, [and] usually seen on the first floor area near the front door. The others were not seen, only heard." When I interviewed Chef Lauren Saltsman in the spring of 2007, he agreed as to the spirits' main locations. "I think the most frequent character is a woman, as there is a dress shape to her image, though I can make out no detail. When I catch a glimpse of her in the dining room mirror—she's there, and then she isn't. I had heard stories of her haunting when I grew up in Johnstown, so she doesn't really scare me. It's like having a sometimes-greeter out there in the foyer, though she seldom is encountered when the inn is filled with guests.

"After closing time, when the doors are locked, she tends to manifest. One night after locking up, I clearly heard the front door open and then slam shut. Can't be, I said to myself, and went out only to find the door still locked. Had she left for the night, or was she just coming on duty?" he asked with a smile. Lauren recounted the many occasions upon which the building's lights dim and then return to brightness. "And there are cold spots too," he laughed. "Once, as I crossed from the taproom into the Presidents' Room, I walked through an ice cold spot in the foyer. Suddenly, my heart began to race, knowing that I'd just walked through the spirit. Who is she? I wondered. Many of our staff have encountered her, and most of us think she is a former maid, but certainly not old Nick Stoner, or even the Indian that he killed.

"One day, we had another strange manifestation: a man dining in that room suddenly felt a firm hand upon his shoulder, though he and his wife were the only occupants of the room. He asked his server if we had ghosts here, showing her the hand-shaped impression still on his jacket. We have a radio in the kitchen which sometimes turns itself on at 3 a.m. and even changes stations. That's more a bother than a fright, though."

Most of the longtime staff members, some of whom have seen the ghostly mist on the foyer stairway, take the spirit's presence with good humor, as the entity never interferes with business.

Peter Zendzian remembered a variation on the door scenario. "Late at night … the main door would be heard to open and then close softly, and each stair tread would creak in the pattern of somebody climbing the stairs. Then the newel posts would make their sound, as somebody would put their hand on them to make the corner … next the third floor door would open and close, and you would hear those stairs creak, footsteps overhead that would slowly become quiet." He remembers that, many times, he'd stand in the foyer and "watch as the soul would travel by, and then die out." He remembers his visiting grandmother describing the same scenario, an event that occurred at least once a month, though the days and times would vary. The DeWitts had told his parents to expect these events, and Mrs. DeWitt referred to the female spirit as a little girl.

Tales such as these are a major reason why I love history. Too many people believe history is "dead." Well, in a sense, it is—everything dramatic that happened in the past seems to still replay itself, especially the traumatic events. As usual, when we don't know the private details of so many peoples' lives, we can't know why the woman walks, why she remains in Union Hall Inn. Inns and hotels retain the vibrations of countless hundreds or thousands of guests, each traveler uprooted temporarily, each with concerns or grievances.

So, when visiting Johnstown and its historic sites, do drop in for lunch or dinner at the old Union Hall Inn. Just entering the foyer and glancing into the dining room on the left and the taproom on the right, your thoughts speed back to less complicated times of the early 1800s. And it is certainly okay to mutter a "Hi, how are you?" as you traverse the foyer—she will appreciate your noticing her. And maybe "unseen others" will also be happy that you care enough to talk to Union Hall's historic spirits.

Alfred's Place

Alfred's Place

With the dangers of Indian attacks long gone, Colonel. Sidney Berry built a home facing the Hudson River in the Town of Northumberland, New York. The old house, dating from the early 1820s and added to by successive owners, still stands on West River Road. Berry had been the first town supervisor and was a founding member of the local temperance society, which, ironically, was chartered in the old Mawney Tavern at Clark's Corners. For many years, the Berry house was the center of an extensive farm. Following the Colonel's death in 1820, the property remained a farm well into the twentieth century.

In 1941, Alfred, a noted and successful hat manufacturer from New York City, purchased the house to be used as a summer retreat, especially during the thoroughbred racing reason in nearby Saratoga Springs. Many years later, in 1998, I met the elderly man at the town's bicentennial celebration, and he showed a keen interest in the ghost story books I was autographing, asking if I really believed in such spirits. We had a nice talk, but I noticed that the nature of his questions implied that he lived with specters of some sort. Though his home was put on my "to do" list, I never got around to interviewing him before his death at age 104 in September 2004.

Following Alfred's death, however, one of his longtime friends gave me permission to wander through the building before its contents were sold off or dispersed. Accompanied by the woman friend and one of my favorite intuitives, Susan, we toured the house on an early spring day in 2005. I discovered anecdotes among my notes that I had written some years before, memories of individuals who had worked for Alfred. Most of those individuals were certain that spirits from the past still lingered in the old house.

Following our normal routine, Susan toured the house alone, seeking impressions in the various rooms and hallways. She returned and I accompanied her, often comparing impressions, as I often become quite sensitive when working with gifted intuitives or psychics. Susan's love is old houses. The fact that many of them have resident ghosts is just frosting on the cake for us both. As we began our walk, she told me that, in meditation the previous day, she'd had the vision of a boy, perhaps eight, wearing shorts and suspenders, digging in the dirt behind the house. "It was probably back in the thirties," she said, "but I don't get any such imagery today."

At first, there were no strong impressions on the first floor, but Susan summoned me to an upstairs bedroom, saying that the energies were quite strong there, near a walk-through closet. I remembered a note card in my records that told of a housekeeper in the 1980s experiencing icy cold spots in an adjoining room. As we neared the top of the stairs, I had received the impression of a servant holding an object, perhaps a basin of water, in the center of the room. Once we entered, Susan also felt strong energies there, though they were non-specific. We moved to a smaller, adjoining room, and Sue got a curious look on her face, constantly looking down at her left hand. "Everything all right?" I inquired.

With an amused look on her face, she answered, "There is a child here, I think a little girl, who keeps pulling my hand. It seems that she wants to take me somewhere and show me something." Staying in that room, we speculated whether it had once been a child's nursery or a dressing room, as it was situated next to the master bedroom. "I can't get much here except the little girl," Sue said. Then, almost immediately, she said, "Now she's giggling at me." That phenomenon continued throughout most of our day in the house. Apparently, the child enjoyed the psychic game of hide and seek with the long ago information we were seeking. We never were able to discover who she was or what family of inhabitants she belonged to.

On the bed were large portraits of the deceased man's parents, waiting to go to family heirs. We noted that the man's face in the painting was particularly stern and strong-looking. Later, in a downstairs room, while holding one of Alfred's old hats, Sue felt Alfred's mother likewise exuded a very strong will. Along with that sensation, she felt Alfred, as a young man in New York City, experienced sadness and a sense of loss regarding someone he loved very much. As many veteran ghost story enthusiasts know, memory energy can sometimes accompany an individual's portrait or personal belongings. Looking at Alfred's mother's image, Sue suddenly felt that Alfred, her son, had lost a true love at a young age, but no further information arose.

In the old housekeeper's quarters on the second floor, Sue felt very cold and visualized a woman bending over a bed. Suddenly, she pictured a ball of light emerging from the closet and moving into the room. She stepped into the closet and quickly emerged, feeling quite uncomfortable, though she was unable to discern the cause. At the same time, our woman guide heard sharp footsteps, though the three of us were stationary on a carpet. Later, I found in my anecdotal records that a former housekeeper, of whom there have been many over the years, had often heard walking on the floors of that room when nobody else was there. The woman had also noted occasions of hearing and feeling concussions on the floor, similar to very heavy footsteps, even though she was vacuuming downstairs at the time.

In the downstairs living room, Susan both felt and saw a static figure, almost like a portrait, of a man standing in front of the fireplace, as if warming himself. "He gives off the same energy that I felt with Alfred's father's portrait upstairs," she said. Perhaps in confirmation of that sensation, I later found information among my notes from an earlier housekeeper who often felt a strong male presence in the house, even when Alfred was away.

The former owner's friend, who accompanied us and was familiar with some portions of the house's history, then recounted a story that she heard from another housekeeper in the 1990s. The employee had spotted another woman, quite likely an apparition, walking out the driveway toward West River Road. Clad in a full skirt, perhaps of the Civil War era, the woman was apparently involved in a long-ago errand. That housekeeper resigned soon after seeing the ghost lady vanish.

Our guide told us that the Williams family, residents in the house during the 1930s, had found strong chains fastened to the wall in a rear upstairs room. Several houses in the area have, or have had, such manacles. It is a popular belief that Saratoga County farmers of days gone by used slaves in their fields by day and shackled them by night until the practice of slavery ended in the 1830s to 1840s. Popular local understanding of such devices seems often confused with the fact that many upstate farmers took part in the Underground

Railroad during the 1850s, though it is difficult to understand why escaped Southern slaves would be put in chains overnight.

I have often noted strong energies in known Underground Railroad "stations," which might be understood if one takes into account the fear and anxiety that the escapees must have felt during their passages. Such fearful vibrations often seem to cling to the structures long after the escapees have found their "jubilee."

In the summer kitchen at the rear of the house and in the nearby cellar entrance, Susan continued to hear the ghost child giggling. As we concluded our visit in the old kitchen, neighbors dropped by to chat with our guide and informed us of the shackles in their attic. They also recollected a brief conversation with Alfred, in which the elder made an offhand remark about seeing "a former owner walk through the house." He gave them no further explanation of the comment, though.

It must have been difficult for a man who was so successful in finance and the world of business to give full credence to the existence of non-physical beings. As with so many people inhabiting old houses, Alfred coexisted with former historical personages but kept his focus on the fast-moving financial world and even faster horses, both of which could doom a man's fortunes if he didn't pay strict attention to matters at hand.

A-Moulderin' in the Grave?

John Brown's farmhouse

Most of us know the old song about John Brown's body, sung to the tune of "The Battle Hymn of the Republic," a Civil War song that inspired many New Yorkers to enlist in the Union Army in 1861 and venture forth to die for national unity. We know where Brown's body now lies, but is his spirit among those remaining in his nearby old house?

For those unsure of their American history, John Brown was an avowed Abolitionist, born in Connecticut, who attempted to raise an army among southern slaves and overthrow the slave-owning system. On the 16th of October, 1859, Brown, with members of his family and other volunteers, captured the federal arsenal at Harper's Ferry, Virginia, hoping to gather weapons to arm the slaves. The U.S. Army, ironically led by Lt. Col. Robert E. Lee, surrounded the buildings and killed or captured the insurrectionists. Following a trial, Brown was hanged on December 2, 1859. Afterward, he became a hero to many northerners but was condemned by most in the South.

Brown made his home for a while (1855-1859) in North Elba, New York, near the village of Lake Placid and (after spending a bloody year in Kansas) returned to the farm for one last time in June of 1859. Then, with several sons, his daughter Annie and daughter-in-law Martha (son Oliver's wife) he went south to his eventual rendezvous with destiny and martyrdom. In nearby Maryland, Annie and Martha kept house for Brown, his sons, and others of their liberation force as they planned their raid on the arsenal. Just before the October attack, Oliver brought the two women back home to North Elba. After John Brown's execution, Brown's wife, Mary Ann, arrived in Charlestown, Virginia, to accompany her husband's body back to North Elba, where the dead sons and Brown are now buried at the farm. Before going south, Martha had learned she was pregnant, but didn't disclose the fact to Oliver, for fear he'd stay in North Elba to care for her.

The State of New York now oversees the John Brown farm as a state historic site and employs Linda Roy as tour guide during the late spring to fall season. "How could one family endure so much savagery and violent death and not leave a ghost or two behind?" I asked Linda when I visited the site. She smiled and took me and fellow investigator, Diane, through the two rooms downstairs and the upper loft space. It's not a big house, but has been restored to much of the condition that widow Mary Ann Brown knew before she departed westward in 1864. Though the Brown farm has been an historic site since the 1870s, other families farmed the land until the late 1950s.

On our tour of the loft, Linda asked me, "What do you get over there, by the rocking chair?" I confessed that my psychic feelers weren't very operative that day, so she revealed that, when working downstairs she many times hears the rocking chair moving back and forth. "I'm pretty sure that I know who it is, because there were two deaths here," she said. "Oliver's wife, Martha, died here soon after giving birth to Olive, then the little girl died shortly after that.

Working away downstairs, when it's quiet, I often hear Martha rocking the baby, probably hoping Oliver will return home soon. Likely she doesn't know that he's buried outside with his father and brothers." I suggested that, on a future quiet day, when tourists are absent, Linda walk up into the loft room and disclose to Martha what has transpired since 1859. The white light should be visible to her, and on entering it, she can find Oliver and many of her other loved ones. "One of the tourists, when coming upstairs a few years ago, asked me whether we have a ghost in the loft, so I told her the story. She, also, had felt a woman's presence. But there is one other here, too," Linda smiled.

"The first one I became aware of appeared during my fourth year as tour guide. I had already heard sounds in the building, but you know how it is—old house? Sounds? When I come on duty, I hang my coat in the cellarway that leads down into the root cellar, but one day, I got a surprise. Opening the cellar door, I discovered a man standing at the foot of the stairs, looking up at me. He was surrounded by a reddish aura. I looked at him and said, or thought, to him, 'Who are you? What do you want?' He vanished as I heard visitors coming across the lawn. Over the next few days I kept thinking at him: 'You're trying to tell me something—what?' Soon afterward, I opened the cellar door and found a piece of foundation mortar on my little shelf. There is just no way it could have floated up to that spot, so, what is it about the cellar that he wants to convey? There used to be a dirt floor down there, but it is now concrete since the furnace was put in back in 1965.

"I have lots of quiet time here between visiting groups, so I can often get into a dreamy state and maybe that helps me pick up ideas. I also have time to get history books from the regional library and use this opportunity of quiet time to learn about the Brown family and their life and time. One day, a woman visitor asked me if I knew about the Hughes family who used to farm this land in the 1900s. 'One of their sons, Billy, was killed by a lightning strike here,' she informed me. And, sure enough, several visitors since then have mentioned seeing a man in the living room window as they approach the house. It could be him," she laughed.

"You might find this interesting, too," she laughed. "While doing my research on this house, I discovered that my great-great-grandmother, Elizabeth Reed, who lived locally, used to work here as a helper to the Browns. Talk about coincidence! Or is it?" she smiled.

Spirits aren't a great surprise to Linda, who grew up in Saranac Lake. She told me of seeing a male ghost standing alongside her bed when she was a child. She thought such events were normal, and thus, at age six, didn't panic when her dead grandfather came to her room, sat on her bed, and talked to her at night. "Finally, I told my mom that Grandpa visited me at night, but she wasn't surprised; he visited her too.

"Not a lot of people know about the Brown site, so we don't get lots of tour buses here," she told me, "but I'm never lonely. I have Martha and maybe little Olive for company, and, of course, there is Billy Hughes, though I haven't seen him in quite a while." How inspiring, I thought, to work at an historic site where the past keeps playing out gently. But, how could the State of New York ever put that in their historic brochure?

Another Viewing

Totten's House

Steve Totten owns a big, old 1840s house on Park Settlement Road outside the Southern Tier village of Owego. There are few records to help him research the building's history, but he wishes he knew more. Asa and Sally Phelps were the first residents and likely the builders of the old Greek Revival house, he learned, but little else is known except that the old farmhouse did double duty as a funeral parlor.

"Like all old homes, it has a central main door," Steve told me. "But there is another door here on the porch, now hidden behind the clapboards; it was usable when my dad bought the house but has since been covered. During death and funeral ceremonies, that second door was used as an entry into the large viewing room on the right. How many of the dearly departed were laid out here, we'll never know, but when my parents bought this house, that large room became my parents' bedroom," he grinned. "Many times they heard voices in there, and once Dad got slapped on the foot when he was sleeping. Many times the doorknobs would turn but the doors never opened. Later on, after my parents died, it became my oldest son's bedroom, and he witnessed the doorknobs turning, though nobody was ever there when he ran to the door to see who was coming in. At times, he smelled the almost-sickening-sweet scent of flowers. You don't need much imagination to suspect that odor comes from the remaining energy of long-ago funerals.

"When those events began, all I could do was share with my son some of the eerie experiences I had growing up here," Steve continued. "When I was thirteen I sometimes heard the chain hit the bulb on a hanging light when there was no window open and no draft. It takes something to hit that chain in order to make the clink, but I didn't want to think what or who was hitting the chain. Finally, in frustration, I yelled at the light and told it to stop and that did it; it never clinked again.

"I also told my son about the time when I was fifteen, and we had a power outage. Suddenly, I heard footsteps coming down the stairs though I knew it wasn't my friend because he was right beside me. I grabbed the flashlight and ran to the foot of the stairs. I turned the light on and shone it on the stairs but there was nobody there," he laughed, "nobody living, anyway. A friend of my son's heard a door slam upstairs when no one else was there.

"During the 2006 flood I was stranded away from home, but I knew my son was coming home and was okay. Later, when I returned, he told me that as he had come into the driveway, he could see the light of the TV on in the living room, so, entering through the kitchen, he walked into the living room without turning on the lights. In the light of the TV, he saw a dark figure sitting on the couch and just then rising to stand for a few seconds before disappearing. He figures that his sudden return home surprised the ghost who must have been watching a program or maybe trying to figure out the existence of our modern entertainment. He couldn't discern any detail on the figure. It was more of a 'shadow figure,'" he said. I told Steve that many people all over the world use just that term to describe such entities, but having a descriptive term does nothing to help us understand who or what they are. Are they just ghosts or something more complex?

He told me that objects many times disappear, only to reappear after a suitable absence. We laughed and I told him the story of "The Ring," which appears in this book. Where do such objects go when they vanish? Is there some cosmic custodian for them? And where, if not on this plane, is the keeping place?

"I am retired now," he told me, "and am beginning to do some investigations of events in the Tioga County area. In an office in an old farmhouse on Route 96 in this county, there are some strange events that happen after the office closes. The daughter of a friend saw an old guy just walk through a wall. Our investigator friends have gotten some very clear voices (called the EVP phenomenon) on their recorders. One angry voice told us during our investigation to get out of the house. These things are a real challenge to me, as I used to work in law enforcement.

"But here is what has me concerned," he said with a grin. "In 2007 I had just climbed into the upstairs of our old barn, and right there on the floor was a shiny Boy Scout medallion. I have no idea where it came from, because my boys aren't Scouts, and neither was I. It's too new-looking to be left from previous residents. What got me thinking was its motto, 'Be Prepared,' written in eighteen different languages. Was that a warning from some of the spirits that still live here alongside us? Things have been pretty strange ever since I have lived here, and now does one of those ethereal beings have something new for us? I can't wait!"

At the River's Edge

Glen Sanders House 1713

Less than an arrow-shot from Schenectady's Western Gateway Bridge, across the Mohawk, in the Village of Scotia, is an historic landmark—The Glen Sanders Mansion. Though modified by more recent additions, the original 1713 core building remains. Within that structure, but not in the newer parts, there is a residue of ghostly activity; history replaying itself, as if the structure cannot shrug off its past.

In 1658, three years before the palisaded fort was built to found Schenectady on the river's south shore, Scotsman Alexander Glen settled on the Mohawk River's northern bank to seek his fortune. Indian trade in furs was especially profitable for Europeans, and with Schenectady's founder Arendt Van Corlaer, Glen was among the first to profit. His stone house on the river's edge was dubbed "Nova Scotia" (New Scotland), though it didn't last long, as Glen failed to consider the depth of the spring floods that, even today, cause consternation for lowland dwellers along the river. Salvaging what he could from the ruined house, Glen at first built a single-room dwelling higher up, on a nearby rise. Soon, he had an expanded structure of three rooms and a large trading hall. That original room has been incorporated into the present structure's kitchen. The 1713 building date, today seen in large wrought-iron numbers on the old building's front, was assigned when Glen's son added a larger east wing. Also clearly evident is the original gambrel roof.

In 1739, Alexander Glen's great-granddaughter Deborah Glen married Albanian John Sanders, and the estate has ever-since been known as the Glen Sanders Mansion. The structure welcomed many colonial notables including George Washington. During the French and Indian War, British officers conferenced there before attacking Ticonderoga, a hundred miles to the north. The Glens occupied the house until 1961, so we assume that much of the energy in the old building today is a residue of that family's activities and experiences.

Pursuing rumors of the mansion's ghost activity in November 2007, I arrived with my friends Geri McDyre, a noted area intuitive, and Bill Getz, a professional dowser and my longtime friend. Each one of us would be seeking house memories or active spirit entities at the old Glen homestead. Cathy, a staff member, guided us through the older parts of the building but gave us few details unless we requested a date here or a name there. Understanding that almost all of the phenomena were confined to the original structure, we chose to first visit the West Cellar tavern room with its cool stone walls. Geri glanced nervously down a back stairway, then looked again—I knew she was onto something. "There's people down there, and boy are they scared!" she said. At the mid-stair landing she announced that there was a long-gone group of three black people at that spot, scared out of their wits at being discovered. "It's like the days of the Underground Railroad," she told us, "and the Glens must have been hiding the escapees here before they continued on to Canada and freedom." Bill quickly brought his dowsing L-rods into position and they instantly crossed at the same spot—confirming Geri's intuition, yes the spirit energy was indeed there. Geri then announced receiving the letter J, though Cathy couldn't connect that with any of the history she knew. It might have been part of the name of one of the refugees. Again, Geri announced that her heart was racing; she had physically taken on the anxiety of the escaped slaves. By the time we had finished the day's investigation, this seemed to be the most powerful energy that our team could find in the Glen Sanders Mansion.

As we moved into the wine storage room, I could "see" a circle of stones in the dirt floor, indicating a well. I checked with Bill and received a positive response from his L-rods. He also showed me a water pipe, likely from a more modern well, several feet away behind a cabinet. Bill told me that he'd been dowsing the staircase again and found indications of energy both on and below the stairs. There was an old board partition beneath the stairs and he felt that escaped slaves might have been secreted behind it on at least one occasion. He also believed (after questioning his unconscious through the rods) that the wooden shelf above the well was once used for kneading dough for bread baking.

In the West Cellar or tavern, Geri spotted a vanished person hanging from an old hand-hewn beam. "I don't think that timber is original to this house, however," she said. "It came from another structure." Cathy quickly confirmed that some of the wood had been salvaged from the early 1685 stone house. She also told us that legend says a tunnel once existed for escaping slaves, which led to the cellar of the present-day Public Library building across the highway. Nobody has yet opened up or excavated that tunnel, though our guide told us that the Mansion's driveway sinks a bit along that line every spring when the ground thaws.

In the East Cellar there appears to be a large walk-in fireplace, but it is only an old Dutch-style arch to support the main floor's fireplace above. Nevertheless, both Bill and Geri picked up energies from former occupants, as if sitting near the arch. Geri felt that someone who long ago froze to death in the snow had been at that spot. When we first entered the room, I had "seen" stacks of hay, but that vision made no sense in terms of the known uses of the room. Geri also visualized men in quiet conversation sitting and planning at a long-gone table there. She felt they were British and planning some military activity. There was a cold spot there, suggesting a spirit. She also heard a voice, "Why do they care?" Was this a ghostly commentary on our efforts? Bill and I didn't hear the voice.

Upstairs there are 20 overnight rooms, but also a number of public and private dining rooms. In the Alexander Glen Dining Room we all felt "family" and the warmth of long-past dinners. Geri found an intense cold spot in the corner. "A happy and proud man stands here," she informed us. "Apparently, he returns to this spot from time to time just to savor the happiness that he knew when living here, maybe as host of parties or as owner of the house." Bill, questioning his dowsing rods, came to the conclusion that a personality from 1943 likewise remained or often visited the room and Geri envisioned a cradle near the room's fireplace.

As we entered the Stockade Room, Cathy told us that the room's partitions had changed over the years. Geri spotted three men speaking quietly about General Washington and the unlikely possibility of his ever coming to the spot. It wasn't clear whether or not the reference was to Scotia, Schenectady or the particular building. The hushed tones indicated that a man standing farther away was not to hear them. Two of the participants felt that the general would come, but the other gentleman was doubtful. [During and after the Revolutionary War George Washington did visit Schenectady three times.] As we surveyed the room, Geri smiled and announced that the Glen Sanders Mansion was full of good will and happy people's memories or energy. "They are non-judgmental and kind folks. Some of them also were happy to take part in rescuing slaves and moving them on to freedom in Canada," she told us. Bill and I agreed that, other than the fearful souls downstairs (by federal law escaped slaves were to be returned to their southern owners if discovered up north before 1865), there was a peaceful feeling, as if vague forms or energies still continued to live their lives despite the intrusion of the 21st Century.

Glen Sanders House

As we descended, Cathy showed us a notch on the main stairway rail, informing us that legend tells of an angry Oneida warrior throwing his hatchet at Mrs. John Sanders. Both the Glen and Sanders families were on good terms (as fur traders had to be) with the Indians, probably inviting many of the braves into their home. Not far from the main house, a large tree once stood, the location of many Iroquois torture ceremonies. Apparently, the homeowners had to permit this savagery (though it was not considered as such by the Indians) to avoid repercussions. Around 1685, the natives captured a French Jesuit priest and committed him to the care of Alexander Glen, demanding that the cleric be confined in one of the cellar rooms until they could slowly murder him the next day after they caroused with firewater all night. Glen, agreed, but had no intention that the priest should ever be harmed. He warned the captors that priests had magical powers and might even slip out a keyhole as if made of smoke. Glen then locked up the captive while the Indians went to test the local alcohol. In the depths of night, when a wagon load of salt casks set forth to Albany, the Indians could not see that one giant barrel contained the priest. In the morning, they discovered that Glen was right—when the captive's cellar room was unlocked, it was empty!

The mansion's receptionist, Rita, told us that the old East Cellar had been used for cold storage. "After 1961 this building was used by a Mr. Ebling to sell antiques and gifts. He and his wife had a small museum here that contained some artifacts of the Glen and Sanders families, which we now have in display cases for our visitors to see. Ebling complained that his lights often turned themselves on and off at will. Donna, one of his employees, locked up one night after dousing all the lights. Later, as she drove past, she was unnerved to see them all turned on again, though the building was locked. During this period, passersby sometimes saw faces peering from the second and third floor windows (which are the original panes of glass).

Cathy then informed us that the hotel's office or conference room is up under the rafters on the third floor. "A former executive worked there but often complained about the static on his hard-wired phone line. A telephone company technician came to diagnose the problem, only to find that the wires were not connected to anything. We often worked up there and sometimes heard conversations echoing from the conference room when there was nobody there. Another time, I heard an eerie voice call my name, though no living person was there that time either. I'm happy to work down here at the desk now," she said with a smile. "On several occasions I've seen a young girl about four, wearing a blue dress over a white petticoat. She seems to roam the building, maybe looking for a playmate. Sometimes, hotel patrons see her and think she's real in our terms of that word."

Donna told her co-workers of entering a back door one evening and seeing a man seated and writing at a desk formerly owned by the Glen family. Finding Mr. Ebling in another room, she asked him the identity of the unknown man. "What man? There's nobody else here," Ebling responded, and when they returned to the desk, Mr. Ebling proved correct and the candle on the desk was no longer lit. As ghost fans know, our furniture or possessions often retain some part of our life energy which, years later, can be spotted by unwary residents or visitors.

Area restaurateur Angelo Mazzone owns the Glen Sanders today and has invested in refurbishing the structure as closely as possible to its historic condition without sacrificing modern amenities. The mansion is a curious place, with us, the living, certainly there, but also with the feeling that we are not alone. It isn't unpleasant at all, and history lovers are certain to enjoy the capacity to live with five centuries of energy at the spot. A dedicated historian and ghost hunter might conclude that to do the investigative job correctly and fully, an overnight stay is called for. To date, I haven't done that. But our small group of investigators sure had fun "dropping in for a visit." The only thing we didn't understand was where the energy of the long-ago horrors of war went. We thought we might encounter reverberations of the Schenectady Massacre of 1690, an event that Alexander Glen must have witnessed from his upstairs windows, as it all took place just across the Mohawk River.

One expectation that we all have, I'm sure, is that love and happiness outlast danger, fear and threats. We found that true at the Glen Sanders Mansion. It is as if old Alexander stood at the door and bid us enter to share in his hospitality. What more could a restaurant want for an advertisement?

Everyone Knows

Van Wyck Hall

It is always a delight for me to hear ghost stories told by public safety officers such as policemen and firemen. These individuals have to be in charge of a situation, often having to write up official reports of incidents. Even so, many times, a skeptical or cynical reader is not inclined to honor such reports if they involve ghosts. As many readers know, unkind comments often result from such disbelievers if their world view is threatened. In this case, however, the Village of Fishkill, New York, takes it all in stride.

"I worked for a period of time in the Village Hall named after our first mayor, Henry Du Bois Van Wyck," a woman named Tamme told me. "I was employed in the Village Police office beneath the old bell tower, and one of the ongoing sounds was of footsteps in the attic above us. Everyone treated it casually, certain that they knew who it was. Though he died in 1901, everyone knew it was Mayor Van Wyck."

Over a century since his death, how could the man's spirit still be striding through the hall which he had built, and more precisely—why?

Born in 1823, Henry's early years were spent in Fishkill, then in New York City, where he clerked in a tobacco sales house. Later, he lived in Michigan, raising sheep and working in the nation's young oil business. In 1849, hearing of the gold discovery in California, he went west and did find gold, though he made a fortune in business ventures there (selling ornate gold pocket watches to gold miners) and in Oregon. He served as colonel in a regiment of California troops during the Modoc Indian wars, later operating a stagecoach line which provided him more riches. Then, partnering with George Gordon, inventor of the famous Gordon Printing Press in Norfolk, Virginia, Van

Henry Dubois VanWyck

Wyck continued to profit and married Lenore, Gordon's widow, after the inventor died.

Because of his business interests there, Van Wyck adopted Norfolk and built a theater, The Van Wyck Academy of Music, in that city in 1880, and also provided for the building of a public library in Norfolk after his death. In 1882, the couple returned to Fishkill, residing at his father, John C. Van Wyck's, house there. Henry became the village's first mayor during that period. Eight years later, he and his wife traveled to California, where Lenore was stricken with pneumonia and died. As a widower, Van Wyck returned to Fishkill and bought land for construction of the dam which created Van Wyck Reservoir. He also built Knickerbocker Lodge, later a popular resort until the 1920s, when it was purchased by J. Noah Slee, millionaire inventor of Three-in-One Oil, and husband of birth control pioneer Margaret Sanger.

Then, in 1899, he built a theater in the village with upstairs apartments that he occupied until his death. Following his demise, which occurred on a visit to Norfolk in March 1901, Van Wyck Hall became the present village hall. It seems that, even today, on at least some occasions, he returns to visit his old upstairs dwelling place.

Henry's was an energetic life, filled with adventure, travel, and great success in business ventures. His laudatory obituary described him as sociable and methodical. Apparently, he loved whatever he was doing on any given day, and it seems Henry simply didn't let an inconvenience such as death slow him down. Local people cannot think of any other individual who would so purposefully stride through the upstairs of the village building.

When I visited Fishkill to speak with Local History librarian Antonia Houston, police chief Robert Bessman, and other municipal employees about the ghostly footsteps, I met another former village employee who told me of working in the present police department office some years ago. "From upstairs, I sometimes heard what sounded like a chiming clock," she said, "though it only struck one musical tone each time. Needless to say, we had no clock up there, so I've often wondered if it is related to old Mayor Van Wyck not knowing it was time to just let go," she laughed.

Tamme, the other former employee, told me, "We heard stuff all the time in that building." And while Chief Bessman didn't elaborate on that point, he admitted hearing noises in the ceiling, especially at nighttime, when all other workers were gone. "In those days, we used to say it was Mayor Van Wyck's ghost still walking through his old theater. But, in later years," he winked, "I came to believe it was just squirrels getting in the roof area."

Too many people, however, have heard the sound of human footsteps, to which all those I questioned agreed. Most of the village employees seemed quite calm in discussing the matter with me, and I met none who were afraid. If, as they suspect, the former mayor's ghost is still at work, Fishkill can only benefit from his efforts.

Hanging in There

Jailhouse Restaurant

At fourteen minutes after noon on a cold January day in 1880, the execution scaffold trapdoor in Owego, New York, opened, dropping the condemned man into eternity. Daniel Searles, whose neck wasn't broken by the fall, twisted and slowly strangled, a process taking eleven minutes. How had Searles come to this gruesome end?

A month before, a jury convened in the old courthouse had found Searles guilty of the June 21, 1879 robbery, murder and grisly slashing death of one Eldridge Rewey, an old farmer from Newark Valley. *The New York Times*, commenting on the execution in 1880, noted that Searles had gained a mere $300 from his victim, who was nearly decapitated in the death struggle. At his trial and again, just minutes before being hanged, Searles freely admitted his guilt, so that was that; an open and shut case with the malefactor punished. Or was it the end?

A local physician purchased the body before Searles' death, as the condemned man was likely indigent, and used it for cadaver dissection. One curious and macabre twist in this story is that the doctor donated the prisoner's head to the Tioga County Historical Society and that item remained a hideous acquisition until the late 1980s, when the New York State Health Department ordered all human remains in historical collections to be interred. As Rewey, the murder victim, had nearly lost his head in the murder, so Searles suffered a similar fate after death. Modern science has no way of ascertaining what lingering consciousness or thoughts remain in those who die, criminals or upstanding citizens, so we can only speculate how or why Searles seems to have found a new and ongoing occupation.

Thirty years after the execution, a new jail and Sheriff's Residence were constructed at what is now 176 Main Street in Owego, right next to the lot on which the scaffold once stood. Using the then-state-of-the-art Pauly Locking System, the three-story brick jail housed the county's prisoners until 1996, when the present modern Public Safety facility was constructed north of the village on Commercial Drive. Building contractor Bruce Nelson purchased the old structure with the intention of creating a one-of-a-kind restaurant beneath two top floors of upscale apartments. Plans changed, though, so today, the old Sheriff's House on the corner has become the apartment, and first and second floors of the jail are used as a restaurant.

Today, the Jail House Restaurant has reopened under its fourth ownership since 1996. Christopher Nowak (who calls himself "the warden") has added a lightness to the old place, where modern guests dine in old cells, on tables made from the old guards' catwalks. He has kept one of the original cages undisturbed, bed and all, for modern visitors to see, and perhaps ponder the wages of crime. Old catwalks and cell doors have been shifted to make this a fascinating place to dine—and speculate about the afterworld.

Today, many owners and operators of public facilities shy away from too close a promotion geared to the world of spirits, in case such disclosures might frighten away customers. However, my personal experience is that there are many moderns who actively seek out venues with an "edge" of some kind. Natives of the village remember and recount tales they have heard of Searles' death, though he predeceased the building of the jail/restaurant. Might having his head in a display case for years be a likely cause for the man's lingering spiritual unrest? Might Daniel Searles still cling, in his self-confessed guilt, to that structure which represented his final disgrace? Or, has he since discovered a new role as entertainer of the unwary staff and diners?

Those who appreciate the old jail's unseen entity call him "George," a very common name for male haunts, I have discovered. The menu from a former ownership of the restaurant used to warn diners, "Don't be scared if you hear a noise from upstairs, it's just George opening the cell doors for his fellow inmates."

Fred Gage was one of the restaurant's early owners who quickly discovered George when paper money began to disappear from one spot, then turn up in another location nearby. Gage noted that such occurrences always took place when he was alone, and it became almost a nightly adventure to locate some bills he had just placed on the counter while cashing out. The spirit never kept the money, but seemed to use the movement to attract Gage's attention—"I'm here, you had better acknowledge me!" Keith Greene, the Historical Society's executive director, interviewed Mr. Gage about the presence, and the proprietor noted, "It always felt like there was somebody else here. But, we had never heard any of the old stories about the spirit, so I really didn't know anything about the history of this building prior to [my] ownership."

Another previous owner found his staff unwilling to descend into a cellar storage room because dry food items (e.g. onions) were sometimes hurled at them by an unseen hand. Hearing of these incidents (and likely having their own culinary "disappearances" upstairs) the chefs finally refused to work unless and until management brought in an exorcist. The person hired for the cleansing seems to have done a fairly good job, as there have been no new reports of onion fastballs zooming through the cellar for a while.

Gage concluded that it was the shift in energy between ownerships that occasioned the spirit upsets, though he didn't use those exact words.

Still, Chris Nowak admits that many of his wait-staff feel nervous or "watched" in the cellar, though foodstuffs are no longer stored there. There has been considerable recent renovation in parts of the cellar, where new prisoners once were signed in, examined, issued new clothing, then escorted up to their cell block. Many ghosts become more active when a change occurs in interior decoration or personnel, and in some cases, just a change in the style of restaurant mood music can aggravate an already-frustrated or resentful ghost.

In his Keith Greene interview with Gage, the former owner stated that, though some kitchen help had experienced no phenomena, other employees still immediately felt the spirit's presence upon entering the workplace, and several also heard their names called out loud. Several workers claimed to have felt cold hands upon their shoulders while on errands in the cellar. George was not above tweaking the behinds of some of the more attractive waitresses too. Since Nowak has become an owner, he discovered that George seems to prefer blondes above brunettes. Many, if not most, of the legendary events have been experiences of the female employees, causing observers to suspect the entity is a ladies' man of sorts. One wonders how ghostly pinches, tweaks, and fanny-pats might look on a Workers' Compensation claim form.

The cellar infestation hasn't halted completely, because workers who visit the storage area today continue to report cold spots or feeling watched by someone invisible. Chris Nowak told me of working alone downstairs and often having a misty shape "whoosh" right up to him. "I acknowledge George and tell him leave me alone, as I have work to do," he said. Chris is a cool character, giving George (or Searles?) little satisfaction in return for his scare tactics. "I have often seen what I call 'flutters' in mid-air since I became manager/warden in August of 2007," he laughed. "Since then, we had a ghostbuster-type person come in and attempt to get a picture on her digital camera. Most of the quiet dining is done in the cells on the second floor, and that is where she got her image, right outside the preserved cell. And, coincidentally, that is where many of our waitresses feel cold or unsettled air.

"Whatever the spirit's identity, I've discerned that he feels trapped when there are too many closed doors inside the restaurant, so he opens them. I know he opens doors because, before we opened, I stayed inside the building overnight. I heard all kinds of strange bumps and bangs and doors opening, though I was locked inside, and know nobody else was here," he grinned. "I slept in that demonstration cell, which wasn't really that pleasant, but it sure helped me visualize the mix of lightness and seriousness with which we'd design our new interior."

I asked Chris if George had a sense of humor, and he became wide-eyed, happy that I had asked. "Look up at all those lights," he said, pointing to the second floor overhead lights, each covered with a stylish baffle, meant to redirect the illumination. "It's almost impossible to reach under those baffles, but we often find the bulbs unscrewed." Sure enough, only three or four of the dozen overhead lights were turned on during my visit. "It's an ongoing situation," he told me.

The Jailhouse Restaurant has a unique and historic décor, one that you aren't likely to find in other towns. Owego is a village very conscious of its history and preserves it. Maybe that is why George (or is it Daniel Searles?) has remained in the old lockup. Perhaps it is the only place that he was ever able to call home. He seems to have a sense of humor (or mischief) and lighthearted ghost hunters should find this the ideal Tioga County site for dining, observation, and conversation. Whether at the first floor bar and reception area, or in the quiet second floor dining area, George might be encountered.

I asked a former sheriff's deputy why the third floor hadn't been used before they moved out to more modern quarters. "The electrical wiring there wasn't up to code," he told me. "Nevertheless, it was up above the second floor cells where we kept what was termed 'juvenile prisoners,' age 16-19. Most of them weren't really bad guys, but one deputy couldn't resist going to the third floor in his off-duty time, and bouncing objects on the floor, just to spook the young men below. Maybe some of the rumors about hauntings came from their tales, once they got released." Maybe, but those pranks could never account for the other experiences of those who work there today.

"Don't blame everything on Searles," a retired deputy told me, "because there were a couple of suicides in that jail, and another guy burned himself to death in a cell before the guards could get it open." So, there is some more history which could lengthen our list of ghost suspects.

If you live in Tioga County, or are just passing through Owego, take the time to drop in and see if George is working or relaxing that night. If Chris isn't busy, he can update you on the pranks that waitresses really don't think are that funny. And before you leave, tell George, "Don't lose your head, now!"

Huguenot Street

1799 House

America is a place of constant renewal, of the old being replaced by the new. This cultural tendency poses difficulties for lovers of history who might wish to tread the streets and explore neighborhoods of two or three hundred years past. However, there is a magic place in a New Paltz neighborhood—Huguenot Street. Here the student of America's past can enter and study a small village almost three hundred years old and hear tales of the French Huguenots who bravely settled the Walkill Valley in the late 1600s.

The Huguenots were French Protestants who escaped from Catholic France where they were persecuted. They sailed to the New York colony soon after the English seized it from the Dutch, and strived to avoid difficulties with the Native Americans. Rather than flourish through military conquest, the Huguenots purchased a section of the valley from the Esopus Indians, then sought a legal patent of ownership from the English King. After that, twelve patentee families arrived in 1677 and began to build a church and houses of stone, many of which are still extant. Descendants of those original families lived in those homes, in many cases, well into the 20th century, and eventually the structures were ceded to the local historical society, who worked to win a National Historic Landmark designation for the old settlement. More than a dozen old stone structures, some modified a bit over intervening centuries, remain near the creek called Walkill and are open from spring to fall for daily tours.

What may not be visible or tangible to the historian or tourist is an ambient energy from long ago—some local witnesses say that certain of these homes are haunted. The story that attracted me to Huguenot Street was that of the old Abraham Hasbrouck House, built in 1721. I had read an article in the *Kingston Freeman* about a shadowy man and his dog appearing in the window of an otherwise uninhabited building. There are records of honest citizens seeing a dark-coated, tall man walking through or into the house, and often he was accompanied by a large black dog. Some wintertime sightings had him entering the house, but when the curious spectator rushed to the door that the elder entered, there were no footprints in the snow, either entering or leaving the portal.

Over the years, the folk legends have expanded, with credible witnesses seeing a screaming man holding an axe over his head in an upper window of the house, apparently about to strike someone or something below window sill level. There is no record of a murder or other violence occurring in the building, but not all such episodes would necessarily have become official records in the old days. By day, the Hasbrouck House is bright and tidy. The guide there told me that old Abe or his son Daniel, or another entity, has stayed on, tending to stay upstairs, out of sight of the causal visitor. The staircase, however, is closed off, and tourists don't get to see the upstairs. As in so many of these old homes, it is well worth the visit to see period furniture and hear the guide's tales of the cleverness of our ancestors' modifications on the buildings.

Alf Evers, a local historian, grew up in the house during the 1920s and recalls a strange but true event. His mother was something of a local psychic, often visited by intuitions and premonitions. One day, it struck her that there were human bones buried in the cellar, and she could not be dissuaded from the inspiration, so the family members began to lift floorboards and dig in the soil beneath. And, indeed, human bones were found, which, upon examination, were determined by a local physician to be those of an adolescent, though the records do not indicate whether they were female or male. The skeleton was displayed upon the kitchen table for some days to satisfy the neighbors' curiosity, but then the bones began to crumble into a fine white powder. Finally, the residue was swept together and interred in the local cemetery, without any attempt to identify the person, the manner of death, or a potential motive if the death had occurred by misadventure.

Other curious features of the building are the hex marks still visible on door latches, carved as deterrents to witches entering the house. In strict Calvinist congregations of the late 1600s, there was still a strong fear of witches harming people or animals, and oftentimes crosses were placed upon windows or doorframes to keep the spiritual darkness out. When cows stopped giving milk, or the cream became unaccountably sour, or if crops didn't grow, a witch was strongly suspected, and the wary citizens were quick to take preventative measures.

Most guided tours of the community begin at the DuBois Fort on Huguenot Street, a large building dating from 1705. During the middle of the 20th century, Elsie Oates operated a restaurant there and lived upstairs. She explained to historical society members that, one evening in the late 1940s, she arose from bed to visit the bathroom. Walking into a partially lit hallway, Elsie was startled to see a female figure "possessing a very small waist, wearing a long brown dress, and wearing an embroidered white collar with a dark ribbon through it." What caught Mrs. Oates' attention the quickest, however, was that the figure was headless! She recounted that nature was calling louder than her fear of the ghost, and she brushed the apparition aside and entered the bathroom. When she emerged, the ghost was gone, and although she never saw it again, strange, unexplained noises were heard throughout the remainder of her tenure in the house. Years after Elsie moved out, a caretaker once more observed the headless woman. Also, a member of the Huguenot Historical Society visiting the building by day spotted a woman's long skirt swishing around a corner. Hurrying to that corner, the witness could find no other person in the building.

Today, the DuBois Fort is uninhabited, except during daylight hours, when it serves as a small museum, orientation center for the site, and Visitors' Center for Historic Huguenot Street tours.

Almost directly across the street is a large Victorian home (the Judge Abraham Deyo House) that, at first, seems out of place in a colonial museum village. Its size and Queen Anne architecture stand out. Until a guide shares this information, one would not know that, underneath the 1894 exterior, a stone house dating from 1692 remains within the building's walls. Again, identifying a particular ghost is never easy, but there are strong suspicions among historians as to who the culprit is here: Gertrude Deyo. Wherever her portrait hangs, the caretakers have found, there is likely to be a disruption that some would call a poltergeist effect.

Gertrude, a daughter of the Deyo family owners in the late 1800s, had her portrait painted to hang alongside likenesses of her mother and father, and all three portraits were once hung together in an upstairs hallway. Soon after the portrait sitting, however, Gertrude contracted tuberculosis (TB) and died. As the Deyo family grew older and members moved away from New Paltz (today there is a strong Deyo family support association that works with the museum), the old house was incorporated into the Huguenot Street Historic District. One museum curator thought that the Judge and his wife (Margaret) should be displayed downstairs, where museum visitors might immediately encounter them upon entering.

Immediately after the parental paintings were moved, a Historic Huguenot Street housekeeper came into the building to clean (as part of the restoration work) and found Gertrude's portrait not just moved from its upper hallway wall but standing against a wall at the top of the stairs. A wag might suspect that Gert was headed downstairs to rejoin her parents. Just to be safe, a recent curator has moved Gertrude to a downstairs location, in a parlor not far from her parents. She seems content in that brighter location and hasn't acted up since. Readers should consider whether anything of a deceased person's energy or consciousness can reside in a likeness, portrait or photograph. There are many investigators who believe it is so.

The Deyo House isn't occupied every day, but often, when a volunteer or curator visits the house on business, there are reports of heavy footsteps ascending the old servants' stairway, and one volunteer actually saw a ghostly woman walking up those stairs. In addition, another worker saw a framed photograph suddenly slide across a table and fall to the floor, while still another guide caught the shape of an unknown person stealing into a Deyo House bedroom. The girl sped to the doorway to see who had just entered, since there was no other way out of the room. It was empty. So there may be more spirit entities afoot at the old Deyo House. For that reason, after visiting the Abraham Hasbrouck House, the avid ghost hunter should make this old home the second stop.

Hasbrouck 1721

The Jean (Jacob) Hasbrouck House, built in 1721, and currently closed for renovations, was also the site of a phenomenon. One day, a guide escorted a small tour group through the interior and, accompanied by two young boys, ventured into the attic to see the hand-hewn ceiling beams. In that space was an old spinning wheel—and it was moving! First, it spun forward, then backward, as if a phantom spinner were working a ball of wool or flax into yarn. That was enough reenacted history for the guide and her two young tourist lads. All beat a hasty retreat.

Old French Church

Next to the restored French Church at the end of the street is an old cemetery with tombstones dating to 1731, though earlier burials date to 1678. The early years of life in colonial villages were perilous ones for youngsters when it came to disease. Often a child stood only a fifty percent chance of reaching maturity, and the old graveyard is filled with many youngsters' memorial stones. Across the street there is a white, two-story building that seems to occasionally house one of those child ghosts. History records that long ago a family wagon, with a mother and her children inside, was being ferried across the Walkill, not far away, when suddenly the craft was upset, and the entire family was thrown into the rushing water. All survived, however, except for a little girl, whose lifeless body was brought to the old burying ground and interred. On occasion, New Paltz police, making their normal rounds, have seen a small child in an upstairs window when the house is supposedly vacant.

Either that little girl, or another child whose life was cut short by death, seems to haunt the LeFevre House, right next to the cemetery. Mr. Heidgerd, a former resident of the old LeFevre House, wrote about his family's experiences with the otherworldly creatures there, reporting that the flow of entities into his house was constant, and eventually the family became used to the apparitions. Many of the deceased, of course, were known to the Heidgerds, and they often could recognize voices of individuals they'd known in life. The man recorded that he often spotted both Margaret Schoonmaker and her husband Daniel Hasbrouck in his house, but he explained it away with, "Well, you see, they are buried closest to this house in the graveyard, so, of course, they'd drop in to visit from time to time."

Over the years, I have noted nonchalance among many people who are regularly visited by ghosts. If the entities don't seem harmful (and most ghosts don't), there usually develops a familiarity between the living and the dead. But, what does "dead" really mean, anyway? For me, it seems to refer simply to "being permanently away from the body," as there are so many recorded instances of personalities continuing on, at least for a while after the body's death. Here, on Huguenot Street, the settlers worked long and hard to grow crops, build houses, tend shops, and carry on commerce. Something that has been worked at so ardently and for so long may take quite a period of time to release. Look at the attachments in your own life—how many of those (possessions, relationships, grudges, etc.) do you think you'll be able to just put aside when you find yourself dead?

If You Need Any Help...

1799 House

Reuben E. Fenton had been a Free Soil Democrat during the tumultuous 1850s, but as the Civil War loomed, the Congressman from Chautauqua and Cattaraugus counties became very uncomfortable. Too many Democrats were willing to allow slavery to continue its spread into the Kansas and Nebraska territories, and many of them stood behind the Fugitive Slave Law of 1850, which required the return of escaped slaves to their Southern owners. By 1855, he'd had enough, and he helped found the New York State Republican Party. In 1864 he allowed his name to be placed into nomination for Governor on that party's ticket, and as a "Lincoln man" he swept to victory. He had always been "the soldier's friend" when in Congress between 1853 and 1864, and instituted many measures to help New York State veterans and their families when the war ended.

Governor Fenton

During the four years he served as Governor, Fenton helped establish a paid fire department in New York City; formulated healthier codes for the city's slaughterhouses; regulated tenement housing within the state; raised the standards for teacher education and established teacher-training normal schools; created the school of agriculture at Cornell; formalized the inspection of asylums, state hospitals and homes for the disadvantaged; and thrice vetoed the NY Central Railroad's demands for higher fares. He regarded himself as a bulwark between big money's power and the ordinary citizen. After losing the election of 1868, Fenton stood for the United States Senate and was elected. He served in Washington until 1875 and then, in retirement, served as president of the First National Bank in Jamestown. In 1885 he died in Jamestown, the city that he loved.

In 1863, he had built an ornate Italian Villa style home on Washington Street. The three-story building remained his family's home after his death, but as with all old homes, the building eventually passed into the hands of others who weren't as interested in its preservation. It wasn't until 1964 that a historical society was formed, and the restoration of the historic house was begun in order to establish a museum of Jamestown's past. That work took many years.

Kristin-Maeve Uschold Noonan, a native of Jamestown, worked on the museum's staff between 1986 and 1987, at a time when the first great project neared completion—that of the Grand Parlor or Grand Drawing Room. She is a sensitive woman who often felt the history in the items she placed on display for museum visitors. A good deal of her work was done on the third floor, in rooms that the Fentons had used for their children's school and housing for the nanny. In later years, those rooms would be devoted to artifact storage. Kristin-Maeve recalled for me a most mysterious event from early 1987, when workmen were finishing restorative work on the second floor.

"My work was interrupted by a horrendous crash from the second floor, so I went into the hallway and peered over the railing. We had a glass display case down on the second floor, which contained a collection of funeral mementos from Victorian days, little objects fashioned as *memento mori* or keepsakes of the deceased person's funeral. There was even a small child's casket inside. Because the items were delicate, the cabinet was sealed and always locked. Well, not this time!

"The first thing I noticed as I looked below was the door to the cabinet standing wide open. Immediately after that, I saw the two workmen scurrying past it with fearful faces and down the stairway to the outdoors. Neither would say what prompted their hasty exit, other than the crash, but they vowed never to work inside the museum again. For the next month or so, they worked only on the exterior. We never found out how the cabinet became unlocked or who had done it. However, I felt that I knew—Reuben.

"Though I normally don't see ghosts (I more often smell or feel their presence), many times I'd catch a glimpse of a tall, male shadow standing in front of the parlor windows, staring out, with one of his hands tucked into the opposite armpit. Often, there would be the scent of tobacco—pipe tobacco, I think, as it didn't smell like a cigarette. Had Reuben been alive at the time, I would have thought it an ordinary pose of a man concerned with great matters, a gentleman who paused to look downhill into his city while musing about these issues. Had I seen Governor Fenton's ghost?"

One valuable feature of a local history museum is that it offers citizens a place to donate historic documents, photos, and other artifacts, rather than leave them to the ravages of time. "As I worked on several displays, I sensed that a strong person stood behind me, surveying my work. Great curiosity marked this spirit's appearances, as if Fenton was just delighted to see his old home restored. I always sensed exuberance in the parlor, as if he was saying, 'If you need any help …' It must have been very hard to watch a luxurious home decay because of others' lack of care, so he seemed to appreciate all we did to bring back the glory of yesteryear.

"We have a large Civil War collection there, too, and maybe his championing of the soldiers' rights keeps him tied to so many of those artifacts. We have a small soldier's jacket there, maybe that of a drummer boy. There are all kinds of military accoutrements, and some of it is stained by blood. Because my sensitivities in the spirit world are strongest in the area of smell, I many times could pick up the coppery smell from human blood emanating from cloth items or weapons. I didn't want to think too much about how that blood came to be there. Cattaraugus and Chautauqua counties sent great numbers of men into battle to preserve the Union and not all of them marched home in victory. I wonder if some of those spirits, too, occasionally come to visit the family photos, the diaries that soldiers kept, the antique firearms, and the uniforms they wore."

Kristin-Maeve noted that she felt the Governor's presence most strongly in the area of the former children's rooms upstairs. "I know he loved those children, and I know he loved the returning veterans who presented their flags to him at the State Capitol in Albany. Speaking to the regiments drawn up before the Capitol Building, he vowed that 'the people will regard with jealous pride your welfare and honor, not forgetting the widow, the fatherless, and those who were dependent upon the fallen hero.' I think he was a man with a big heart, and that heart keeps him attached to his soldiers, his home and family, and to Jamestown."

Any one of those three attachments is enough to keep a departed soul tethered to the physical plane, I've learned. Here is a good example of a spirit remaining on the earth out of love, respect, and obligation.

Isabelle/Isabella

To date, I have interviewed almost nine hundred people who have apparently had ghost experiences, and I'm often surprised at the determination that so many of them have shown in attempting to identify the entities through historical research. Here is such an example from Bloomington, New York, once a part of West Hurley, and now located in Rosendale, Ulster County.

Tamme Stitt and her husband moved into the old farmhouse in 1992, attracted by the building's ornamentation and by a strong desire to restore the historic property. The restoration work was nearly done in late 1999, when Tamme discovered she was expecting a baby. She and her husband often discussed potential names for the child. "I knew, all of a sudden, that it would be a girl and that her name must be 'Isabelle.' We don't have anyone in our families with that name, so I thought it rather odd that such a name would suddenly spring into my mind, but Isabelle it was certain to be.

"When Isabelle was about three, I began to notice little odd events, not scary, but just plain odd," she told me. "When she was an infant, I would put Isabelle's sleeping blanket on the floor, where it was safest. There was always a baby monitor near her while she slept and I worked in the kitchen nearby. Many times, while in another room, I'd hear a woman's voice humming or quietly singing what seemed like a lullaby, though the baby was alone and asleep whenever I hurried to check. Must be my imagination, I thought. After a few more years, figuring that I must have a spirit or two in the house, I began to study numerous old deeds of the property in order to theorize about the spirits' identities. From a still-living, former owner, I learned that a woman named Isabella Baumfree once lived briefly on the property.

"First, I was amazed at the possible inspiration for my daughter's name, but (in the light of events since then) I was even more surprised when I checked on the identity of the first Isabella. She was a slave born in Ulster County in 1797 [N.B. New York State permitted slavery until it began freeing all the state's slaves in 1827.] and one who suffered much at the hands of cruel owners until she left Ulster County at the age of thirty-two. The world knows Isabella as Sojourner Truth, a name that she adopted in 1843, when she began to work with the Abolitionist movement across America. Wow! That sure was inspiring; even more so because I began to suspect that this woman's spirit still drops by for a visit and briefly might take up her former role as a nanny, this time to my little girl.

"My Isabelle used to walk alone down the driveway toward the barn, holding her right hand up in the air, as if some taller person held it. [N.B. Sojourner Truth was almost six feet tall] Once in a while, I worried, as if some unseen being was 'leading her away,' but, of course, Sojourner Truth indeed did encourage slaves to free their masters in the time before the Civil War.

"What is it with that barn? I began to wonder. One day I saw the famous psychic Sylvia Brown on the Montel Williams Show, so I contacted her to get a psychic reading. About a year later, I finally received my phone reading. Ms. Brown had never been to Ulster County, but she remarked that long ago a woman had killed herself in my bedroom from whose window a person can see the barn. Now, that's the only window in the house from which the barn can be viewed; how could Sylvia have known? And who was that woman? Apparently, Sylvia said, the woman had killed herself because both of her children had died of diphtheria. If true, then the woman sure wasn't Sojourner Truth, who died in Michigan. Later, when I began my search, I couldn't find any evidence of a woman and two children dying in the house—not of any cause. Yet, here was a theoretical second woman, and one who loved and missed her children.

"Then my research did turn up a child's death—a girl named Jenny. A researcher discovered that both of little Jenny's parents, Felix and his wife, had died by 1892. The records aren't clear or are missing, so we can't explain how Jenny acquired a guardian named Silas Schoonmaker, but the house was willed to the five-year-old. For some reason, the little girl lived only seven months more.

"I hired a young woman to search county courthouse records for children's deaths on my property, but hadn't told her why I wanted to know. She related to me that at the moment when she found little Jenny's name she was suddenly overcome by an intense cold chill. I have a bad feeling about Silas, and have begun to suspect that it was he, rather than Sojourner Truth, who was holding my Isabelle's hand, perhaps luring her to the barn. I haven't been able to determine how or precisely where Jenny died, but I suspect she met her end in an 'accident' in the barn."

Tamme told me that she suddenly began to mentally connect some prior events which she had formerly ignored. Ever since Isabelle's birth, Tamme had noticed a small shadow traveling through the house—always out of the corner of her eye. "She never went beyond my front hallway, though, for some reason. And every time I felt or noticed the child, she suddenly 'blinked out' and was gone. I also discovered that Silas sometimes listed Jenny as his daughter: Jenny Schoonmaker, but could find no evidence of a legal adoption.

"So, what's with that barn, I wondered, and, gathering up all my courage, I decided to sleep there one night. I was in a twilight sleep early the next morning when I began to hear women in conversation. As clear as day I heard them talking happily, probably gossiping about village matters, though I couldn't make out the precise words. In my mind's eye there were three or four of them and clearly were close friends. My neighbors have a house behind the barn, so I assumed it was those folks who were up early. I forced myself to wake up and go outside, noting that it was 3 a.m. on my watch, but it was pitch-black and nobody was around. Later, my tenant told me that she once awoke in the night to find someone standing at the foot of her bed, just watching her. She wasn't a believer in ghosts, so the experience woke her right up!

Another event from when Isabelle was three is that I often had a bad feeling that we shouldn't dig the hole for our in-ground pool, so I told the workmen to stop immediately if they found 'anything.' Isabelle one day took my hand and led me to a small stone marker near our property line and obscured under some bushes. Was it a grave? And, if so, whose? Since that day, the bushes have been removed, but I cannot find that marker—it's just gone! This had been a 'cement town' and some grave markers, I was told, were used.

Also, some folks said that the deceased were often buried on a property line if a regular cemetery wasn't used. Since that time, I wondered if my daughter was "led" there, and if so, by whom? Is it possible that there is an unmarked grave in that part of the lawn?

"After a big pool party sometime later, when the guests had all gone and we were upstairs asleep, I awoke at 3:30 a.m. and looked out into the yard. In the moonlight, I spotted a man sitting near the pool and smoking a cigarette. I was irked because I had a 'no smoking' sign clearly posted near the pool. I hurried down to berate the man, figuring he was a straggler from our party, but when I got into the yard, nobody was there, though I could smell smoke. I'm sure it wasn't imagination because, another night, a neighbor called to say someone was smoking near our pool and did I know who it was?

"I know that Fred, the previous owner of our house, died here in his office, which is now my office. I also know that he was a smoker because there were smoke stains everywhere and it took a long time for me to get rid of them and the smoke smell in our house. Many times during our life here, I have actually seen or smelled smoke indoors, but I've learned to just say, 'Put it out now, Fred!' And the sight or smell immediately vanishes, so my guess is that Fred comes and goes from the old homestead from time to time. Likely, it was hard for him to leave for good, as we know he loved this house."

Tamme smiles when she says that these occasional spirit-friend visits don't bother her, but Silas does. She is watchful of her two children today, though she suspects that Isabelle has had more experiences than she talks about, while her son often sees Jenny and thinks it's neat to have a second "almost-sister."

Lending a Hand?

Hand Home

Augustus Cincinnatus Hand opened a law office in Elizabethtown, Essex County, in 1831. He later became Postmaster, then served as Judge of the Essex County Surrogate Court. In time, he also was elected a State Senator and afterward represented his congressional district with one term in the U.S. House of Representatives between 1839 and 1841. In his later years, he was elected to the New York State Supreme Court. His legal duties were performed in a small frame office on River Street, and he built a stately brick home to the east. The old house and office have been beautifully preserved.

Hand's three sons likewise entered the legal profession, and his two daughters were educated far beyond the level of their Adirondack peers. Richard, the youngest son, was the last family member to live in the house, dying there in 1914. That doesn't mean that he was the last Hand resident, however, because Ellen Hand, Augustus' daughter, had died young, shortly after her marriage. It is possible that her spirit stayed on as it seems certain that some ambient energy or spirits have been preserved at the historic site on River Street. Some staff members of the non-profit organization occupying the house today think Ellen is the likeliest candidate for the house ghost.

Since 1914, there have been incidents of sedate ghostly activity in the building, though none of it would be considered improper behavior for a well-bred Victorian daughter. First, any grand old house that lies abandoned, as the Hand house was during the 1960s and '70s, is normally a prime attraction for vandals. Yet, this old home was never broken into, likely because local juveniles believed it to be haunted. Subsequent phenomena seem to validate that belief.

Once the Crary Foundation, the building's present owner, took possession of the house in 1979, the

Ellen Hand

staff began to inventory its contents. Joan Youngken began to notice strange "coincidences," such as the time when she sat writing up a report on the historic Hand family dresses stored in the upstairs rear rooms of the house. Taking a break from her intense work, she went downstairs and, perhaps intuitively, opened the drawer on a desk. Inside was an old letter from a Hand family member and as she read it, Joan was stunned to recognize that it described the very dress that she had just inventoried and put away. When she expressed her astonishment at the various coincidences to other workers, she received smiles and heard similar tales.

Some told of catching glimpses of people from the corner of their eye, but when they looked directly at the entities, there was nobody there. Others told of hearing or seeing doorknobs turning, though no living person ever came into the room, and no one stood outside when the viewer checked. Several times, upon entering otherwise empty rooms, some of the workers caught sudden glimpses of human forms that suddenly evaporated.

Another woman resident in the house during that period used to place her handbag on the bed in her bedroom and lock the door upon exiting. At day's end when she returned, she found the handbag empty and all its contents carefully arranged on the dresser. Yet, the room's door was locked before she entered and there was clearly no other entry. It was almost as if an invisible hostess were bidding her to stay. Who or what energy was at work?

One day, William Savage, whose wife was a member of the Hand family, came to visit and the woman, excusing herself, unlocked her bedroom door and tossed her jacket and handbag on the bed. William observed, "Mother (likely referring to his deceased mother-in-law) would never stand for that. Once a bed was made, you did not put things on it." So, finally, the woman resident had a likely culprit for the room's phenomena.

In 1984, Hannelore Kissam, Director of the Crary Foundation, became ill, though she wanted to remain on the job. It was suggested that she stay in an upstairs room, and for four weeks her son joined her, sleeping in an adjoining room. "I saw at least one of the ghosts," Hanne told me. "I was asleep one night and heard footsteps in the hallway—too light for my son's feet, I judged. Then the doorknob rattled and turned, but nobody came into the room. I couldn't stand the suspense any longer and got out of bed and opened the door. A bit farther down the hallway, I saw a petite young woman with dark hair walking toward the room at the end of the hall. I also noticed two other things.

"First, as the girl passed a hallway mirror, there was no reflection of her movement. Secondly, there was a unique odor, a combination of unwashed body scent and perfume. You know, in the old days, people didn't bathe as often as today and just used doses of perfume to cover body odor. From time to time after that, I'd smell that particular combination of smells, though I didn't see her. Curiously, I'd often smell it near the dining room door, which is the room where Ellen Hand's portrait now hangs. The figure I saw in the upstairs hall very strongly resembles that portrait."

In 2003, Hannelore, who recently retired as longtime director of the Crary Foundation, told her experiences to Elizabeth Folwell of *Adirondack Life Magazine,* and noted that these scents might belong to present staff members, but maybe they didn't. She observed that old houses often have evanescent historical odors, and she was entirely comfortable with both explanations.

In the summer of 1998, two young men and a clergyman who were attending a local function stayed overnight in the house and met the invisible "whoevers." The young clergyman heard footsteps in the hall, then sensed a sudden presence in the room, just following the sound of a turning doorknob, though he hadn't seen a door open. Next, he felt a pressure, as if someone had just sat down on the bed, and finally, an unseen weighty object or person laid itself out atop his body. Frightened, the man became totally awake and, struggling to breathe under the pressure, found the weight suddenly lifting and departing from the room with an audible closing of the door and footsteps receding in the hallway. Needless to say, he remained awake throughout the night and left quickly in the morning. Two others in the room had peacefully slept through the entire episode.

None of the staff that I spoke with felt that ghosts or spirits or hauntings had much to do with the present function of the house. All seemed broadminded enough to suspect that there was some leftover energy from the time when the Hands lived in domestic peace there. All of today's Foundation employees are intent on carrying out their mission, which lies in granting over five hundred scholarships to deserving students each year, to those needy individuals who don't otherwise have a "ghost of a chance" of entering college.

Music in Hunter

Haines Falls R.R. Station

When railroads began in New York State, they followed the easiest terrain, such as river valleys and lowlands. The state's mountainous areas presented

111

engineering problems and increased costs of construction and operation. So, it wasn't until the 1870s that the Ulster and Delaware Railroad completed tracks into and through Haines Falls in the Greene County Town of Hunter. By that time, the Catskill Mountains were already famed for the vistas that had invited Thomas Cole and other artists of the Hudson River School of painters.

There were already great mountain resorts, such as the 1823 Catskill Mountain House and the Laurel House, in existence when the U&D tracks reached Haines Falls. The Mountain Top branch spur, however, allowed even more of the remote farms to move their dairy products to city markets, along with the ice, forest products, stone and coal from the uplands. In return, by 1880, a steady flow of well-to-do tourists came to the Catskills to bask in the cool air and idyllic setting. The U&D built two new hotels in 1881, the Hotel Kaaterskill near the famed falls, and the Grand Hotel in Highmount, and these thrived for many years.

Eventually, with the popularization of the automobile, summer visitors went elsewhere, and by the end of World War I in 1918, the hotel business, as well as the number of passengers coming by train into the mountains, declined. Spurred by losses in the Depression, the U&D went bankrupt in 1932. For some years, the closed station was abandoned, and then was sold to a private investor who converted the structure into a three-bedroom dwelling, adding interior hardboard walls and obscuring the old wainscoting, and also changing the position of the windows. Did some unrecorded, yet enduring, history take place during those years?

Between 1991 and 1994, Bridget lived there and had a number of uncanny experiences. "It was a place that immediately attracted me," she told me. "It was comfy and distinctive. An old school mistress had lived there before me, though I know little about her and her habits. What interested me most was that, in 1992, I began to hear faint music. Taking time to search for the source, I was stumped. The sound came from nowhere and everywhere inside, especially the living room. When I stepped outside either the front or rear exits, there was no sound at all. Inside, however, it seemed as if I heard ragtime piano music, perhaps like old Scott Joplin pieces.

"Our living room was the former passenger waiting room, I learned, but such passenger accommodations, even at the height of the Victorian summers, never included piano entertainment. It was strange to sit in my living room, then, and hear ghostly, but nice, sounds. The ghost, though I never saw him or her, seemed happy—and helpful. Might it have been the old school mistress performing in her time?

"One night," she told me, "I awoke to a crash, and turning on the light, discovered that a large curtain rod had somehow jumped out of its u-shaped bracket and fallen to the floor. I had a big old shag rug on the bedroom floor at the time, and noted what appeared to be a mist on its surface. Suddenly, I recognized that it wasn't mist or ectoplasm, it was smoke! My floor heater had just started a small fire in the carpet pile, and had the curtain rod not fallen so loudly, I might never have been able to extinguish the fire. So, did a ghost save my life?"

Once, when her mother was staying over, the woman complained to Bridget, "Turn that music down!" "I had to explain to her that it was impossible to do so because it was a ghost sound. She gave me some look! A skeptic might suggest that the sound was all in my head, but a friend who stayed over one night heard it. And my dog became nervous whenever I opened the cellar door. He just wouldn't go down there, though it never troubled me to do so, and I never felt anything sinister in the cellar." Sometimes, Bridget said, she could hear a faint laughter behind the music, and it was such a happy place to live. Nevertheless, she had to move in 1994.

A few years later, the public-spirited citizens of the Town of Hunter formed the Mountain Top Historical Society and began the restoration of the old station. Replica wooden benches were made and installed. The old gypsum board interior walls were removed, exposing the old hardwood wainscoting, which the historians cleaned and polished. Lecture space and temporary seating was developed for programs dealing with railroad history or history presentations. In essence, a historical campus was begun, though the old iron rails have been long ago removed and the old "puffer billy" steam trains no longer make a refueling or passenger stop.

"If I ever had a chance to return to Haines Falls and could purchase that building, I would, but I've never returned. It was a place where I gained some education about ghosts and it is now the place where the Greene County citizens educate visitors about the old U&D and the people who lived in that beautiful scenery." Seldom had I heard such a loving and longing for a ghost site.

The Midnight Lover

In the 1760s, before the Revolutionary War, Thaddeus Crane built a house near the junction of what is now Route 121 and Baxter Road in the town of North Salem. The Westchester County area soon became embroiled in the American fight for independence and Crane took command of the Fourth

Regiment of the New York State Militia, composed of Westchester County men. During the war's early years he also served (1777-1779, when the prospects for independence seemed bleakest, and when Crane lost his wife and two sons) in the New York State Assembly. He certainly was a mover and shaker in the Town of Upper Salem, as it was known then, until his death in 1849.

As with most historic structures, the Crane house passed to new ownerships and the old home was a rental property in 1982, when Fran Corey moved into a small house on the property. "It was a nice, quiet place for several years before my first experience," she told me. "In 2003, I awoke in the middle of the night, aware that something was just not right. As I sat in the middle of the bed, I became aware that standing in the bedroom doorway was a man. The bearded figure sported a mustache and light brown hair, and I noticed his outfit was a khaki color. Because of our area's historic past, I wondered if he might have been a soldier, as I already knew he was a ghost. Nevertheless, I wasn't scared, just intrigued. I'd heard about ghosts, but this sighting was a first for me. However, whatever his identity, I didn't see him for quite a while after that, though my cats did. Many times I'd see them rolling over and over, purring, as if stroked by an invisible hand. The ghost seemed to make them happy.

"Then, awhile later, I was sick with a winter cold, and tossed miserably in my semi-conscious state, with a stuffy head and headache. During that long night, I half-woke to turn over, and when I did so, there was my "soldier," sitting beside my bed, almost as a caregiver. When I awoke in the morning, as you might guess, he was gone."

Fran was fascinated by the unseen world and wondered at that time if books about casting spells were accurate. She tried a few of the more common ones, attempting to influence physical objects in the house. One of these magic formulas involved the use of a needle and candle, but after hours of no success, she left the needle stuck deeply into the candle on the mantelpiece and went to bed. In the morning she was astonished to find the needle placed neatly alongside the candlestick. "It would have taken some effort to pull the needle out," she continued, "so I know it didn't just fall. Was this my visitor's commentary on my spell-casting? I wondered."

Some months later, Fran had a very vivid dream in which she watched the man enter her bedroom door, cross to her bed and then sit beside her. He tenderly leaned over and kissed her on the lips, she said, but it was as if he didn't know how to kiss. "I don't know how people kissed in those old days, but his skills were sadly lacking in our time," she laughed. I suggested that it may be quite difficult to give a good kiss if one doesn't have a solid body, and we both laughed.

As this was a "romance" that was going nowhere, and as her life changed, Fran moved from the old Crane house in 2005. Before leaving, however, she was visited by Maggie, a friend who called herself a "good witch." Maggie walked about the old house and then pronounced that the spirit visitor was named "David." Assuming that the spirit might be from Revolutionary times, both Fran and I did research on the Cranes, but neither of us could find a David in the Crane family who would have worn that old homespun style of clothing.

"I did figure that he might be an ancestor of the McKeon family, however," she told me, "because my landlord at that time was a McKeon."

NEW YORK STATE GHOSTS

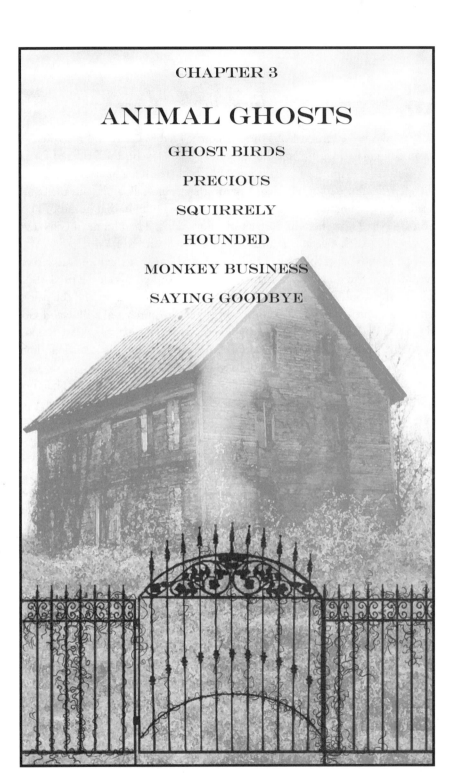

CHAPTER 3

ANIMAL GHOSTS

Ghost Birds

When he retired from the Air Force, Fred Wickert and his wife, Tae, became fascinated with tropical birds, and when a lovebird was offered for sale in a Cobleskill shop, they bought her. Shortly thereafter, a man in Duanesburg offered a Double Yellow-Headed Amazon that could talk a bit, and the couple became excited about owning a talking pet, so they bought that bird too. Then, soon afterward, they bought Barbara, a Yellow Wing. Their home in Gilboa was a lively place with several beautiful and talkative feathered friends.

Barbara's previous owner told Fred and Tae that the bird was very active, often playing on a swing that he had made for her. When she tired of that activity, she would play with his Military Macaw named Augie, and the pair often spent hours grooming each other. But then, he purchased a Blue and Gold Macaw named Andrew, and Augie grew jealous and bit his owner. So, the man put Augie up for sale with a pet dealer in Niskayuna named Joan. Joan loved Augie and, rather than sell him, chose to keep the bird as her pet.

A few months later, Joan bought a pair of baby Amazons that had been shipped from Texas, but in just a short time, the two developed Parrot Fever and suddenly died. The veterinarian notified the U.S. Department of Agriculture of the contagion, as the law requires. Parrot Fever can be virulent and easily transmitted among birds, and the USDA prevented Joan from selling any more birds. A month later, no more birds became sick, so the government agency allowed area owners to remove their birds from Joan's shop, but, for some reason, Augie was on the USDA's hit list. Late one night, the government agents came to Joan's shop with a seizure warrant and euthanized all her remaining birds. The agents expressed amazement at the struggle that Augie put up, and also the amount of time it took him to die.

That night, not knowing of Augie's execution, Fred and Tae noted Barbara doing something strange. On her swing in the doorway, the bird was swinging and talking, when suddenly she stopped. "Barbara froze and got a very puzzled and confused look on her face," Fred told me. "Then, she said, 'Hi, Augie. What are you doing?' A minute later she repeated her question to what appeared to us to be an otherwise empty room. Then, apparently confused, Barbara sat motionless for three or four minutes. Finally, as if nothing had happened, she resumed her playing on the swing." It was difficult for Fred and Tae to believe Barbara's reactions which they later computed had taken place just as Augie was being killed forty miles away.

Fred sold his mother's old house next door and used the proceeds to buy a pair of baby Macaws and some new cages. Romeo was a Blue and Gold Macaw and Juliet was a Bolivian Scarlet Macaw. The two birds became good friends and spent many hours with each other, often playing and preening. At day's end, each was returned to its individual cage.

Following a flood on the Schoharie Creek that destroyed their house, the Wickerts moved into a new home on higher ground, having been fortunate enough to save all their birds. In their new domicile, Romeo and Juliet shared the same cage. Not too long afterward, they discovered that Romeo had developed several large tumors on his breast. The veterinarian found them to be malignant and inoperable. Romeo died and was buried.

"Two weeks later, I saw Juliet stop what she was doing and look to her left. She said, 'Hi, Romeo, what are you doing? Hi, Romeo. I love you.' Continuing to look in the same direction for a couple of minutes, she then returned to her regular activity," Fred told me. A week later, the scenario repeated itself, exactly as before. It has never reoccurred since, and Juliet has never spoken his name again. "It makes me wonder whether or not birds' spirits can remain for a while as ghosts. It surprised me that they can see one another's spirit or energy," Fred told me. He is a down-to-earth guy, but knows what he heard and saw.

Precious

Lovers of ghost stories well know the role of an apparition or a surreptitious movement, or even the sudden "theft" of an object in sparking our interest in the spirit world. Sounds, spoken words, sudden frigid drafts, and even smells that evoke the memory of the deceased are common indicators that another world of sensations awaits us after death. But how about dreams of the departed? These leave no tracks, cannot be photographed, recorded, or measured on an EMF device. Can we, should we, take these as genuine contacts with the spirit world and evidence that life indeed continues after body death?

My study of dreams has concluded that when we sleep, we tend to put our conscious mind (which usually demands "proof" of our visitations) on a shelf of sorts, more fully exposing our unconscious mind to the stimulus of subtle energies, which ghost contacts usually are. In the dream state we seem to get messages and imagery that we more often need, than the experiences we seek when we are fully awake and ego-centered. Dreams are a fruitful source of information about both our waking and our sleeping lives.

Here is a simple, yet instructive, story from my friend Lori in the upstate Town of Ballston. "At the end of February 2008, I lost my 19½-year old cat, Precious. She had been my friend and companion for so long, it seemed as if she would live forever, but by October of 2007, her respiration began to fail. For four months she lived on in intensive care.

"Finally, in February, the vet informed me that the end was near; Precious' time had come, as her lungs were filled with fluid, a new problem that she hadn't experienced before. Having sat with my husband Bob's uncle when he died of lung cancer, I knew we couldn't let her suffer, so we agreed to let her go. It was only a few weeks later that I had a scary experience one night as I lay in an alpha state just before dropping into deep sleep. I suddenly found myself in a huge water tank. To my left was a drain pipe through which the water would flow out of the tank, and at the end of that pipe, I could see a bright light. I thought the illumination must be the sun.

"I panicked for my safety as I knew myself to be almost submerged in the fluid, with my mouth barely above the water level—there was nothing for me to hold onto to keep my head above the water. All I could do was to 'umpf' myself up into that pipe, and the dream suddenly ended. When fully awake, I pondered the dream's message or meaning, and concluded that these were the physical symptoms that Precious had experienced at death. It wasn't a dream about danger to me, but was much more likely a sensation communicated to me by Precious. Two weeks later I had a short dream in which I walked to the back of my parents' house, went inside, and there sat Precious, alert and healthy on her favorite cushion."

Lori told me that her husband was visiting a counselor shortly afterward, on an unrelated matter, and used part of that session to share Lori's dream with the man. David, the counselor, agreed that it was a death dream and concurred with Lori's conclusion. Where had the message come from? In some far-off eternity, had Precious reassembled her memories of the just-ended life, and communicated the experience of her passing to Lori, her longtime friend? Or had some part of Lori's psyche, still grieving for the loss of Precious, reached out into the ether to understand what all creatures experience in the final separation from a physical body? For me, as I have done dream analysis, the main point seems to be the light at the end. Likely, that illumination (a final goal for us all) is still too profound for us to comprehend its ultimate essence.

"I was blown away by that dream or communication," Lori told me, noting that she has had other profound dream experiences. "The counselor told Bob that it means I had a strong attachment, which is a good thing, with my parents! I have had a connection with my dad, who was deceased, where he came to me and we talked to one another through our minds. I also believe I have been in a thin place (a place between the worlds of life and death) on two occasions. The most memorable of those was when I held Bob's uncle's hand as he stepped over into the next place on his journey from life into death. I felt the utter peace of heaven."

For readers who have had close relationships with their pets, no more needs to be said. These owners who have become "owned" by their pet's love already know the deep sense of loss when the animal or bird passed away. But many of these people have afterward been gifted with dreams or other spirit experiences, as was Lori. And for these individuals, there remains the certainty that there is more, and that no love connection can ever be broken.

Squirrely

On Valentine's Day in 2008, Russell got a surprise. He lives north of Utica in the cold and snowy southern Adirondacks and knows well the wildlife that inhabit his neighborhood.

Following a night of snow flurries, at 1:00 p.m. he ventured out onto his porch and surveyed his yard. A grey squirrel suddenly appeared and made three quick hops across the snow toward his bird feeder, but then disappeared. "I wondered if it had perhaps burrowed into a snow drift, as the surface snow was quite powdery. That critter was headed toward my white pine trees, and it should have continued until it reached them. Nevertheless, it just vanished. This was only a small mystery, but I wanted to solve it, so I went out to check his tracks—where had he gone?

"When I got to the area there were no tracks at all, as if the squirrel had never been there!" he laughed. Russell is no stranger to ghosts, as he has often taken photos of ectoplasmic energy in area cemeteries and has had one-on-one meetings with them, including a grandfather who refuses to leave his house; thus, he pondered the possibility of a squirrel ghost in his yard. "I remember shooting a squirrel that wouldn't leave my bird feeder alone last fall right there. Is that what was going on here? The ghost of a robber squirrel who wanted to continue raiding the birdseed? The one that I shot died instantly, so maybe he doesn't yet recognize that he's dead." Russ scratched his head in wonder.

Russell then pondered the vision that he'd just seen, and remembered that the vanished squirrel had been a darker grey than the usual neighborhood squirrels, who are light grey, with white patches on their tails. At the time of this writing, Russell keeps his camera ready to capture the animal if it shows up again. A ghost squirrel? Really?

In the middle of March, after promising to keep me updated, Russ wrote that the mystery is deepening. He set a baited trap out on his porch, with tempting seeds inside. Checking his lure a few days later, he found many of the seeds eaten, though the trap locks were still secure. If, indeed, a varmint had gotten into the cage and had eaten the seeds, the locks would have retained the animal inside the cage. There was no way that, once inside, the animal could escape. Yet the seeds continued to be eaten. In mid-summer I called Russ once more, hoping for a plausible resolution to his problem, but he told me the seed is still being stolen by something that can't get into the cage, but does.

One always looks for a down-to-earth explanation for any strange phenomenon, but such a thing is pretty hard to find in this case.

Hounded

Janet Singer from the Adirondack hamlet of Olmstedville lost her favorite Daschund in 1992. Holly had been a good and faithful friend and it was with much sadness that Janet and her husband buried the dog. "I thought, well, that's it—she's gone," Janet said, "but that turned out not to be the case. Every so often, when I walk around the kitchen, I almost trip over her. She still walks behind me, helping me in her own way. After fifteen years—now that's loyalty," she chuckled.

"What I most wanted to talk about is my father's experience with his dog," she continued. "Growing up outside of Brentwood on Long Island, I enjoyed life. Our house on Wicks Road was in a rural setting (though it is all built up there today) and across the road from the very old Taylor Farm.

"Dad was best known for his work in local politics, being the Town of Islip Highway Superintendent for many years, and he finally became the Town of Islip Supervisor. Before those years of public service, however, he worked longer hours and enjoyed each day's end, when he could walk our dog Buster. Buster had a personality problem and some said he was vicious, though he was sweet and gentle to members of our family.

"In any case, each night before going to bed, Dad took Buster out onto the dark old stretch of road in front of our house. There were no street lights then, so the only illumination was the night sky and the moon. One night, my dad returned from his walk very excited—we all had to sit down and hear his tale. Once out of the house, and with Buster not on a leash, Dad said that he had looked up the road and spotted someone walking—a man, it turned out. As the stranger got closer and closer, Dad began to fear that Buster would chew him up. On the shoulder of the road Dad and Buster stood, watching the man approach. Then Dad noted that the walker was oddly dressed, in a Chesterfield coat. Nobody had dressed that way since Victorian times—who was he?"

Reaching for the dog's collar in order to restrain him, Mr. Pearsall awaited the inevitable growl and lunge. But it didn't happen. The stranger came closer and closer and then passed by within a foot of Buster. "Dad said that he thought the man's pant leg might have brushed against Buster's nose, but the dog kept looking straight ahead, obviously savoring his nighttime stroll. The stranger kept walking and was soon lost to view. The experience was so upsetting for Dad that he had to wake up everyone in the house to tell us of the mysterious encounter," Janet smiled.

A real dog and a ghostly man—sometimes the characters in such encounters are reversed, providing the tale of a ghostly canine surprising a living man. What is illustrative here is that people's lives are so often filled with these mysterious mini-events that most folks seldom recognize that they have just encountered a spirit. It's easier, perhaps, just to conclude that this time Buster didn't bite, but Mr. Pearsall knew what he'd experienced. While our pets are many times very sensitive, Buster hadn't even seen the ghost.

Monkey Business

One of the nicest old villages in Oneida County is Holland Patent, and the Toomeys are lovers of antiquity. Kevin and his wife   appreciate the craftsmanship of early America and sought a nice old "tall case clock," which many Americans know as a "grandfather clock," to complete the décor of their home on Wynn Road.

They were very pleased when their friend, Rome, New York, antique dealer Ed Lannigan, told them that he'd located a nice old 1812 item in New Hampshire. The craftsman, Silas Hoadley, former business partner of famous clockmaker Seth Thomas, had long ago built the timepiece in his Plymouth, Connecticut shop, and it was currently in the possession of another dealer in North Conway, New Hampshire. In some forgotten way, the clock had migrated from Hoadley's shop to a farmhouse in Guilford, New Hampshire, then was sold to the local dealer.

Sight unseen, the Toomeys instructed Lannigan to make the purchase, which was completed at a very fair price. Once installed in their living room, Kevin told me, they took great pride in the beautiful clock face and pewter hands of the rich wooden-cased antique. For quite a while the couple experienced some strange phenomena that at first they couldn't conceive might be connected to their new possession.

"From time to time, after we'd gone to bed," Kevin told me, "we would be awakened by the living room stereo suddenly blaring away. One of us would have to get up and shut it off, though we both were certain that it had been off at bedtime. Then, other evenings, as we sat watching television or listening to music, I'd spot a dark patch of something going up or down our stairs. At first, I assumed it was our cat, but when I looked over, I'd see kitty in my wife's lap. What could it be? If it was a ghost, it certainly wasn't of human size. The activity persisted, however, so I got back in touch with Ed, the antique dealer.

"He did some research with the New Hampshire dealer from whom he'd made the purchase and determined that the Guilford farmer had owned a monkey. Before Ed found the clock for me, it seemed never to run for very long. Then, maybe," he said with a grin, "we discovered why. While awaiting sale in the North Conway shop, several customers had told the owner that they saw a dark figure run up to the clock. But the figure walked with a strange gait, almost as if it was a chimpanzee. Then the owner confirmed that the original owner, the old farmer, had indeed owned a monkey as a pet. It seemed that the spirit of the monkey, upon its death, had for some reason attached itself to the clock. Great! I mumbled, how does one get rid of a monkey ghost?"

Kevin told me that it was as simple as turning the clock to face a different wall. Not understanding the mechanics of how it works, he was happy that the process did work, and the Wynn Road house has been quiet ever since. As all beings and objects carry electrical fields of varying strengths, it is possible that Kevin's turning of the timepiece may have eliminated some of the energy that powered the monkey's spirit, preventing the creature from reappearing.

Saying Goodbye

When I do storytelling, especially to children's groups, I find great interest in whether or not a favorite dog, goldfish or canary has survived body death. In a world filled with bombings and murders, youngsters are already consciously or unconsciously at work, deciding about the meaning of life and the fearsome word "death" that causes so much anxiety among adults.

Here is a story that should provide some ease for young people and those of us elders who have lost a favorite pet.

Stephanie Torkilson Bambina remembers that, in the summer of 1981, a young boy was biking through Red Hook in Dutchess County, when he noticed a brown grocery bag in the road. He stopped to investigate and discovered three small tiger kittens that someone had discarded. He took them home, keeping one (named Bartlett because he was pear-shaped) and giving the other two to Stephanie. She named them Fenimore and Cooper.

By 1998, Cooper had died and Fenimore was seventeen, and troubled with a thyroid condition that required daily medication. Though he was an old male by then, Fenimore was an excellent parent to kittens that Stephanie brought to her new home in Kingston. She smiled wistfully when she remembered, "He was an excellent parent to the three kittens that I brought home, and boy, was he adept at getting into things—there was not a door or cabinet in the house that he couldn't open! Fenimore studied with her when she was in graduate school, was chief lookout when she took a shower, and slept on her pillow each night.

Though he was old, he seemed healthy enough to be left behind when Stephanie was ready to leave on vacation with her husband that year. However, a few days before the departure, he refused his thyroid pill and ate only irregularly, passing up his favorite—duck liver pâté. Worried, Stephanie took the cat to her vet, but he found nothing wrong except for his age and the thyroid problem. Nevertheless, the doctor agreed to keep him at the clinic during her absence, so that medical help would be available if the situation worsened.

"We left our vacation phone number with the vet, but I remember experiencing a terrible sinking feeling as my husband (who was less emotionally connected to Fenimore) and I drove off. I called the vet each day from our hotel, though we were late returning to our rooms on Wednesday night and the vet was closed. So, I called early on Thursday morning," she told me, "only to hear that Fenimore had just died. I screamed so loudly that they must have heard me from one end of the hotel to the other! Reluctant to break off his vacation, my husband tried to carry on, but I was inconsolable, so he gave in, grumbled, and we returned home on Friday."

Stephanie was filled with remorse at Fenimore's probable suffering and bewilderment that she wasn't there as he readied for death. Her husband dispationately reminded her that she wasn't God and couldn't have prevented Fenimore's passing, but she still ached because she wasn't there to comfort her old companion when he died. Stephanie had no children, so Fenimore had been her "baby," and she agonized over her loss. Her husband worked late to avoid her self-recriminations and weeping, so when he was home, she learned to cry only in the shower, where she couldn't be heard and she could dry the tears before walking out of the bathroom. As a school teacher, she doubted that she would be able to return to her job in the fall. The only way she could do so was to get counseling, which she did.

Her therapist suggested some excellent coping techniques for Stephanie whenever she felt assailed by grief and depression. She worked with the counselor for a year and learned to cope, but there was still a black hole in her heart, a place of emotional emptiness because she'd never see her companion cat again. Finally, in the summer of 1999, she chose a vacation spot that permitted visitors to have pets. Determined to bring all her kitties with her this time, she set off, knowing that beneath the sunny skies and ocean water environment, there lurked what counselors call "anniversary grief" which can suddenly leap out and unexpectedly ambush even the happiest person. July 23rd was the unhappy day of Fenimore's passing, and Stephanie was anxious about its arrival.

"But then, early in the dawn of the 23rd, the most amazing thing happened," she laughed. "I had a truly wonderful dream in which Fenimore returned to me. I intuitively knew (in the dream) that he could only stay with me for one hour. I accepted, in the dream, that he was dead, but I had been granted this hour with him as a gift of love. Fenimore had raised Willow, a kitten, and in the dream, he followed the other cat around the room, then rubbed against and licked me. Then he jumped into my lap, purring, and I could feel the softness of his tiger fur. I could see his green eyes and white feet and bib, all spotlessly cleaned." She remembers the hour ending as she held her old friend, and as she said, "Thank you, God," she awoke.

Stephanie found herself sitting up in the same position in which she left off at dream's end, a position in which she'd always cuddled with Fenimore in life. "Now, for the first time in a year, I felt a deep sense of peace. Though I had dreaded July 23rd so much, I had been gifted with a dream of joy."

A skeptic or individual who has never owned a pet will likely scoff at this tale, certain that Stephanie's unconscious mind had confabulated the entire scenario as "compensation." But pet owners who have lost a loved animal know what the truth is here. In my archives I have many stories of "a pet's last goodbye." So, if death inevitably takes our pets, then, at our end, The Creator certainly will take and sustain those of us who have loved those pets. Luke 12:6-7 relates that not a sparrow falls from the sky without God's notice.

CHAPTER 4

GHOSTLY APARTMENTS

FORMER TENANTS
STAIRWAYS
ADVENTURES ON ALLEN STREET
DANCING
HIGHER EDUCATION
SLOW EXIT
UNHAPPY TENANT

Former Tenants

"I grew up in Queens and have lived there most of my life," Jack Abbott told me. "In the years I have lived here, I have had two experiences that I can't explain—I can only tell you about them, and you can decide what really took place.

"In 1968, I had a newspaper job in Greenwich Village and commuted from Queens. Thus, when Richard, my close friend, told me he was traveling to Spain and needed a sitter for his apartment, I readily volunteered. For two weeks I could be closer to work and I also could be near my favorite party spots in lower Manhattan, so I jumped at the opportunity. Giving me his key, he told me to move in on Friday night, as he was flying overseas that morning. I stopped in and looked the place over, then returned to my home in Queens, gathered necessary stuff and brought it with me to 333 East 18th Street the next morning. Convenience—that's what I was thinking of, and maybe also a chance to be closer to the pretty women in that neighborhood."

When he returned to his new lodging that night, he had been partying and needed his sleep, and really didn't need to be awakened in the middle of the night, but that's what happened. "About three a.m. I awoke to the sounds of a woman sobbing—the sound was unmistakable. Must be a lady out in the garden, I thought, and tried to dismiss it. Nevertheless, it continued, so I got up to investigate. I turned on the bedside lamp and the sounds ceased. Maybe it's a cat who likes the dark, I considered, maybe it hides out during the daytime and only comes out at night. But it really wasn't like a cat's cry, and there was no cat in the apartment or anywhere else around there. The next night, about the same time, it happened again, with the same result after I turned on the lamp," he told me.

"Maybe the third or fourth night, when the cry came, I left the light off, I got down on my hands and knees and crawled out of the bedroom and down the hall, hoping to find a cat underneath some piece of furniture or on my window sill. By the time I got to the kitchen counter that divided the living room and kitchen, I hadn't spotted anything, so I looked toward the living room. Suddenly she or it was there—a bluish, translucent human shape without much physical detail, except that it was a woman. And her filmy arms were raised to the position of her face, moving as if to wipe her eyes. I heard the sobbing even louder. Then, as quickly as she appeared, she was suddenly gone, seeming to have sensed me. What had I just seen? I asked myself as I stumbled back to bed."

Jack told me that he was dating someone and, seeking a second opinion, invited her to stay over with him. As soon as she came into the apartment, the hallway light blew out. It seemed that whenever he entertained women overnight, he told me, lights blew out; "I'd open the front door and the hall light would blow out; I'd go to the bathroom and that light would blow out!" In fact, during his ten-day stay (he didn't last the two weeks) in that apartment, he had to replace thirty-three dead bulbs. He smiled as he told me that he had bought every light bulb available in the corner grocery. The blow-outs occurred not only when women visited, but as a regular event. As a numerologist, that "power number" or "master number" of 33 caught my attention, but I continued to listen to him without comment for as long as I could restrain myself. I also noted the street address was 333.

"My friend Kathy came over and we were fooling around, when we were startled from our affections by an explosion. We turned on a light and, stark naked, stumbled from the living room, down the hallway to the bedroom, searching for the source of the loud bang. As I passed down the twenty-foot hallway, I turned on the light and glanced into the bathroom. I noticed something white oozing down the wall and into the sink, so I opened the cabinet. I discovered that a can of shaving cream had exploded and had filled the cabinet's interior with foamy shaving cream. Was that a joke? Was that somehow symbolic? What would Freud think? I wondered. Suddenly, two more light bulbs blew out. Kathy ran, got dressed, and fled out the door in less than two minutes, wishing me 'Good luck!' as she slammed the door. Was there a someone or something in that apartment that didn't want me dating women? And why hadn't Richard warned me about the crier? I lost several potential relationships that way," he told me. So, I had to inform him that the number 33 in numerology referred to "love and relationships, perhaps even unconditional love. It also denotes overcoming fear with love." The symbolism caused Jack to laugh. He didn't ask about the symbolic nature of light bulbs, but maybe they related to his "not seeing the light" in some aspect of his life or his relationships.

"On my first weekend there, I awoke in the middle of the night with a craving for an Italian sausage sandwich; don't ask me why, I just knew that was what I needed, so I dressed and walked down to St. Mark's Place," he said with a grin. "Near one of the all-night restaurants I encountered a beautiful woman and was immediately struck with the possibilities of the situation. She looked lost, so I said hello and she looked directly at me, then her face took on a look of terror and she screamed. I freaked out; how could I blow a relationship with just one word? I grumbled, as I slogged home. I still have no idea why the woman screamed. When I got inside, the overhead light blew out.

"The next day I got in touch with another attractive woman who was interested in visiting with me overnight, but hardly had we gotten to bed than the doorbell rang. I got up to answer it but found nobody in the hall. When I told my guest that the doorbell incident was like some of the strange experiences I was having, she too fled my apartment, even faster than my previous girlfriend.

"Later that night, after my friend left, the crying resumed, causing me to crawl out of bed to find the source. It was one thing to be screamed at, but now came the crying—all the same night. I stumbled into the living room, griping out loud, 'Why are you waking me up? Why are you bothering me?' Suddenly, there was a man there—a guy dressed in 1800s style, with a tall, starched collar and suit, and wearing a mustache and beard. The filmy woman was there too. In an instant, she pointed toward the marble fireplace and communicated, 'He shot me.' I moved closer to the fireplace as the two spirits vanished. There was an indentation or crack where she had pointed. Might a bullet have broken that façade?

Then, never mind the history or an explanation—I suddenly decided that was it! I had had it. I packed and moved back to Queens. And when Richard returned three days later, I asked him about the woman. 'Oh, I didn't think that you'd see her. I'm gay, and I never brought a woman home.'"

A few years later, even Richard had to leave the apartment, as Beth Israel Hospital purchased the site and did considerable renovation of the premises. Maybe the new hospital usage will help heal the afflicted nighttime crier.

Leaving that apartment seems to have been a major step forward for Jack, as he eventually found a new line of work and met Mary, the woman of his dreams. He proposed and she accepted, and they picked out a pleasant place to live in Sunnyside Gardens, in Queens, when they married.

The seventy-seven acre utopian community had been built in 1924 through the efforts of public-spirited idealists who recognized that the Borough of Queens needed affordable housing for the working people, many of whom took the train to jobs in Manhattan each day. And the second floor apartment was affordable for the about-to-be-married couple.

"We moved in and started emptying boxes," Jack continued, "and began placing furniture and putting things away. I remember we were walking from a back bedroom, past the stairway, and toward the living room, when suddenly I stopped just past the stairway. What had I just seen? I turned to Mary and asked, 'Did you see that?'

Apparently she had, as she asked me, 'I think so—tell me what you saw.'

'I saw a man and his cat walking out of the apartment,' I responded. She nodded; that was exactly what she had seen. Fortunately, that was it. We only had that single experience there, but Mary believes all the other tales I have told about those years working in Manhattan. She is my soul mate and we really communicate well—fortunately," he laughed. "I have had two experiences in my life that I can't explain, but I think they belong in a book about ghosts."

Stairway

605 Auburn

Monica Gartler and her sister grew up in a house on Auburn Avenue in Buffalo. Later in life she would write her first novel, *Beyond the Horizon* (Published by Tate Publishing Co.), a metaphysical tale of a young girl's search for answers about life and death. "I have some of those questions in my own mind," she told me. "Maybe that is why I wrote the book."

"Before we left that house, we discovered how old it was, as it dated to 1860. That is plenty of time in which people can live out their lives and then move on," she said, "but I'm not sure if one of the former tenants did leave. My sister and I often worked or played separately in the house so, at first, we didn't

131

realize how odd it was that we'd hear heavy footsteps on the stairs to the second floor. Each of us suspected the other was trying to fool around, so the sounds didn't scare us. Nevertheless, when we were alone in the house, we still heard the heavy plodding. Knowing it wasn't our parents, we decided it had to be a heavy-footed man, but no one ever appeared in the stairway. We also knew it was definitely the footfall of a human being, and not some noise from out on the street. Years later, when we compared notes and realized neither of us had been teasing the other, we became a bit nervous about the implications of that infrequent event."

There was another side to life there, one that caused Monica to wonder if the ghost or the house itself might have possessed her parents. The longer they lived in the house, the more depressed their mother seemed to become, and she spent much time alone in her bedroom. "At times, she would emerge, foaming at the mouth or screaming, and sometimes stark naked. We just didn't know what to do about that. Also, my father began to spend more and more time just sitting in the bedroom with no lights on. All that abnormality became normal for my sister and I," she recalls. Her mother later died in a nursing home.

By that time, fearing she might become possessed by what she viewed as the strong spirit of her mother, Monica became estranged, and only her sister was with their mother at her death. Curiously, the sister later did exhibit many of the depressive moods of her deceased mother. Monica counseled her sister and a new, more positive "born again" atmosphere can now be found in the sister's home.

Their father died as a broken man, worn down by his wife's unpredictable and often violent episodes. The family was forced to move, though the ghost didn't come with them. The spirit was likely a former resident of the house, perhaps the builder. There is also a strong likelihood that the ghost remained immersed in deep depression or a stupor of some sort, and at the time Monica's family lived there, was still unaware of its body's death. Thus, it is likely that Monica's father might also have come under the influence of the melancholy personality. In such instances, either the house has to be cleaned of its negativity or the residents may need psychotherapy. Sometimes both.

When Monica began to lead her own adult life, she became friends with a very nice young man; sadly, he was brutally murdered, leaving her bereft. "That first year without him, when I lived on Bidwell Parkway, was terrible. I would spontaneously remember the funny little things we used to say to one another, and the serious conversations we often had about our future together. One thing I remember was him telling me that I should never cut my waist-length hair. But now he was gone, and my heart ached. Bit by bit I began to cope with my grief and I tried to put my life together again.

"The downstairs of my apartment house was home to another single woman, though I didn't often see her. Nevertheless, one evening I decided to cut my hair short. I was going to make a new start and become a new me. I looked in my bureau for my scissors and they were gone. My house is very organized and there was no way I could have misplaced them, but they weren't there. I walked downstairs and asked the tenant if I might borrow her scissors, but she only had pinking shears, so I dejectedly began to walk upstairs.

"As I reached the top, where I had little stuffed animals as decorations, the stairway behind me began to shake and quake violently. I had to grab onto the railing to keep my balance. The bear and the little squirrel were shaking back and forth, but what totally unnerved me was seeing my scissors leaning against the animals. I was so scared that I just couldn't think rationally about what was taking place and ran into my apartment, to the far end. There, I prayed to Jesus and God to deliver me from it all. I asked for protection. Nobody followed me into the apartment and nothing else happened. Only later, just in the few minutes I allowed myself the thought, did it occur to me that it might have been my old friend returning my lost (or had they been?) scissors. Was that a sign? I just couldn't cope with seeing him again, but maybe he knew this and only appeared as an apparent shaking stairway. Nothing more happened after that."

Today, Monica lives in Williamsville and has moved from her Catholic upbringing to the Pentecostal religion and then onward to a non-denominational congregation, where she feels surrounded by love and the concern of others. It appears that she has, indeed, gone "beyond the horizon" that fear can impose on us. She now stands at the threshold of discovering how much more powerful than fear is The Creator's love.

Adventures on Allen Street

A mile east of Buffalo's famous La Salle Park is Allen Street, which was once an ordinary business and residential street for the city's merchants and business leaders. Here and there, theaters were built among the facades of small stores and brownstone mansions on the short street. After the boom of World War II shipping days, the city began to decline, as the better-off residents fled to the suburbs. Allen Street was a part of the downturn, and it was only in 1978 that art lovers decided to restore the remaining residences, stores and theaters in that area. The Allen Town Historic Preservation District was formed, and a wonderful restoration effort commenced.

"I visited there before that restoration began," Faye told me. "My uncles Mac and Stuart were pioneers in that renovation. They had purchased an old building and decided to remodel it, to make the structure more up-scale, knocking out some connecting walls to create apartments. As they opened up the interior walls, I wonder if they didn't also open up something less visible.

"In the early 1970s, when I visited them to watch their progress, they gave me a bedroom on the second floor. I enjoyed that because my cot permitted me to look out onto Allen Street's rich night life. The other floors were not yet ready for occupancy. That first night, I suddenly heard a rustling, but wasn't sure where it came from. Likely it's Uncle Mac reading his newspaper in the other room, I suspected, and rolled over.

"All at once, I could feel my feet, then my legs becoming numb. What's this? I wondered. Then, as the lack of feeling crept up to my waist, I heard a woman's voice loudly demanding, 'Who are you, and what are you doing here?' Nobody was in my room, I was sure, so I was instantly terrorized and screamed as loud as I could! By the time I got to my feet, looking hurriedly around the room, I could see nobody else in the room."

Her uncles hurried in and snapped on the lights, and Faye poured out her scary story. The two men looked somewhat abashed at each other. "Faye, I guess we'd better level with you," said Uncle Stuart, "some visitors and party guests here have seen a ghost woman dressed in black and white taffeta, only to have the woman vanish as quickly as she had appeared. We didn't want to alarm you, but I guess we should have told you. Come over here and I'll show you a spot on the wall that is always icy cold, even in summer. At other times, we smell coffee brewing when the pot isn't even plugged in. It's like a smell from the past, I guess."

Uncle Mac then joined the discussion and reminded Stuart of the big chandelier that had once fallen from the ceiling, to crash onto the floor, though it had been installed properly. No cause was ever found. "Tomorrow, I'm going to call a psychologist friend at the University," he said, "and let you talk with him. He knows all about our unseen lady." "True to his word, the next day, my uncle dialed the professor," Faye said, "and the first words out of his mouth were, 'She's a *****, isn't she?'

"Yes, that's exactly my feeling about her attitude," Faye responded. "The professor had visited my uncles many times and explained that his studies indicated the ghost was a woman who didn't like other women and, in fact, I was the first single woman to stay overnight in the building since my uncles bought it." "Now, you have to stand up to her," the professor told Faye, "and don't let her scare you, because she's the dominating type and will push you further if you're timid. And," he chuckled, "if you don't back down, and things come to the worst, you can just tell her to go to hell!" He laughed a bit, then added, "That threat is a very frightening concept to a spirit, you know.

"Spirits are like people," he continued, "attracted to their favorite situations and atmospheres. Look at your uncles—they are talented men who appreciate architecture. Many of the classy furnishings in the apartment came from Buffalo's secondhand shops. Often, old furniture retains the energies and maybe the consciousness of former owners. Here, you have age and beauty, and lots of deceased individuals try to hold onto those things forever."

"After chatting with the professor, I understood the situation better" Faye told me, "and was determined to give the ghost lady what-for if she showed up again. But I didn't see her any more on that visit. When I got home to Albany, it took me almost six months before I could walk into a dark room again without becoming panicked. I also knew I had to acknowledge that what had happened did, though, intellectually, I couldn't manage to do so."

A few years later, Faye met a legendary blind healer from Troy, Sam Lentine, who claimed (and from the author's experiences with the man, did have) the ability to see and read through the palms of his hands. Sam had worked with a nationally-famous seer from Buffalo named Carol Ann Liaros, who continues to help the handicapped develop their innate sensitivities. Sam considered it a challenge to send the domineering woman's spirit away from the Allen Street house, and seemed successful. "But then, with the most powerful spirit gone, others who had once inhabited the building began to appear," Faye told me.

"Sometime after Sam cleared the lady out, I went to visit my uncles again, taking my two young sons. Uncle Stuart took us on a house tour and I loved the restoration work. As we walked through the basement, one of my boys blurted out that it must be really cold inside one of the cellar rooms, which had a window in its door. I asked why he said that, and he told me the white curtains inside the window were blowing strongly. I opened the door and showed him that there were no curtains inside, but later, I figured he must have seen something filmy and white, and to me that sure sounded like a ghost."

In the 1980s, Faye found more time to work and study with Lentine and felt less threatened on her summer trips to Buffalo, where she often visited the famous Allen Street Art Festival or the Nina Freudenlein Gallery. "At my uncles' building, I now could sense presences, leftovers from the past, but I experienced no phenomena," she said. "At one of the gatherings there, I met an older man who told me he'd lived in that building as a child and teenager. He smiled when I told him of my experiences in the second floor bedroom, and he related being so scared in that room that his parents had to move his bed to a back room because of all the frightening things. Then, the man suddenly broke off the conversation, not wanting to remember too much of his past.

"Shortly after that, Uncle Mac died and I traveled once more to Buffalo to attend his memorial service. Uncle Stuart gave me the back bedroom, and when I turned off the room light and turned on a small nightlight, I began to hear noises outside my bedroom door, and then in the adjoining room. It was as if someone was moving about whenever I was about to drop off to sleep. Finally, I said out loud, 'Cut it out and go away.' But the noises continued, so I said, 'Halloween is over—go away!' Now the noise grew louder, sounding as if someone was moving furniture. Fed up, I said quite loudly, 'If you don't stop and leave, I will tell you exactly where you can go, and you won't enjoy it!'

"Suddenly, everything became very quiet, and I settled down—at last! Then, just as I was dropping off to sleep, there came a great crash in the next room. I jumped up and opened the door, and discovered a large section of the plaster ceiling had fallen onto the floor. I guess whoever it was, just wanted to get in the last word," Faye said, smiling.

In later years, she developed her intuition much more strongly, helped by Sam Lentine, who has since died. Faye went on to other exploits and experiences, but told me that the adventure on Allen Street was her initiation to the other world.

Dancing

"As a child, my greatest fear was that I'd see a ghost," said Ray Karpicki. But in 1968, at the age of thirteen, when he finally did see a ghost, he saw not one but three. "But there was nothing scary about this at all, perhaps my disbelief kept me calm."

At the time of his vision, Ray was living in a very old (about 1870) home on Richmond Road in Staten Island. Though the exterior of the house has changed dramatically since the late 1960s, the intensity of his youthful experience is still fresh and vibrant.

"It was sometime in the night when I awoke thirsty," he said. "As my bedroom was in the front of the house, it was necessary to walk through the living room, the dining room, and then the kitchen to get a drink. Upon entering the living room, I saw her—a woman dressed in a blue Victorian gown. She was

136

gracefully dancing around the dining room table. Her image was solid-looking but a bit smoky, and under her dress could be seen a white slip, revealed by her gay movements. I remember trying to make out the details of her face, but all I could see was a sort of 'fleshy wash' with no definite features. She remained a minute then disappeared. There were no sounds."

Ray was still in awe of his ghost visit a few nights later, when he got to meet another nocturnal resident of his house. Thirsty again, he ventured through the living room and discovered "a man dressed in black, wearing a top hat, walking from the kitchen into the living room." Sleepy, it didn't occur to Ray that he was seeing his second ghost, and he continued toward the kitchen door. "As I approached the kitchen, he stood to the side, bowing as a butler might, to let me pass. Then he disappeared. Who was he? Who was the lady?"

Later, in conversation with his mother, he discovered that she also had seen the two people together. She had seen the pair floating across the room in the embrace of a dance, then dancing right into the wall!

But there was at least one more covert resident of that house, and Ray came to know of his presence by hearing scraping footsteps in the basement. Ray named the spirit "Old Man Footie," as if to allay fears about yet another unknown dweller. The scraping sounds in the cellar became so frequent that "we used to yell out, 'Hey, Old Man Footie!' Then they (the sounds) would always stop…for a while."

Ray believes that he saw this old man once during a family picnic in the backyard. Turning from his work at the barbecue grill, the youngster spotted an old, hunched-back man who sported a large growth or bump on his forehead. Dressed in black, the stranger ambled down the outdoor cellar stairs. "I ran in after him but found no one," he remembers. Returning to the party Ray sought some confirmation of the old man's reality, but he could find no other guest who had seen the specter.

A few years later, the family moved, leaving Ray wondering about the reality of ghosts but sure of his own sightings. He prefers to remember them all with the image of the dancing pair upstairs, still enthralled with the dance and each other.

Higher Education

"Though I grew up in Massapequa and got my education there, I learned a whole lot more when I reached college and rented an apartment in Hicksville," Gail McKenna told me. There had been no more than the usual "unexplained" incidents in her early life, and like most of us, she was inclined to ascribe these to "coincidence" or perhaps a faulty memory.

"The world of 'the others' came to me suddenly in my Senior Year of college, when Karyn Goldberg and I briefly rented a first floor apartment on Kuhl Avenue, not far from Cantiague Park. Originally, it had been a single family house, but previous owners had converted the cellar into a second apartment, which seemed ideal for two girls who would soon graduate from Adelphi College.

"I remember, as if it was yesterday, the day we moved in and began selecting bedrooms. When I first walked into the front room, I suddenly felt a presence—someone unseen who made me a bit upset, so I left there and chose a room in the back of the house. In passing, I realized that the apartment's front door was visible from my room, and shortly afterward, I also realized that I was glimpsing movement at that doorway—was it someone entering or leaving? I couldn't be sure, but it didn't aggravate me enough to count noses and determine whether or not it was Karyn.

"One evening, she told me that she had been resting with eyes closed on her bed, waiting for her boyfriend to arrive. Then there came the sound of footsteps on the porch, the front door opening, more footsteps across the floor, and someone sat on her bed. Certain that it was her beau, she opened her eyes, only to find herself alone on the bed. With all our college preparation, we never found an explanation for that. On other occasions, we began to notice that the apartment lights would turn themselves off and on. I also often found my television or stereo unplugged. Thinking that my housemate had borrowed the device and taken it temporarily to her room, I told her that it was okay to borrow it, but just to plug it in again when she brought it back. She looked at me wide-eyed, denying that she had ever borrowed either item. How to explain that? Was there an invisible someone pulling plugs, and if so, why? In return, my friend confided that she, also, occasionally found electrical devices unplugged in her front bedroom."

Gail remembers asking questions of the landlord and neighbors: what residue of a previous owner might still remain in the house? By that time she was willing to consider the presence of a ghost, which didn't particularly scare her but, as an educated woman she wanted answers and explanations. Eventually, she learned that the house's previous owner, before the rental apartment was created, had been electrocuted while doing electrical wiring there. Also, the man's widow had died of natural causes in that front bedroom area; it might be either one or both, denying that death had occurred or had separated them. Was this what it was like to live in a haunted house?

"As the semester went along, other disturbances occurred. I had placed a throwrug in front of the bathroom door in the hall. Yet, on many occasions, I found it moved to the center of the hallway. Though I'm not too fussy about such details, I was puzzled, and asked my friend, who denied moving it. I have to admit that I never actually saw it move, but only the result. Somebody, maybe Mrs. Harris, wasn't happy with my decoration scheme. One night, one of Karyn's friends visited us and casually mentioned seeing a man standing near the front door. We checked, but nobody was there, so we made light of it. Another tidbit of décor was our sugar bowl, which I always left on the kitchen table. Many times we'd find it on the counter instead, and my roomie asked me about it, but of course, I didn't have a clue about that phenomenon either.

"On another night, I was semi-awakened by the barking of the dog next door and by my thirst. Opening my eyes, I could see a white figure at the foot of my bed. It seemed that she spoke to my mind telepathically, 'It's okay, you can go out to the kitchen. The dog is on a chain—go get your drink.' Not recognizing the improbability of the scenario, I walked to the kitchen with the figure (who seemed female) following me. I turned on the faucet, got my drink, and then turned—nobody else was there!"

Perhaps content that the ghost woman (or woman and man) had made their presence known, the incidents tapered off until, with their lease expiring, the girls prepared to move out. "I was tired and had trouble getting to sleep one night because of the loud partying taking place in the cellar apartment. I got angry with their lack of consideration and prepared to get up, go down and complain. Suddenly, I heard those downstairs residents' car pull into the driveway—there had been nobody downstairs at all!"

Gail graduated and went on to a professional career, but in Hicksville she received an extraordinary "advanced course" in the continuity of life.

Slow Exit

"I have a story for you," said Ann Smith. "Between 1995 and 1998 I lived alone in a basement apartment on 128th Street in Queens, off Parsons Boulevard in Whitestone. It was a nice, old Italian and Greek neighborhood filled with old buildings that dated before 1900. I especially liked the quiet. City life can be hustle and bustle, but this promised to be a peaceful place.

"Well, that didn't last for long. One sunny afternoon I had been using my hairbrush and placed it on the table, to attend to some matter, but I was back in just minutes. The hairbrush had vanished. Since then," she smiled, "I've

139

learned that, in such events, people who have a ghost almost always assume their memory is faulty, or they have forgotten some detail. People usually fall into blaming themselves for the unusual events, and I was one of those people. But, when I returned to the room not long afterward, I became even more confused because the hairbrush had reappeared—right where I had left it. I try to rationalize the events in my life, so I concluded it was a case of faulty memory. But then, other things disappeared, sometimes for short spells and other times for much longer."

She awoke one night to find the lights turned on in another room, she told me. It was hard to rationalize this event because she was certain that she had turned all apartment lights off when she went to bed. Nevertheless, she got up and switched the lamps off. The next morning, still trying to find a logical explanation for the previous night's experience, she concluded that there must be a timer switch somewhere on the apartment walls, though she could never find it. This discovery of all lights being turned on in the morning occurred at intervals, but one morning Ann found not only lights ablaze but her dresser drawer had been pulled out and was now situated on top of the dresser. "That was the end," she said, "I now knew I had a spirit. I laughed out loud and exclaimed, 'I know you're here now!' Immediately afterward, I said a prayer for whoever it was.

"A few days later, I got out of bed, readying to go to work, and entered the bathroom. I found the toilet seat up. Now, a single woman is never going to raise the seat, so I shouted out, 'And now I know you're a guy!' But there was no response. The events kept up. My closet door would mysteriously open and when I was in bed, I sometimes felt a weight on the other side of the mattress. For some reason, my sense of humor won out. I never felt endangered or scared; the whole thing was comical. I bet the ghost man got a kick out of me and my reactions. I told my boyfriend about all these incidents, but he didn't know what to think. I suppose he couldn't believe such a thing could happen in this day and age, but that changed.

"I had to go away for a period of time and asked my boyfriend to stay in my apartment to keep an eye on things. When I returned, he was a new guy, telling me he didn't know how I stood all the racket. 'First night, he (the ghost) went through the china, rattling plates and dishes. Then there were all those other noises. I had to get up and turn the light on to make him stop—my poor boyfriend became a believer!

"Knowing that this couldn't continue, I addressed the spirit and said loudly, 'Okay, you got my attention, but you can't stay here. You have to go to the light!' A few days later, I went upstairs to chat with Theresa, my landlady, telling her about my spirit activity. Theresa told me that her mom and dad had lived there for years and the noises all seemed to be their normal day-to-day bustling around. 'But, of course, they are dead,' she said. So, I concluded that, at least Theresa's father was still in residence. I didn't have any phenomena that I could attribute to her mother, but her dad sure loved a prank. It was with a mixture of relief and sadness that I finally moved out."

She never had ghost experiences again, but her sister then moved into the basement apartment and continued to have occasional experiences similar to those that Ann had endured. But her sister by then knew the old man was going to require some more time before he left, so she lived peacefully with the strange goings-on.

Unhappy Tenant

Catskill house
with permission from Dover Publications

"I don't live in Catskill any more, not since early 1978," Stephanie told me, "but my four months in that old house gave me the biggest scare of my life." She spoke of the old three-story Victorian apartment house on William Street that she moved into in the early fall of 1977. It was an ornate old structure then, but it clearly had seen better times.

"I shared the apartment, one of two on the second floor, with a roommate. We found it cozy at first, as the big fireplace promised warmth when winter came. We used the old dining room as our living room. One night as my boyfriend and I cuddled on the couch, he nonchalantly said to me, 'There is something in the fireplace, and it's looking at us.' At first, I thought he was

141

NEW YORK STATE GHOSTS

teasing, so I laughed it off. He couldn't give any details of what he'd seen, but he just knew there was an unmoving 'something' there." He became too nervous after that, and didn't come around any more.

Stephanie got a new roommate, Jane, and peace seemed to return to the apartment, but only briefly. Within weeks, Stephanie returned home to find the burners on their gas stove all lit, and she knew that Jane not only hadn't ignited them, she hadn't been home all day! When Stephanie informed Jane about this, her roommate abruptly packed her belongings and moved out. Hardly had this transpired when Stephanie, who wore her hair in braids at that time, felt a sharp tug on them. It hurt! Nevertheless, she knew she was alone.

"I started to yell at whatever being was tugging on my hair, and its only response was to toss most of my clothes out of the closet when I was away. So, whenever I got upset at the spirit's pranks, I'd yell, 'Get back in the closet,' and that would calm things. Nevertheless, I knew the trouble was escalating, and when I once saw all the clothing in the closet come flying out into the bedroom, I decided I had to go. I gave the landlord my notice and began to pack. During that time, I went upstairs to share my experiences with the third floor tenant. 'I'm not surprised,' the woman told me, 'most people who rent that apartment don't last much more than a few months. There are little things that go wrong throughout this old house, but the mischief seems most concentrated in your apartment.' I moved out of the building in January 1978 and never went back," she told me.

When I interviewed her, Stephanie said that she has had other encounters with the unseen world; some of the activity clearly seems ghostly while other events are just head-scratchers. "At the time, in 1973," she told me, "I didn't quite understand what was going on, but now I understand and accept my sensitivity to negative vibrations. My friend worked in Coxsackie and we wanted to find a rental somewhere between there and Catskill, so we drove to an old house on Route 9W that he had learned was available. But once we entered the driveway, I got so shaky and unnerved that I couldn't even get out of the car to inspect the house. It was almost sickening and I felt paralyzed by the vibrations there. He couldn't believe that I reacted in that way, but we left without even looking at the place. Years later, I overheard a Catholic priest saying that the building needed an exorcism, but I don't know whether or not one was performed. The old house later burned to the ground."

Many readers have sensitivities to the unseen world but don't immediately connect their discomfort to the presence of a discarnate spirit. Remember that many individuals who die without making peace with their just-finished life can be in turmoil at finding their earthly existence vanished forever. Some will refuse the help of spirit guides in transitioning into heaven or eternity, and instead will attempt to remain on the earth plane on whatever terms they can manage. Their frustration and anger can be aimed at living people on the premises. Thus, amateur ghost hunters are advised not to enter reputedly haunted properties without first asking for protection from The Higher Power.

NEW YORK STATE GHOSTS

CHAPTER 5

BAD GUYS

Always Open

Many metaphysicists believe that psychic ability is a significant part of the spiritual gifts spoken of in The Bible. Of course, any gift or talent can be used in love or in selfishness, but an enhanced awareness of the invisible dimensions interpenetrating our physical world is truly a gift from The Creator.

Many individuals don't want to acknowledge such abilities, lest they be held accountable for the manner in which they are used. Thus, many potential healers hide their gifts from society. Others, who were never told such abilities can exist, shrink in fear that something is wrong with them when intuition begins to manifest itself. When clairvoyance, clairaudience, clairsentience, psychometric skills, healing, precognition, retrocognition, or "dreaming true" suddenly appear, a person's life can be thrown into turmoil.

Nevertheless, what might a person's life be like if, from their earliest years, he or she had regular experiences with the other world? What if the child's parents didn't dissuade him or her from using or developing such abilities, so that the youngster felt secure in employing those gifts when and where they seemed needed?

One of the people I have met through my newspaper ads, wherein I seek those with some familiarity with the spirit world, is a young woman named Kathleen from Horseheads, N.Y. "Ever since I was little, I've been able to hear and occasionally see ghosts," she told me, "so I have always believed they exist. Eventually, I think I've become something of a magnet for them. My first memory of a ghost was when I saw a little girl downstairs in our house. At first, I assumed it was my sister, but no, upon looking again, I knew it wasn't. The other child wore a light pink dress and walked through a closed door, carrying a small teddy bear. My mom saw it too, but didn't comment at that time. The ghost girl didn't interact with me then, and I was just a witness to her passage through our house."

As a youngster, Kathleen had always enjoyed the dark and, when she turned twelve, she grew more adventurous and invited any ghosts to come visit her. She immediately heard a genderless voice comment, "You really don't want to do that," but she didn't understand why not. Then one night when she was thirteen, she saw another girl in her bedroom and assumed it was her sister sleepwalking from her bedroom next door. And Kathleen noted that her dog, sleeping on the bed beside her was awake and staring, his ears flattened against his head. "It was the dog's sudden movements that had awakened me. I heard the walking figure laugh a strange laugh that wasn't my sister's, yet I turned on the light for my sister so she didn't trip, but she must have still been asleep next door in her bed, as no one was there. Realizing that I had seen a ghost, I sat up, terrified, the rest of the night. The next morning, it was hard to believe it had all happened. Was another spirit helping or protecting me?"

Soon afterward, Kathleen, her sister and parents drove south to Virginia to visit grandparents. "When we returned to Horseheads, something subtle seemed to have changed. I noted certain ornaments on our Christmas tree spinning when there was no breeze. There were also movements by other decorations in the house which couldn't be explained. My sister and parents noticed these occurrences but never commented on them. I wasn't sure whether or not I should talk about those events because my parents were professionals and might not tolerate my new attitude toward spirits.

"When I was fourteen, my sister had a dream of a young girl who was killed in a hit and run accident, and awoke with the name Rebecca Rose in her consciousness. I also had dreams and, between us, we filled in much information on a girl who died in Virginia. Had her ghost come back to New York State with us? we wondered. From our accumulating information, we determined that Rebecca, who seemed like a nice person, had come from a very religious family and felt guilty that she hadn't been paying attention to traffic and had taken a step out into the road where she was hit and killed. We never saw her directly, though my sister saw her gravestone in an online web site. Once, when I opened the comments page on that memorial web site, I felt suddenly chilled and felt a touch on my hand, which suddenly grew warm. Then the sensations stopped."

After the sisters found the web site and had their brief experiences, Rebecca seems to have moved on, content that she had been able to let at least two young women know of her tragic death.

"Another spirit that came to me was Rachel, who seemed quite unfriendly at first. She presented herself as unattractive and I believed that she wanted to scare me. "I was prettier than you are," she taunted me. Then I got upset and bawled her out; after that, she was nicer. She told me psychically that she had been kidnapped and murdered, though she provided few other details of her life."

Dedicated spiritualists appoint an individual in the spirit world, terming that trustworthy being a "control" or "guardian," to serve as a filter for the desperate entities who badly want contact with humans. Just because such beings are there, doesn't mean that we should be seeking them out unless we are prepared to help them. Spirits are no wiser than they were when they had bodies. One can be just as murderous, greedy, grasping, manipulative or hateful when dead as when alive. It appears that Kathleen, among the dozens of spirits who have been drawn to her, has drawn one good one, who she was able to help, and another one who still "hasn't seen the light," in so many ways.

Old-timers have heard the saying that "the proof of the pudding is in the eating thereof." From that bit of folk wisdom I conclude that one must think critically about what we term paranormal experiences and evaluate them. St. Paul told his students to "test the spirits," and evaluate them for what they were. If I were to open a bottle of supposed fine wine and then find it to be vinegar, down the drain it would go. I wouldn't keep negotiating with it, trying to bring out its best side; likely it wouldn't have one.

To date, most of Kathleen's spirit contacts have seemed either neutral or menacing, though she has not been hurt. My advice to her is to recognize that few of these contacts serve her well being. She herself wondered to me if she unconsciously might have invented some of the entities. "I was a pretty lonely kid," she said. Yes, the mind can "compensate" for what we perceive to be our weaknesses or deprivations. Thought imagery can be as "real" as the physical sights that we see each day. I believe I will suggest to Kathleen that she seek more uplifting or healing contacts and, in a year, re-evaluate how her gifts should be focused. In the meantime, she is a student at a Southern Tier college, seeking a higher education in worldly matters.

Enough Already!

Southern Monroe County boasts of its wide open spaces and rolling hills, where one can experience rural comfort in close proximity to urban Rochester. It is a peaceful setting that poses few questions to the visitor, especially in the Town of Rush. Mysteries and ghost stories are found in all areas, however, as former residents who have not fully passed over continue to notify the living of their ongoing existence upon our plane. Here is one tale told to me by a puzzled and sometimes frazzled housewife who has contended with ghosts for almost two decades.

Karen remembers that her first experience came on the night of November 23, 1988, the day her mother died. Deeply stirred by the sadness of the day, she went to bed later, but lay awake in the darkness. Suddenly there came three very loud knocks on the wall above her bed. That was it—just three knocks. Could that have been Mom, now freed from an ill body and anxious to let her daughter know she was still there?

"Our house was over a hundred years old and my husband and I recognized that some modernization was needed, so we began the remodeling," she said. It would have been more comforting to pretend that one of the workmen was still laboring away after dark, but it just wasn't so, because, from the roof above her bedroom came the sound of walking. "It continued for two hours each night, for quite a long period," she told me. "Then, since that time, we continue to hear the walking sounds about once a month. There are also loud knocks almost weekly. My husband doesn't hear the walking, but he sure hears the knocking."

She told me that a psychic once visited them and decreed that the spirit was not of their family, but one "brought in on a laborer." Many readers aren't aware that a person can pick up a spirit just as we pick up a virus or infection. Much of this seems to depend on the host individual's mental state, which can invite such an infestation without the host person's awareness. Constant anger, pickiness or condemnation of others is sure to invite such attachments because it establishes a negative atmosphere.

Despair or long-term depression can also create a cleavage in the individual's energy field. Like it or not, there is much negativity afloat in this world, and one should strive to remain positive and pro-active, and work to prevent and overcome despair of any nature in oneself and one's companions. Often, this requires being connected to a belief and activity system or religion that links us to a higher power, because none of us is so omnipotent that we can handle serious attacks. Those enslaved by addictions are also likely to serve as hosts to dark energies or spirits, though these individuals might never suspect they have "company."

Tick Gaudreau's fine book *Spirit Rescue: A Dowser's Ghostly Experiences* (available through Amazon.com) can be a down-to-earth eye-opener to those just entering into the study of ghost phenomena. Tick is a true professional who has done yeoman work in helping afflicted people whom I have interviewed.

Karen's son, Jimmy, has also heard the walking on the roof above his bedroom. There is nothing in his high school studies that can easily or scientifically explain what he knows that he has experienced for nine years. Jimmy has also had another strange encounter. Several years ago, on a warm summer night, the boy ventured outside onto the porch and spotted a figure dressed in black moving rapidly in his direction from the wooded area near the yard. Though the figure never reached him, Jimmy will never forget the fright of that night. Green-faced entities are not supposed to roam people's yards if it isn't even Halloween! On occasion, as he entered adulthood at age nineteen, the boy also heard the sounds of feet shuffling across his bedroom carpet and fingernails softly tapping on the dresser top. The being never revealed itself any more clearly though.

"Ten years ago, though I had some doubts, I invited a psychic to visit our home, though I only told her ahead of time that we had been 'hearing things,'" Karen remembers. "After a bit of pacing, the woman told us she had seen 'someone sitting on the house roof as she drove up to the house, which somehow didn't really surprise me. The psychic identified the spirit as 'Rion,' [or Ryan?] a male spirit who must have once been passing by in the spirit high-ways, who liked their family and now doesn't want to leave. I asked her to smudge (a Native American practice of burning sage to purify a space) my other son's room, as that had originally been my husband's and my bedroom, where we'd first heard the knocks and roof walking. A lot of sounds had been emanating from there," Karen told me.

In November 2006, she returned from several days away from home and, completely tired, fell into bed. Almost asleep, she suddenly felt fingers grip her upper left arm. An hour later, the phantom grabbed her thigh. She is quite sure that this being is not Rion. When one is worn out, it is easy to convince oneself that such feelings are "just imagination" or muscle twitches. But then, during a summer night in 2007, when she had difficulty falling asleep, she lay on the couch. Almost immediately, two hands "like liquid," she said, crept from somewhere behind or underneath her and moved beneath the front of her pajamas, then across her chest and upward. "It felt like fluid moving hands that continually flowed," she told me. We agreed that the American "right to pursue happiness" did not extend to ghosts or malevolent spirits getting their jollies, and that a house cleansing was needed. It can be very difficult for the scientifically minded in our "modern" society to believe that such events can happen, yet there are countless verified reports.

Not all spirit world residents are nice grandmotherly or Casper-type individuals. If you are touched or threatened (this doesn't necessarily include being startled) there should be the certainty that this isn't a spirit to be reasoned with. Almost always, expert assistance is needed to chase the being out of the house for good. Anyone so put upon, as Karen certainly is, should not treat the matter as cute or entertaining, which Karen certainly does not. The physical, mental and/or spiritual attacks can only increase in seriousness if not dealt with—they never get better all by themselves, despite your use of prayer or amulets. You need help!

That is what I told Karen, and she agreed. She has made an appointment for her pastor from church to visit and do a house blessing. That is always a positive first step. But, the essence of the attack is spiritual—the being is pushy and unwilling to obey a simple instruction to depart. This type of individual thrives (as perhaps he/she did in life) on bullying people. The spirit world is populated with (among others) drug and alcohol addicts, cheaters, murderers, and sex addicts whose highest ideal is their limited-scope of self-gratification. So, the usual solution must be spiritual in nature, whether or not the attacked person is "religious" or not.

One must not assume, unfortunately, that all pastors are equally proficient in removing disturbing entities. Specific training is needed and good intentions alone are not effective. Do consult a clergyman or clergywoman, but also recognize that there are some very effective Native American healers or lay people who also have a very high success record. And many times, to end such attachments, all the members of a household will need to take part in the exorcism.

I recall a man (non-religious) in the Adirondacks who became the host for the invading entity after his house (but not the man, himself) was exorcised by a priest. Later, in his new home in California, the man discovered he was still hosting the entities. Fortunately for him, he found some learned Franciscans who performed an effective cleansing ceremony. I recommend only those "cleansers" who come personally recommended; I don't think the good ones are found in the Yellow Pages. Find someone you can trust.

Though young Jimmy shared his mother's experiences, her husband, a scientifically trained professional, wasn't quite sure of her revelations until he had an unquestionable experience. Karen told me, "Last summer I was sleeping, and in the middle of the night, a decorative ball, which always sits on our bedroom blanket rack, bounced off the rack and onto the floor. The ball hitting the floor woke me immediately, and I watched it roll up next to my side of the bed. My husband awoke and could clearly see the ball's new position. He knew I hadn't gotten out of bed to get it."

Then in early March of 2008, as she worked at home and alone at her computer, she heard the unmistakable sound of the lamp chain in her dining room being pulled. "It makes a distinctive sound, as you must know," she told me. "I got so irritated at this continuing activity that I shouted 'Knock it off!' from my chair. Just five seconds later, I heard a loud knocking sound from the dining room."

"Sounds like a wise guy ghost," I ruminated aloud, so we went into a defensive plan. I agreed to set certain events in motion on my end, (seeking talented "cleaners" in that area) and Karen commenced her own activities to finally rid the house of unwelcome guests.

This story also highlights the difficulty that one spouse can have in getting the partner to accept that such phenomena are really taking place. Many of you ghost story readers already know the isolation that can occur in the lives of sensitive individuals who have apparitions, voices, moved objects, or horrific dreams, to say nothing about physical or psychic attacks, unless your loved partner agrees to help you with the problem, or even admit that there is a problem. Such experiences can strain even the most loving relationship. Fortunately for Karen, there is plenty of family love and support.

Quite a Racket

"I've been here for twenty-seven years now," Lynda told me, "and I am just about ready to give up. I take care of foster children and, thankfully, most of them have not been bothered. But, you know how it is, when you have children to raise and care for, every noise in the house might represent a difficulty. So, almost as soon as I moved in, and when the noises started, I was on edge.

"Somebody, I'm sure it must be the ghost of a man—an angry man— would stomp up the stairs in the middle of the night. At first, I thought someone must have broken into our house here in Bayport. Yet, when I'd get up to investigate at night, there was nobody else here. Then, I would hear faucets turning on full force in the kitchen or bathrooms, and had to get up to turn them off. These events didn't happen every night, so I never knew what was coming next or when I'd get a full night of sleep.

"Sometimes, when I'm upstairs, I'll hear the heavy footsteps in the downstairs or on the stairway, but it has become so much a part of running this house that I seldom go to investigate any more. When I'm downstairs, I sometimes hear the footsteps upstairs, yet I know there is nobody up there…nobody alive, anyway. I hear the kitchen cabinet doors opening and closing, but there is never anything or anyone to see if I go to check.

"This house on Third Avenue isn't that old. It was built in the 1950s," she said. We talked for a while about how houses acquire a spirit, but Lynda said she is sure that the male spirit was already there when she moved in. At first, though, she knew nothing about the previous residents. "But I did see him—twice," she exclaimed. "So I have a good idea what he looks like. First, in 2002, I awoke to see him sitting on the end of my bed during the night. He wasn't scary looking; in fact, he looked like someone you might pass on the street—an older man wearing a suit. He was there motionless for a few minutes, and then disappeared. Again, in 2007, I saw him in the same position. In five years he hadn't changed a bit," she said with a frown.

We talked some more about it always being "today" for ghosts. "They are always in their own time," I told her, "and the ghost man may be puzzled to find you in his house, like the three bears finding Goldilocks sleeping in their bed. Obviously, the man either doesn't know he is dead, or stubbornly won't admit it. He seems to keep on re-creating his former daily or nightly routine, going upstairs to bed each night and often rummaging through the house as he did when alive."

"Well, that's all well and good," Lynda responded, "but I have kids to raise here, and I've put up with this nonsense for too long. My kids all have some physical or emotional challenges, and the older ones are now tuning in on this invisible resident and I can't explain the noises away much longer. I have to do something now or move out!"

I asked what little she knew about the previous owners, and she said that, in the 1980s, when she bought the house, the neighbors had told her of the couple, both alcoholics, who had lived there. "They said the police were here all the time, so there was probably domestic violence of some sort," she said ruefully. I told her that addict spirits are often the hardest to remove from a house, but it can and must be done.

When a person dies with an addiction (their limited version of heaven, which likely has become an inescapable hell), he or she will keep trying to get inebriated or high. Without a body, they will seek to enter other bodies (thankfully, it hasn't gone that far in this case) in order to encourage their hosts to drink or shoot up. Many people become temporarily possessed in this manner and truly have no knowledge afterward of what they have done or why.

"This guy has frightened my sister so that she doesn't want to babysit here any more, and the ghost man has recently taken to knocking on one of the upstairs windows at two in the morning. I don't know what it means, though," she said.

We talked some more about the need to send ghostie on his way. "If you had termites, you'd get an exterminator, right?" I said. "Ghosts aren't any different; they're irritants. Get someone to chase him out. Start by addressing the guy verbally. Tell him he's dead and can't stay here any longer. Tell him that you own the house now and will take good care of it, but he has to go onward now," I continued. "Tell him about the light that is available to all who have died, tell him to walk into its brightness. If he was an alcoholic, then he still is," I said. "Expect him to be stubborn. If you are religious or are willing to be helped by the clergy, get a priest or minister to come and do a house blessing (a step short of a full exorcism) and see what that does. Many ghosts were bullies in life and try to continue that way," I said, "so get someone with more power, spiritual strength, to bully them and do them a favor at the same time."

Most religions urge us to be a good neighbor to all. Few today realize that we are obliged by our faith to render that service even to those who have died.

Surprise!

Most people are surprised (to say the least) when they first encounter a ghost. Very few of us, when we're young, are ever told that the essence of life is spirit and that the physical world is only a part of that larger, enduring world. If all people knew that spirit continually interacts at our level of existence (sometimes visibly and oftentimes not), perhaps we wouldn't be so alarmed when that sudden recognition is thrust upon us.

Jessica Simpson and Michael Vessio, Jr. rent a house in Levittown on Long Island, which they have called home since early 2007. The community was a post-World War II phenomenon of the Levitt & Sons Construction Company which, from 1947-1951, built about 18,000 homes for returned veterans of the war. There is a sameness in appearance and construction, though that mass-produced construction initially made these houses affordable to many families. The house in question here, on Sprucewood Drive, is significantly different, however.

Someone else is there; a someone who is disruptive and difficult for the couple to live with. "We don't really believe in ghosts," Jessica said during our first interview, "but we sure do have a lot of surprises here. The first of these was the continual raising and lowering of both the volume and channels on our TV set. At first, we thought it was a technical issue, but that proved to be wrong. The electrician also examined the house in order to determine why the lights often flicker, but could find nothing wrong in that respect either. While we were still engaged in that puzzle, Michael saw a wall light detach itself from a wall and fly across the room, directly at him. It seemed as if that invisible force had it in for him. Yet, we couldn't consider that it was ghostly."

Michael is of Italian heritage and Jessica's background is Argentinean and British. The couple had never before had any contact with the spirit world and, lacking that experience, were deeply irritated that the comfort of a nice half-century-old home was disturbed. These events don't happen continually, but only sporadically, almost as if the being was determined not to let the pair ever get comfortable there. Their two dogs are also upset, staring and barking at something invisible.

"On one occasion, both Michael and I saw a dark shadow with no detail in it as it sped across the room, but we both agreed that it was short, about the size of a child or very short adult, about 3½ feet tall. Though Michael is of Italian heritage, we're not particularly religious," Jessica said. "So I did go out and buy a statue of the Blessed Virgin and some crucifixes to place inside our home. In the end, though, I don't think they did much to help us resolve the disruptions. I later discovered one crucifix turned to the side, and I know Michael and I didn't do that.

"One day I set a portable heater on a chair for a moment. Instantly, it turned itself on, became very hot, and then flew off the chair, almost as if tossed aside by an unseen hand. Spare change that I had set aside on a dresser suddenly became airborne and flew across the room. But what got us deeply concerned, though, was that Michael awoke with a bruise on his eye one morning. At first, we didn't connect that incident with a spirit, but the following morning, when he awoke with a bruise on the side of his face, we knew we were in trouble, as if being assaulted by something invisible. Later, he awoke again with a third bruise."

Thus far, I had listened to Jessica's story, trying not to interrupt her, but with the mention of the physical contacts, I became very concerned and had to confirm that she did indeed have a ghost there, and a very unhappy one at that. "Whenever the being engages in 'bad touch' of whatever nature, you know you have to take action," I said. "Physical assaults are a form of aggression and intimidation by an unhappy soul, and you must make every effort to send them away if you are to enjoy your peaceful home. One cannot remain neutral or hide their head in the sand, hoping the entity will just leave. These situations always get worse unless dealt with," I noted.

"I was touched, too," she continued. "One day, I felt a distinct touch to my left eyebrow, followed immediately by an icy cold. Both Michael and I occasionally hear whispers, though the half-heard words don't seem to be directed at us, but more of us overhearing a faint conversation. Our once, briefly happy home is now filled with a distinct negative, depressing energy, which we feel most days. Michael and I increasingly find ourselves quibbling with one another, whereas we were best buddies for a long time. It's almost as if the invisible person wants us to fight and be depressed, and you know what? It's working. Another recent mystery is how water in a hot pot can boil when it's not plugged in. Some personality seems very upset with us."

I estimate that the majority of our loved ones who pass on will do so peacefully. Some will have brief periods of reckoning before passing into Paradise, however. But then, there are those who were likely unloved, perhaps because of their attitude toward life.

I felt it necessary to explain to Michael and Jessica some basic information about these unhappy people remaining unhappy spirits after leaving their physical body. People should understand this while they are still alive, I reason, because death does nothing to cure our earthly situation; it often doesn't even end the troubling matters. If traumatized while alive, we will remain so after death, until we're ready to objectively review what happened during that chance or opportunity called life. The angry remain angry and the greedy remain possessive. The aggressive ones and bullies turn out to be discarnate gangsters. There should be no mystery about that, but most people are surprised to hear of the carryover of negative emotions. Fortunately, these unhappy ones aren't that numerous.

Suicide, likewise, solves nothing, but only makes a person's consciousness more depressed, as the person has now also lost a physical body that might have helped remedy their situation. Thus, it's all carried into what we call "the next world." Of course, positive people, if they remain near this plane after dying, can be happy ghosts. There are several stories of that nature in this book.

I gave Jessica and Michael some basic instruction as to how the spirit should be evicted, since it may never be possible for them to discover which former resident of Sprucewood Drive is the culprit. "First," I said, "talk to the entity, and tell them that their body has died. Tell them that they are no longer welcome in the house and that they must go. Don't ever use wishy-washy words such as 'should' or 'ought to go.' Inform the discarnate one that a bright light exists and that they need to turn around and see it, then walk into it. It will relieve their inner turmoil.

But understand that many beings, both living and dead, just love to hold onto their gripes and complaints. Unless we have previously devoted some time to our afterlife while we're alive, many individuals hold desperately onto what they know; what they've always done; what has always worked for them before they died. When one is depressed, it's hard to be creative or accept new patterns of thought."

Cemeteries are places where many spirits can be found (and often videotaped by modern ghost hunters) because, in spirit, they just cannot yet let go of their physical body and its former concerns. Some of these individuals never truly permitted themselves to consider that the body must one day die; now they're faced with what feels like a disability. Other spirits try to regain a physical body, even if it means they will continue in their inner turmoil or grief—body life is all they know, or want to know. This attempt to hold onto the past and the physical world can lead to a mini-form of possession unless a person learns to protect him or herself (through prayer, for example). Psychology researchers should seriously consider researching the many cases of chronic depression to rule out a spiritual malady as the cause. In Michael's case, the attempted possession may have already begun because of the physical wounds. This must be stopped in its tracks.

"Secondly, if it becomes evident that the spirit hasn't left when you commanded it to do so, then raise the ante: send them out of the house in the name of Jesus or God (as Jessica has a religious upbringing). Take a few days to see if that works. Bullies often fold up their act once confronted by a higher power. Non-religious readers should consider what force they think is higher than the human being, as they might need to seek that help in time of distress.

"So, thirdly, if the turmoil remains, go to your local priest (or minister or rabbi or imam) and ask the clergyperson to visit your house to do a 'house blessing.' Many clerics understand what you're up to," I told Michael and Jessica, "but would rather not hear the details of your infestation. Most know what to do and do such blessings well. Of course, as in all professions, some of the religious aren't good at this sort of thing. I have heard of a few cases where clergy flee the house and refuse to perform their function. If, after the house blessing is done, the spirit still remains, then a formal exorcism must be done." It is trickier to find a good person to do that final exorcism. When it isn't performed, people eventually find habitation in the house to be impossible. That may be why we so often picture haunted houses as being abandoned.

A non-religious individual can have a tougher time in finding an exorcist, but there are a few lay people who can do the job. You want to see their credentials first, however, because an amateur can make your situation measurably worse. As in all matters in this world, you need to find a bigger power than the opponent possesses. Don't be surprised if the clergyperson insists on exorcising all the residents of the house as well as the structure. That is the only way to make sure the spirit has nothing and no one to hold onto when it's forced to leave.

"I never knew these situations were so common," Jessica responded, though I assured her that many homes all over the world are blessed, cleared, and exorcised each day.

So Michael and Jessica began their attempt to pacify their house guest. A few days after the initial interview, Jessica called to tell me that she and Michael had read the riot act to the invisible ones. "At the moment, nothing happened. But then, two hours later, we heard faint laughter and other noises.

The television volume first went up then down." To us both, it seemed that their ghost was going to be a hard case. So then, they began their search for a clergyperson who could more forcefully inform the spirit of its condition and then cast it out. "Nobody has to live in a haunted house," I told her. She seemed relieved.

Curiously, as I plugged my intuition into this matter, I visualized a ruddy-faced and stocky businessman, grey flannel suit and all, and carrying a briefcase. He perspires a lot, constantly having to remove his glasses to wipe his brow. He is exasperated at both his family ("They don't appreciate what I had to go through to provide this house; none of them appreciate it!") and also either the government or his boss, who had marginalized him and his need for achievement in life. He seems to be a gentleman still "on the make," immersed in hoping to pull one more fast deal or sell one more of something; perhaps to ink one more contract. He died completely unready to release this world. So intense is his concentration that he brushes aside all people and issues that don't fit his drive for success. Mister, the game is over; the train has left the station.

"My cell phone turns itself on too," Jessica said at the end of our interview. "That's bad enough, but how can do this if there are no batteries in the phone?" For sure, I don't know the answer to that one. Maybe the ghost is still trying to make one last successful business call and is drawing positive energy from Jessica or Michael. Let's see what they can do to permanently retire this guy.

What I Did

I often seek stories by placing ads in local newspapers. "Have you lived with ghosts?" the ad inquires. Some of the responses sound a bit desperate, as in this case.

"I had a bad situation here," said Cami from Wantagh on Long Island. "I got to the point where I considered selling my house."

"Let's review your experiences," I said. Cami then answered my usual questions as to the building's age, how many previous owners she knew of, and whether or not she knew any of those residents.

"The house dates from the late 1940s and is a typical small Cape Cod style," she said. "I know that there was an original owner, then several renters before we came here as tenants in 1969, with the option to buy. The house was in pretty bad shape, and in some parts, someone had punched holes in the wall." In the light of the frustrations that she enumerated, I could understand that some prior resident might have attempted to resolve his experiences by force. But, when one is dealing with ghosts, one must rely on a force different than the physical.

"At first, almost every night, I heard what sounded like children running back and forth on the mostly-unfinished second floor," she continued. "My husband and I thought it might be squirrels or raccoons, though our inspections never turned up an animal intruder. We kept a watch, however, on our children's bedrooms across the hall from ours. Then, before I could grasp it all, my husband moved out, leaving me with two children that were no longer toddlers.

She decided that it was time for the children to have their own upstairs bedrooms, but those upstairs rooms had no closets. Cami had two closets built in each room, pushing through the old walls to provide storage space under the eaves. The children's former bedroom downstairs now became their playroom. But something or someone else came to play upstairs. At first, she attributed those strange upstairs noises, if not to animals, then to the house settling. Maybe it was her imagination, she tried to believe. Then her children began to question the strange sounds in the house.

"I set up a play area near the laundry room in the cellar for my daughter. One day she called upstairs to me, expressing wonder that I'd been able to come upstairs without her hearing me walking, as she had just heard me in the laundry room. I became a bit unnerved because I hadn't been in that room. Another time, her friend R. came to visit and I prepared a lunch for the two of them and my son, who I could hear playing upstairs. R. went to the bottom of the stairs and called for the boy to come down. To me, the upstairs sounds seemed to indicate that my son was playing with toy soldiers and banging around and rolling on the floor—likely he was playing out a battle. When he didn't respond, R. went up to get him.

"Soon, she came back down to the kitchen with a scared look on her face, saying, 'He's not there!' I knew what the girl was experiencing emotionally, as I'd felt the same way dozens of times with those noises, so I tried to soothe her. Just then, my son walked in the back kitchen door with his toy shovel, indicating to me that he'd been digging out there. R. looked at him, then back at me with a bug-eyed expression, hoping that I had an explanation. She was a bright girl and not about to be put off by my casual dismissal of the incident."

Just then, she told me, she and the children heard a hissing sound by the steps going upstairs. "My legs went week," she recalled "because they all were looking to me for an explanation. I assured them that a baby garter snake, which were not harmful and were abundant in our neighborhood, had probably gotten mixed up and came inside looking for its mommy. I encouraged them to look for it," she frowned. "Eagerly, the children ran up and down the stairs, searching for the snake, but they were unsuccessful. I never learned the cause of that hissing sound.

"A few days later I heard my son's feet racing down the stairs, across the living room, and into the kitchen where I was working. He wrapped his arms around me, saying, 'I am never going into that room (his new bedroom) again. My Action Jackson doll just flew across the room by itself.' That event, also, was never explained.

"A few nights after that, I was watching TV in the new playroom, when I head a crash in the kitchen. Nervously and very, very slowly," she said, "and with much trepidation, I finally worked my way into the kitchen. There, in the sink, I found every dish that I had just washed twenty minutes earlier, but they were no longer in the drainer. The dish drainer hadn't moved an inch; just the dishes. All my clean dishes were back in the sink!"

She was very demoralized and anxious after those events. "What does one do? I thought of calling the police, but what could I tell them—they should arrest the dishes for disturbing the peace? Then came the final straw, an event that caused me to call a priest to come and do a house blessing. My daughter came home from school one day and went directly upstairs. Suddenly she screamed as if confronted by a burglar or worse. I ran upstairs quickly as she continued to scream. As I entered her bedroom, the poor child, frightened out of her wits, continued to scream while pointing to six tiny handprints, each about an inch in size, in the left hand top corner of her bedroom mirror. We both were absolutely frightened, convinced that these marks were something sinister. As I stood there almost paralyzed, I shouted to her, 'Get the Windex. Get the Windex!' On some level of consciousness I felt that the danger would pass if we could only obliterate those handrprints."

The priest came soon afterward and went through the house sprinkling the holy water and performing the blessings. Throughout his journey, Cami noted, the man kept asking where the children slept "Where are the children's rooms? Where do they play; where do they stay?" Likely the cleric understood the potential for danger to the young ones. Finally, he finished his services and she invited him to sit and chat in the living room. "But it was clear that he was searching for answers as profoundly as I was," Cami continued. "Finally, he inquired about me and my personal life. Among other things, I told him I was divorced.

"'That explains it!' he almost shouted. Very quickly he departed. I never fully understood the meaning of all that. This was the 1970s and maybe he thought I was some kind of kook. He was an older man and maybe he had little appreciation of how many American women were having to raise families alone."

Cami told me that it took her several more weeks to calm down, always waiting for strange sounds to erupt, though none ever did again. "The house that had made us so afraid, uneasy, helpless, vulnerable, insecure, frightened and unprotected became a warm, comforting and happy haven. It truly became, with God's blessing, a home sweet home, and has remained so to this day!" She gave a big smile and her relief was evident.

This story is most instructive, as it shows the disruptions that an unhappy spirit can cause. It is easy to see, judging by the amount of fear created by such intrusions, why frightened people can believe in demons. In fact, a very unhappy soul was forced to leave an innocent family alone, and the priest even did a favor for the entity by forcing it to confront the Absolute Goodness of the Creator, against which it could not stand. Hopefully, the being surrendered its rigidity and capacity to cause fear in others, and maybe now it is also at peace.

NEW YORK STATE GHOSTS

CHAPTER 6

MORE HAUNTED HOUSES

In the Woods

In the summer of 1974, Rick and his first wife, Mary, began building a rustic home on a hill overlooking Spier Falls Road in the upstate Town of Moreau, New York. By wintertime the building was enclosed and comfy in the December cold. They invited the priest from St. Michael's Church in South Glens Falls to visit their house and give a blessing, which he did. Mary died of a seizure less than six months later, and had little chance to enjoy her new home. There had been an earlier warning of her fragile health in May, when Mary collapsed and appeared dead, but was quickly resuscitated. Family members noted that a dome clock on the mantelpiece had stopped at the moment of her falling. The timepiece was restarted and kept proper time for the next few weeks, but when she died on May 20th, the timepiece stopped immediately. Rick remarried a woman named Jean a few years later.

During their growing up years, the four sisters and one brother of the newly-mixed family often quarreled and feuded with one another, and there was little real sharing of life's experiences. In later years, as the children grew up and began sharing youthful experiences, it turned out that each child had undergone powerful and frightening episodes along the path to adulthood. And each was prone to blame the sometimes-terrifying events on another sibling.

When little brother Ben was four, his parents forbade him to go upstairs into the attic for fear he'd fall and hurt himself on the steep stairs. Christine, his older sister, working in the attic one day, was upset to hear the child start up the stairs. "Dad! Ben's coming up into the attic," she yelled. Rick rushed to the foot of the stairs as Christine looked down from above. As the boy retreated down the stairs, he suddenly lurched forward and fell, though he landed at the foot of the stairs without injury. Immediately, he arose and blamed Christine for having pushed him. "Somebody pushed me, and it was Christine!" he said, pointing at his step-sister, who had never left the stair top. Christine pondered the incident for years. If, indeed, Ben had been pushed, she hadn't done it, so who had?

When Catherine was in junior high school, she had a powerful experience that seemed supernatural. Someone had left the upstairs hall light on that night and she was fitfully trying to fall asleep in her bedroom. Opening her eyes, she looked at the doorway and was startled to see a man's silhouette framed in the lighted opening, and it wasn't her dad! "We had always heard footsteps walking around in the house, usually on the stairs, so I wasn't surprised at this presence; however, it was the first sighting I'd ever had. The figure seemed to rush toward me and I couldn't move. He stopped just a few inches from my face and I closed my eyes tightly. Two seconds later, I opened them and he was gone. That was enough for one night!" Catherine remembered.

Christine continued, "When I was about thirteen, I had a girlfriend, Joanie, stay overnight. Before we went to bed, we were in the basement playing the piano. I played the song 'Do-Re-Mi,' from *The Sound of Music*, as that was the only number I could pick out. Suddenly, Joanie grabbed my hand away from the keys and ordered me to stop playing. As I was playing, Joanie had been hearing a woman humming the melody alongside us. It scared her and she never went into the basement again when she visited me.

"Another friend, Heather, who had long blonde hair that she always wore down, sometimes came to the house after school and we used to chat about school and boys and that stuff. One afternoon I was in the kitchen while she sat in the living room. She suddenly screamed and said that she had experienced a sudden drop in temperature and felt icy cold, though it was an Indian Summer day outside. All at once her long hair was lifted completely away from her back by some unseen force. We never figured that one out. She didn't like to be left alone when she visited after that day."

In time, conflicts arose between Rick and Jean and it was thought best to divorce. "During that time when my father and Jean were going through the divorce preparations, my sister Helen and I were coming up the basement stairs after school one day, and heard someone running down the attic stairs overhead, screaming and swearing. Our stepmother was under a lot of stress and we assumed the screaming was hers. Helen said, 'Oh great, now Mom's home.' But when we got upstairs there was nobody else there. With the marital tension and ghostly episodes, we were used to just enduring matters. But when this event occurred, we were so frightened that we called the neighbors to come down and help us search the house. This was very embarrassing for us because they found nobody else in the house, plus my bedroom was filled with piles of clothes that I hadn't put away, and now the neighbors knew that I had other secrets," Christine said with a frown.

Then she added another tale. "Once, when we had house guests sleeping in the guest bedroom, the man heard a knocking on the bedroom window, followed by a woman's voice crying out, 'Let me in!' He dismissed it and told his wife to go back to sleep, but he was fully awake and heard the woman's voice repeat the request. All he knew to do, he later told us, was to tell the spirit to go away in the name of Jesus. And it did."

It wasn't until years later at their summer camp in Essex County that the siblings shared their eerie experiences, which each one had guarded from the others. One of the sisters told Catherine of seeing a shadowy man pacing quickly back and forth in the hallway upstairs at night. "I got chills, because she was describing the very man that I had seen and had never told about," Catherine said. She then remembered and shared another scary experience with her sisters.

Catherine recalled feeling someone's hand roughly grasping hers while she slept. Though she couldn't see the attacker, she felt the hand to be bony and pulling her down off the bed. "At first, I couldn't be sure it was real, as it seemed so dreamlike. I was able to pull my hand out of its grasp, but made sure after that to never let a hand or leg dangle off the bed."

Christine then revealed another experience as the sisters sat on the beach at Paradox Lake. It had been ten years since her sister, Catherine, had moved away, and each young woman had stifled many scary adolescent memories and never shared them since that time. Christine remembered three incidents of an oppressive weight suddenly coming upon her chest at nighttime. "I could not lift my hand or sit up and had much difficulty breathing. Then I heard and felt someone running directly at me, stopping just in front of my face, but nobody or nothing was visible. These events seemed to last for hours, though they probably didn't extend for over twenty minutes each."

Catherine, hearing her sister's experience, interjected, "And then that Indian man went, 'Boo!'" It seems that Catherine had actually seen the spirit entity rushing at Christine at that time. The two sat and just stared at each other in the sudden recognition of a shared fright. "You know, the force or person rushing at me stopped when I was in my late teens, about the time I became a Christian," she told me. We later concluded that the family's home stood in an area that the Mohican tribe known as "The Palmertown Indians" had once inhabited.

Christine remembered another occasion when numbers of faceless entities rushed out of her bedroom closet, though she had no idea who or what they were. All three of the daughters, it turned out later, had experiences of dreaming their house was surrounded by monsters of some sort.

"I had one especially strange experience too," said Rick. "After Mary died I was worn out. The girls weren't very good about picking up after themselves, and I was frustrated. Soon after I went to sleep one night, someone or some thing suddenly lifted the foot of the bed off the floor then dropped it. It sure woke me up, and I was mad! I yelled out, 'Look, you so and so, if you've got all that energy, then turn on the vacuum and clean up this place!' The bed stopped moving, the room became suddenly quiet and the incident never happened again. Maybe I turned the tables and scared the ghost, instead of the other way around!" he beamed.

Today, Rick has remarried. He and Sue live in the hillside home which is now quiet, as the negativity has vanished, leaving the family scratching their heads. This was likely a series of events in which an ambient spirit energized itself from the stress of the high schoolers. The tensions and anxieties of the children also likely constellated into a force that apparently joined with the spirit energy. As the passions calmed and each child moved on into adulthood, the house became what it was designed to be—a quiet and happy retreat in the woods.

Holding On

During the late 1960s, tragedy struck the Z family on County Highway 126, outside Hagaman, New York. Most of the family members died within a few years. The husband and wife had a son and daughter, and the wife's mother came to live with them. Within six years, the husband and his mother-in-law both died of heart attacks in the house. Shortly thereafter, the widow's son died in an automobile accident during his graduation weekend. A year later, the widow's daughter died in childbirth in St. Mary's Hospital in Amsterdam. Grief-stricken by the multiple deaths, Mrs. Z sold her home and moved to Florida.

Joe Bonk and his wife bought the old house which death had too often visited. When the Bonks moved in, Joe began remodeling and modernizing the house. With awnings, more modern windows, and new paint in a striking color, the house bore little resemblance to the home Mrs. Z had sold. When she returned to visit Montgomery County, Mrs. Z. was angered at the renovations. Knocking at the door, she cursed the Bonks for the changes they had made, enumerating all the alterations that she found repulsive. Then she sped away.

In less than a month, strange events began to happen. Lights all over the house began to mysteriously turn on after Joe's family had gone to bed. He called an electrician to check out the house's wiring, but the man could find nothing amiss. The Bonks' daughter's bedroom in the basement seemed to be inhabited by an unseen person who frequently turned the room's lights off and on around 10 p.m. Discussing the phenomenon with neighbors, Joe discovered that not only had his daughter's bedroom been used by Mrs. Z's deceased mother, but that the woman had died around 10 o'clock at night. The daughter continued to experience other strange events during the night—someone or something made impressions on her bed quilt, as if a phantom had lain down.

The plumbing also acted up. One night at 1 a.m., Joe heard the water pump in the cellar turn on—a faucet was open somewhere. Checking the house, he found the kitchen sink faucet flowing and turned it off. Returning to bed, he was startled to hear the pump turn on again. Returning to the kitchen, he found that faucet off, but then, searching the house, he discovered the bathroom faucet was running and shut that off.

The Bonks' pets fared no better. Their collie dog spent hours trying to corner an invisible something or someone in the daughter's bedroom, while the cat avoided the room entirely, scampering away in fright.

Neighbors also noticed strange occurrences. Several reported the window blinds opening and closing, as if someone inside the house were peering out, though they knew the Bonks had gone for the day. Workmen hired to continue the renovations were startled to see magnets on the refrigerator door slowly sliding sideways.

"Eventually, it got ridiculous," said Joe. "One night, as I sat playing the organ in the living room, someone slapped me really hard on the back of my head. Angered, I turned around, only to see an empty room. By then I figured we had a ghost of some sort, and whoever it was seemed to be a music critic!" As good Catholics, the Bonks sought advice from their priest, but the cleric didn't believe the tales. "So my wife got a really nice picture of The Sacred Heart and hung it in my daughter's bedroom. That seemed to end it. We never figured out if our ghost was Mrs. Z's dead mother or the result of Mrs. Z's curse, but the house has been quiet ever since. Maybe the ghost recognized it was up against a Higher Power," Joe concluded.

Strange Events

"I'm sure my experiences are typical," Kassy told me when we met. "Ever since the first episode, I've felt certain that my visitor is female. This isn't an old house, because it was built in 1992, so I have always figured the strange events come from somewhere in the past."

Kassy lives on Kellogg Street in inner city Syracuse, on a typical street of aging houses that Hollywood would never choose as a movie set, yet it is in everyday settings that so many people experience personalities from the past.

"I had only been living here for a few months, and, while seated at the table, I heard an infant cry. I don't have children, so to hear such a sound in my own house was really a mystery. I got up and, just for the heck of it, looked around. Of course, there was no baby inside the house. Okay, I said to myself, the noise could have come in from the street, except that I had no open windows and there didn't seem to be any pedestrians outside. To complicate the issue, the sound was definitely coming from inside my house. I sat down at the same spot to contemplate the matter, and immediately heard the cry again. I jumped up to find the source while the crying was continuing. You may find this hard to believe, but I discovered that the crying originated within the wall next to where I sat. Strangely, I have never heard the crying since that day."

Then, slowly, the phenomena became more numerous. "One warm day, I sat in front of my fan, which was not turned on at the time. Suddenly, the knob turned itself up to high speed. And that was the first of the electrical events that I've experienced," she told me. Her lights many times switched themselves on, as did the radio and television, though whatever the cause was, they were never switched off. Yet, these are such commonplace ghost activities, probably an attempt to be noticed by a departed soul, that she didn't think too much about the events before we met.

"I never saw any ghosts or filmy beings here, but I'm sure my spirit visitor is a woman. I'm an intuitive," she told me, "and I continually feel that another woman, but not in any way threatening, at least visits me, if she isn't here all the time. The only ghost I've ever seen was when I was a fifteen-year-old. Two of my girlfriends and I decided to have a séance, and as we went through the Ouija procedures, I suddenly saw a mist taking a human form and we all felt a cold draft," Kassy remembers. "I wondered aloud who it could be, and the cloudy figure began to take on details, such as a hat, and he appeared to be like a bearded Southern planter in the pre-Civil War times. His face also seemed familiar. We plied the Ouija with 'yes and no' questions, and afterward began to read through the encyclopedia, searching for something similar to what we had seen. Eventually we found that the spirit resembled film actor Joseph Cotten, and we all agreed strongly that the figure was him, perhaps in some film role."

Prompted by the actor's name, I researched Cotten's filmography and raised an eyebrow or two at his 1943 film title, *Journey Into Fear* and a notation that, in the 1980s he had a television series entitled *Tales of the Unexpected*. Interesting, but there was no real proof of the misty form's identity there.

Where to go with this story? Could the phantom figure be a prior dweller at the site? I recalled writing (*Ghosts of the Northeast*) some years ago about an episode in a dormitory at the U.S. Military Academy at West Point, where a dead cavalry instructor (whose house on that spot had burned with the officer inside in the late 1800s) occasionally continues to show up at the very spot where he died, which is now on the first floor of the present-day barracks. The appearances and frigid cold make the room unusable by the USMA, so the space is used for storage at the last report. Had someone died at this Kellogg Street spot, maybe long before her house was built?

Kassy and I talked about the property itself. "An old timer in our neighborhood told me that, before there was the vacant lot on which this house was built, there had been a house here, and that it burned." This looked like a possible cause for the spirit manifestation.

Recently, Kassy has begun to smell burning wood, though a search of the house reveals no likely cause. Maybe the ghost woman is getting excited that her story is going to be told. My next step was the Syracuse City Clerk's office, to check prior deeds for the property.

The City Clerk was very helpful, pulling out old property records for the house, which indeed had burned in October 1986 and was quickly torn down as a hazard. The last owners of the property had been Raymond and Martilena Terino who, for some reason, appear to have abandoned the building at least three months prior to the fire. Following their departure, neighborhood youngsters vandalized the interior and it became a hangout. It is entirely possible that the fire was generated by the young people. But what of the Terinos?

I contacted some distant relatives who told me that Raymond had died of a heart attack soon after the fire. Martilena, a Puerto Rican native, then returned to the island and hasn't been heard from since. Is it possible that she has died in the two decades since leaving Kellogg Street? Probably I can never document a solution to the "woman ghost" that Kassy experiences there, but it is possible that Martilena is the culprit. And why not? When one has to abandon a home, which if often her prime source of feeling secure, how can one just walk away without emotion? And if a woman's husband then dies, leaving her without many resources, might that grief compound the situation? If a person dies with that level of grief, it is entirely likely that she can take a while to adjust after death.

That You, Mom?

"I lived in an old house at 67 Fowler Avenue in Newburgh between 1969 and 1979," Tammy told me. "All I knew at the time is that the former owner, a woman, had died. I knew that her son lived elsewhere in the city, but I didn't think much about previous ownership until I began to hear noises when I was alone in the house. Of course, like most people, I went to discover the cause: maybe a window left open or a machine still turned on. The mystery grew because I could never find a reason for the sounds.

"One day I was in the basement and heard someone walking across the floor above me. It must be one of my family who has come home early, I thought, so I went upstairs. Nobody was there and my doors were still locked. Even then, I didn't consider the "g word." Like most people, I thought there was a simple explanation. Then I began to feel a presence of some kind—as if there was an unseen person watching me or moving through my house. Though I couldn't see anything to explain the sensation, still, I wasn't frightened. I began to consider that maybe it was a ghost, but the energy or presence didn't seem scary or intimidating.

"A few years later I remarried and had to tell my new husband about my suspicions," she told me. Her mate laughed and laughed—outlandish, he said. Who ever heard of such a thing? Ghosts were for movies and television but didn't exist alongside real people. "You have lived alone here for too long," he told Tammy, "that's all it is—just your imagination!"

His awakening came when the couple finished watching television in their bedroom one evening. Soon after clicking the set off, they distinctly heard two steps on the stairs creaking. They knew the sound; somebody was coming up the stairs to the second floor! To make matters worse, they knew that those two stairs were near the top, and whoever made the noise would soon be upon them. Quickly, her husband jumped out of bed, snapped on the lights and went to the stairway, only to find nobody there. How could stairs creak without a human stepping on them? "One night a short time later, he had to conduct another fruitless search, and then finally had to admit that a somebody or a something was living in the house with us," she smiled.

"A year later, at night, when I was quite upset over some matter, I heard a woman calling me. Figuring it was my sister-in-law at the door, I went over and opened it, only to find the doorstep empty. Who could it have been? I finally had to conclude that it was our invisible ghost woman. I heard her speaking or calling my name at times when I was especially out of sorts, almost as if she was comforting me. Maybe, I thought, she wanted to tell me that things weren't so bad, or maybe that they really didn't matter. Finally, I had to conclude that it was the deceased former owner. How nice, I concluded, her hanging around in order to soothe my thoughts and emotions. Our relationship continued over four years. Suddenly, they ended as abruptly as they began.

"Searching for a reason or cause, I noticed that she last came to visit me at a certain date, and the newspapers from that week carried the obituary for her son. Maybe she was just biding her time, knowing in the spirit world that her son didn't have too long, so why not wait around and help somebody else who had a difficult life?

"After the son's funeral we never heard an unexplained sound again for the six years in which we lived there. How can I not believe in ghosts? I had one for a housemate!" Again, Tammy smiled confidently.

The Dark Thing

Soon after the British captured the Dutch colony of New Netherlands and changed its name to New York in 1664, the new colonial government was organized into twelve counties, one of which was Ulster County. It quickly became one of the most agriculturally productive areas in the Hudson Valley. And it is one of those old farms that is the scene of this story.

"When we came here, we moved into an older modular house on a Clove Valley Road farm in High Falls," Anita Gehrke told me. "An older couple, the Nersessians, and their son had lived there for years, but had sold to my sister, and we rented one of the two houses on the property after the old man died. Nevertheless, we were happy in the rural setting. Soon after we moved in, however, I often noticed an ethereal object moving through the house's interior. For want of a better name, I called it the 'Dark Thing.' First, I'd notice it out of the corner of my eye, then if I looked directly at it, the dark shape would dart away. But it didn't seem harmful, so I didn't mention it to my husband or little son, as I didn't want to scare them. I certainly wasn't scared of it, as I noticed that it always appeared in the same way and at the same place.

"My son, Clay, was about five when he said to me, 'Mommy, there's a black thing in the house.' I responded, 'I know,' not wanting to make it a big issue. Soon afterward, he commented on the apparition again, telling me that he saw it in the same spot every time, and I was amazed, because that was the location where I always spotted it. The figure didn't scare either of us, though it appeared to dart or run from place to place. When Clay was eleven, we moved into a new log cabin house less than a half-mile away, and it seemed that we had left the Dark Thing behind. I noticed nothing spectral in our new house, and that situation seemed confirmed when Clay told me that the Dark Thing hadn't come with us."

Nevertheless, a few months later, while the children were in school and Anita walked through the house, she paused at the foot of the stairs. "I knew I wasn't alone and felt compelled to look up the stairs. There it was, stationary for a minute, then the dark, opaque but wispy energy vanished. Hmmm, I

172

thought, why is it here? While I was still pondering the situation, just a few days later, Clay told me, 'It's here, Mom.' I told him that I'd seen it too, though I had purposely left out its location. 'Yes, it's right up there!' he responded, pointing to the top of the stairs."

Anita never found the presence to be troubling and, recognizing that ghosts or spirits are vestiges of some people's lives, she spoke to the entity, acknowledging its presence and saying that the figure was welcome to stay around if it felt a need to, but suggesting that it move on to a better situation.

Quite a bit of time passed before Anita recognized that she hadn't recently seen or heard the being, and its most recent appearances had been static and less energized than in the old house.

Anita and I talked about her experiences and she told me that, only recently, her husband admitted that he had also seen some of the ghostly activity in the old house, but it had always been in peripheral sightings and seemed not worth mentioning. Their son Clay had seen the figure, but their other boy had not.

Now, as there didn't seem to be an entity there to contact psychically on Clove Valley Road, we tried to ascertain who the individual had been and what it had wanted. The obvious candidate for house ghost was the old farmer, Mr. Nersessian, as he had only recently passed on when Anita and her family moved in. Many souls require a great period of time to let go of all activities or objects that fascinated or tormented them in body life. In many cases, too, there is a strong love or concern for surviving family members—"Can they carry on without me there to help them?" The amount of grief expressed by the survivors often acts as a magnet, pulling the deceased's consciousness into the earth plane and holding it there. Many researchers use the term "earth-bound" for that state of being. For this reason, grieving family members need to work through their sorrow, so as to set the newly deceased person eternally free.

Then, there is also the issue of uncompleted work—items that the deceased feels still need their attention. Oftentimes the spirit will attempt to get the inhabitants of the house to do one last thing for them. It is best to try to talk to the spirit, informing them that none of these concerns matter any more. They don't always believe you, however.

Also, many of the deceased are surprised to find themselves (as consciousness) still "alive," and they want to communicate to someone that "I'm still here." Another variation on this theme is the passing of a relative, whether or not the person lived nearby or not. Just letting some family member know of their continued existence is often enough for the soul to release its hold on the physical world. In this instance, Anita couldn't remember any relative who had passed over just prior to their living in the old house. In any case, the spirit had found an affinity for Anita and her family, maybe because several of them acknowledged its continued existence, and therefore were part of the spirit's "way out" of this world. Anita's friendliness seems to have been enough to release the spirit.

The Housekeeper

The Dutton House

Cassandra Cottone readied to leave from the old Dutton House at 107 River Street in Middleburgh, N.Y., in 1978, and friends gathered to help her sort and pack belongings for her imminent move to North Blenheim, N.Y. Ken Rossi and his then wife, Elizabeth, were among the helpers. It was exciting to help their friend prepare to relocate, but it was also a bit sad, as she had lived in the stately, old 1828 Greek Revival house for almost fourteen years.

After a hard day's work packing items, Ken headed for a small bathroom in the front of the house as night fell. Leaving the dining room, he entered the center hall and walked to the back of the living room, where he turned on the chandelier to light his way to the small bathroom. Elizabeth and Cassandra remained in the back of the house, so he left the bathroom door open and didn't turn on the light inside as there was enough illumination from the living room to suit his needs. As he was engaged in his business there, Ken heard footsteps crossing the wooden floor of the living room behind him. Then the bathroom door opened and the chandelier went out, plunging him into darkness. It must be Cassandra, he thought, but she knows I'm in here—why would she do that? he puzzled. Finishing up, he returned to the kitchen through the dark living room and dining room. Both women were still busily at work, hardly noticing his return. Neither admitted to having left the room during his absence.

When the van was filled and they prepared to drive to Cassandra's new home, she expressed her concern that, with the drapes removed from the windows, the house's interior was clearly visible to passersby. She asked Ken to double-check all door locks before they departed to North Blenheim in the moving van. As the last one out the door, Ken turned off the remaining interior light and double-checked the door lock. The trio drove to Cassandra's new house, off-loaded their truck, then returned to Middleburgh. As they approached the house, they could see at least one interior hall light lit. Ken did some head-scratching, certain that he'd turned out all lights. The trio opened the doors and set about packing some more boxes for another run, then suddenly found all the downstairs lights on. Who did that? They all claimed innocence because the "g word" was not an issue that any one of them wanted to consider.

Filling the last empty box, Ken volunteered to go up and get more in the attic. Entry into that space was gained by a ceiling trapdoor on the top floor, a trap that was counterweighted and whose pulley squeaked every time the door opened. Taking up more boxes from the attic floor, he returned to the ground floor. "That ought to do it for tonight," he told the others. "I'll go up, turn off the attic light, and close the trap," he said, starting upstairs. At the first floor landing, he heard the loud squeak of the trapdoor, and when he got to the opening, he found the door closed and the light inside turned off. Moreover, the door seemed latched from above. Disturbed by the antics of the unseen person, he returned downstairs and asked Cassandra if she had a ghost. She admitted that several times during her residency she had observed a filmy presence darting through the house. "But Ken, such things come with old houses, for heaven's sake!" she said, and moved on to another task.

Present residents of the house have had no such experiences, a situation, then, that may create skepticism about this ghost experience, as it does in so many similar cases. It seems obvious that various tenants of old buildings have different degrees of sensitivity. Each person also brings his or her own bioelectric field into a house, perhaps upsetting the former balance there. Ken, however, had ghostly experiences in other houses during his life, and may therefore have acquired a sensitivity that was shared that night by the two women.

The old house became "the Dutton House" in 1901, when Asa Dutton, retired and, enriched by ownership of a button factory in New York City, came to Middleburgh and bought the property. Asa had twin children, Asa, Jr. and Alice, who continued to live there after their father died in 1910. One old timer in Middleburgh said, "Old Asa had a most disagreeable disposition and more than likely was a pinch-penny. However, his daughter, Alice, who never married, might more likely fit the antics of that ghost. She was prim and proper and might well have taken offense at Ken's using the bathroom without closing the door. She also lived on a tight budget and may have continued to turn off apparently unneeded lights after her death." The best candidates, then, for the Dutton House specters are curmudgeon Asa Dutton and his spinster daughter. Today, almost forty years after the haunting, it seems the spirit or spirits have finally left their abode in the Schoharie Valley house.

Vestiges

"My friend, Matt, dropped by my place of work in Pittsford, N.Y., back in 2005 and asked if I'd join his crew in modernizing an older house," Peter told me. "I had helped him on some other construction and demolition jobs, and, as I had some free time that June, I helped out on weekends."

Peter told me that the house had been built in 1951 and had become a bit run down under the ownership of an elderly woman, who finally sold the property to Nick, Matt's father. Nick and his son were hoping to renovate the house and place it on the market. "The crew had pretty well finished scraping and sanding the exterior, so I spent my first week helping them paint the outside of the house," he told me. "Our crew of eight young men was full of energy. It was rewarding to restore the house, as it had a nice, secluded back yard and patio, and we expected the house would sell quickly.

"The second part of the job involved three other guys and me preparing the interior walls and ceilings for painting. There were almost no furnishings left inside, so we moved right along, though there was a mustiness throughout the interior that made me uneasy. While working in the kitchen one day with Chris, another painter, we heard walking from somewhere in the house. We knew that, barring an intruder, no one else was in the house that day. So, because footsteps were clearly impossible, we chalked it up to imagination and kept on working."

As the house was secure and because Peter was watching his expenses, Matt gave him permission to move into one room of the house. Peter would serve as a watchman and his commute to work would be short. The house was still a long way from being finished when Peter moved into an upstairs bedroom. "One night, when I was sure that I was alone in the house, I heard footsteps ascending the stairs and then pausing outside the closed bedroom door," he remembered. "I opened the door and checked, but no one was there. I checked every corner of the house, but to no avail—except for myself, it was empty.

"There was a major intersection not too far from the house, but nevertheless, I knew I wasn't confusing traffic sounds with footsteps—those steps and the movements in the hallway outside were real! I recognize that older houses sometimes creak, but the sound of those footsteps was not faint, but a sustained sound. After a while, I gave up checking out the hallway, but I was certain that real feet were walking on those steps. It had to be a ghost, but I wasn't about to share my suspicion with my co-workers. On another occasion, when in my bedroom, I clearly heard someone drop a metal pipe down in the cellar. When I checked it out, the basement was empty."

I asked Peter how he could stand to live night after night with the unknown. "Well, David, I'm a Christian man," he told me. "I believe in God, who is more powerful than any ghost or spirit, so I wasn't ever fearful, but just curious as to how it could all happen. I believe God is greater than whoever or whatever was making the noise, and that is what kept me from being afraid."

The house renovation was almost completed by late October and the work was concluded in early December. "I had to move out then, as the house sold quickly, once it was put up for sale, and I never returned," Peter said, "so I often wonder whether the unseen being continued on after the new people moved in. Maybe, someday, I'll drop by and ask them what's up," he laughed.

What's On Tonight?

Several years ago, when living in an old 1850s house in Salem, N.Y., near the Vermont border, my family had some unique experiences with a former resident.

When I married my wife, who had owned the house for about ten years, she informed me that there was a "knocking ghost" that rapped on the front door perhaps twice a year, always in the dead of night. Looking down from an upstairs window over the door, she never saw anybody at the door, she said, though the rapping or pounding still resounded in the stairwell behind her. I figured that, in time, I, too, would experience that ghost for myself, but I never did.

In October 2000, I narrated nighttime ghost tours in Saratoga Springs until late at night, and it was close to midnight when I arrived home. Returning home one night, I found the rest of the family had gone to bed, so I walked quietly in the back door and through the house to the front hallway without turning on any lights. Turning left, through a doorway, and then right into the hall itself, I took one more step and walked into a powerfully pulsating "something." It had no coldness, as one might expect, but vibrated as if I had grabbed onto a live electric wire. I instantly bounced back a step or two, not scared, but surprised that we had "one" in the front hall. For a minute, I suspected that this might be the "knocking ghost," though it didn't make sense that the spirit had now come inside the house. Genuine ghosts seldom show adaptive behavior or change their "act."

Again, I tested my perception by taking one more step forward into the energy field, and again my entire body vibrated. Knowing that this area of the hallway had forty years before been the entryway to old Dr. Bangheart's office and waiting room, I considered that the phenomenon's origin might lie in some unresolved medical situation from the past, or indeed from the door knocker himself having moved indoors. But I was also tired out, so I just said, "I don't know what you're going to do, but I'm tired, and I'm going to bed!" Walking through the vibrating energy, I turned and went up the stairs to bed. No one in the family had ever experienced this manifestation before me, and no one else did afterward.

Some weeks later, my wife awakened me in the middle of the night, convinced that someone had broken into the house—she heard the television blaring downstairs. I puzzled that a burglar should take the time to watch infomercials and sit-com reruns at 1:30 a.m., but went downstairs where, sure enough, the TV was on. A thorough search of the house disclosed no open or unlocked doors. Attempt as I might, I could not convince myself that someone had left the TV on, as I was the last one upstairs that night and knew I had turned it off.

On an irregular basis over the next few months, the TV would turn on, usually around 1:30 a.m., and someone had to venture downstairs to turn it off. One night I decided to simply call out, "When you're finished, turn it off." We laughed and went back to sleep, but in the morning the TV was off. Subsequent experience showed us that it always turned off before 4 a.m. So this phenomenon apparently had intelligence behind it and did evidence the capacity to respond to voice commands. Most ghosts, I've learned, will do so. Just tell them what's on your mind.

I also discovered that our TV turned on at three minutes before noon on some days, too. I considered this glitch must be caused by a passing car, perhaps someone triggering a cell phone or car radio—after all, the Sheriff's Department was located right at the end of our street. So for several days, I stood at the front window at 11:55 a.m. and waited. If the TV was to turn on, I'd hear it do so behind me while I scanned the street outside. Day after day, when it did turn on, there was no car on the street outside—no town or country trucks or law enforcement vehicles.

My ten-year-old step-daughter was apprehensive that her peers would find out she had a weird step-father and/or that she lived in a strange house. But what harm could there be in doing homework with a friend on the living room rug in the afternoon? The girl and her friend worked on math homework at four p.m. one afternoon, and, all of a sudden, the TV snapped on over the girls' heads. Blushing and mortified that her secret was out, my step-daughter testily turned and pointed at the set. "Off now!" she commanded. The TV obediently snapped off as her poor friend, who hadn't witnessed our ghost in action before, stood shakily, round-eyed, and started walking toward the kitchen. "I don't think I like this house," she said. This is the only time the TV or ghost ever responded immediately to a voice command.

In June 2002, as my new book, *Ghosts of the Northeast*, neared publication, and as I raked the lawn, I spotted my neighbor, a retired airline pilot. We said hello, and he then asked how the new book was coming and when it would be on sale. Then, "David, you don't have any…ghosts…in your house, do you?"

Matter-of-factly, after experiencing two years of ghost activity, I answered, "Well, our TV seems to turn itself off and on—sometimes twice a day." He scowled. This was a tale he'd never heard from my house, though he'd lived next door for twenty-five years and had known the former occupants, a doctor and his wife and another family. As a former pilot, my neighbor was a logical and critical guy—such events had to make sense if he was to accept them. Then he brightened, with a big smile on his face, and said, "Why, that's Mary!"

"Who's Mary?" I asked.

"Why, that's the old doctor's widow. Yes, she was in failing health after he died, and, for entertainment, her family bought her a new TV set with a remote control. However, I think she was getting senile and confused with modern technology because, most days, she'd come over here with the remote in her hand and say, 'Hey, I can't get the TV to turn on. Come fix it for me!'" And this kind-hearted man did as requested, but after a few weeks it became wearing. "I pondered going over there and permanently disabling that set," he said with a smile. Then he broke up laughing, "It sure looks like she's learned to turn it on by herself now!"

He went on to note that it wasn't long after getting the new TV that Mary needed more intensive treatment and left her house to enter a senior care facility, where she later died. The house sat empty for a while before getting its new inhabitants. But that new family seems to have had no TV problems before

NEW YORK STATE GHOSTS

I joined them. This indicates how subtly the energy in a house can change, with the addition or subtraction of a single person. At that point, a phenomenon can suddenly begin or end, just because of the addition of a new individual's energy to the household.

Now, with a name for our ghost, we felt closer to her and tried every remedy we could think of to evict her into The Light. But Mary, having finally mastered control over her entertainment, was in no hurry to move on. On some nights when the TV would snap on, either my wife or I would trudge down and give Mary a lecture on the advantages of Heaven and suggest she leave town for the Promised Land. Nothing doing. Each New Year's Eve, we held a little ceremony with holy water and a candle and opened the front door, inviting Mary out of the house and onward to more sublime experiences. Not a chance—she had found a good thing and was dedicated to enjoying late-night television.

In November of 2003, I helped a friend examine a house on Main Street that he intended to buy. I had felt there was a woman's spirit upstairs when I entered. The friend had hired Doug, a talented building inspector from Pawlet, Vermont, to do the house inspection. Doug traveled through the house with us, noting a few items that would need improvement, but otherwise gave the building a clean bill of health. At the end of the inspection, we stood in an upstairs bedroom, and Doug asked us if we required anything more. Jokingly, I wished aloud that Doug could get rid of the ghost lady.

He responded, "Oh, you saw her, too?" We were astonished and replied that we hadn't actually seen the woman, but had felt her presence. "Do you want her gone?" Doug asked.

"Sure," I replied. "My friend ought to start his life here with an empty building."

Doug then sat motionless on the window sill, and we discovered another of his talents. We didn't understand what he was doing at first, but, after about four minutes he suddenly straightened and smiled, "It's okay now, she's gone." Dumbfounded, we looked at one another, and I was certain that we'd just been scammed. Doug hadn't waved his arms, burned any incense or sage or uttered any chants, spells or prayers, so we were pretty dubious about the result. We did learn later that the seller's first wife had died in that house some years before, and had likely stayed around in a confused state of mind.

"What did you do?" we asked Doug.

"Well, my grandmother helps me. She died in 1968, so I get into a meditative state and call on her. When she comes, I mentally tell her we have a ghost woman trapped here, and she convinces the spirit to move onward to the greater glories that await. She just asks the spirit 'What are you doing here, honey? Don't you know that something better awaits you?' Then she escorts them away. Doug then asked, "Anything else?"

"Do you have to be in a house to do this removal?" I asked.

"No, what else have you got?" he inquired.

"Our house is about three hundred yards away, and we have an old woman ghost that we think is named Mary, and she keeps turning our TV off and on."

"You want her out?" Doug asked.

"Sure, if you can do it," I said with fingers crossed behind my back.

Again, he sat quietly and then, after a few minutes, brightened and opened his eyes. "Okay, she's gone too!" We thanked and paid him, and parted ways. My family, skeptical that Mary's eviction was accomplished so easily, eagerly returned to our house, awaiting 1:30 the next morning. Nothing happened then and not a single TV interruption ever occurred again. It was fascinating to live through the entire episode and then move on.

So a talented individual or clergyman can often free a trapped spirit, permitting the soul to return to the place of glory from which it originated.

Who's Got the Button?

Gilboa farmhouse

When I was a kid, we used to play a guessing game at children's parties called "Button, button, who's got the button?" I can think of no more appropriate title for this story, shared with me by my friend, Fred Wickert from Gilboa, New York. Fred is not one of the "true believers" who one often encounters in researching ghosts. He is, instead, a very practical and down-to-earth guy, an Air Force veteran and former law enforcement officer. Yet, he has had to contend with many strange events throughout his life. Here is a simple, but intriguing, one.

Fred retired from the Air Force in 1973 and, with his Japanese wife, Tae, returned to the Catskills. They bought the old Stryker House not far from the Schoharie Creek, a Shaker style building that was more than 200 years old. It had been in desperate condition when Wally Stryker bought it in 1933, so he restored and remodeled the house before finally moving in during 1939. By 1973, the Stryker children were grown and had moved away, so the parents built a smaller house elsewhere and moved away.

"Our first night in the old house was May 1, 1973, and it was quiet and nice for a few weeks," Fred recalled. "Then, one day, I commented to Tae that I'd heard my name called, though it wasn't her calling. Her face lit up and she responded that she had experienced the same thing, but couldn't find me when she responded to the summons. Who was calling us? We were the only people there!

"I had a favorite suede leather and camel hair sweater that I loved, and when cool autumn weather arrived, I went to the closet in our master bedroom to put it on. I took it off its hanger and discovered that all the buttons were missing. They were round leather-covered metal buttons. I considered that, this being an old farmhouse, field mice might have gotten in and eaten the fabric, but certainly not the metal. My sweater now looked as if it never had any buttons! Since I couldn't fasten it, I re-hung it on a hanger and stored it in a large closet at the rear of our second floor. We weren't able to find any trace of those buttons," he said, still in amazement at the thirty-five-year-old mystery. But the mystery had another twist to be discovered years later.

"Tae had a favorite red winter coat with large, fabric-covered brass buttons," he continued, "which also hung in that closet. When cold weather came, she went to get the coat, only to find that it was missing all of its buttons. So, that coat also went into the back bedroom closet."

The Wickerts have always had pets and have raised show dogs and tropical birds (see "Ghost Birds" in this book), and Fred told me that Pudge, his foundation stud Cocker Spaniel, was the most beautiful Cocker Spaniel that he had ever seen. Pudge got to sleep in the master bedroom, where he guarded Tae and Fred at night. On occasion, the dog would rouse and stand snarling, on guard in the bedroom doorway, his neck hair raised and his fangs bared. Awakened by Pudge's sudden growling, Fred told me, he always got up to check the hallway outside, but there was never any living thing outside. "At other times," Fred remembers, "Pudge would be about to enter a room, but then would suddenly stop. I would enter and check out the room, to see who or what was inside, but I never discovered what repelled the dog. After I had entered, Pudge would follow me in, as if nothing was amiss. In later years, we had a poodle who often stopped short in her roaming, almost as if she had run into an invisible fence between me and herself."

Over the years, these episodes came less often. Then, in 1991, Tae's daughter and her children were coming from Japan for a visit. Wally Stryker had added a wing to the house in the 1950s, so Fred quickly did some remodeling, fixing up the previously unfinished second story of that section, cutting through the big old storage closet to make a doorway to the upstairs, which formerly was reachable only through an exterior door. He also added a deck and exterior stairs to provide outdoor access to the small apartment. Preparing to cut through the closet wall, Fred began the removal of the boxes and clothing stored inside. Moving his favorite old sweater, he discovered that the original buttons had somehow been restored!

"Then I picked up Tae's favorite red coat, and it, too, had mysteriously had its buttons returned! We were astonished, and could only figure that we had a ghost with a good sense of humor," he laughed.

Having grown up with grandparents who had known the Depression and hard times, when nothing was thrown away, I remember the incidents when all buttons were cut off garments before they were disposed of. Old buttons could be sewn onto homemade garments. Perhaps a thrifty farm housewife's consciousness remained in the house, still attempting to salvage every last usable item, though her body had long ago gone to its grave.

In January of 1996, the Schoharie Creek rose well above flood stage and the old farmhouse was so badly damaged that FEMA purchased it and razed it. "When I visit the site of the house today, I often recall that, maybe a hundred feet behind the house, was a cemetery for early Schoharie Valley settlers, mostly burials from the 1700s and early 1800s. Most of them, I remember, were children. Do you think some youngsters' spirits tried to get our goat by getting our buttons?" Fred laughed at the prospect.

Him and Her

"Most of my life has been filled with some kind of strange experience," Barbara told me. "As a kid, growing up in Churchville, New York, I had a UFO sighting experience in the park—it was an object that many saw back in 1967. The main outcome of that event was that I came to realize how sensitive I was to the unseen parts of life. Not long after that, I noticed that I was hearing distant conversations that were usually unintelligible, but they were almost like a radio playing in the background. To this day, I can tune in, occasionally catching a word or two, but I've never been able to make any sense out of what I'm hearing or why I hear such things." We talked about the potential for severe psychiatric disorders (as is common for those who "hear voices"), but Barbara has otherwise carried on a normal work and home life, so she doesn't fit the psychotic diagnosis. Her feet are firmly on the ground.

This phenomenon, comparatively rare as psychic gifts go, is termed clairaudience (or "clear hearing") which can sometimes be a wondrous gift, but if not developed (when it can be) the activity can seem a burden. It is another ability or technique for hearing into the complex invisible world of life that surrounds us—a realm that we perceive only in part.

Living in two worlds has sometimes been troubling for Barbara, as she told me of her first ghost experience. "When I lived in Henrietta in 1983, I remember getting ready for bed one night. As I sat on the edge of my bed untying my shoes, my sewing machine light suddenly turned on with a snap, followed almost immediately by my bedroom lamp clicking on. That startled me, but then I became extremely frightened, as a strong force pushed me back onto the bed and then laid upon me. Whoever or whatever it was, I couldn't move. I sensed it saying, 'I'm going to tear your heart out!' There was a huge shadow over me, as if it was a big man. I turned to look at my husband, but he seemed in a trance or dead until the episode ended. Later, he told me that he'd felt paralyzed.

"What allowed this scary event to stop that night was my continual recitation of The Lord's Prayer. I hurt very much afterward and, the next morning, believing that I might have had a heart attack, I went to the hospital to have an EKG done. The doctors found my heart rhythms normal and sent me home. But then, I became even more scared when my eight-year-old daughter informed me that she had undergone the same experience during the previous night! What should I do? I wondered. How could I protect myself and my daughter? As the child didn't know of my experience, I was able to calm her by saying that she'd just had a bad dream. Later that year, I wrote of my experience in a "true experiences" column in FATE Magazine.

Fortunately, after those two events, the spirit molestation stopped. "The only phenomena that occurred afterward were small things such as my TV going on and off during the night," she said in great relief.

We talked about the experience, since it is fairly common, and often assigned to the "evil spirit" or "demon" category of spirit. Each of these situations is likely unique and must be studied individually. As a rule of thumb, however, readers should never permit a physical relationship to develop with discarnate entities. Such events can only be regarded as assaults or attacks, and the individual experiencing these should get professional help, likely the ceremony called "exorcism" (or cutting out) performed by a clergyperson or trained professional. I don't perform these and rely on talented individuals who know how to protect themselves from the negative energy as they do the procedures.

In my conversations with such "cleansers," I have learned that, usually, not only the house but also all the inhabitants living there need to be purified at the same time, so there remains no "handhold" for the entity to cling to. In simple cases, the Native American ceremony of "smudging" (burning of sage throughout the house or apartment, followed by a firm instruction to the spirit to depart) can be done by ordinary residents. But the attacked person must be certain that they want the entity or beings to go; there can be no wishy-washy 'Gee I wish they were nicer, so I could keep them around.' You don't need and don't want such beings to remain where you live and sleep. And, even then, an unskilled layperson might be unable to chase out a determined bad spirit, so a professional must be called.

I noted also that she instinctively did the right activity to repel the aggressor. Having read many UFO abduction cases, I note that those experiencers say that keeping one finger moving (or one idea, such as a prayer, running through the consciousness during the attempted assault) deprives the attacker of succeeding in their nefarious aims. There is a powerful force in the human will, though too few of us exercise it daily in determining the flow of our life and its experiences. Prayers for protection each night before you sleep can also be a powerful deterrent. Visualizing oneself surrounded by a brilliant light also is helpful.

Some years later, after her husband's death, Barbara moved to a new apartment in West Henrietta, but shortly afterward found herself with a new, if gentler, ghost. "The first thing I noticed, three years ago, was that someone or something would sit on the side of my bed most every night when I went to bed. I could both feel and see the mattress go down or up when the being sat or rose. I have never been frightened by this thing because I don't feel threatened. I was told that a former resident, a woman, died in this room, but that doesn't trouble me, though I think the woman never fully departed. It seems that she is still keeping up her normal routines and may not be aware that I'm here," she wrote.

Barbara hears walking in her kitchen during the middle of the night (Prior to death, many ill people experience difficulty in sleeping, perhaps due to pain or another difficulty such as breathing. Following death, until they understand that they have passed, many continue their "sick routine."). Sometimes she hears the refrigerator open and close, while the bathroom medicine cabinet can be heard to open and then slam shut, and "several times I have found my makeup missing, and it never returns. The same opening and closing occurs with kitchen cabinets. Three nights ago," she told me during our interview, "my cat Puff sat on my lap and we watched the bedroom doorknob turn back and forth. I could also hear the movement, so it wasn't an illusion.

"Puff and I sense our visitor, usually sitting or standing just to the left of my recliner, in the corner. If I talk to it, the shape or energy flies all over the place, and I watch Puff shifting his head to follow the movements. When I am speaking to Puff, there is no reaction, but when I address the lady ghost directly ("Hello, how are you tonight?") it goes all over the place. I asked her not to scare my cat so much, and have also asked the spirit to move up and down (as Puff will follow the movements with her eyes and head) allowing me to know that the answer is 'yes' to the questions I'm asking." Barbara figures that she wasn't very successful in training the ghost.

Think about this, though. Consider that you are sick, perhaps terminally ill, and are unsure whether or not life goes on after the body dies. Maybe you are fearful, yet determined (as so many that I've known indeed are) to keep your remaining days structured and as close to normal as you can. Now, imagine that you hear someone speaking to you. Perhaps you think you see a seated ghost lady, sometimes with a cat, in your living room! If you got all upset as a result, what would that look like to an observer? Something like the experiences that Barbara or Puff have? Which of you is truly real? Or is that not even the word to use in a universe where everything is One?

In April 2008, Barbara wrote me, "I spoke very firmly to it four nights ago and told it to move on to the white light (as you had suggested, I told it that it was dead). I have not in four nights experienced the usual nightly visitation, and my cat is very calm now. It was the first time I really asked it to leave, and I think it may have worked. Time will tell." Not every one has to have an advanced academic degree to be a ghostbuster, though you do need to watch out for the spirit's potential to trick or lie to you.

If, indeed, life is eternal (and Scripture tells us that it is) then what real part of us can die? Barbara seems to live on the cusp between the two worlds, having known the terror of a horrible personality who passed into spirit and likely still seeks revenge on others. But she also was afforded the opportunity to lovingly serve as a healing presence for "the other lady," and may even have had the chance to help that woman acknowledge that the unreal part of her being has passed, and that her true, eternal self can now take its place in the light of Forever.

CHAPTER 7

GRANDPARENTS

NANA'S HOUSE
GRANDFATHER
THE BIG HOUSE
OLD TIMERS
UP AND DOWN
REJOINED

Nana's House

85 West Chester, Kingston

"My grandparents, Tom and Vivian Hughes, owned a beautiful old Victorian house at 85 West Chester Street in Kingston," Cheryl told me. "It was awesome to go there as a child because the big old porch frightened me and there were parts of the upstairs that I was uncomfortable with, but it was always nice to see my Nana. I now recognize that I was quite sensitive as a child and had many experiences in that old house every time I visited. At the time, I could never imagine that I would live there one day."

Cheryl Olsen spoke of this sensitivity focusing sharply for the first time when she was sixteen, and a young male friend had died in a car accident. "Later, after the funeral, someone visited me in the night and told me everything was okay. At first, I thought my mom had come into the bedroom to reassure me, but at breakfast the next morning, she denied coming into my room. After a while, I came to believe that it must have been that young man's spirit," she said seriously.

When she was older, Cheryl married and, with her new husband, moved into Nana's house on West Chester Street. There were things to fix and modernizations to do, but with every piece of wallpaper stripped or wall knocked out, there were strange objects found—gaudy paint on wall surfaces, old murals, and strangely-painted ceilings. The couple later discovered that, before Nana's time, the old 1873 building had been a house of ill repute. Other than that, Cheryl did no research on the property, though it was very near a house that had burned to the ground.

What made her afraid as a child was, in part, her great sensitivity to the "other world." There were children's voices echoing through the building from time to time, as well as children's laughter outside a closed door. "None of that was scary to me as an adult, because I understood ghosts could exist," she told me. "One of the strange things was finding an old Ouija board in the attic, and on its back were four burned figures. We learned that somehow, though it had been in a house that was totally destroyed in a fire, the board survived. Nana couldn't remember how it might have come into her attic.

"My husband and I often worked that Ouija board and received strange messages from its pointer, though none were scary," she said. When I interviewed her, I wanted to be sure that Cheryl had experienced spirit events before the use of the Ouija, as sometimes the introduction of Ouija board use in a house can bring in entities who don't want to leave.

She told me of occasionally seeing a threesome of children wearing Victorian clothing walking or playing in the hallways. "One day I knew I was alone in the house and was showering before beginning my day. There I was, soaking wet in the shower stall, when I realized I hadn't brought a washcloth with me. Now, what to do—go out dripping water all over the place? Just as I began to wash the shampoo out of my eyes, a dry washcloth fell onto my hand. At first, I didn't think too much about that, but as I cleared my eyes, I was startled to see a small, dark-haired boy about nine on the other side of the glass shower door. Still, I knew those spirit children were around, so it didn't scare me. I finished showering and then came out to dry myself off, but the boy was long gone.

"At another time, I saw his older sister, who wore her blonde hair in ringlets, and another time, I spotted their younger brother, maybe about five, who wore brown knickers and a brown vest. I often heard music echoing through our house, though I never could discover its source. I also know my little dog heard and saw things in the old house too. It was as if there was another happy family living there alongside my husband and myself.

"It was a big house and costly to maintain, and we knew we couldn't afford to fully restore its Victorian elegance, so we put it up for sale. Sometime before we moved, however, I began to notice dark shapes moving through the house, but they vanished if one looked directly at them. Our living room began to feel uncomfortable and a visiting friend, who spent the night in that room, told me of suddenly feeling an icy cold draft there. And when she awoke, she saw a dark figure with what she called 'soulless eyes' staring at her from the foot of the sofa sleeper. At times, when I roamed the upstairs, it was as if I could imagine a huge portal up there where spirits entered the house at will. Because we were going to move, I didn't do anything about that; I mean, no exorcism or such.

"And the new family who bought and restored the building, have reported no incidents at all. One curious thing, though. When we moved out, I seem to have carried many of the sounds and voices with me, as if they wanted to leave with us. I got help from a physician, who gave me some medication, and that world hasn't moved into our new house." Because Cheryl is obviously psychic, sensitive and receptive, I shared with her some of my stories about others who "took something with them" when they moved.

Cheryl now works from home in her newer 1963 house, where she loves selling clothing and helping people prepare for exciting events, though most of her biggest excitement was left behind. "From time to time, I do see little spurts of energy in this house, almost like cats' spirits. If I look directly at them, they disappear." Then she laughed when I asked her about the strangest events at her new house. "Well, one night I awoke to see a man dressed like a hobo slowly drifting through the air. He looked at me and waved, but kept right on going, and I haven't seen him again—wonder who he was and where he was traveling to?"

This seems to be the story of a woman who was very sensitive, even as a child, and when she moved into a house thus open to paranormal events, she had many, many new and more powerful experiences. Now that she has left Nana's house, she has a more modern home. But her native sensitivity still opens from time to time, beckoning her to remember times gone by.

A few months later, when I stopped to photograph the old house, I was fortunate to find Jim and Betsy Scheffel, the new owners, at home. "We don't experience the things that Cheryl did," Betsy said, "but we have visitors who occasionally hear the children." Maybe that is the way it should be, with each owner of the house hearing what they are most comfortable with, I concluded.

Grandfather

In the late 1960s, a man I'll call Bill Sayles operated a liquor store on Water Street in Newburgh. "He lived downstairs under us when we lived in the Heights area of the city," remembers his granddaughter Irene. "I was his beloved grandchild and always enjoyed seeing him and chatting with Grandfather in the morning before I went to school and he went off to his job.

"One winter night in 1969, when I was 13, he didn't return home on time, and when it grew late, my dad, an ex-cop, went down to the store. He found the street door open and entered, only to discover Grandfather badly wounded and lying unconscious on the floor. A wrapped bottle of liquor stood on the counter, but no robbery seemed to have taken place. Apparently, the robber or robbers must have panicked and fled after shooting my grandfather. Dad called the ambulance and Grandpa, who was 68, was rushed to St. Francis Hospital in Poughkeepsie. He lingered a short time and then died on New Year's Day of 1970.

"I was filled with grief and had a hard time accepting that he was gone. Eventually, two guys were arrested and ordered to stand trial for the robbery and murder, but that didn't make me feel any better."

But then, Irene told me, just a few days after her grandfather's funeral, she was surprised to hear the downstairs toilet flush in Grandpa's apartment, just as it had done when Grandpa was alive. Shortly after that came the sound of a downstairs door slamming. How could that be? she asked herself—the apartment was empty; Grandpa had died. Over the next few weeks, the sounds that Grandpa had made daily echoed from below. Footsteps resounded from downstairs and kitchen cabinet doors could sometimes be heard banging, yet, the apartment was locked!

"Then, the two robbers went on trial. They weren't convicted, however, because there had been no eyewitnesses and there were other legal technicalities. When the trial ended, so did the sounds from Grandpa's apartment. Apparently, he realized that all that could be done had been done, and knowing that his old home was in good and loving hands, he went on into Heaven to see what came next," she told me.

As we discussed the brief but poignant story, I told Irene that such leave-takings are more often the rule than the exception. Many individuals who hadn't intended to die suddenly or violently seem to need some time to accustom themselves to remaining alive, though not having a body. And, in this way, I suspect, most of us will need a bit of adjustment to new conditions as we prepare to move further into Eternal Life.

The Big House

"My grandparents had a large, forty-acre farm near Saranac, New York, in the Riverview section," Maureen told me. "Their large home was old when they bought it. Our family's house, however, was a smaller building, which we called 'The Little House' on the edge of my grandparents' land. Growing up there, I had a strong connection to family, as we went to a small one-room school not far from the Big House. My sister and I were the third generation of the family to live on the property.

"Ghost stories were not unusual in our family, and I remember, as a child, walking in the nearby woods with my cousins, sharing the strange stories passed down by our mothers from the family's past. Some of my aunts were probably psychic, I have since come to understand. I never had any doubt about the truth of those stories that we heard, though we never heard any from Grandma," she told me.

Maureen said that her grandparents often left the Big House for several months each year to visit family in other areas, so their house sometimes sat empty and alone. It was during one of those periods that this story tells about. "When my sister, Sheila, and I were fifteen and sixteen," she said, "we had to do intense review for the upcoming State Regents exams in French and geometry, and our parents said it would be okay for us to go to the vacant Big House to do our study. It was agreed that we'd fall into bed when tired, then awake ourselves in the morning to catch the school bus. Because Sheila and I were good students, we were excited to be 'grown up' enough to be trusted to do our own study."

She told me how their excitement continued as the sisters drove up the hill to the Big House with their load of schoolbooks. At the kitchen table, they settled in for a long evening of studying formulas, proofs, and French conjugations. Finally tired out, they went to bed upstairs in Grandma's bedroom. Morning seemed to arrive too quickly, but they did catch the bus to school. The first night of study had gone fine.

The next night, as the girls left the kitchen at the Little House and hurried over to Grandma's, they ascended the driveway sensing that something was markedly changed. "I was filled with a sinking dread," Maureen continued, "and forty years later, I can still re-experience the tightness in my gut, the shortness of breath, and the weight on my shoulders. Small hairs on my neck were stirring and my heart seemed barely able to beat. What was wrong? What had changed? The big, old house seemed strangely darker than usual, almost as if a terrible tension was emanating from the building, but I didn't mention my dread to Sheila.

"I tried to overcome my unease by concentrating on our new freedom to study away from the blaring television at home; I was now a grown up, after all. The two of us focused intently on our studies, but I knew I was in no hurry to go upstairs to bed. When we got too tired to concentrate, Sheila decided it was bedtime, so I followed her up the stairs. I was amazed that, despite my uneasiness, I could still make my legs move toward and through the living room—it was almost a paralysis. Upstairs, I dropped my jeans and hopped into bed, not taking time to don my pajamas.

"My sister and I tucked in and lay silent for about five minutes; suddenly, Sheila asked, 'Do you want to go?' I readily agreed, jumped out of bed, got dressed, and we started through the hallway and down the stairs toward the living room. Apprehensively, I leaned over the banister as we descended and became certain that the living room was filled with spirit entities. As we entered the room, nothing or no one was visible but the feelings of being watched, even inspected, were powerful, and it was as if the spirits only grudgingly gave way to let us pass. How could this be? This was Grandma's house! As we hurried through the kitchen, where we gathered up our books and papers, the energies were less palpable, but we hurried to the car and drove quickly to the safety of the Little House."

At home later, the two sisters compared notes. Though each had at first remained silent about their sensations, it seemed that they had experienced the same thoughts and feelings at Grandma's. So many of those childhood stories told by their cousins' mother and their own mother came back into sharp focus. "Sheila and I came away from that experience amazed that we weren't imagining the phenomena; we had both had the same sensations at the same times and places there.

"Years later, Mom stayed with her aging parents in the Big House, caring for them, but if she had any frights, she never disclosed them to us. The people living there in the Big House today have never commented on any concerns, so what was it?"

As we talked, Maureen and I determined that her grandparents were not the original owners of the house, so whatever negative energies she and her sister ran into may have arisen from those first owners, or perhaps from a Native American activity predating the arrival of the whites. Very few pieces of property come with a record of all the physical and emotional activities that have taken place there since the earliest settler days, so sleuthing for ghosts' identities is my joy.

It is possible also, when two adolescent girls are the main life energy in a building, that they acquire a reinforced sensitivity to subtle or long-dormant energies. There are stories where ghosts interact only with children, or men, or just with women. "One of my aunts later disclosed that, seven years before Sheila's and my experience, she had heard a bed creaking in an unoccupied room, which scared her," Maureen remembered. One also has to write off the suspicion that what Maureen and Sheila encountered was some form of hysteria or that they had anticipated something scary there. At the outset, both were grounded and serious about schoolwork. Also, Grandma's house had always been a place of comfort and safety. We searched in vain for any frightening event that could have predisposed the girls to fright. As it was, it still is unexplainable, thought the sensation of "others" was very strong, and it was the first such event in the girls' lives.

As I've written before, though a writer would love to wrap up a story with a likely, convincing solution, many times the exploration of a ghost story leaves the reader or listener with more questions than answers.

Old Timers

In a span of two hundred years, most houses become patchworks of construction. Additions are created or old sections removed. Doorways and window openings can be changed, and rooms can be renovated, which changes their function. Such is the case with a wonderful old house outside Remsen, New York. Edward and Emily have lived there for ten or more years now, and are gradually uncovering the renovations made by previous owners. Not only those changes, but in some cases, the individuals who made them seem to remain or visit from time to time.

"The upstairs is a long space with three rooms, one leading into the next," Emily told me. "Our bedroom is on the end and the center bedroom, where the baby sleeps, comes next, then our son's room is on the other end. Most of the time we keep the door to the baby's room open, just so we can check on her during the night. Six years ago, I was napping in the afternoon with the blinds closed, and Edward was downstairs. When I lay down, of course, I had taken my glasses off, so I couldn't see clearly, and at one point I roused just enough to glance toward the baby's doorway and saw a shadowy figure there. Figuring it was Edward, I rolled over and went to sleep. It couldn't have been five minutes later that the baby began to cry. I looked, but Edward wasn't there. Fine thing! I sputtered to myself—he came up and woke the baby. So I went in and picked her up and walked her.

"I went downstairs, where he was working at the computer. 'Why'd you come up and wake the baby?' I demanded. 'Emily, I haven't moved from this chair for hours,' he told me. Then, who had come upstairs? It certainly had been an adult shape," she concluded.

Several times she has heard footsteps walking from her son's room and into the baby's room, even when she knows her son isn't in the upstairs. It has been puzzling at best and quite frustrating at its worst, she told me. There are both front and back stairways to the upstairs, so she guesses that if there was another person in the house, they might have gone back down the other stairs. But the problem is, there hasn't been any other adult in the house at the time of hearing the footsteps.

In 2003 a friend came to babysit for the baby and took a nap on Emily's bed. When she returned home, the friend told Emily of seeing a woman in a long gown going down the stairs as she dozed. Who was it?

Exploring an old house often can be fun, and sometimes is rewarding. In late 2004, as she and Edward explored the barn, they discovered an old photo of a middle-aged woman on a shelf, and brought it into the house. "It was a tough time, as we were having a run of bad luck, but I tell you, immediately after we brought that photo inside, things turned around for us in a major way. So we framed that lady's picture." Then, in 2005, as she repainted the room, Emily took the framed photo down for a while. And again, family income turned downward, so she hurried to hang it up again. In doing so, Emily noticed vague writing on the back of the picture, some inscription that might be read as "Black" or "Bertha." Later, she searched the Remsen area cemeteries and discovered no burials of a family named Black, though there were several Berthas.

There is also a small apartment off the kitchen, and Emily's sister-in-law stayed there late in 2006. Before long, however, she asked Emily whose voices she was hearing in her rooms. There was no logical answer for that puzzle, nor was it easy to understand who the woman had heard giggling outside her bedroom. Shortly afterward, Edward related hearing a female giggle as he sat in the living room. There seemed to be no other conclusion than that a ghost was present, so the two women attempted to get some evidence of the presence. Emily knew that the present apartment had once been a woodshed, then was renovated, as was the attic space above it. They set up a tape recorder, as they knew of EVP (electronic voice phenomena). On the one tape that showed anything at all, there is a lot of background noise and a few vague, unintelligible voices. But there is also one short segment of the tape in which a distinct male voice is heard to laugh, "Ha, ha!" An energy memory from some past event?

The pair then did some research on the house's history—had the building been the scene of any memorable parties? In fact, they found that it had, as a former owner (termed a "socialite" in an old newspaper story) was recorded as dying there at age forty.

Then, Emily heard of a local man, Russell, who is something of an expert in taking photographs of ghosts and is also gaining psychic ability to tune in on haunted sites. Russ was happy to oblige and came to the old house, taking some pictures and sharing with Emily some of his intuition. She told him of having taken a photo a week before, which showed an orb outside the front picture window. Russ took his own pictures, some of which showed a mist outside the house, and in that mist were several images that resembled human faces—one being very lifelike, though appearing in black and white tones. Also, in that imagery, Russ spotted a dog. "It seems to be an Afghan hound," he told her. "Here in the southern Adirondacks?" she puzzled. Afghans are not common in rural areas, as they are more show dogs. "I think you are wrong, Russ," she said, but agreed to ask questions of the neighbors.

It wasn't long before a neighbor remembered that, yes, the previous owners indeed had an Afghan! Russ's interpretation of the photo was correct. So, was there also a ghost dog to go with the mysterious ghostly male? Russ couldn't have known that, soon after Edward and Emily had moved into the house, Edward's mother had seen a woman's and small girl's spirits wearing long gowns in an upstairs bedroom. Now Russ, visiting that room unaware, spotted an older woman's spirit there, about age seventy, he guessed. Then he saw a shorter figure with dark hair. He interpreted the child to be the older woman's servant.

"She is showing me a brick fireplace here," Russ continued, "between the kitchen and dining room," though the room currently has none. Emily remembered that wall had once faced the house exterior before the addition was put on, so it seemed possible that a fireplace may once have stood there. "She seems to live in this room and shows me porcelain dolls and images of a special horse in a stable outside," he continued. Then, "Now she shows me an image of a small window with the walls angling down on either side of it." Emily immediately recognized his description of an attic window overhead, in a space that Russ hadn't yet entered. When he got there, Russ also spotted a male figure with red hair who didn't move.

"I get the woman's name 'Karen,'" he went on. "As far as I know, there has been no Karen associated with this house in the past, though there was a Katherine who lived here once," Emily told me. Her research has turned up information that Katherine lived there from about 1828-1868, before the addition was built. She was quite well-to-do for an immigrant from Wales, and her family is buried in the nearby cemetery. Russ also intuited a servant girl there who had a friend named Sarah.

Getting used to their home of ten years has been both enjoyable and a bit strange, Emily said. "Edward has many times heard giggles in the house when our kids are either sleeping or not home. Once, while I was in the shower, I heard a child's voice call out, 'Mama!' Is there a ghost child, then, along with the ghost woman and ghost dog?" Emily gave a big smile. "It's not really scary, but it is so puzzling. Our children are old enough to have very vivid dreams. One morning, my daughter told me of having dreamed of a man with dark hair who identified himself as a schoolteacher. And our son dreamed of a character named Hank standing by a fireplace, followed by a fire breaking out and burning him. "I discovered that a W. Howard Richards once lived here around 1900, a man who liked parties. Is it possible that his friends might have called him 'Hank'? What do you make of all that?" she asked.

For individuals who are dead to this world, the phenomena continue, leading Emily to consider the spirits as almost alive. She noted that when her sister-in-law moved out, things calmed down a bit, but then she herself heard a giggle on the kitchen stairs when she was in the attic. She looked down the steps and spotted the cat playing...with somebody.

As with most ongoing experiences of hauntings, I urged her to continue to take notes and compile more of the house's history that seems to keep playing out in the 21st Century. Nobody has been harmed at the old house, and maybe some remaining energy or consciousness of the former owners is attempting to educate the family about the building's past.

Up and Down

The two-story house at 78 Hoffman Street in Kingston doesn't look very different from its neighbors, but one former resident discovered it to be a structural history book, filled with beings from the past who haven't yet moved on.

Joe and Helen Dempsey lived in the house's downstairs for much of their lives, and raised a family there, having inherited the house from Joe's grandfather, Patrick Dempsey. Joe and Helen worked hard and Maureen's parents (Gerald and Jackie Dempsey) moved in upstairs after their 1973 marriage. "I grew

78 Hoffman Street

up there with my sister, Christine," Maureen told me. "As the oldest girl, I was probably the first to notice what appeared to be a long, white dress floating through the second floor hallways. When I finally got up the nerve to ask my parents about the sight, they laughed, and told me it was only Grandfather Joe's mother, Mary, who had died in the upstairs years before my birth. Instead of going to Heaven, she seemed to prefer continuing the daily life that she enjoyed there in the early 1900s. They weren't afraid, so I wasn't either," she told me. When Christine was four, she, also, spotted the filmy figure moving and asked about it, so I told her what my parents said, and that seemed to end her curiosity.

"As I grew older, however, the phenomenon really puzzled me. As Irish-Americans, we always took it for granted that a person went either directly to Heaven, or elsewhere, when they died. There wasn't any in-between world, so how and why could my ancestors still cling to the old house? Of course, my parents couldn't explain it, but Dad remembered some odd events from his growing-up years there. In childhood, he and his two sisters often awoke at night with some unseen person tapping them on the shoulder. No living person was ever there, even when they awoke to the bedside light turning itself on. At first, the three siblings thought it was one of the others pulling a prank, but when it became clear this wasn't the case, they just accepted it as an unexplained event and never brought it up again."

As a young adult, Maureen heard another strange story about the house from her father. Grandfather Joseph, it seems, had almost a conscious link to the other side, and would often close his bedroom door at night to talk to his deceased mother. "We weren't allowed to disturb him or ask about it," Gerald told his daughter, "but my family could hear him chatting away inside the room, though they could never make out what he was saying." As I heard this, I wondered if Grandfather's conversational link hadn't encouraged Great-Grandmother Mary to hang around even after her son passed away, perhaps on the assumption that if he needed her advice, maybe the other Dempseys would too.

"When Dad's parents (Joseph and Helen) died in 1989, the downstairs was vacant for quite a while. In our upstairs apartment, the white dress apparitions became more frequent and the spirit dress seemed more opaque," Maureen remembers. It was as if the invisible person needed their increased attention, though they couldn't figure out why.

Needing an absolutely quiet place to study her college courses, Maureen used the downstairs kitchen for a reading place, and eventually, Christine found it was a good spot for her to study in. "It was a strange set-up," she told me, "with two kitchens. Christine and I studied in the front kitchen, but one day, a movement in the rear kitchen caught our eye—the wall lamp back there suddenly turned itself on. How did that happen? I wondered. All I could remember about that particular spot was that Grandpa used to sit beneath that light and listen to his baseball games on the radio. The hair on the back of my neck rose up and I got goose bumps, but I chose to be cool, and just walked back there and turned off the switch. That should do it, I reasoned.

"I returned to my study, but a few minutes later, the light came on again, and Christine got really scared because of that. I walked back to examine the back door and found it locked, as were the windows; nobody could have gotten in to play a prank on us. What the heck, I decided, and left it turned on. Five minutes later it turned itself off. Was someone trying to get our attention, and, if so, why? Nevertheless, it was spooky, so my sis and I packed up our books and papers and ran upstairs. My mother said it probably would be wise just to avoid the downstairs for a while and study upstairs, where she'd promise to keep it quiet."

Family life for the Dempseys resumed without incident for at least several weeks more. But with only one bathroom in the upstairs apartment, schedules often didn't mesh, and Maureen's dad, Gerald, decided to use the downstairs bathroom one day. "When he returned and found Mom, Sis and I watching television, he got huffy and asked which of us had come down and banged on the bathroom door three times. The three of us all told him we'd been upstairs, and he was imagining things, so he agreed, and things returned to normal.

"A month later, however, it happened to me. I was in the downstairs bathroom when somebody rapped three times on the door. I yelled out, 'Please wait. I'll be right out!' Then, two minutes later, it happened again. So I got up and quickly opened the door, but the downstairs was absolutely quiet, and of course, nobody was in sight. When I returned upstairs, the rest of the family was playing cards. Even so, I asked who had come down and knocked on the door. They gave me the strangest look, so we concluded that it was the ghost again. Not long after that experience, we moved to a new house."

Her aunt retained the house and began to make renovations. In less than a week, the workman, who was staying in the downstairs apartment until the job was finished, abruptly quit. He claimed to have awakened in the night to see a mustached man standing over his bed, checking the time on a pocket watch which he took from his vest pocket. "That old guy looked so serious," was all the workman would say. We considered that it might have been Grandpa Dempsey, but didn't tell him that. So, our family sold the house "as is" in the early 1990s and the Hoffman Street stories ended.

"But then, you see, I moved to an apartment on South Clinton Avenue," Maureen told me, "and I had some new experiences!" She lived there peacefully with her boyfriend for almost eleven years until the first episode in fall 2006. Then she began to notice a slight movement out of the corner of her eye as she worked at her computer. Eventually, she spied more detail and was surprised at what she saw. "Twice I've seen a man standing between the kitchen and living room. All he does is look at me with an intense stare. He wears a cowboy hat and dirty brown pants and shirt, and has a mustache. Whoever he is and whatever causes him to stare at me, I don't know, but I feel the power in that piercing glance. Even so, when it happens, I just act cool and pretend I don't see or experience anything.

"Then, in March of 2007, my boyfriend died and I was alone. What happened next probably wasn't the cowboy's doing, I think, and probably it was my boyfriend's energy. When brushing my teeth in front of the bathroom mirror, I noticed the lights flickering and looked around. There was no bright sun outside and no reflections from the street. The first time this happened, I turned out the light and left the room, and then came back a half-hour later, flipped the switch, and turned the lights on. There was no more flickering right then, but since, it goes through a flickering routine at least once a week.

"One day, I mentioned it to my neighbor downstairs, a guy who was one of my boyfriend's friends. He was surprised at my story, as he, too, has had that experience. But then, in June of 2007, he moved out. With what might have been a short circuit taking place, I asked my landlord to check the building's wiring, but he found nothing wrong. So, the next time it occurred, I talked to the energy, saying 'hello' and 'I can see what you are doing.' That's when it stopped." As readers know, all that many departed spirits usually want is for us to acknowledge that they still exist, then they can depart. Maybe they are just double-checking their perceptions, so if we will interact with them, then they know they exist and can continue on, perhaps exploring what appears to be their new environment. There is a very good chance that the flickering was Maureen's boyfriend sending a last message, both to her and to the downstairs friend.

In the process of discussing the building with her landlord, she discovered that the South Clinton Avenue building played quite an active role in the city's Prohibition days. Apparently, there was a "speakeasy" in the cellar, where alcohol was illegally sold to those deemed trustworthy by the former owners. The landlord told her of noted gangsters and smugglers frequenting the place during the 1920s, and of a rumor that the bar patrons were supplied by a pipeline that ran from the milk factory on O'Neil Street, and another that ran from or to the present YMCA building on Broadway. As violence was often a part of the illegal distribution of booze, perhaps there is more in the building's history that might explain the cowboy character and his disreputable appearance, but Maureen and I agree that we'll take the romantic route to understanding the flickering lights.

Our own "lights" will flicker out one day, that is one of the sure things in life. Yet, from the great number of ghost stories (I, myself, have done over 900 interviews to date.) we can be sure that even individuals who die in a troubled state make the journey to the next world when they are ready, though some move very reluctantly and very slowly.

In the future, Maureen may have new experiences to relate, as she seems quite sensitive to "others" who have chosen to remain behind, at least for the time being. How about the old house on Hoffman Street? I stopped by one day to photograph the house, now owned by artist Charles B. Barnett III, and asked him about strange events. He gave me a quizzical look. "Here?" he asked in surprise. "Nothing abnormal has happened here since I bought the place. All that is here is me and my inspirations," he smiled. That was good enough for me, as it seems that Maureen was tuned to a "different level of reality" than many less-talented people are.

Rejoined

Lynne's father died in 1964 when she was eight years old and living in Queens Village in the Borough of Queens. It was a shock to the third grader to suddenly be without a loving parent, so, she told me, it seemed like a dream when his smiling face first appeared to her at night. "Back then, when he came to me in the night, I thought I was dreaming. Children don't have a big enough vocabulary to express the nuances of different nighttime experiences so, if it happened when I was in bed, it had to be a dream. That was also my conclusion," she said, "the second time he visited me. Looking back on over a half-century of life and experiences since then, I know those weren't dreams.

"In 1976, my son Christopher was born. He was such a joy, and my mother's first grandchild. My mother was a very independent woman, so when Christopher got old enough she would take him places. She thrilled to each of his accomplishments and enjoyed each new achievement through his growing-up years. 'I'm not leaving this earth,' she used to say, 'until Christopher graduates from high school.' She'd grin, but despite her occasional bouts with illness, we knew she was serious. When Christopher neared the end of his senior year, Mom had to go to the hospital, then from there to a rehabilitation facility. Was she failing? I wondered. Will she reach her goal of seeing Christopher graduate? Then, it happened again.

"One night in the middle of June, I awoke suddenly to someone shaking my arm. What emergency was this? I wondered, quickly coming to my senses and sitting up in bed. And there was Dad, just the way I remembered him! This time, however, he wasn't smiling much. He told me that he loved Mom so much and hated to see her bedridden in a rehab facility, so he was going to take her with him. Not at all frightened by his sudden reappearance, I cautioned him with the story about Mom's often-stated desire to see Christopher graduate. Suddenly he vanished, but came back the next week, with graduation only days away. Again, I told him that Mom wouldn't go, because it was so important for her to see her grandson graduate. Tuesday, June 28th, finally came and Christopher graduated. Mom was so proud of her first grandson and we all celebrated.

"But Thursday morning about five a.m. the nurse could not waken my mother. She was in a coma. Then the phone call came from the hospital about six a.m. telling me Mom had been taken to the hospital. The doctors surmised that during the night an aneurysm had burst and it was just a matter of time. She died at one p.m. on Thursday, June 30, 1994. Thursday night after all the funeral arrangements had been made I was tired and went to bed, but during the night, someone woke me up. This time it was both my parents. Then I saw them both with my father's arm around my mother's shoulders, standing at the foot of my bed, smiling and so happy. They had been apart for thirty years and now were reunited. They were glowing." She smiled, then added, "They still come to visit me from time to time, just to see how things are going. I couldn't be happier for them." I told Lynne that this single event was definitely an example of how our loved ones watch over us after their passing. It clearly was an experience of a lifetime.

"But wait, there's more," she smiled. "During my second marriage, I had a second son, John, who was only three when we moved into this new house in Bellerose Manor. One morning he came down to breakfast saying that he was unhappy and wanted to go home—back to our old apartment. He said that there was a man in his bedroom, a man who said his name was 'Grandpa.' John couldn't have known my father, who had died in 1964, and hadn't even seen photos of him, but I asked my son to describe the man who had visited him. I thought it might be my husband's father, but no, John said the man had 'light eyes,' and my dad's eyes were blue. John described my dad to a tee, so I explained to him that even when some family members have passed away they sometimes drop in to let us know that they are still watching over us and they are never far away from our thoughts.

"It wasn't long afterward, though, that John had another story. While watching me iron in the cellar, he thought that someone was watching us. I told him I have seen a man, dressed in a brown jacket and dark pants, out of the corner of my eye. That sure wasn't my dad or even my husband's father, so who had come to live with us? Was it some former owner of the house? I just wish while he's downstairs he could at least do some ironing.

"Not too long after that, while I was instant-messaging a Connecticut friend named Ellie, telling her of little John's vision. Ellie got a phone call and asked me to hold on a minute. The call, it turned out, was from one of her California friends who is psychic. Apparently Ellie mentioned our conversation of the moment to the California woman, who advised Ellie to Instant Message me to go downstairs with my digital camera and take five photos. I did as the woman suggested, not knowing the purpose of it all. Looking through the photo file I spotted a single bright orb in the fourth picture, so I walked back upstairs to the phone and had Ellie relay that fact to her friend.

"The California psychic, hearing of the bright orb, told Ellie to tell me the man's name was Alex. That stumped me for a minute, as I thought I didn't know anyone by that name. But then, I suddenly remembered a distant relative of my husband's, a man by that name who had been missing for some time. Apparently, the man had died though his body had not yet been found, so he had come to us, as John was open to spirit visitations. Later, the body was discovered, and we had no more such sightings downstairs."

"Tell me more about John," I asked Lynne. "Is he still pretty sensitive?"

"Oh yes," she said while laughing. "A few days ago, just like in the old days, he came down to breakfast scratching his head. 'Mom, did you come into my bedroom this morning and whistle, then leave, closing the door?' I told him no. I think he knew it wasn't me, so maybe we have a new boarder," she chuckled. "We're going to have to see on that one. Maybe it's someone we can help."

How nice it is, if such be the case, that those who die alone and away from their loved ones, can find peace and be rejoined in heart and mind with those who remain behind. I believe that those individuals who help the dead rejoin with the living are especially blessed.

NEW YORK STATE GHOSTS

CHAPTER 8

GHOSTS IN RESTAURANTS HOTELS AND INNS

PRECIOUS RUBY'S
ALL AMERICAN
HARRY
PARKED
THE LONG FELLOW
THE LAKEVIEW
THE POND
TIP TOP CONDITION
HIDEOUT
MOLLY
NO PLACE LIKE IT
THE ORANGE INN
THIS BUD'S FOR YOU

Precious Ruby's

The Catskills can seem wild and filled with endless forests. Yet, just north of the Catskill State Park is the busy little Greene County vacation community of Freehold. And in that hamlet is a gem of a restaurant that is worth a visit for those seeking great food, good times, and perhaps (if you arrive at just the right time) and encounter with those who used to live or visit there. In my world there are no coincidences, so when I stumbled upon Ruby's Hotel while searching the internet, I knew I had to visit and explore.

Frank Sporer is a tile artist who creates wonderful Nigerian ceramic drums. He was drawn to Freehold by his first wife, who loved the old Meyers Hotel just west of the crossroads. It had been closed for twenty years when he first visited in 1999, "Yet, I knew it was a diamond in the rough," he told me. "Through the windows I could see the old art deco soda fountain from the 1920s, and behind that, through the dusty windows, I could make out a wonderful old bar, with a large dining room behind that. All the tables and chairs looked original when we inspected them in the attic, so I didn't know whether to make it a museum or a going business establishment. In any case, we bought it," he grinned.

"Not long afterward, my father-in-law drove by and spotted a dark-haired woman looking out the attic curtains," Ana told me. "We knew there were no inhabitants at all. Ever since, though we don't know her identity, we call her Ruby, a nickname that friends once gave me in college. Several visitors have since seen the woman with long dark hair strolling through the place, though we never find where she has gone. Thus we knew we had more history here than we had expected."

There are three serviceable guest rooms upstairs, though upon my visit, my group and I found many more hidden away places, all holding memories or energy from long ago. Frank told us that after his first marriage had ended, he met his current wife and chef, Ana, and as a chef in the Big Apple, she became excited at the prospect of bringing her New York City cuisine to the Catskills. "Even in 1999, when I arrived, I knew we had spirits, here," she told us, "as I could hear the frequent tromping of footsteps up the front stairs. Their steepness indicates that the building probably dates from the 1880s. All we had to do before opening our doors was to bring the original furniture down from upstairs, clean a bit and do some painting, which our young artist friend, Frank Broderick, helped with. Friends who stayed with us in those first years reported people walking in the hallways at night, though we all knew there was nobody else there.

Henry and Chilly Meyers had run the hotel for years, mainly to provide lodging and meals for summer visitors, but when they closed in the 1960s, everything was preserved, even the old neon sign that was repaired and reinstalled on today's hotel. What else has been retained in the building? Ana told me that there is a strange cocoanut scent that permeates the upstairs when the building is quiet, and she once heard a cat's meow up there, though the couple has no pet. When the upstairs renovations are completed and the guest rooms are ready to let, it should be interesting to hear what lodgers experience. "None of it is scary," Ana told us, "it is just that several time periods seem to overlap here. For instance, look at that red neon light over the soda bar. It's been there, working away for over sixty years!

"When we opened, Frank Broderick, who died in 2003, at age 28, was our bartender and helped with renovations. He had quickly become our friend and we missed him, so one day, after we had placed his photo over the bar, I stuck a candy bar behind it for him, where nobody could see. A few days later, I checked and it had disappeared," she laughed. "We named our new second-floor art gallery after him, and he seems to be a continuing presence, as doors are heard to open and close upstairs, though we aren't yet ready to rent those rooms. A week after his death, I had a vivid dream of Frank, and in that dream he told me he was reminiscing. I told him he couldn't do so, because he was dead, but he responded, 'No, I'm alive!' Several friends who have stayed over have had similar experiences with him.

That first phone interview with Frank and Ana was enough for me, and with sensitive friends Peter and Sue, I visited Ruby's on the occasion of the Broderick Art Gallery's opening, when drawings by B. Goode were on display. We'll just go and have a meal and see what we can pick up, we agreed, after all, it will be crowded. Hardly had we taken our dining room seats, though, than a young dusty-haired spirit man stood to my left in his waiter or bartender's apron. "Glad you like it," he communicated to me before he vanished.

On some level I'm sure we did like it. Frank had just finished explaining to us the history of the downstairs paintings, done by German prisoners of war in US Army prison camp where he father was chief of medical services in Aix en Provence, France, before the end of World War II. The prisoners had donated their work to Frank's dad, and they provided a bit of Continental charm to our dining room. But Peter visualized those artists at work.

"I get four to five men and two women sitting and working quietly, apparently not upset at the war's progress," he offered. "They discuss painting styles, though the women aren't painters, but only coupled with two of the Germans. Both women and men have no apparent interest in the war's outcome or politics, and are disgusted at the war's interference in their lives. A thin man of less than six feet in height, a bit of a know-it-all serves as the group's leader or spokesman."

Sue felt both male and female energy in a nearby corner of the dining room before the female left. The tall and slim male in the spirit world, she said, wants to be thought of as sophisticated or elegant, though he's from a simple background. "He laughs at us trying to understand him," Sue said quietly to our group, "and he continues, 'Good luck!' His connection is to this building, however, and not these paintings." she said, "and he wants to communicate that life is much more complicated than what we think. 'Your concepts of God are not what I have found them to be, as yours are too simplistic,' was the end of the figure's communication."

Our waitress arrived with the entrées, which were delicious, and we turned off our psychic receptors while the opening night crowd began to build in the bar and main dining room. Throughout the meal, however, I received a succession of names, such as Tony, Arthur, Karl and Arch or Archie. Were those names related to the prisoner painters or former residents or owners of the building? Or, as anyone who is intuitive must always self-examine, are these just my mind working overtime? After finishing our meals, we decided to visit the upstairs before the formalities began up there. The two main display rooms already had a dozen people circulating and commenting on B. Goode's works, marveling at the intricate details.

Peter said quietly that he was somewhat jostled by a younger spirit man behind him. "He seems proud of his upper body or shoulders, and by pushing me a bit, made his point, but also wanted us to know he was especially proud that with his physical prowess, he was yet capable of making such delicate painting strokes." Was this Frank Broderick? As yet, we had seen no photo of the man. "He has a girlfriend, Peter continued, but she takes a back seat to his painting, and I find him too self-absorbed. He was immediately upset that I wasn't paying enough attention to him, but then relaxed. I see him as a man of short life and flashes of annoyance."

Sue kept looking at a closed door in the second room, certain that someone was behind it. We later determined that the door opened onto a small stairs back into the lodging rooms, though when we got there, nobody was visible. As I strolled among the drawings, I received the image of a cleaning woman standing there and wondering what to do next. I don't believe she would have been in Frank and Ana's employ but, from the clothing style, must have been from the early 1900s. I mentally asked the apparently befuddled woman who she was, and she told me she was a farm wife employed there on some occasions.

That seemed to be it for the two gallery rooms, but then I found the door to the guest rooms slightly ajar. Crooking my finger to the others, I motioned them to join me. First, inside the door, was a maroon-painted room, available for Frank and Ana's friends, but not yet ready to rent. I sensed a man with a small mustache standing at the foot of the bed. He seemed to be a smoker and told me he was going to die; the doctors had told him to quit, but he refused. Though his appearance differed markedly from Broderick, Frank told me later that such was his old friend's attitude, and Broderick had died of respiratory failure. Peter and Sue, however felt the presence of a woman there. Sue felt the lady held the essence of the true Ruby-type, perhaps the image that Ruby's places on their business card—a vamp in furs, yet nobody's numbskull. Peter categorized the presence as "taking charge mentally and sexually, in charge of money or finances, though pleasant enough." In old hotels, with hundreds of past patrons, it is almost impossible to identify the individual spirits.

Each of those rooms in the rear of the really large building (though, from the street, Ruby's seems rather small) had its energies or memories, but none of the others seemed very strong. In a back (green) bedroom, I received the image of a dejected balding man, seated and worrying about his "accounts." Also I got the name Ethel, who seems to have died there, or just after visiting there somewhere in the past.

Returning to the gallery, Peter felt his "strong man" from fifteen minutes before used to have a desk to the left of the gallery arch, a place from which to look out at Basic Creek which flowed outside. We later confirmed with Frank Sporer that there used to be a vanity there, and it is likely that Frank Broderick would have enjoyed the quietly-flowing stream below.

As we prepared to leave, Frank Sporer told us of their opening night, when a large Broderick painting had been re-hung to face all visitors entering the front door. "It suddenly crashed down onto the floor, yet, when we inspected it, there was noting wrong with the hanging wire, and neither was anything amiss with the hanging nail on the wall. Had Frank Broderick signaled his displeasure with its placement? We took it back to where the dead artist had originally hung it."

Though it was gallery-opening night and both the gallery and dining rooms were now filled to capacity with happy revelers, Frank still found time to de-brief us, validating many of the sensations that we had experienced, though many of these may never be verified. Still, I was impressed that our group could maintain an inner quiet as we moved among all the visitors. Frank opened another small room for us and showed a photo of Frank Broderick, which seemed to portray a heavier version of the aproned man who greeted me in the dining room.

When all is said and done, however, this isn't just the story of ghosts. It is the tale of a vibrant business that has helped reinvigorate Freehold, one that caters to urban visitors and locals alike. It is a place of entertainment and culture and of good times for city people and suburbanites alike. The past is simply present here, whether it is apparent or not.

Though the gallery exhibits may change, and Ana will certainly create imaginative and innovative entrees for the menu, these cannot replace, but only will add to the century and a half of art deco charm. When you come to dinner, do walk upstairs and say Hi to Frank Broderick, who is likely still mulling the decisions that he made in his brief life, and also probably plotting how to inspire lovers of the arts who visit. Look for the neon sign, the happy, chatting people and the filled parking lot when you come to this small village—you've found a jewel called Ruby's.

All American

Native Americans knew of the mineral springs long before white men formed the Town of Sharon in 1797. Magnesia, sulphur and chalybeate minerals surged to the surface in the fertile valleys of northern Schoharie County, attracting primarily German and Dutch settlers before the Revolution. Westward-moving New Englanders came next, and the first crossroads boarding house opened in 1825, permitting visitors and travelers to partake of the healing waters over a protracted stay. Then, as curious health-seekers thronged the resort, even larger hotels were constructed in the village before the Civil War. To the northeast, both Ballston Spa and Saratoga Springs were luring visitors with bigger hotels and gambling and/or horse racing, but those villages excluded Jews. Not so Sharon Springs, which welcomed all foreign and domestic visitors, and by 1900, European Jews found this Mohawk Valley village a peaceful haven for their desire to "be well."

By the early 1930s, however, local railroad service was suspended and the Depression hit full force, causing most of Sharon Springs' big hotels to close or fall dormant. A decade later, large, full-season hotels were no longer in vogue when World War II ended, and motels became the fashionable mode for vacation stay-overs. Sharon Springs lay almost abandoned as a vacation resort.

But then, in the early 1990s, the local historical society gained recognition for the weathered and abandoned old hotels. Much American history had been lived out in the valley, and a determined effort was made to save the remaining buildings and bathhouses from the past, even as they burned or collapsed under the weight of winter snowfalls. Additionally, new waves of eastern European Jews had arrived at America's shores and discovered the beautiful old buildings and springs, many of which are now being restored. Up-scale Americans visiting the Cooperstown area historic sites and the Glimmerglass Opera, also discovered the quaintness of Sharon Springs.

Among the most beautiful of the restored inns is the American Hotel, currently being renovated by Doug Plummer and Garth Roberts. The old hotel came to my attention when I learned from a friend that there were "other non-paying guests" in the old building. On the day of our appointment, the new owners welcomed me and my professional dowser friend, Bill Getz, in the early winter of 2007. "Go ahead, the building is yours," Doug and Garth said, "take your time and explore each floor." They smiled, as if hiding a secret that we would have to discover.

It was immediately clear that only the ground floor, dining room, bar and the second floor had been restored to a late 1800s décor. Bill, with his waggling dowsing rods went one way and I went the other. Was some long ago visitor still here? I asked myself. Or perhaps more than one? Before the day ended, we found ourselves immersed in many dramatic scenarios.

Scanning the bright dining room, Bill walked to a window table and got a reading of a woman spirit presenting herself as a fifty year-old, sitting at a no-longer-visible table. "I have the sense that she enjoys sitting here in the morning sun, watching people of long ago strolling to the stores and shops," he said. However, he was unable to communicate with her, and we chalked that experience up to a "building memory." We decided to visit the second floor restored rooms first.

The greatest amounts of energy seemed to be in Rooms #6 and #7. I felt "on" as I visited Room #6 alone. My mind's eye showed me a dark-haired woman in a maroon gown or housecoat stretched across a single bed, whose headboard was vastly different (much taller) from the present double bed. I sensed her depression and mentally asked her what was wrong. Her consciousness let me know that there was an impending death, so I asked whose. "I have just been diagnosed with uterine cancer and there's nothing they can do," was her response. Inclined as I am to doubt such intuitions, I asked Bill to come into #6 and take a reading with his dowsing rods. "The time period here is 1933," he told me, "and yes, there is a woman here, about forty-five."

As Bill provided a tentative confirmation, I crossed to that room's bathroom, getting the name "Stanley" as I walked, though I was unable to determine if that was a man's surname or given name. Intuitively, I knew the entity was interested in architecture, either as a career or an avocation. His consciousness expressed great concern over "the herring," but I couldn't decipher whether or not it was an entrée from a long-ago menu, and if so, whether or not it was cooked correctly. By now, it was clear to Bill and me that we were dealing with Jewish vacationers and, likely, a kosher menu.

Then I got the name "Dolfuss," though I knew we'd never be able to confirm that as the name of a hotel visitor because the old visitor registers no longer exist. As he crossed and recrossed the hallway, Bill got the impression of an affair taking place between a woman in #7 and a man in #6. Again, we ended up with more questions than answers, as we couldn't determine if Stanley and the dying woman in #6 were the participants or whether this was a long-vanished intrigue involving other guests.

Those were the most active energies on the second floor. Later, Doug told us that last year a woman psychic visited The American and also discovered much energy in #6, as had another male psychic. As an historian, I'm happier to discover a distinct troubled personality rather than just an anonymous and uncommunicative mass of energy. Knowing that others from yesteryear also struggled with overwhelming problems is somehow comforting in our own troubled times. Before we left Room #6, I instructed the dying woman that her pain and death had long ago concluded, and that she was now able to be pain-free if she wished to be. And that would permit her to now be "gathered to her ancestors." Bill and I encouraged her to release the depressing news of her vanished life in the flesh, look around, and discover the new eternal surroundings in which she has now surely been "healed."

We then opened the door to the third floor. Before we had entered the hotel that morning, Bill had spoken with Tony Daou, owner of the Black Cat Café, across the street. Tony recalled that he sometimes saw lights in the third floor of the hotel when it was closed, a fact that he reported to Garth and Doug. Now, Bill was anxious to see the electrical layout of the upstairs.

The top floor of the American Hotel is currently undergoing restoration and, though the floor is littered with broken plaster and strips of lath, new wiring is in place and a modern sprinkler system is operating. But the first thing Bill noticed was that there wasn't a single light bulb on the third floor. So what illumination was Tony seeing in the upstairs?

The third floor is a bright but currently unheated space, so it was cold on the day of our visit. We turned into a room at the left of the stair top and it seemed colder by at least twenty degrees than the hallway. Cold, of course, is oftentimes an indication of a spirit presence. My only sensation there was somebody's anxiety over money or finances; I couldn't perceive a defined personality. Bill's rods told him of a forty-five-year-old woman and another person aged sixty-four still clinging to that space in a long-gone era. He received a hint that one of the two had committed suicide, though not necessarily in this hotel.

Moving down the hall, Bill found a presence in the southeast corner end room, where he sensed a small writing desk which the entity likes. Across the hall, I sensed a small girl hiding behind the open door, fearful of what she called "an older man." It was unclear if the gentleman was a relative, spouse, or stranger. My sense was that she was a very young bride and that the marriage hadn't been her desire. Bill's dowsing rods confirmed at least the presence of this energy, but he was unable to determine the girl's identity. On the floor we found pages of a 1930s newspaper printed in Hebrew.

So, how much of this information could be refuted or confirmed? Our hosts didn't deny our suppositions and, in fact, offered some fascinating sidebar stories.

Doug was still puzzled over a recent problem with the hotel's showers, which had suddenly gone cold on January 14th. Investigating in the cellar, he had found the temperature gauge on the boiler turned to its lowest setting. "We'd never have done that, and nobody else goes in the cellar, so how can you explain that?" he asked. "We installed this modern system as part of our renovations and it has never done a self-change by itself. Then, just two days later, all our motion sensors in the cellar went off. Do you think there is an unseen energy moving down there?" he asked. Bill and I surmised that was the most logical conclusion, though a hard scientist would have a very hard time with that assumption.

Heidi, the receptionist, told of catching vague movements in the dining room when it is empty. "It really isn't a ghost, at least not what I think of as a ghost, anyway," she told us. "But it is a something." She also told us that a quickly disappearing man is sometimes seated at the bar when no bartender is present. Who could he be?

Garth then told us that two visitors in Room #3 as well as some of the hotel's employees have heard running on the third floor, but having just visited that level, Bill and I knew for sure that nobody could run up there—too many construction obstacles! Sometimes the running definitely sounds like a child's footfalls. "We had an American Indian psychic visit us not too long ago," Garth continued, "he was the first one to discern the energy in Room #6." The seer reported the spirits of many early 1900s guests, and apparently had a psychic conversation with one of them who reported just returning from the mineral baths.

"Also, we had a woman psychic visit here and she spotted a Jewish boy lying on a cot in a corner of Room #6, apparently bleeding. The woman experienced the anguish of the boy's father, as nothing could be done to save the child's life. Now, that woman could not have known that Doug and I discovered a cot with dried blood on it when we bought this hotel; she couldn't have known that."

What a fascinating "living history" museum the American Hotel is. Before we left, Bill's dowsing concluded that there were at least eight spirits currently in the building, probably reminiscing about personal traumas that are no longer known to the living. Within another year, the third floor should be ready for occupancy and we wondered what experiences the guests will have up there. We met Joe, a sous chef during the season, doing some of the renovations on the third floor, and asked him what his feelings were as he did his work. "The cold. The absolute cold," he said, "even in the summertime." I turned to Doug and joked, "Well, at least you can hold down your air conditioning costs."

Sometime soon, try a weekend stay in the old hotel that is becoming new again. The delicious, hot gourmet meals in the dining room are enough to offset any "other sensations" you might experience.

Harry's House

"You have to meet the Fosters," my friend Ed Gazel told me, "and you have to see their marvelous house!" Ed never steered me wrong yet, so, making an appointment by phone, I visited "Ruah," the Fosters' exquisite bed and breakfast inn in the Adirondack hamlet of Hague. The beautiful 1900 house sits on a knoll overlooking northern Lake George, and was the creation of artist Harry Watrous during the first four decades of the 20th century. Legend says that architect Sanford White contributed to the design.

Peter and Judy Foster welcomed me to an old home that is both Adirondack and country gentry in décor. Many of the antiques collected by former owners embellish the large dining and living rooms. "Tell me more about Harry Watrous," I asked. Smiling, Peter and Judy informed me that Watrous (1857-1940) had been a real character: a painter, world traveler and adventurer of sorts. Many of his early paintings were of idealized or seductive women, though he also did landscapes and still-lifes. His art schooling in early life had taken him to Paris, where he allegedly shot a man during an argument. Back in the United States and making a name for himself, Watrous married painter and author Elizabeth Snowden Nichols, and built the house in Hague on land that he had won in a card game.

In June, 1904, Harry repaid a prank by his friend, Col. William Mann, producer of a New York City scandal sheet. Determined to top Mann's Lake George "big fish" stunt, Watrous crafted a five-foot-long wooden monster's neck and head, fashioned from metal scraps, telephone line insulators and paint. He developed an intricate pulley system to permit his contraption to surface and swim across parts of Lake George, then dive out of sight before it could be photographed or fully inspected. "George," the lake serpent, was quite a tourist attraction, as Watrous installed it at several locations on the lake in subsequent summers. Later, in 1934, the entire adventure was revealed as tomfoolery. Harry's eyesight had slowly begun to fail after 1905, so he concentrated on producing mainly night scenes and landscapes. Another feature in his works was the occasional detailed image of insects or birds, especially crows and ravens.

"Do you think Harry's ghost is still here?" I asked the proprietors.

"Did you know that he shot and killed another man here?" Judy asked me. "In June, 1913, two local fellows got drunk and decided to burglarize this house one night. Hearing a noise around midnight, Harry grabbed his pistol and headed downstairs with a flashlight. He saw two forms moving in the dining room and one lunged at him. Harry fired twice and the man crumpled. The other dove through a window and fled. At the Ticonderoga hospital, a wounded Frank Cardinal, from Hudson Falls, confessed to the break-in before dying. In daylight, the other man's trail was followed and the burglar was discovered hiding in a shanty near Silver Bay. He turned out to be Frank's brother, Joseph, from Glens Falls.

At the coroner's inquest, Watrous was cleared of any wrongdoing, but the artist remained troubled by such a tragic ending to two young men's drunken misadventure. He hired an attorney for Cardinal, and the burglar received a suspended sentence. Then, against all odds, Frank Cardinal went to work at the Watrous estate, doing odd jobs and grounds-keeping for Watrous for many years afterward."

Harry was a complex man who enjoyed the night life around the small lake port village, where graphite was transported from the local mine to the Dixon Pencil Company plant in Ticonderoga. He and Elizabeth had separate bedrooms, and Harry often used a private exit at night to saunter to the horse barn, mount his steed and ride down to the local "watering holes," the better to inspect the local "models." The northern end of Lake George was far quieter after his passing in 1940.

The Guryan family then purchased Harry's "Camp Inn" and lived there for many summers. Phillip Guryan owned a company, Neuman Ticket Agency, a forerunner of the Ticketron Corporation. "So, we are just the third owners of this property," Judy told me. "Indirectly, we bought it from the Guryans, who were here over 40 years. Actually, our purchase contract was with Manhattan College, to whom Ann Guryan had willed the house and land after Phillip's death. Ann and Phillip had two sons, one of whom attended Manhattan College and was supposed to inherit the property, but the young man died in his twenties. When Ann became too infirm to care for the second son, Richard, a man with Down's Syndrome, she hired a woman named Betty as Richard's companion and nurse. Betty thought she was to inherit the estate but, because of an omission by Ann in her will, the house went instead to Manhattan College, and we bought it from them.

"As part of our purchase agreement, Peter and I agreed that Richard and Betty could come and spend a week each summer in this old house which he had known and loved so much. Peter and I used that week to visit in New York City," Judy told me, "though sometimes our son remained here in a room on the third floor during that period. One night in 1985, Betty called us at our downstate house, and she was boiling mad, telling us our son had locked himself in his room, turned up the stereo or television full blast, and that it was so loud that the noise could be heard out on Route 9N. I looked across our living room and there was my son, who had come down for a visit; so it wasn't him. I told Betty it must be a break-in of some sort and to call the State Police.

"An officer came and found the third floor bedroom door locked, so we told Betty to call Inge, our housekeeper in Hague, as she had room keys. Inge came, the policeman opened the door, and sure enough, the television was blaring—but there was nobody inside! Additionally, there were pillows strewn about the room, while one bed pillow had the impression of someone's head in it. A thorough search of the premises turned up nothing unusual. A few nights later, Betty called again with the same problem. 'Are you trying to scare us away?' Betty demanded angrily. Apparently, she feared we were going back on our agreement that Richard could visit each summer. Politely, I told her it was a police matter, and we loved having Richard visit his old home.

"A friend of ours had a memorial service in the Hague area, so one day, while Richard was staying in the former Guryan house, we came up for the service, and then dropped in to see Richard and Betty. There sat Richard on the couch, moving a non-operating electric shaver across his chin and conversing with someone that couldn't be seen. 'He's talking to his mother, he tells me,' Betty explained, though Ann Guryan was long dead. When I told Inge the story, she laughed. 'That's Ann, for sure,' our housekeeper said. 'She never liked Betty and is probably trying to drive her nuts so she'll leave!' That autumn, after Betty and Richard left, the young man died in Michigan, so the pair never came again. We wondered if Ann's spirit was responsible for the loud noises on the third floor."

"What is the strangest thing to happen here?" I asked Peter. He smiled and told me of finding a large painting in the attic when they bought the house in 1984. "It had the initials H.W. on the bottom, though the theme sure was unlike any Watrous works we had ever seen. There were serpent heads and gargoyles, and we thought it was something Harry had composed on a bad day, and had then banished it to the attic. It would have been nice to have an original Watrous (as these sell in the thousands if not hundreds of thousands of dollar range) but this wasn't anything we wanted our guests to see.

"Then we learned of Livingston, a Watrous relative on Nantucket, where we also have friends. So, we took the painting with us on a visit and delivered it to Livingston and Alicia, who were happy to have it, and they filled us in on some of the other facts about Harry Watrous' life. Afterward, when Livingston Watrous went to stow the painting in his car, he opened the back hatch, and suddenly a black crow swooped down from nowhere, lit on his shoulder and started pecking at his collar. Livingston put the painting inside while brushing the bird away. The bird then flew to the front windshield in front of Alicia, who was sitting inside, and hissed at her and kept pecking away at the windshield until they drove away. Livingston called the Fosters the next day and again thanked them for the painting, and then said, "That bird was just like Uncle Harry, always up to his pranks!" Okay, the Fosters thought, if they want to believe Harry was changed into a bird after his death, that's their right. Some months later, when Peter scanned a collection of old Watrous paintings in a book, he found an image showing a woman seated at her dressing table, while a black crow looked on. Hmmm, Peter thought. Black crows were then found to have appeared in several other Harry Watrous paintings.

In 2003, as she washed dishes, their housekeeper, Tracy, heard "What are you doing?" She turned to Judy Foster and answered, "I'm washing the dishes, of course." Judy looked up and asked, "What did you say, Tracy?" The domestic said that she was just responding to Judy's question. Judy hadn't asked any question, so whose was the female voice?

With the Betty issue resolved and Ann Guryan's spirit now apparently at peace, and with no evidence that (other than the crow appearance) Harry had remained on the earth plane, I asked if the house was now quiet. Judy laughed, telling me she and Peter had established a bed and breakfast there in 1995. She remembered a recent guest who came to breakfast inquiring if there were spirits in the house, as the man had seen a vague shape or shadow pass in front of a mirror in his room.

In another incident, a guest who had stayed several years before met Judy at the Glens Falls Hospital. In the conversation, the man, a physician, remembered that he'd never told the Fosters about being awakened by a loud crash during the night of his stay in Harry's former bedroom. Astonished, he had leapt from his bed, turned on the lights and found a painting (not one of Harry's) that had hung on the western wall of his bedroom, now leaning against the front, eastern wall. The picture was not harmed in any way, and upon examination, the man found the hanging wire intact and the hanger on the wall was still in place. Unable to comprehend the situation, he'd gone back to bed, and then forgot to tell the Fosters about the incident.

In early December 2006, I returned to the house, bringing my intuitive friend, Susan. As we crossed the verandah toward the front door, Susan received the strong impression that a woman in a light grey or blue dress had just crossed in front of her. "I think the dress is made of linen and is in an early 1900s style," Susan said, "and she is very refined." We wondered which of the former residents or visitors she might have been. I believed it was Mrs. Watrous.

Peter gave us an extensive tour of the house, and Susan had a powerful impression in Harry's old bedroom after Peter revealed the "picture frame" incident to her. Once he had related the picture tossing incident, Susan seemed to tune in on the who and why of that activity. "I sense a woman entering this room through the closet. She looks at the empty bed and swipes at the picture on the wall, sending it crashing against the room's front wall. There is a sense of frustration and anger in her, as if to say, 'He's gone out again!'" Peter then shared the story of Harry's nocturnal forays in search of models, and we concluded that the energy, when it does infrequently appear, must represent Elizabeth Watrous' rage at finding Harry off on one of his "scouting expeditions." Peter told us that he believed the present closet had once been part of a hallway extending between Harry's and Elizabeth's bedrooms. Photos in the Fosters' collection always show a plump Elizabeth Watrous appearing to hide from the camera's eye beneath her wide-brimmed hat. She certainly didn't resemble the lithe young women that Harry painted.

"There is another energy here, though I wouldn't call her an ongoing presence," Sue told us. In the northern second floor bedroom, with its beautiful view of Lake George, Susan experienced the feeling of ownership and a quiet satisfaction with the old house. "She isn't the woman I met on the front porch," Sue explained. Later, when Peter leafed through a photo album that he and Judy had created for the house's past, it seemed to the three of us that this "matronly woman" was a dead ringer for Ann Guryan. "She isn't here all the time," Sue said. "It's just like she occasionally returns, looks around and remembers, then moves on in confidence from her vantage point in eternity."

So, yes, there are occasional "situations," though no guest has run off in the night, and no more crashes or blaring televisions punctuate the night. I asked about the name of the place today, Ruah, as I knew it to be a Hebrew word for "spirit or energy" or even "Holy Spirit." The Fosters told me the name was an inspiration of their son, as he studied religious scriptures in college. Spirit—yes, that's for sure. Harry's inspiration and energy abound in the painting-filled living room. On the cold day when I first visited Ruah B&B, a cheery fire burned in the large fieldstone fireplace. Traffic down the hill on Route 9 had dwindled from its summertime frenzy. And maybe, just maybe, the kind spirit of Ann Guryan visits on occasion, seeking assurance that Betty hasn't returned.

Open all year, Ruah is best enjoyed in the dead cold of winter or in the fragrant last days of spring. If there are spirits about, those would be the times they would want to kick up their heels.

Parked

Concluding research on several ghosts in central New York State, I headed south to Hammondsport, at the southern end of Keuka Lake. I mulled my acquaintance with a village native, Robert (Gus) Tillman, a classmate of mine at the State University in Albany a half century ago. Another alumnus had told me last year that Gus had died, but like me, had taken an interest in history and had written a book or two in his later years. It brought back nice memories of our freshman year in 1955.

I soon arrived in Hammondsport, home of American aviation pioneer Glenn Curtiss, to follow up on a lead at the Park Inn, suitably located on the village park. When I entered the building, I already knew that there was reputed to be at least one spirit lodging there, and maybe two. The establishment has catered to travelers since 1861, though it has been partially modernized today. Twelve original rooms have been combined into five two-room suites, decorated in an antique quilt and furniture theme today. When unpacked, I entered the large dining room and, because it was still early, I enjoyed relative solitude, though I thought I saw a husky man with jet black hair by the front window. Later, I thought I saw a vanishing woman in a Twenties house dress as she stood in the large dining room doorway wringing her hands. Maybe she expected more diners at that time of afternoon, so her concern seemed to be financial. And an intuitive, such as I am, never can be quite certain where the images come from, or if they are, in this world's language, "real."

Learning that Carla, the barkeep, was a custodian of many of the establishment's strange stories, I waited until most of the regulars had departed for the evening, then introduced myself. When I told her my goal, she gave a half-smile that many witnesses exhibit, almost as if they aren't sure their story will be believed. "Right back there," she said, pointing to a room between the bar and kitchen, "that's where the icy chills happen—not every time I walk through, but a good deal of the time. Sudden icy cold is a ghost experience isn't it?" she asked. I assured her it was, especially when it happens on a warm day.

Overhearing our offbeat conversation, Bill Fries, one of the regulars, came over and introduced himself by telling me that I had just scared him out of his wits when I entered. "You look like the ghost of my old friend Gus Tillman!" he said. Bill's jaw dropped when I told him that Gus and I had been Albany classmates, and my jaw dropped when Bill told me much of the similarity between Gus's later life and mine, affirming that his old high school friend had indeed died a few years back.

"As we're talking about ghosts, and because you grew up in this town, Bill," I opened, "does a black-haired, stocky man in this building mean anything to you?"

"Oh sure, that's my grandfather, Harold Lee, who could often be found here with his friends, Charlie Lott and Deb Chase, and his brother Fred Lee. You saw him, did you?" he responded. "He died a number of years ago."

"Yes, just sitting there in the front of the dining room or lobby—he seemed to move around while I dined out front," I said.

"There are a lot of Saturday night/Sunday overnighters here," he told me, "and at one Sunday breakfast, I heard a woman testily telling her scoffing husband, 'I did hear it!'" Bill had introduced himself to the couple and said he couldn't help overhearing, then asked her what noise had troubled her. The woman responded that, several times in the night, she had heard walking in the hall outside her room, and got up to inspect the hallway. Each time, however, the hall was quiet and not a person was in sight. She told Bill that the footsteps had seemed to be those of an adult.

"I grew up in town, as I told you," Bill reminded me, "and I would have expected her to say those were the footfalls of a child. There is an old legend about this place, which some overnighters seem to have confirmed, of a child playing or skipping through the hallways at night. The story is that a little girl long ago fell down the stairs and died, and remains here, even though she probably knows that she's dead." Okay, I thought, there's something to look forward to for tonight. John, the proprietor, had put me in Room 4, in the center of the back hallway, once he learned I was ghost-legend hunting. Why did he choose that room?

"Well, here's another one for you," Bill continued. "My son, Joe, used to work with me in my electrical contracting business, and we came to the Park Inn because they had an electrical problem of an urgent nature here. Inside a wall we found a smoldering wire. Joe got into the space and then pulled out the wire. It was unconnected to anything on either end, yet it was smoking! It may not be a ghost story, but nobody could ever explain that event."

Carla rejoined us as the customers gradually left; it was getting late, and even Bill had to bid us adieu. "Another thing about that back room," she continued, "is that once, as I pushed through the swinging door, it suddenly kicked back at me—hard! So, I pushed again, hard, and found that it opened easily. And strangest of all, there was nothing behind it; there was nothing for the door to catch on, much less to push it back at me! Another mystery, which maybe a person should expect in an old hotel or tavern, is that I went down into the cellar earlier this year, and a filmy shape walked past me. I know that nobody living was down there, and it gave me the willies.

"I could go on and on," she added, "because it's like we have a custodial staff that isn't real here. Not much of it is scary, but it sure can be a nuisance," she grinned. "See the pictures on the wall in the dining room? We have to straighten them out at least once a week, as they seem to tilt themselves. And there is no heavy traffic outside on Sheather Street to jiggle them crooked. I've also never felt the building shake, so how does it happen? Maybe once in a while a diner might brush against a picture frame, but the odds are just too great to have that happen every week. Now look over here," she instructed. "Notice how the tables are set with the knife and fork parallel to one another. Either Cheryl or I always set the tables that way, but once in a while, we come into the dining room and find all the knives and forks crossed into an X pattern. If a ghost is doing that, what could it mean?" We discussed the matter but couldn't resolve the mystery.

It was getting late and Carla had to close the bar and head home, so I thanked her and went upstairs, hopefully for a visit by the child ghost. In short, though, I'm not sure if the little girl arrived. I woke several times in the night, realized that I was "on the road," but wasn't this the most comfortable bed I'd ever slept on! Then, I returned to sleep. A final time, I half-roused, popped open an eye, and saw that it was almost dawn. I had an early appointment farther south and grumbled that I'd have to leave the bed's comfort soon, but then dozed once more.

Gently, at that moment, I realized that I was in the lobby of a big, old-fashioned hotel, certainly not the Park Inn, and was seated in a maroon over-stuffed chair. From my left, came a little girl, whose hand was held by an adult who I couldn't quite see. The child was dressed in a blue dress reminiscent of the Twenties or Thirties sack style, and had her hair combed straight down, though she might have worn a single ribbon or barrette. She had no expression, but slowly reached out and touched my left cheek. Something about her cheeks—what was it? The skin seemed wrinkled, almost elderly. She withdrew her hand and took one step forward, as if to exit the room, and in that instant, the dream ended and I awoke. Realizing that dreams are often places of spirit contact, I quickly reviewed the details of the imagery before I moved a muscle, so as not to miss recalling any aspect of the experience. Was this child a ghost?

The girl seemed to have had the guidance (angelic, parental, spirit guide?) that a deceased person might, probably does, have. She also seemed to be leaving the hotel under that guidance. If that is a correct analysis, the spirit might have been signaling the end of her haunting at the Park Inn and imminent progress to the next level of reality. If so, that would make for quieter nights at the Park Inn.

Old inns and hotels, as well as present day bed and breakfast inns, clearly retain diluted energies from yesteryear. I call these "house memories," as the energy we expend today, being a form of matter, cannot be created or destroyed. Our thoughts, words and activities are eternal in that respect.

The Park Inn is a worthwhile place to spend the night. You will enjoy your meals and the camaraderie of the regulars in the bar. You may also encounter former customers who enjoyed their stay too much to depart any time soon.

The Long Fellow's Garden

"This area called Interlaken today was a place of holiness and joy to the Iroquois and their predecessors, the Ancients," Sue said, with a faraway look in her eyes. "As long as I've lived around Saratoga Springs, I've been drawn to this place because there are still many Indian souls here. I've developed the ability to contact them, learn some of their names, and to discover what energy holds them here."

One winter day in 2005, I interviewed this woman who has worked in the educational field for many years, and who has strong intuitive abilities. It is very important to her that modern people understand the reverence that our native forbearers had for the land and waters of New York State, so that we might preserve a healthy environment for our descendants. "When the whites came to Saratoga County, they discovered that the Indians maintained silence when crossing Saratoga Lake, as they considered it a grave offense to talk in the midst of its beauty. Of course, we can see what European society did to this area after colonization.

"It's all developed today, with townhouses and restaurants and camps all around the lake, especially here on the northwestern shore. The Indian spirits tell me that they used to come to this spot without weapons to play their games and compete with one another in friendship. They were eventually driven out by white men who believed they owned the land, but after death, the Indian souls returned to maintain a vigil here."

In 2002, I had written about the famous Longfellows Restaurant, which is located in the Interlaken neighborhood, delineating the ghost stories associated with it. In *Ghosts of the Northeast*, I provided a history of the summer activities of the Victorians, the Prohibition era comings and goings of entertainment figures, gamblers and gangsters at the famous Arrowhead Club, Newman's, Riley's Lake House, and other notorious establishments. After the U.S. Senate Kefauver Hearings in the 1950s, New York State made gambling illegal, and within just a few years, all the old "lake houses" had burned or been demolished. But the old dairy barns were converted into a popular restaurant known as The Caunterbury.

Years later, under new ownership, the name "Longfellows" was given to the restaurant in honor of a legendary thoroughbred by that name. Soon, however, a number of ghost stories (formerly known to just a few former employees) began to circulate. Maybe those originated with the old undertaker across Route 9P having stored his deceased customers in the dairy barn's ice house. Maybe the ghosts were a residue of dead bootleggers that energized the disquieting vibrations. And maybe some of the Indian presence was misunderstood.

Soon after 2000, the two large barns were combined into a restaurant and rnn, and a new wing was added to the Inn in 2003. "I remember that back barn. It was used mainly for storage of tables and firewood before the Inn was created," former waitress Candace told me. "Once, something invisible touched me in there, so I went in only when I absolutely had to. Also, up on the dining room balcony, I once saw a Victorian man and woman; she had a closed parasol resting on her shoulder. And there were many nights when Frank, the manager, and I closed up for the night. Once we reached the parking lot, however, we sometimes saw the lights turned on inside again and had to unlock, re-enter and turn them off again.

"I was also one of the first employees to see The Captain, as we called him—just a ghostly head that floated in the air by the bar or entrance foyer. One night, another waitress and I sat taking a break at the bar. 'Wow, that guy must be really tall,' she said to me, pointing down into the entrance foyer, 'If we can see his head above the floor over there, he must be eight or nine feet tall.' I took a look, saw the bushy black hair and long fuzzy sideburns and told her, 'Naw, that's just The Captain.' I told her that it was one of our restaurant ghosts, and she was very unhappy to hear that," Candace laughed.

Former waiter Nick told me of his responsibility to close up both establishments at day's end. "One night, I had just secured the restaurant's doors and went to the back office, right next to the wine room. I sat at the desk, facing the door, and immediately heard a rustling noise behind me. I turned just in time to see wine bottles falling. Maybe a dozen or so smashed on the floor, but it's physically impossible for this to happen, as they are stored in horizontal racks. That scared me, and I ran out to the bar and got our Dutch bartender, Hans, to come and witness the event. He witnessed more bottles sliding out and falling five minutes later. I'm glad I had someone else with me!"

Nick recounted another strange experience in the second barn, which is now a part of the Inn. Making his closing-time walk through the upstairs, he heard his name called three times in an empty hallway outside the office. Nobody was there. I also interviewed a chambermaid who often cleans rooms in the downstairs, and she told me there is one room that she just won't stay in. "There is an ice cold feeling there, even on hot days. And out in the hallway, where there are many framed historic photos hanging on the wall, I always find pictures tilted, even when no guests have walked by to jar them loose."

Recently, I met a man named Chris, who spent several years in the pest control business. "You know that restaurants have to be very careful in that area to keep the State Health Department happy, so I often visited Longfellows. Of all the buildings I had to attend to, the area near the wine cellar always gave me the willies. I'd feel an intense cold, I'd get goose bumps, and the hair on my neck would rise. I don't know what took place around that wine room before that building was a restaurant, but it must have been powerful. I'm glad to be in a new business, now," he laughed, wiping his brow.

The Inn's manager, Dan, told me of another strange event. "One day, the chambermaid had cleaned up Room 108, and it was ready for guests. All of a sudden, at the switchboard, several of us noted an outgoing call from that room. The chambermaid wasn't in there—I even checked. Yet, the call button kept lighting—it was eerie. A clerk went to the room and replaced the phone, but that phenomenon continued the rest of the day and then abruptly stopped! We never figured out what was happening there."

One local psychic suggests that nefarious activities which took place within the barn during Prohibition might have left a dark energy pattern behind. In the old days, as the barn was being converted to an inn, a former employee said a local woman sat with the jackhammer crew and read "The Song of Hiawatha," burning sage for the peace of the souls that might fear the loud mechanical noise.

"In the place between Longfellows and Saratoga Lake, there are many Indian spirits," Sue told me. "I met a man in Interlaken, a newcomer to our area, and I shared my knowledge of the Indians with him. He showed me a beautiful arrowhead that he had just found on his property. As soon as I touched it, I knew an Indian named Mourning Dove had given it to him as a gift and reminder of the sacredness of this place. He was very excited to hear this, and I'm sure the man is now a believer in these entities that he can't see."

Sue even shared with me a third interpretation of the name "Longfellows." I had always thought Saratoga was a classy place, to name a restaurant after an American poet. But no, someone told me a few years ago that the name came from a famous thoroughbred that ran at the Saratoga Track in the late 1800s. "Maybe so," Sue said, "but the Indian spirits around here refer to The Creator as "a long fellow," or a being of tall or mighty stature. So maybe they inspired the current owners of the restaurant in the choice of a name," she grinned.

In any case, my sensitive friends assure me that the area between the lake and the hilltop on which Longfellows sits is an active location for spirits from many time periods. It might be interesting for ghost fans to visit the restaurant and meet The Captain, or dine in the dining room where staff and diners sometimes feel "energy." To cap it off, I'd recommend spending at least one night in the Inn's naturally cooled Room 108, "just to be sure."

The Lakeview

Mayville, the county seat of Chautauqua County, grew up during the late 1800s, and at 13 Water Street in that village can be found one of its oldest buildings, The Lakeview Restaurant and Hotel. The Lakeview didn't always look as inviting to travelers as it does today, and maybe some of the old days remain as energy there.

In 1993, Ray Marsh and his wife, Ruthabeth, retired classical musicians, bought the aging building, hoping to refurbish both the interior and exterior, and reopening the rooms upstairs for rental. The old foundation had deteriorated so badly that the couple had to invest in a new one made of poured concrete. Because of higher-than-expected expenses and too little time, they never fully accomplished their dream, however.

Ray told friends that, one day in 1995, he was working on the outside of the establishment when a dog, apparently a stray, came to visit and never left his side for three weeks. At night, the canine would sit in the bar and observe the operation. Then, as quickly as the animal had appeared, the owner was found several blocks away, and the man reclaimed the dog. Shortly after that, Ray died. At first, the apparent stray seemed to have no importance worth relating in a story on ghosts, but subsequent events caused many of Ray's friends to scratch their heads in wonder.

Ray Marsh's wake was held and, that evening before the funeral scheduled for the next day, the small party of mourners, including Ruthabeth, retired to the hotel's taproom, of which Ray had been proud, especially of the horseshoe-shaped bar. A member of the group named Dave looked up and saw Ray's old canine friend sitting attentively outside the front door. As the animal had been a "regular" for a while, Dave got up and invited the dog inside, whereupon it strode to Ray's old sitting spot at the end of the bar and sat, from whence it took up its surveillance of all the visitors.

A short time later, Ruthabeth entered and the dog walked over to her and attempted to climb into her lap, an activity that he had never attempted while Ray was alive. She had to push the animal away, and as the gathering broke up and a car came for Ruthabeth, she again had to discourage the dog from trying to enter the rear seat with her. Such strange behavior for a dog that had always maintained his cool! Finally, resigned that he couldn't be with the widow, the animal returned to the bar, entered and sat quietly for another twenty minutes at his observation post. Then, slowly he rose and went to the door, where one of the party let him out. That was the last time any of the group ever saw the animal.

The bar was sold and reopened a few months later, with a man named John as the new manager. Sitting alone in the bar on dark nights, John was often distracted by movements and the sight of a man standing in the shadows. It sure looked like Ray, he told others, but the lighting was so dim that he couldn't be sure. With a new owner, new customers were drawn to the lakeside restaurant, as it faces beautiful Chautauqua Lake, one of the prettiest bodies of water in New York State. The old hotel was a comfortable place to watch the setting sun's reflections on the water, and many of the old regulars came to stay well into the idle hours.

Inside the front door was another door that used to lead to the second floor, a stairway that permitted lodgers of old to return to their rooms without having to enter the bar. That second door caused much consternation for the new manager, as he often found it standing ajar, though there were no overnight guests upstairs. The portal had a deadbolt lock on it so, many times, either John or Dave, the new owner, or later on, Dave's girlfriend, Donna, would rise to shut and lock the door, which never wanted to remain closed. Was this the ghost energy of a long-ago traveler, returned to his room briefly?

From time to time, one of the customers would remark at how much Ray had hoped to refurbish the upstairs. Was his spirit afoot, still seeking bids on the construction work? Donna also had the experience of hearing a man walking through the dining room and then circle around behind the bar. As the lighting was subdued, she couldn't spot the strider, though the sound of walking was there. On one occasion, she was so sure the walking was caused by her friend, Dave, that she called out to him. Dave suddenly emerged from the kitchen on the other side of the room and asked, "What did you want, honey?" Dave told me that Donna's expression was one of astonishment. Surely, they had a ghost, and almost surely it was Ray, at least for a brief time.

This story points up a fairly uncommon phenomenon, where the departed spirit of a human being grasps at the opportunity to manifest once more, if only briefly, in the body of an animal or bird. I have recorded a number of these tales, though the spirit never seems to stay in this new lodging very long, but only in an attempt to communicate with bereaved survivors. Many of the deceased hate to leave their loved ones.

Today, Ray and Ruthabeth's dreams have been realized—the upstairs has been remodeled, and the guest rooms are open. The Lakeview is now truly both a restaurant and a hotel. The almost-two hundred-year-old building seems sparkling new and attractive, but the old framework is there. Many energies of yesteryear also seem to abide in the darker corners and remote parts. Those who seek the ghosts of the past might enjoy a lunch or dinner there, perhaps on the veranda on a nice warm summer's day. There may still be some historical energies to experience. If he could or if he can, Ray is certain to come by and greet you, to assure himself that you like his restaurant.

The Pond

Between the Berkshire Mountains of Massachusetts and New York State's Catskills there is a broad valley that has been farmed since the days of the Dutch patroons. This story takes place in this southeast part of Columbia County, not far from the state line. Going south from Hillsdale, we turned right onto Route 3, the road from Route 22 to Ancramdale, and we found a restaurant readying to open. "As far as I know, it has always been called The Pond," Linda Warner-Marrish, the new owner told me. With her husband, Larry Marrish, she purchased the now-seemingly-new building four years before and began its renovation. "But don't let our Lincoln Log exterior fool you," she said. "Underneath the new poured concrete foundations and shiny exterior, there is an old cider mill dating back to 1818."

Her daughter, Tonya, had approached me at a ghost story event a few weeks earlier, and told me of this wonderful old building that is approaching a new life. With my dowser friends, Bill Getz, Frank Hoenig and a newcomer to our crew, Doug Dean, a retired engineer who lives nearby, we visited the soon-to-open business. By the time you read this, ghosts not interfering, you can visit the site and dine there, while listening intently and, with your psychic receptors turned on, perhaps looking over your shoulder from time to time.

"The first story that I heard about ghosts here," Linda said, "involves an older man who lived in a trailer out back, kind of a watchman during the years that this place was closed. One day, a neighbor spotted the old guy, fishing pole in hand, headed for the Roeliff Jansen Kill, a stream that isn't far away. What unnerved that neighbor is that the old man had died and was buried two weeks before," she said with a laugh, "yet, there he was happily walking to the fishing hole."

"When I had already fallen in love with this place and decided to renovate the building and reopen, a neighbor dropped by and said, 'Oh yeah! They got ghosts there.' Another visitor told us of bumping into a ghost when the restaurant had been open long ago. Then, various local people stopped by to tell us of the property being used by bootleggers during the Twenties. 'See that hill over there?' they said, 'whenever the booze was in and the Feds were gone, someone would raise a flag on top of Crogan Hill and the locals knew what to do.'" This didn't faze Linda, who had owned a successful restaurant (the Hearthstone Inn in nearby Hillsdale) and was now ready to begin anew. She learned that, following its incarnation as a cider mill, the old building had been a private home for many years and had only been converted to a restaurant about 45 years ago, when a side wing had been added.

Our group members didn't want to know many more specifics, as we prefer to use our divinatory tools or system or just plain intuition to see what can be "picked up." "First, let's go down cellar," Linda urged, as the carpenters were busy on the main floor, noisily transforming the place. In fact, most of the "old" is no longer visible inside, as new sheetrock walls cover old beams and studs, ceramic tiles have been installed on the floors, and coils of wire were everywhere. This old place is sure going to be hi-tech, I observed. We passed through the new stainless steel kitchen and down the cellar stairs.

As soon as we were on the old dirt floor in the basement, I mentally spotted a young woman, perhaps eighteen years of age. She uttered something about this being her place and gave a name that began with H; I intuited that she was from an old Dutch background, and her clothing seemed to be from a period before the 1850s. Doug Dean observed that The Pond is located not far from the boundary line between the old Dutch Van Buren and Livingston families' estates.

Bill was immediately in action, hoisting his L-rods to seek energy fields. Then I turned and spotted Frank doing the same. Bill quickly observed that there were two spirit entities there: one up under a cellar crawl space and another attached to an antique-looking weathervane configured to appear as a sulky driver and his horse. "That came from our other place, the Hearthstone Inn," Linda cautioned, "and it is only about 35-45 years old, so it's not antique." Nevertheless, Bill felt that the weathervane, stored temporarily in the cellar until it was ready to grace an upstairs dining room, had attracted a young female, about fifteen, who might already have been in the house. Could she have been the girl who I had spotted? And, if so, what ancient memory of hers drew her to the horse and driver? Bill said, "She also could have been a person of recent years, who saw the weathervane and admired it, attaching her energy (perhaps the desire to own the object) to it."

I got only another partial name (J-O-_) for the entity in the crawl space, who seems not to have manifested again that day, though Bill picked up a hint that the figure was female and about twenty-two years old. Continuing his dowsing scan, Bill asked (rather told) Linda about another well on the property. Strange, I thought, as we could see the cover of her primary well in front of us. Linda agreed that, yes, there was another drilled well beneath the banquet room. Frank interjected that he picked up a total of five spirit visitors to the house or cellar, "But they aren't permanent dwellers here," he observed, "some are mischievous or restless and only come here sometimes."

"One story that I have to relate to you," Linda interjected, "because we are right here at the well cover. One day we came here to do some work and the contractor announced that there was no water. 'That's impossible,' I told him, 'because the well is full and we have brand new equipment here.' So I came down to the cellar and, in the electrical box here on the wall, found one item (which Doug identified as a capacitor unit) missing its insert. The missing object sat on a cellar ledge about eight feet away." Doug observed that the item (something like a large BUSS fuse) requires considerable force or energy to remove from the unit, to say nothing about then moving it through the air to the ledge.

`   "We had a sensitive man come here recently," Linda continued, "who told us that he picked up two spirits in the building: one in the banquet hall upstairs and a mischief-maker down here. Maybe it's true, because on another day when we had no water, and we suspected that the pipes had frozen, I came down here to inspectand found a valve turned off back in the crawl space, a difficult place to get into, and an operation which one would have to do manually. I was ticked off and shouted, 'Show yourself!' but nothing came forth. Then, a few weeks later, I came in and all the lights upstairs suddenly went off, but I said out loud, 'Okay, this is not a good time to show yourself!' I couldn't handle an apparition that night," she chuckled. Another day, as she came through the front door, she heard a man speaking clearly in the dining room. As soon as she came into the room, however, the voice stopped and she has never again heard that speaker, she told us.

They have two dogs there, and Frank asked if the dogs ever register any upset. Linda responded that the dogs are quiet during the day, when there is plenty of construction work taking place, but the animals sure get worked up at night, scurrying around and barking at unseen beings or energies.

"Don't forget to ask about the bower," a voice said to me. First, I had to recall what the word meant, and remembered that it used to refer to a trellis or latticework upon which vines grew, often to provide shade. "Was there such a thing here?" I asked Linda, though she didn't know. But Doug, who is a lifetime local, remembered that in the early days of the former restaurant, such an object used to stand out back. So, why is this important? I asked my intuition, but got no answer.

Linda also told us that a former cleaning lady from the previous ownership had once found all her cleaning materials moved from one room to another when she came to work one morning, even though nobody else had been indoors since she had left the previous day. More ghostly activity? More mischief?

Such miscreants often seem to prank us in ways that make us think, causing us to realize that we can't see everything around us.

Someone asked about the restaurant's name, and Linda responded that, as far as she knew, the place had always been known as The Pond, likely due to the nice fish pond in the front yard near the restaurant's sign.

So, what is it about The Pond? The ghosts seem neither more helpful nor more troubling there. As in most haunts, it seems that they want us moderns to understand that they are still there. And, if Einstein is right, that there really is no time, and all events in the universe are taking place simultaneously, maybe we appear as spirits to those of another time period.

The day we inspected the old building, we noticed many old, weather-beaten clapboards and timbers stored inside, where they will likely be reshaped and reused in the new restaurant's decor. And each of these can carry memories and energies of long ago, of settlers and businesspeople and rumrunners, as well as a half-century of satisfied diners, who have come to this beautiful valley and loved what they found. Our crew decided right then and there to come back when The Pond reopens and have a nice dinner and perhaps a glass of wine, and see whether spirits of another type will enliven our meal.

Tip Top Condition

"I don't know when the restaurant got its name," Perry Paul said, "but when I bought the place in 1985, I kept what was on the sign. I know it had been a little grocery store in the 1940s before Charlie Dare opened a bar in the building, so maybe he was the one that christened it. After 1951, Art and Del Roberts were the owners, and then Lucille (Del's daughter) and Eddie Solar bought the restaurant in 1969, while Art and Del lived in the upstairs apartment. Then Bebe Gargiulo and his wife, Audie, ran the place for about a year before I made my down-payment in December 1985. I ran the place until December of 2004."

The Tip Top became a legendary watering hole for the folks in Gloversville and Johnstown, and Perry regularly served up the finest chicken wings in Fulton County. But he suffered a debilitating leg injury in a car crash, forcing him to give up the business in 2004, when he sold to Dennis and Christine Draper. The reason I am listing the previous owners is that one of them before Perry's tenure must be the ghost in question.

"I never thought much about the ghost, and never used 'the g word,'" Perry told me. "Service to my customers was always paramount, so the ghostly stuff was only a distraction and a nuisance at times. My dad, Harry, and my mother, Beverly, when they retired, became part of the business, often bartending and waitressing, so they also witnessed some of the odd goings-on. The first hint of a presence was when my wife, Rebecca, working at the end of the bar, heard a woman call my voice while I tended bar. I looked down to her end of the bar and asked what she wanted. 'That wasn't me, but I know I heard some woman call your name.' There was no other woman in the bar at the time! On other occasions, both of my parents heard the woman. I concluded that it must be the spirit of Del Roberts, a woman who stayed very close to the minute workings of the restaurant during her ownership.

Occasionally, a customer known as "Dollar," who was a big strong guy, would pick up on these events. Dollar could handle himself physically with any human being, but admitted to getting goose bumps when the ghost was heard. And hearing was the biggest part of its presence at the Tip Top.

"During my ownership, my sister-in-law, Mary, and her family lived in the upstairs apartment for almost ten years," he told me, "and occasionally, her daughters would hear the strange upstairs noises. Mary always deflected their curiosity by joking that it was just the furnace man downstairs, but it must have been difficult for her—hearing footsteps passing her in her own apartment. From time to time, downstairs, customers such as Denny H. could hear someone pacing in the apartment overhead, though we knew the space was empty at the time. Old timers, who had known Art and Del, told us that Del was a worrier, and that she continually paced the upstairs floors when she wasn't downstairs tending to the restaurant," he smiled. "So I have always thought of the ghostly presence as a woman, and specifically as Del."

I asked Perry if the phenomenon was limited to footsteps, and again, he grinned. "Well, let's see. First, there were the problems with lights. Several times, I had middle-of-the-night calls from the police, reporting that all the lights in the Tip Top were blazing. One late night, even I, while driving by, spotted the lights on inside, though I was certain that I'd turned them out when I closed up." Mr. Paul estimated that there must have been over fifty strange incidents during his nineteen years of ownership.

Another phenomenon was the TV set glitches. The Tip Top had three TV sets in various parts of the restaurant, so diners could watch different programming, usually sports. "Many a time, I'd open up in the morning and find at least one of the sets turned on, and several times I found all three noisily entertaining my empty restaurant. A man might forget to turn off a single TV when he closed up, especially if its volume was on low, but nobody could miss the three!" He told me that he might expect such uncanny events once in every two or three months.

I asked if he ever witnessed incidents, and he grinned again. "One Sunday afternoon I was tending bar and the customers were watching a football game on the bar TV. An ashtray on my left suddenly moved under its own power right across, in front of me, and several feet farther. A customer sitting there was amused and dared me to pick it up, but I figured I wasn't going to argue with the ghost; if he or she wanted it in its new spot, that was okay with me!

"Another incident I heard, though I didn't witness it. We heard a crash over by the dining room salad bar, and when I went over there, thirteen salad bowls were sitting on the floor—all sitting upright!" I speculated for a minute on the odds of not a single bowl being overturned, and suggested that the ghost had simply wanted to get his attention. Another baffling event was Perry finding all the salt and pepper shakers moved to a single table when he opened the Tip Top one day. "This just wasn't the way I left the place the previous night when I closed up. Shakers would be refilled after closing, then moved back to their tables, so we were ready to go at opening time the next day." This sounded to me like something Del or a previous owner, now deceased, might have done in the old days, and still kept doing while living on in his or her time. The person might have gotten forgetful about returning the shakers to their rightful place. Or, maybe the spirits had used up all that day's supply of ghost energy in getting the shakers to that table, and then couldn't get them returned.

Perry told me that, in retrospect, he had had other experiences when young, such as hearing voices in his home when nobody was there. He also had a strange experience when descending the stairs there. "I was coming downstairs and suddenly passed over three or four steps. It's not that I slipped or fell, but I did feel a little push from behind just before the incident. I landed on the bottom step and kept right on going, though I sure was scratching my head as to how it all had happened."

Perry told me that the locked outside cellar door at the Tip Top would sometimes be found unlocked by nighttime police patrols, though he was always security-conscious and kept the door locked.

"When we took over the Tip Top, we did quite a bit of remodeling, and I thought afterward that all those changes might have gotten the ghost active. One of the first oddities I noticed was that our ceiling fans would unaccountably be turned on, though one had to flip a wall switch to activate them. And when we found them on, I always thought back to the previous night's closing, sure that I had turned them off," he said.

233

Some restaurants with a ghost often find an oven or stove top turned on, so I asked Perry Paul if he had experienced that. "No," he replied, "just our fryer. I never thought too much about that, however, because I could always imagine that someone might have forgotten to turn it off the previous night. Yet, while the fryer was found turned on, it was never at the high level of heat where we did our frying."

Del Roberts left the restaurant in 1969, Perry told me, so he had never known her. I, however, hearing of all the goings-on during his ownership, figured that Perry had gotten to know Del, simply by her continuing "help" around the restaurant.

"When the Drapers bought the Tip Top in December 2004, I told them of the ghost," he said, "but I suspect they thought I was pulling their leg, so we all laughed." Apparently, the Drapers didn't make a go of the business, though, and the old Tip Top sits for sale today.

"Do you think the ghost is still active there?" I asked Perry. He raised his eyebrows, gave a smile and leaned forward, as if imparting confidential information to me. "You know, from time to time when I drive by the old place, in one of the windows, I swear, I can see...." We both laughed.

Apparently, the ghost remains in tip top condition even without customers to wait on.

Hideout

Rock Hill, in the southern Catskills, was pretty much wilderness, traversed only by State Route 17, when Frank Porporo, Sr. converted an old farmhouse on Lake Louise Marie into a rural restaurant called The Dodge Inn. But it was its remoteness that attracted individuals from the world of organized crime during the 1920s and '30s, as Rock Hill was only a couple of hours drive from New York City. "My father knew them all but was very closed mouthed about his relationship with them," Frank recalled. "When I got out of the service in 1945, I came to work there, but those old days were gone.

"Some say that the spirits of long-dead mobsters such as Al Capone may still roam the property. I grew up calling Capone 'Uncle Al' but he was gone when I took over the restaurant from my father in 1948," Frank told me. "This place also became a rendezvous for illicit love affairs; the Dodge had four quiet rooms upstairs. We didn't ask questions, but just served great food. Then, the place burned to the ground in 1967, leaving only a great fieldstone chimney in the ruins. I liked it up here in the mountains because it wasn't the Bronx, where I grew up, so we chose to rebuild. That fireplace and chimney are the only part of the original structure remaining from the old Dodge Inn. Within a year, we had rebuilt and opened again in 1968. Still, I wonder whether some of those former personalities remain on the grounds," he mused.

His son, Frank, Jr., took over the rebuilt inn in 1981, and operated it until 1993. But the son experienced noises that couldn't be explained by any feature of the new structure. In the back kitchen, there were water faucets that wouldn't stay turned off. Interior doors that the Porporos closed at quitting time were standing open in the morning. Old timers told an unsubstantiated tale of a woman's son drowning in Lake Louise Marie, across the road, and it was commonly believed that she remains on the property, still seeking the boy in the spirit world. Others are sure that the disembodied Capone still roams his favorite eating place from time to time, as he once had a hideout house on the lakeshore.

In 1993, Randy Reznik bought the restaurant, now dubbed "The Rock Hill Country Grill." A few years later, the Strauss family purchased the restaurant and operate it today. "What I can tell you about," Marc Strauss said, "is that there are still phenomena here. One of our waitresses discovered a man dressed as a cowboy, sitting in what we laughingly call 'The Mafia Room.' Though his western dress didn't fit the Catskills, she had the impression that the ghost was a bounty hunter of some sort. She described the apparition as tall, maybe six feet four inches, with black hair and mustache. Suddenly, he vanished, even before she could pass him a menu.

In our interview, Frank Porporo, Sr., now living in Arizona, told me that there were other candidates for restaurant ghost. When the Catskills were a Borscht Belt resort area, the big names of show business got away from the Concord or Grossingers, and came down here for a quiet meal. Milton Berle, Tony Bennett, Red Buttons, and Phil Silvers were regulars here. Marlene Dietrich was here from time to time, along with Alan King, the comedian. He once praised our place on national television as one of the few places where he could truly relax. Lee J. Cobb, the actor, dined here, as did Rock Marciano, the boxer."

"Any one of them, now in spirit, might visit occasionally to partake of our spirits," dining room manager Gary Strauss told me. "One night a year ago, near closing time, I sat here on a barstool, chatting with the last customer. Over there," he pointed to the back bar, "see that bottle of Grey Goose Vodka? As the man and I talked, its cork top flew two feet upward out of the bottle. Now, vodka isn't a carbonated drink," he observed, "so where could vodka find the energy to pop that cork? It only happened once, though.

"Still, especially at night, just before closing, when I'm alone, I'll spot a dark shape walking across the dining room. Nobody is here; even the chef is gone, so I know I'm alone. But alone with whom?" he asked with a grin. "We try to honor the ghosts and not to bother them," co-owner Heather Strauss told reporter Victor Whitman of the *Times Herald-Record* in nearby Middletown. Gary and Marc echoed that sentiment. "The ghosts don't bother us, though they do make pots and pans fall off their hooks in the kitchen. Once, an entire dishwasher tray of glasses fell and shattered when nobody was in the kitchen. Faucets in the ladies room seem to turn themselves on, and then there is the cigar smoke. As with most New York State restaurants, the Rock Hill Country Grill is a non-smoking establishment, but we still smell fresh cigar smoke here from time to time," Marc recalled. "One day, we had no water, and when I went to check the water lines, I discovered the main valve turned off. But it took a heck of a lot of work to turn it on again, as the space where it's located is very narrow and hard to get into. Who would do that and why?" he smiled.

Here again is human history, playing out from time to time by some of the most famous Americans on an old byway of Sullivan County. Interstate Route 17 (soon to be I-83) is only a few hundred yards away through the trees. How many Catskill visitors zoom through the wooded hills, not recognizing that the great players of life's drama are still relaxing at the old Dodge Inn?

Molly

"Did you ever hear of a ghost named Molly?" my friend Peter asked. "Sue and I are headed up to a Fulton County restaurant to see what turns up if we attempt a contact—want to come with us?" Recognizing that there are too many ghosts that I've never heard of, I was game, so my friend Diane and I went to dinner with Peter and Sue. My expectation was that we'd enter and investigate a quiet restaurant before the dinner crowd arrived, but such was not the case. The place was full when we got there.

This foray was one of the strangest investigations in which I've taken part. There were too many nice people to meet and converse with at Kristel's Lodge, just north of Broadalbin on Vunk Road, where the owners, Jeremy and Maura Kristel, have been proprietors only since 2005. The wooden building looked quite new and, as we drove up the driveway, I wondered how such a modern establishment had acquired a ghost. That was just one of many misperceptions on my part that evening.

The restaurant wasn't noisy, but neither was it a silent site where one could meditate or muse to make spirit contacts. Sue is a tested psychic medium as is Peter. I, also, have some sensitivity at times, but Diane was our grounding element. Though she is interested in the subject, she has had little experience other than her interest.

So, we all chatted with members of the Kristel family and smiled at the children and newborns. The atmosphere in the dining room was that of a big happy family of customers, many of whom knew one another. The bar, with its own clientele, was reached through swinging doors and was separated from the dining room.

"So who or what is Molly?" I asked those assembled as our orders arrived.

"She is a female ghost who often appears in the dining room," Sue told me, "though she has never been spotted in the bar." The meal was a delicious distraction from our quest, though I occasionally questioned various members of the Kristel extended family, seated with us, about the history of the apparently new building. "It's not new," one of them told us, "but I don't know how old it really is—maybe a hundred years old." So, figuring that any other history had to emerge from my intuition, I paused, staring into my mashed potatoes, and asked about the place. "I got an almost Victorian image of a woman with her disarrayed hair done up in a Gibson Girl arrangement, haying in a large field. She paused and wiped her brow on a long-ago sunny day, and stood her large hay rake up on its handle. I tried to "go inside" her consciousness and was met with a bitter emotional response: "He's drinking again!"

Other than that, and seeing an old house amid acres of hay, I received nothing else. I wrote the vision in my notebook, then looked over at Peter, who was also writing on a piece of paper that he'd borrowed from me. A few moments later, he passed the paper to Sue, who immediately began her writing without reading her husband's work. So that's the way our little séance is going to take place, I realized, and rejoined the conversation while smiling at little Cassie, who served as our table's chief entertainer.

"Should we go into the bar to see Molly?" someone queried. I didn't understand the question and responded, "I thought someone just said that Molly has never been seen there." Two family members responded that the Molly in the bar was an image discovered beneath a bar chair seat by the former owner. Knowing that people tend to seek order and images even in clouds, I asked a waitress to take me to the bar where "Molly" could be viewed. The woman was a bit nervous and told me, "Every time we take that piece of wood down from behind the bar, the lights in here start to flicker and sometimes go out."

Nevertheless, when we walked behind the bar and she lowered the circular piece of wood for me to inspect, the lights stayed steady and I beheld a close resemblance to a woman's face. It was not as if someone had painted the image, but likely, when a workman long ago brushed some glue onto the approximately 15-inch-round piece of wood, the "face" remained. Bar customers, well aware of the legend, cautioned us against keeping the old seat down for very long. "She puts out the lights," one patron warned.

Family friend Al, when I returned to the dining room table, asked if I'd seen Molly and I responded yes, and he stated that all members of the family have taken the opportunity to inform themselves about the story during the two preceding years. "A Mr. Vunk, an Amsterdam cop during the 1920s, and after whom this road is named, had a sixteen-year-old daughter named Molly, who died of leukemia. She was buried in her dance or prom dress. People who have seen her say that she always appears as a long blonde haired girl in a long white dress. She doesn't stay long and won't go into the bar." That caused me to reflect on the farm wife's upset that somebody had been drinking—one of the Vunk ancestors.

Al's friend, family member Jan, remembered that the restaurant building had originally been a hay barn, then a dance hall and then a restaurant. She also said that Gary, the former owner, would come in to talk with us later.

I took a minute to read Peter's writing, which began with feelings of heaviness in his body, and a lump in his throat, which meant "past relationship issues" to him. Many sensitive people learn to identify their own physical changes that occur in so-called haunted atmospheres, and also to analyze what these refer to, as perhaps they mirror long-ago emotions of the haunt. Peter felt the girl (whom he judged to be between eighteen and twenty-four) was happy to now be divulging her young adult life to us. "She is happy to be around a happy crowd, as her own short life was happy," he wrote. "Probably she knows she has died, but doesn't want to move on because she fears to meet one whom she loved—someone who broke her heart when he ended the relationship, and she never had another." Peter sensed a younger girl, likely a sister, with Molly. "I connected with her because of a similarity between her life's issues and mine. Others will connect with her on different levels because of their own backgrounds or experiences." That made sense to me.

Turning to Sue's writing I found: "A slight, fairly short young girl with long dark hair. She won't go into the bar, but has been greeting each group of diners as they enter the restaurant tonight. She seems particularly interested in the children. The girl is somewhat sad, as she knows she is being drawn by the energy of all the people who love to visit her here. I get the idea that she was a summer visitor to this site, but didn't live here." But if our Molly (as many others saw her) was blonde, then who had Peter, Sue and I visualized?

Lisa, our waitress, stopped by to see how we were doing, and told us that she has said good morning to Molly every morning since her first weekend of work. "At that time, I spotted a girl playing peek-a-boo from behind a dining room chair, so now I always greet her when I enter. I also once saw two plates moving on the kitchen countertop and reached them just before they crashed onto the floor. Molly, or whoever it is, keeps adjusting our kitchen radio up or down in volume all the time, and our toilet sometimes flushes itself," she smiled. "We also have a dry eraser board in the kitchen and one day I saw the pen fly upward out of its socket and hit one of our staff members." She raised her eyebrows, smiled, then moved to the next table.

Jeremy stopped by our table, aware of the search that we were attempting. "I got here early one morning," he said, "and the cook pulled up beside me in the parking lot. 'I see your wife's already here,' the man said. 'She's not,' I responded. 'Sure she is, I just saw her in the window!' the cook answered. But I knew I was there alone, the first person to arrive."

Maura told us that she often saw what she termed "passing shadows" in the dining room, but only in her peripheral vision; when she looked directly at the movement, there was nothing or nobody there.

She introduced me to Gary, the former owner, who had just entered the restaurant. "This place wasn't insulated when I bought it," he told me, so I rented an insulation-blowing machine to do it myself. I began over there," he pointed, "then worked around the outside of the building, but over in that northwest corner, the machine burned out. After I fixed it, the plug continued to pop out of its socket. Joe was a cook who worked for me in those years, and he always had some kind of problem with that corner. Later, we discovered that the barn doors had been there.

"When I bought the place, I found all the dining room chairs stacked up, so I took them down one by one, and cleaned them. One chair fell over and its seat popped off the frame. When I picked it up, I saw Molly's face (that's what I call it) on the underside. That surface would have been inside the chair and couldn't be some kind of graffiti done by a customer. Several times before we got our liquor license, I spotted a woman in a white dress entering the open door, but each time I searched the entire building to find her, there was nobody there. One day, I sat at a table chatting with a saleslady and, startled, she exclaimed, 'Somebody just came in.' I responded, 'No, they didn't, I was looking at the doorway the entire time we've been sitting here.' The poor woman couldn't take that, as she was certain of what she saw, and, jumping up, she searched the entire building. A while later she returned blushing and mumbling that she knew what she'd seen.

"But, in the end," Gary said, "I believed her because I've seen Molly quite often, even after I sold the place to the Kristels. I just didn't want to let on that I saw a ghost because I was afraid the State of New York wouldn't give me a liquor license!"

Thus, there is a nice old restaurant not far from the Great Sacandaga Lake, where friends and family gather every evening to create a happy atmosphere while enjoying good food. It's not hard to understand why Molly would enjoy staying on. We didn't try to send her on her way, as there are beings of pure light who can assist her to transition when she is ready.

If you are in the area of Vunk Road, just off County Route 110 north of Broadalbin, you can initiate your own ghost hunt at Kristel's Lodge. There is no downside to such an investigation, because the food is great, and maybe you can have a chat with Molly before you leave.

No Place Like It

In 1845, Joseph Hotchkiss and Joshua Collar built The Wells House Hotel in Pottersville, at the junction of Olmstedville Road and the main road from Albany to Montreal (today N.Y. State Route 9). The pair figured to profit from the growing traffic of merchants and city people venturing into the Adirondack Mountains, and they did. With the growing popularity of Schroon Lake summer hotels to the northeast, an overnight stay with meals was necessary for passengers disembarking at the Riparius railroad station, then traveling by stagecoach to those small hotels and lake houses at the lake.

In over a century and a half, there have been thousands of travelers who have come and gone, and dozens of proprietors have run or owned the Wells House. Eventually, the Northway, Interstate 87, siphoned off most of the north-south traffic and the railroad station at Riparius closed, today catering only to seasonal and vacation travel. Pottersville became a backwater along the Schroon River, often ignored by travelers rushing to Adirondack ski resorts or Canadian vacation spots farther north.

Imagine yourself as a character in a Hollywood horror film: It's a dark night, with heavy rain and lightning flashes. You're dead tired, or perhaps you've had motor trouble on the Northway—all the ingredients of a scary film story. All of a sudden, perhaps guided by the local tow truck driver who came to your aid, you discover Pottersville at Exit 26, its streets filled with pleasantly lit modest homes, a small restaurant, churches, an antique shop, and one major edifice—The Wells House. "They have rooms there," the driver tells you, "and pretty good meals." Not expecting much, you climb the steps and enter a brightly lit foyer, only to be greeted by a gigantic moose head affixed to the wall. Music echoes from somewhere down the hall, serving as the background to quiet and happy talk from unseen people, perhaps in the dining room. Then something unique happens; there is a shift in mood and maybe "something else." What is it?

"I've worked here for over a year as Day Manager, Johnna Brennan told me, "and it never fails to happen. No matter what cares I'm burdened with, and no matter what grave concerns occupy my mind, once I enter this wonderful old hotel, I'm in another world!" Of the many individuals whom I interviewed, that is the consensus—there is something different there, and it's peaceful and happy.

I asked Marian McCann, who with her husband, Vin, has owned the establishment for a year. "What is that change in atmosphere that occurred when I just walked in?" Marian, a New York City transplant, couldn't be specific, but answered that she had felt the same shift when she first visited in 2007. Paul and Shirley Bubar were selling, and she felt a sudden, powerful urge to be the buyer. "What a change from city life," she exclaimed. "So Vin and I became the new innkeepers."

The Bubars had made major changes in the internal structure, combining what had been 22 small rooms into 11 beautifully decorated modern, yet antique, rooms and suites. Readers understand the implications of such renovations, but Marian, who had almost no previous contact with spirits, was slow to catch on. "The first thing that came to my attention was that the lights on the second floor had gone out. We have funny wiring here, and many of our lights are never off. Nevertheless, I got a new bulb and the stepladder and went to change the apparently burned-out light. However, I discovered that the bulb had simply been unscrewed to the point where it wouldn't illuminate. It wasn't likely a prank, as one cannot reach the fixtures from floor level. Hmmm, I thought. Still, that bulb is often unscrewed," she said with a grin.

When locals heard that the venerable old restaurant was again in operation, they visited and were thrilled by the bill of fare. They told stories, some of which were scary. "Remember the time when a woman was cheating on her husband and had taken a room upstairs for herself and her lover? The husband snuck in during the night and killed her as she sat in the bathtub!" Today, though, the woman's name is no longer remembered, perhaps because the murder was only a fable, but the event was probably the last violent deed or thought there. If true, however, it is good ghost material.

Travelers and tourists, spotting the hotel's new gilded sign from the Northway, stop in for a snack, and more than likely will reserve a room for the weekend. One of these guests descended for breakfast recently and inquired if there was a ghost in residence. "I heard lots of laughs and people moving around near the end of the corridor until very early into the morning," the man observed. Marian was hard-put to convince her guest that nobody else was on that hallway, and that the office staff had departed from downstairs well before 11:30 p.m. The man went to breakfast, telling her that the memory-foam mattress was indeed comfortable, anyway, once he dropped off to sleep.

Not long afterward, a guest from the second floor asserted that there was indeed a ghost there. "A little blonde girl, laughing and scampering around in my room," he joked. "Is there an extra charge for that?" It was the first that the McCanns had heard of the child, but not the last. The girl seems to show up simply to cheer guests, then as quickly departs. She is much like Zuzu, the house feline, who (when no larger than a human fist) wandered in the hotel door on Marian's first workday. Since that time, Zuzu has become the official greeter and unofficial porter, escorting you to your room, or to her favorite upstairs sun porch.

It doesn't much matter whom one interviews; the bartender, for example, will tell you of spotting a tall, thin gentleman in a "funny hat," waiting at the café's door. When the barkeep looks again, a second later, the stranger is gone. "He comes and goes," Johnna told me with a laugh, "so, when we see him, we know he isn't going to stay long enough to need a menu."

Meantime, former owners' family members visit, bringing tales of the days when the present café was a social room and was thronged with Friday night square dancers. "We didn't know that at first," Marian told me. "But that explains why some of our employees hear music and the shuffling of feet down the hallway and in the café. So far, no such sounds have been heard from the formal restaurant, but the McCann's ownership is still in its early stages.

"I can't say for sure just how I came to work here," Johnna offered. "It's a 25-mile drive from my home to Pottersville, so gas costs might seem prohibitive. Yet, when I came to apply for the job, I was immediately entranced by that certain atmosphere here—it's almost like coming home, to work with friends or guests that I've never met before."

"That is what so many of our guests say," Marian added. "Complete strangers will encounter one another here in our lobby, or down in the café, or even on the stairs, and in less than an hour, they are conversing like old friends—acquaintances that have left the cares of the world elsewhere."

Johnna, as day manager, agreed with the McCanns that, though the atmosphere should be informal, the working staff should be neatly coiffed and dressed. And, all of the women and girls who have worked here, or do work here, absolutely feel it's right too. "We may not wear the cute black dresses and white aprons of a century ago, but we are always at our best in appearance. Imagine, then, that a former worker came in one day and reminisced about 'the old days,' before World War II, when the wait staff women had a special room upstairs, where cosmetics were carefully applied, street clothes were shed, and the formal uniforms were donned. And I just picked up on that need the minute I first entered here!" With her Irish roots, Johnna cannot hide her natural intuition.

A woman who once stayed for a week heard piano music echoing from the café room and went to investigate. But, each day, she was unable to find anyone in that room and the piano seemed untouched. Is there another spirit out there, waiting to audition for a job?

Shirley Bubar had come into the lobby on the day that I visited, to inform Marian that the lights had been on and the blinds open in the Adirondack Room on Monday night. "Did you have a guest there?" Marian smiled and shook her head. Apparently that was another of her secrets about the hotel's night life. "Zuzu took me up to the enclosed sun porch the other day, and when I let her into her favorite place, I noticed that all the porch windows were unlatched. We always keep them locked, but nobody could account for them being opened." Shirley smiled in return, as if she might have a few more "secrets" to impart to Marian someday. "Guests come back—and they bring friends," she told me. "There is no sophisticated pretense here."

I cannot recall a happier and quieter "haunted site" in over thirty years of interviewing and investigating. Nobody was the slightest bit unnerved at the prospect of unseen guests. No one had an even partially scary tale, even the one about the alarm clock in the Beige Room, which seems to have a mind of its own. It's just a wonderful and relaxing atmosphere. For an interview, it was easily the nicest of my career. And, as one overnight guest on the verge of tears said to Marian not long after New Year's Day, "This was the best time I've had in over a year. You have something here." Behind me, I thought I heard the moose concur.

The Orange Inn

"I grew up in Goshen," James Hill told me. "Besides hearing all the stories from the town's racetrack (famed for its horse trotting and pacing events), the other tales, really weird ones, came from The Orange Inn. So many of those accounts sounded fantastic and hard to believe when I was young, so I could never envision being a chef there one day."

Nowadays it bears the address of 159-167 Main Street, but in less organized times, beginning in 1740, this site was the address of His Majesty's Courthouse and Gaol (jail). The oldest section of the present building is made of stone, quarried in the nearby hills. In the cellar that runs beneath the ancient section and the large, three-story clapboard addition to its right were the jail cells and a stairway that rose directly to the prisoner's dock in that courthouse, which was redesigned and rebuilt in 1773, shortly before the local citizens declared loyalty to a new nation.

After independence, about 1790, a new prison was created for Orange County, and a tavern was established at the Main Street site. Taverns being what they are, many long-forgotten stories must have originated there. Certainly there were brawls among the taproom patrons from time to time, but it seems that it is the former lodgers from upstairs who have remained to taunt and tantalize modern patrons.

Once graduated from high school, James intended to make and sell software and began that career. Later, however, he decided that culinary activities called more loudly to him, and he entered a cooking school begun by the gourmand James Beard. "Things came together for me and some friends in 1995, and we figured we could make a go of running the old Orange Inn, though it had been vacant for a dozen years. We called our new place 'The American Bistro at The Orange Inn,' giving us an aura of the old and the new. Growing up, I'd heard of ghostly horses galloping on Hill Street alongside the Inn; would I now hear those? No, I never did. My job was as chef, so I heard only a few of the stories from the upstairs part."

By 1995, the rental units and rooms upstairs had fallen into disrepair and were home to many transients. One never knew if their scary tales were fanciful or true. Nevertheless, it was in his kitchen that James first encountered ghostly activity. "We had begun some major renovations in the kitchen and, in June of 1997, it was hot. Imagine, then, how surprised I was to encounter very cold spots in the kitchen—a kitchen which can itself be warm, but in June? I wasn't sure that this uncanny experience was real and, like most who experience ghosts, I guess, I tried to find logical explanations. As the weeks went along, I began to have more such encounters, often followed by someone or something tugging on my sleeve! That really terrified me when it first happened, because I knew I was the only person in the kitchen.

"Then came the giggles! It was as if some spirit stood there invisibly, making fun of me or taunting me in a way that I couldn't see. This was more than I'd bargained for, so I told my wife, Carol, about it. 'It's a friendly place,' she assured me. 'Just talk to them.' Well, it's very strange to talk to empty space, but I did it—I told the spirits out loud that I was busy doing my job there, and they were making that job difficult, and to please stop this joking around. And that is all it took—I never again felt a pull on my sleeve, though I still did hear giggling from time to time," he told me.

"There is a long hallway connecting the kitchen and the dining area of the restaurant, and we often heard someone running rapidly in that space, though nobody ever burst into the kitchen on our end, or into the dining room on the other. Who was running, or if the sound all came from the past, who needed to run there in the past?" He never figured it out.

At one time, when he and his friends first opened the Bistro, James said that upstairs lodgers had access to the kitchen and, during off hours, they'd sometimes come down and whip up a meal. "I put an end to that. I was now a professional chef and wanted things the way I wanted them. I didn't want to be looking around for a pot or pan or a ladle and find it dirty in the sink, or missing. Nevertheless, I had to consider this previous access by the tenants when the strange things began to happen later in 1995.

"We had a woman visitor in 1998—a living one," he said with a grin. "She seemed to have some intuitive or psychic abilities and asked if she might tour the building, especially the basement. We told her to go ahead. When she emerged from downstairs, she told us a number of things that seemed to be true. First, she said, because of its age and the great number of lodgers and patrons over two centuries, the building is (or was now) something of a meeting place for spirits, most of whom had once enjoyed themselves there. Secondly, the cellar (where the cells had been) now contained some very negative energy, though she wasn't any more specific than that, and for my part, I'm glad she wasn't.

"Then the entire building was put up for sale by the owner, so we knew that New Year's Eve of 2000-2001 was going to be our last day of work. I had assembled a great bunch of workers and helpers, and we were a bit sad when the last customer left. As we often did, we sat around in the dining space, facing the fireplace, hoisting our last drink. First, I need to say that, although we were tired after a busy night's work, none of us had been drinking when the incident occurred.

"A woman dressed in the height of late 1800s fashion swept out of the dining room that we knew was empty. As she passed my workers and me, she smiled a strange smile, nodded to us, and left the room by walking right into the fireplace (a gas-burning type) and disappeared. None of the guys said a word. Silently, we all drained our glass, stood, and walked out. No one said anything! And what could we say? Still, it's nice that a former customer chose to spend her New Year's Eve with us on our last night. I'd like to believe that she bid us a silent, 'Good-bye and good luck; well done!'

Even today, though he is cooking in another area restaurant, James occasionally sees some of the old Orange Inn staff. "All we have to say to one another is, 'Remember New Year's Eve?' Everyone breaks into a smile."

Following that interview, it took me a time before I could visit Goshen to see the old inn for myself. And it had changed ownership again. On the awning is "Limoncello, at the Orange Inn." Clearly, the old building is enjoying an Italian-style incarnation. Luigi and Victor Kapiti are the hard-working owners and I arrived in the midst of a luncheon, but Victor took time to host me and smiled when I asked him about "strange events."

"Our light here in the foyer sometimes turns itself off and, when I go to the circuit breaker box, I find the switch thrown. So I snap it on again. I haven't seen that ghost woman yet, but she'd fit right in with our décor, so maybe she'll sit and order our famed loin lamb chops when she comes again. Right now, the lights are our main problem, but I'll keep an eye out, now that I know more of the history."

Before leaving, I stared down the long hallway. Was that a sound of rapid footsteps or might it have been Victor cutting a loaf of fresh-baked Italian bread in the kitchen on the other end?

This Bud's for You

While breakfasting with my friend Bill, our conversation was interrupted by a man at the neighboring table, who heard us discussing ghosts. "My name's Spike Barton," he said. "Are you serious about ghosts?" I assured him that both of us believed that life goes on even after body death. "Then I've got a place for you to visit," he said, "go over to Philmont, near Hudson, and find The Vanderbilt Inn. I heard unbelievable stories when I dined there last week!"

Bill, a professional water dowser, and I invited fellow dowser Frank Hoenig to join us at the Vanderbilt Inn after owner Ken Hussey invited us to do some investigating. "We'll be interested in what you turn up," Ken told me on the phone.

A week later, we three investigators descended on the 147-year-old hotel. It isn't a glamorous restaurant, though it does wear its age well. Bill had done ghost dowsing only once before with me in Sharon Springs, while Frank was a neophyte, fascinated at the prospect of finding energy fields rather than underground streams.

When I arrived, I found that Frank had already dowsed the underground streams on the property and, as dowsers do, had asked his "source" many questions about the building and grounds, using a system of yes and no answers, to which his dowsing rods responded.

It was a quiet morning, with Ken setting up the bar and Del, the handyman, doing some touch-up painting, and no customers were present to interrupt our very serious search. We told Ken's wife, Marcy, that we preferred not to know any of the phenomena or building history, and Ken gave us free rein to investigate the building from top to bottom, as The Vanderbilt Inn no longer takes overnight guests, so there would be no one we could bother upstairs. Bill and Frank went their separate ways, while I walked across the barroom to what appeared to be the old front door.

As I approached it, and even recognizing that I have a great imagination, I still was surprised to feel brushed aside by a sudden influx of busy men dressed in Edwardian finery. As I tuned in to what I perceived as their conversation, I discovered much earnest political conversation. I got the surname "Pelton," though it's impossible today to prove that such a man did or did not once enter that doorway. "We're Lincoln men," I heard a male voice state. Did this place date back to the Civil War? I wondered. Then walking to the stone fireplace in the lobby, I visualized another spirited conversation among males, with one speaker earnestly propounding some belief. Was it more politics? That was pretty much the active energy that I encountered by myself.

Upstairs, I found Bill about finished with his building tour, and we compared notes as we entered an almost empty, pink guest room. I sensed an invisible presence near the far wall, against which was a small baby's cradle. In the cradle were two antique dolls and a stuffed rabbit. "Anything here?" I asked Bill.

His dowsing rods twirled for a moment, then pointed at the cradle. For a moment, he asked himself silent questions, then told me that the cradle seemed to date from 1850, which pre-dated the building. Getting more specific, he dowsed each of the objects within the cradle and found one particular doll, underneath the two on top, was generating or retaining all the energy. Had some long-deceased child imbued the doll with her hopes, dreams or fears? "These dolls are not as old as the cradle," he stated.

Bill remarked that "in the hall, opposite to the blue room, and in the blue room itself, I had the sense that someone had died. My dowsing rods picked up an energy field inside the room. Down the hall, in the room where they store the paint, there is another energy form, but I can't communicate with it, so it may be a fading memory or consciousness. Also, in the big room over the dining room, I got another positive reading. It is frustrating to get these pockets of energy, most of which are stationary and all of which are uncommunicative. We want to know their story."

Then Marcy appeared and offered to walk us up a narrow staircase to the attic, but, for the first time ever, she couldn't get the light to work. "Funny," she said, "it has always worked before!" We guessed that if an entity or two was dwelling up in the very dark attic, we could leave them undisturbed.

Bill and I then descended into the cellar, which is large, dirt-floored, and not very cluttered. I first spotted the large walk-in cooler and, almost immediately, saw a man with white hair spanking a small boy nearby; then the vision vanished. Bill hadn't shared the sight.

In a far corner, Frank was taking photos of what appeared to be an empty corner, with only the fieldstone wall in sight. Later, when his picture was developed, he showed us the shadow of a bird cage on that wall, something that had not been visible to the naked eye when he'd snapped the photo. There was no bird cage in the cellar. How can nature produce a shadow of something that isn't physically present in the first place? We still don't have a theory, though it's possible that a long-ago owner stored a bird cage in that corner, and some faint energy field remains at the spot. Marcy had told Frank that Bud, the previous owner, had expressed a dislike for going downstairs into the cellar. As ghost enthusiasts know, many times an energy or object invisible to our eyes can show up in a photo, especially if a digital camera is used.

We all returned to the bar upstairs and said to Ken, "Okay, so tell us what you have experienced." The owner smiled and told us that he and Marcy had only purchased the old building in 2004. "But," he continued, "we formed an opinion of what's going on during our first week here.

"The building dates from 1861, just as the Civil War was beginning," he told us. "The Vanderbilt family, owners of the New York Central Railroad and the New York and Harlem Railroad, built this old hotel for use by railroad executives and work crews on the NY&HRR, and you see, we're almost across from the old station," he pointed across Main Street. "Marcy and I are the eighth owners in the Inn's history.

"The previous owner of this place was Bud Wildermuth, who had died a short time before his widow sold to us. During that first week of our ownership, I saw Bud here in the bar, then in the hallway, and later, out in the barn. So, we're pretty sure that he is one of the main characters still around. One night, as she approached the bar, Marcy saw Bud behind the bar just as the waitress came from the kitchen out back. The waitress looked and screamed. Grabbing her camera, Marcy got a picture of some misty, cottonlike substance floating over the bar here, but we have never been able to download the image." His wife then displayed the picture on her digital camera viewer for us. It sure looked ghostly, but there weren't any details that would identify Bud as the spectral culprit.

"Now, come out into the kitchen so I can show you just a little bit of what I've experienced here, and you can see where it happened," Marcy continued. "I came into the kitchen one day and found that small window (about 7 feet high, approximately 2½ feet long by 1½ feet high) out of its frame and lying on the floor twelve feet from the opening. The glass was cracked but the frame was intact; it looked as if it had made a 'soft landing' here. See that jar?" she pointed, "I once saw a fork fly out of that jar, cross the room, and hit the refrigerator. Nobody was within ten feet of it! According to physics, it can't happen, but I saw it."

Del, the maintenance man, stood listening, and then volunteered some of his kitchen experiences. "I was taking down some ceiling tiles in here one morning. I was all alone, up on a ladder. Suddenly, three soup ladles flew off the wall and past my ladder. A minute later, three more flew by. Of course, I knew about the ghost or ghosts, so I just said out loud, 'You want to help?' But that was the end of the fun for that day. I've seen Bud several times inside and outside the restaurant and I figure that he's still trying to run this place, doing what he can. It must be tough to toss those ladles when he doesn't have physical hands any more," he joked.

"This kitchen is usually quite hot," Marcy said, "but even so, every so often there will be ice cold spots, even on summer days. And so many times, there are footsteps going up and down the stairs, though we don't rent upstairs rooms any more; they're just used for storage. Another day, I was on the phone out here in the dining room and heard an awful crash in the kitchen, which I knew was empty. Entering, I found a pile of plastic storage trays on the floor. What force could have moved them? And that's all that was moved." Frank was shaking his head, as his dowsing rods provided no response that morning when he asked about energies in the kitchen. Bill's rods picked up an energy field near the steam table and plate table. "I think it's a child who is a bit bored, and wants to help out," he said.

Moving to the lobby and bar area once more, Ken said that he calls the disturbing energy "Jeremiah," because he doesn't know whether or not it's Bud. "On my first night as owner, nevertheless, I spoke aloud here in the bar, telling Bud that I was going to take good care of his old restaurant. I've seen doors open and close here so many times that I've lost count," he smiled. "Now, Fletcher here," he pointed to the dog, "sits and stares at someone or something that the rest of us can't see. Once or twice he has barked when a door has opened or closed itself, when a Sheriff's deputy and his wife were dining here."

Frank remarked that rooms #6 and #9 were places where he found the most ambient energy. And the cellar, of course. He was unable to determine who or what was the source, but was fascinated to get a reaction to more than underground streams.

CHAPTER 9

SPIRITS AND RELIGION
FRANCIS TO THE RESCUE
ASK AND YOU SHALL RECEIVE
HELP AN OLD MAN
YOU ARE NOT YOUR BODY

Francis to the Rescue

Many people dearly wish for a ghost sighting and are frustrated when these don't seem to occur. Never underestimate your dreams though, reader, as I'm convinced that all of us have had powerful contacts from deceased loved ones who come in our sleep. It is more likely for these events to occur then because that period is not filled with as much conscious doubt, and we can be "taught" or "approached."

My good friends Vincent and Kathy Lombardi are outgoing and interesting people who supplied me with some never-to-be-forgotten ghost stories (see *Haunted Saratoga County* and *Ghosts of the Northeast*) from the days they owned and operated Lombardi Farm B&B just north of the resort city of Saratoga Springs. Every so often, Kathy remembers another incident from their exciting lives, and I want to share one of those.

After eighteen years of bed and breakfast proprietorship, the Lombardis decided to retire, putting their old farmstead up for sale. They had rescued a wonderful old house, a former stop on the Underground Railroad, from its miserable state, and modernized it into a showplace. Now, with retirement and a smaller home in the offing, they advertised the business on the local real estate market. No buyers were to be found, and many prospects realized the great amount of labor needed to retain the Lombardis' quiet, hospitable atmosphere.

Lombardi Farm had seventeen rooms and ten acres of pasture to maintain, and their two children had gone on to careers: Grace to the corporate life and Vincent Jr. into the field of medicine. Sadly, Vincent Jr., a nurse-anesthesiologist, had died suddenly several years before their retirement. Still grieving the loss of their only son, and failing to find a buyer through Saratoga real estate contacts, the couple made one last effort and placed a small ad in the Albany newspaper.

"The night that we placed that ad," Kathy told me, "I had a very vivid dream. I saw myself sitting at the kitchen table with my son, and he told me, 'If you want to sell the farm you must pray to St. Francis.' I replied to him, 'I don't know anything about St. Francis, and I am not going to pray to somebody I don't know.' Then, the next morning's mail brought me a card, the kind you sometimes receive from funeral parlors at someone's wake. Strangely, though, this card had no deceased person's name on it, so it couldn't have been something mis-sent. I looked closely and saw a picture of St. Francis on one side, with the famous St. Francis prayer (I've since learned by heart) on the back.

"'Lord, make me an instrument of your peace. Where there is hatred, let me sow love. Where there is injury, pardon. Where there is darkness, light, and where there is doubt, faith. Where there is sadness, joy.' I read it through just once and felt comforted by those words I'd never read before. How neat that all was—a coincidence?

"Just a short time after the mail arrived there came a knock at the door. Two women passing by told me they had seen the newspaper ad and had fallen in love with the farm even before coming in. They toured the interior and then we sat down to talk. They paid cash and the entire transaction took just thirty minutes. Vinny and I discussed the matter over and over. Maybe our deceased son could get a higher view from where he was in eternity, and St. Francis has been near and dear to our hearts ever since then," she laughed.

Ask and You Shall Receive

13 Melbourne Ave.

Dorothy Laselva grew up in the mill town of Hudson Falls, New York, in the 1920s. Those were hard times, and her father was lucky to have work, though the family was crowded into a small apartment at 13 Melbourne Avenue. Her mother was ill, and Grandmother had come to live in the apartment to help care for the woman, even though Grandmother, like Dorothy's father, her son, was "a black Protestant." Dorothy's mother, a staunch Roman Catholic, raised Dorothy, age five, and her brother, seven, to attend Mass, know the prayers, and say them morning and night.

At the time of this story, in the cold winter of 1927, the doctor had come to their house and examined the mother who lay, very pale, in her bed. Around a corner ten feet away, Dorothy could hear the doctor's words to her father through the wall, "Well, sir, if she can make it through the night, she'll live." The little girl panicked; she hadn't realized how sick her mom was, and she began to pray aloud to her favorite saint, Therese of Lisieux, "the Little Flower," who had died just thirty years before. Holding her small statue of Therese, Dorothy prayed aloud, "Please help save my mommy." She knew her Protestant grandmother, who didn't believe in praying to saints, was listening, but Therese had always been her friend and guide, the personification of a God-loving girl.

Finishing her prayer, Dorothy rolled over in her iron crib and prepared to sleep. Suddenly a movement caught her eye. There, across the room, where the doorway to the closet was obscured by a curtain, the fabric was moving! Through the veil suddenly stepped a beautiful young woman in a nun's garb. Dorothy knew the face—it was her beloved Therese! The apparition moved a few feet in her direction, just out of reach. The little girl elevated herself on an elbow and begged Therese, "Please help me—are you St. Therese?" There was no response, just the nun's tender smile. Once more, Dorothy pleaded, "Can you tell me if my Mommy is going to get better?" Again, the nun smiled, but then retreated behind the curtain, and out of sight. Dorothy called out, "Please come back!" but the curtains no longer moved. She sat in wonder. Has anyone else seen the lady? I don't think so. Will my prayers help? she wondered. Before she knew it, she had fallen asleep, confident that something good would happen.

In the morning the girl awoke to familiar sounds, footsteps and Grandmother sliding the teapot across the top of the kitchen stove, and Dorothy smelled the aroma of hot cocoa. There were happy voices coming from the kitchen; her father and grandmother were speaking rapidly and happily. Dorothy sprang from bed and peered into her mother's bedroom, where Mommy was awake, giving a weak smile and wave. It seemed certain she would get better, and she did.

"I always prayed to St. Therese for the rest of my life," Dorothy told me. "I feel certain that my vision was of her spirit or ghost, if you want, but it was a real presence that came into my bedroom. I hope you'll tell this story in your next book about ghosts," she told me, "because that was the happiest ghost I ever met."

Since telling me her memorable story, Dorothy went beyond the veil in 2005, and now she has plenty of time to converse and laugh with Therese, and maybe strew some roses on others' path.

Help An Old Man!

One genre of ghost is the so-called "hitchhiker ghost," an individual who is encountered momentarily, then vanishes en route to the viewer's destination. In 1968, when I became interested in ghosts, I met Professor Rod Roberts from the State University of New York in Oneonta. Rod told me of his collection of such tales from all over the world; he had recorded 1,000 hitchhiker ghost tales at the time. "They exist everywhere," he said, "and there is no city or country in the world without at least one such story." My personal experience since then bears that out, especially following a personal experience that I recounted in *Ghosts of the Northeast.* Here is one such story from my friend Theo, a sensitive, in New York City.

"I was a projectionist at the old Times Square Theater on 42nd Street between 7th and 8th Avenues," he told me, "and I had an unforgettable experience after leaving there on a cold February night in 1982. Our last show usually let out around 3:45 a.m., and I was finished by 4. That night however, as I left the lobby, I had a sudden sensation of being not quite all there. Something inexpressible had changed, but I couldn't figure what that was. Once I got onto the street, the eeriness increased. This is no time to have your head in the clouds, I told myself. The sidewalks are icy, and the wind is bitter cold—you'd better watch that you don't have an accident. I picked my way over the frozen snow and ice piled along the curb and headed across 8th Avenue. There were many street people wandering about, so I also had to watch who was nearby.

"There was some unreal quality to the night, but attempting to ignore it, I kept my head down in the cold wind, hurrying to my destination. On the other side of the street, when I did look up, I could see a hatless old man in a tattered coat standing there and calling out to passersby, 'Help an old man.' Again, he begged loudly and plaintively, 'Help an old man over the ice.' I figured he was a wino and made no effort to comply once I crossed the street to his corner. Twisting away from his grasp, I brushed past the man. The whole atmosphere on the street was unreal, though, so I chalked that sensation up to imagination, the cold air, and my tiredness.

"I walked just a few steps, but immediately felt the greatest guilt and shame for having avoided the old guy. Immediately, I knew I couldn't ignore him, so I turned back, ready to smell the reeking scent of his unwashed body and alcohol. But, strange thing, when I got close to him, I smelled nothing! I looked into the guy's bright blue eyes and told him I'd help, so I took his hand

255

and he gripped my arm, and we crossed. It was a real, solid arm and he was three-dimensional—a real man. People went by us, though, and no one even looked at us. That was odd—at that time of the night on 8th Avenue, you always looked at who was coming near you. We got to the other side of the street and he let go but never said a word—no thanks or anything! Go figure, I thought to myself, and walked back across the street to head home.

"After about twenty feet, I looked back. The guy was still there, looking at me, and he hadn't moved a bit, so I hurried on farther, and glanced back once more. He was still there and hadn't budged. I began to get the feeling that the entire situation was uncanny or supernatural. So, I just had to look back a third time. He was gone—vanished! I could see for an entire block in any direction, and there was no one on the street! He was just gone, nowhere in sight!"

Theo, being of the Greek Orthodox faith, related the story to his priest a month later. "What color were his eyes?" was all that the cleric asked.

"Blue. Very blue," Theo answered.

"Jesus had very blue eyes according to legend," the priest smiled, and that's all he said.

I just never knew what to do with that idea—that I had helped Jesus across the street. Had I? If not, even if it was an ordinary ghost, where did he go? So, to this day, I tell myself it was just a regular ghost. But then…," his voice trailed off, and we stood silently, pondering the meaning of it all.

You Are Not Your Body

Those are the words spoken to me by a unique woman soon after our ghost story interview began. A Buddhist yogi, who grew up in the Finger Lakes area and now resides in Syracuse, Tashi gave me that phrase as a summary of her lifetime's experience. You see, she has been clairvoyant all her life, and thus doesn't know how not to see and experience ghosts.

"What was your first paranormal experience?" I asked her, knowing full well that immersion in "the other world" was now a normal day's experience for her.

"My mother noted that in early childhood, I had continual conversations with my 'friends,' what most folks call 'imaginary friends.' Many adults think it's cute for little children to indulge in these harmless fantasies, but they were real beings to me. I remember that, at age seven, I was told of my Uncle Nick's death. A few days later, my mother got me dressed up to go to his wake.

I didn't know the term and asked her about it. She explained that my uncle had died and he would be in a big box for people to come and say goodbye to.

"At the funeral home, we walked to the casket, but I didn't recognize the person inside. As I sat on the kneeler, Mom asked if I wanted to say a rosary for Uncle Nick, but I said 'No, I don't need to—Uncle Nick is over there, standing in the corner.' That was a surprise to her, and she looked but couldn't see him. I guess that is when I began to realize that this death stuff really wasn't what a lot of people supposed."

As she grew older, Tashi occasionally offered information to her teenage friends and, although many were helped, her clairvoyance made some uneasy. For example, her friend Joe's father died. Two weeks later, the teenagers sat around discussing life, and one offered the certainty that Joe's father had gone immediately to Heaven upon his death. Tashi looked over at her friend, Joe, and spotted his father standing behind the boy. "There was always the question as to whether or not I should disclose what I saw," she said wryly.

As life passed, Tashi found the teachings of her childhood religion didn't fully explain her visionary experiences or many physical events that she observed. She began a search for meaning during the difficult years of the Vietnam War and, perhaps influenced by the horrors of the conflict, found both solace and understanding in Buddhism, specifically in its Tibetan form.

"Harm no living thing," said The Buddha, and Tashi felt this to be the most palatable of life's choices. She met a Vietnam veteran who had experienced the loss of four close friends in Vietnam, and noted that the four were still clustering about him in spirit.

"I learned that when one visits haunted places, there are several common explanations for spirits' tenacity. On some occasions, the spirit of the deceased just can't let go of the person or location because he or she loved it so much. Hollywood ill-serves us by portraying most ghosts as fearsome. In such cases, the spirit has to learn to lovingly let go of their earthly love in order to find an even more encompassing Love. There are other ghosts inhabiting places of violence and sudden death," she told me, "places such as murder scenes or battlefields. Other souls are as yet unable to detach from places of sudden death or suicide. I see all types every day. Sometimes, I try to help them."

Fervently moved by Buddhism's ideals, Tashi sought deeper involvement in that religion and hoped to move to British Columbia, to work at the Buddhist center in Surrey. "When I got there for my interview," she told me, "I immediately encountered an old man ghost who paced back and forth. I couldn't get his name, but he told me clairvoyantly that he had to retrieve something from the loo. Not knowing that this word was a British euphemism for the bathroom, I was still scowling when ushered into the office of my prospective boss. Could I, should I, reveal this experience to the woman? Might it jinx my application? Yet, somehow, the woman surmised that I had second sight.

"'Who is it?' she asked me after a few minutes.

"'It is an old man who tells me that he has to get rid of stuff in the loo,' I responded.

"'You know that this building used to be a nursing home?' she asked. 'Well, let's see which loo it might be, as we have five in the building.'

"'It's the one by the back door,' I responded, suddenly aware of the location.

"We entered the bathroom and explored the contents. Nothing was visible. Then, I suddenly became inspired, dropped the toilet seat, then stood on it and reached up to the dropped-ceiling's tiles. Pushing one up, I felt around in the darkness above. Suddenly, I uttered an 'Aha!' and handed down to her a pile of pornographic magazines. Evidently, the old man was feeling some remorse over that episode in his life and needed to redeem his self-image in the disembodied life. I guess we took care of that for him.

"Not too much later, knowing that the woman was impressed, I felt free to divulge my impression that there were several wandering entities in the building, and one of the most active was an old woman. I experienced her traveling about and bemoaning her inability to find someone named Lucille. So, I told my prospective boss and she invited me to tour the records file with her. We discovered that, in the nursing home days, there had been a nurse with the name Lucille, who cared for the terminal patients, injecting their morphine painkillers as needed. I have discovered that the old woman slept her way into death and just didn't understand that she had died. Many of the spirits that I meet are in that state of not suspecting that they have passed."

"It must be a burden to have so much knowledge," I suggested.

Tashi smiled and said, "I remember, a few years ago, sitting in an auditorium and listening to the Syracuse Symphony tuning up before a concert. The room was still buzzing with conversation as we all awaited the conductor coming on-stage. I explained to my companion that this clairvoyant flow of voices is similar, almost continual in my head if I permit it. And, if a spirit knows that you have seen them or are aware of their presence, they often are all over you, with messages that they want delivered to the living, often family members.

"There is a funeral directors school in central New York State that I often drive past, and there, especially, I encounter such individuals whose bodies have been embalmed but not yet transported to their local funeral homes.

Sometimes, I have to pull over and sit quietly in meditation in order to contact those individuals and explain what is taking place, also to encourage these souls to move on into the Light," she told me. "One such man didn't want to leave me until I agreed to take a twenty-pound turkey to his relative. Imagine a stranger showing up at your door with a free turkey from Ralph, and you know Ralph has been dead for ten years!" she grinned.

"Around Christmastime, maybe from the 15th of December to New Year's, there is a surge of entities wanting to contact their loved ones. One discarnate man came to me and I recognized him as the father of one of my childhood friends. The man was very upset that his son had not talked to his sisters since the father's funeral. So I visited that adult son and found a way to tell him of his father's distress, but the son was not very receptive to my message and chased me out, refusing to make the Christmas Eve phone call. Well, lots of the living don't want to hear from their dead loved ones; others are even less inclined to follow the messages."

I asked Tashi if she had other experiences that I could share with my readers. "I often can share my foresight of a person's death with their loved ones because I can see almost an amber glow around those about to pass. I discovered this ability when I was in high school, when one day in 1966, I spotted this dim light around a coach, and two days later he was killed in a car crash. Maybe this is the dim light spoken of in the *Tibetan Book of the Dead*.

"It speaks of the Bardo Thodol, a dimly lit dimension between earth life and heaven, a place where all the dead must go. It can be a launching station into the Everlasting for some souls, but for those who cannot detach from a particular person, object, sensation, or scenario out of their just-ended life, it becomes a place of discomfort. We call these seemingly trapped individuals 'hungry ghosts'; they still hunger and crave for something that never was real in the first place. Souls passing through the Bardo, we say, are 'riding the rapids' emotionally or spiritually. That is why the *Book of the Dead* has a technique called phowa, which the monks employ to give comfort to souls commencing that journey back into their true identity."

At the end of our talk, she gave a great smile, which reminded me of so many statues of the Buddha, always smiling. Perhaps that is because he knew something that we all should know about death…and life.

NEW YORK STATE GHOSTS

CHAPTER 10

BUSINESS GHOSTS

Julia

Julia

The McGregor family was well-to-do and could afford the best of residences in 1885. They built a beautiful home near the top of Market Street Hill in Amsterdam, New York, and adorned it with the finest in woodwork and paneling. Bronze grates were installed to channel warm air to the upper stories, and a brass servant call-bell system reached to the third floor. One room was appointed in birds-eye maple and another in oak, with a third in walnut. Decorative patterns with mythological scenes were inset into the fronts of the building's five fireplaces, and marble sconces provided light along the stairways. The exterior gables were a showpiece of Victorian gingerbread architecture.

Elizabeth K. McGregor, according to historians, dominated life in the mansion as the family matriarch. When her daughter, Julia M. McGregor, found a suitor and planned for the nuptials, Elizabeth intervened, sending the swain on his way and dooming her daughter to spinsterhood. Not satisfied with managing her daughter's life, the woman also destroyed the marital hopes of a granddaughter, Julia K. Moore. After many years, Elizabeth finally went into the arms of Heavenly Love, but the discouraged granddaughter, young Julia, could not bring herself to venture into matrimony. She lived on as an old maid in the mansion until the Eternal Power called her home in 1974. For a while, the house sat empty while the estate was settled. Then the electronic age came to the Market Street hilltop.

Radio station WKOL took over the quarters and operated a modern radio station in the rooms that once entertained the gentry of the Carpet City. Modern pop and rock music now blared forth from rooms that once hosted piano and violin recitals for the city's upper crust. And somewhere in the hustle and bustle of modern communications, one of the former residents began to assert herself. There has been some discussion as to which of the three McGregors remains, but the odds heavily favor Julia K. Moore, the house's last occupant. Electronic glitches at WKOL became more frequent as some energy began to interfere with the normal functioning of the broadcast equipment.

In 1985, former station account executive Mark Scott told Schenectady's *Gazette* reporter Patrick Kurp of the day that the station simply went off the air. No excuse or cause could be found. Then, after a few minutes, the broadcast resumed. Sometime later, afternoon show producer Steve Savage watched as a commercial tape cartridge machine suddenly turned itself on. Such machines require a modicum of pressure to insert a tape, but no human hand touched this one. Afterward, Lloyd Smith, the station engineer, was able to clear up some of the mystery to his own satisfaction, as he noted the cart machine was likely triggered by a static discharge from the floors. He also believes the station going off the air was the fault of the phone company, which occasionally tested their "feeling current" line to the transmitter, causing an interruption in the broadcasts.

One afternoon, a disc jockey was taping some material for insertion in a future program, but as the tape ran, the man suddenly gasped and momentarily walked away from the mike. He returned to tell listeners that he had just seen a beautiful woman in a pink dress move past his console and into the next studio. She had clearly been visible through the glass window in front of him. He had dashed out to intercept her in the hallway, but no one was there or in the other studio when he entered. The station's employees tried very hard not to panic as, after all, ghosts were the object of ridicule to modern scientific broadcasters. Nevertheless, someone suggested that a psychic be called, "just in case."

Tom Kearns, a Capital District psychic who calls himself "The Centaur," visited WKOL and went into the attic, accompanied by station manager Ellyn Ambrose, Tom's assistant, Michele, and Ellyn's dog. After a quiet prayer, Tom popped a cassette of quiet musical chanting into his portable tape player. Then, as the vibrations slowed in the attic space, Kearns entered a light trance as the Top Forty played quietly in the on-air studio downstairs. Those assembled heard the psychic converse with an ancient Mohawk Indian who used to sit on the hill centuries before, admiring the river far below. The spirit said he was agitated that he could no longer see over modern day buildings. Whether or not this aggravation was enough to cause the electrical glitches wasn't discovered.

Kearns then saw a small girl, perhaps seven or eight years of age, skip into the attic room and suddenly fall to the floor. Rising, the child, dressed in a long blue gown, walked to Michele and slapped her lightly on the face. Michele's face registered a wide-eyed look, as nobody (human, anyway) had come near her. Later, Tom and Michele consulted city historians and became convinced the slap was a jealous fit by the house's last owner, who showed her lack of power in life by appearing as a child. [N.B. Ghosts seem able to project themselves to be any age of their past life, and ghost hunters should pay attention to the projected stage of physical development, as it might provide a clue to who the spirit is and why it appears.] The city historians said that Julia's heart had been broken by Grandmother Elizabeth, and Julia's soul couldn't leave the house because of her ongoing, unresolved grief. Kearns, well-versed in activities of the spirit world because he is an ordained Spiritualist minister, claimed that the high power of the radio station helped to energize Julia's spirit.

After Kearns' visit, the phenomena continued unabated. Steve Savage, who worked the 7 p.m. to midnight shift, saw the phone line lit for an outgoing call, though he was certain that he was alone in the station. Before he could fully comprehend the situation, the line went dark. He put on another song and toured the entire house; perhaps a salesman had come in? No one else was there, and the outside door was locked. No human could have made the call.

On another occasion, Savage was sure he saw the gorgeous young lady in a pink dress watching him, but before he could react, she vanished. Ms. Ambrose, determined to get to the bottom of the matter, hired an American Indian psychic to investigate the house. It was the seer's impression that the hubbub was caused by the spirit of a chauffeur who had killed himself in the old McGregor garage. But if so, why did the psychics only see girls or women?

After eleven years, WKOL (1570 AM and 97.7 FM) turned in its call letters to the FCC and ceased broadcasting, and again the house stood empty. In 1989, Leonard Fiore and his wife, Fran, purchased the old house and began to restore it as headquarters for Fiore's company, The Mohawk Valley Management Corporation. The dingy, blue-grey walls were repainted, and the grey commercial carpet was stripped away. Panels that obscured stained glass windows were removed and temporary partitions were taken out to once more restore the openness and elegance enjoyed a century before. Woodwork was stripped and sanded, and the hand-painted tiles on fireplaces were scrubbed shiny again. Metalwork was polished, especially the antique brass plaque on the front door that still bears Julia Moore's name, and the new company went to work.

Working conditions became more tolerable, though Noreen Langford, the company secretary, had her irritations. She told Sam Zurlo, local newsman, that "I've been alone at night catching up on some work, and I'm not afraid." Nevertheless, she had to put up with a shutter on the window behind her desk which kept falling down. She'd put it back up, and a minute later it would fall again. In exasperation one day, Langford said aloud, "Julia, please leave the shutter alone!" It never fell again. Apparently, Julia, as with most ghosts, simply wanted recognition that she still owned the house. On another occasion, Langford's pen disappeared from the center of the desk, and no amount of searching could bring it back. Finally, she spoke aloud, asking Julia to bring it back. Two days later, it appeared, right in the middle of the blotter.

Eventually, the real estate company ceased its operation in the old house and the building was sold to a property management company that rents out various rooms in the house as apartments. One wonders what tales these unsuspecting tenants will provide.

Licensed to Haunt?

My friend, Bill Getz, and I sat reminiscing one day, when he turned to me and asked, "You want to hear a strange experience that I had over twenty years ago? I don't know if it's a ghost story or not, but that's the only category that I can put it in." I responded, "Of course," and grabbed my notebook and pen.

"In the middle 1980s, maybe 1985, my wife and I had rental property in the Oswego County village of Pulaski. It was an apartment building that required maintenance from time to time, so on that particular weekend we worked on a vacant apartment, especially rebuilding the small deck outside. I used a pry bar to pull some of the old nails, and as I tugged on a very reluctant one, I suddenly felt a muscle in my lower back tear. What pain! I collapsed onto the planking and was unable to move. I knew I was hurt bad, but felt that I might be able to get across the street to visit the chiropractor whose office was there. I asked my wife to phone to see if the doctor would give me an emergency treatment, though his specialty was bone adjustment and not suturing torn muscles," he remembered.

A few minutes later, Bill's wife returned with a grave expression, saying, "Bad news, Bill. The answering machine said that the chiropractor is out of town on vacation and won't be back for two weeks." What am I going to do? he asked himself. I have a job to go to on Monday, and that's down in Albany; I'll never make it. "Well, check and see if there's another chiropractor in town, or maybe over in Mexico or in Oswego—I've got to get some relief," he instructed his mate.

"Okay, I've found another man, down on Bridge Street," she said when she returned, "it's a Doctor John MacDonald, so I called and asked, and he said to come right down." Feeling lucky, Bill and his wife struggled downstairs to the car and she drove him to an old building on Bridge Street. His wife parked and Getz shuffled inside, feeling as if his back was being seared with hot irons.

"There was an old sign with MacDonald's name on the door, so I entered his waiting room. Had I not been in such pain, I would have turned right around and left," Bill said, "because there were dust bunnies under the chairs and old magazines strewn on the chairs. What kind of professional man would want his office to repel patients? There was a noise from another room, and all at once there was an old man, who seemed to be about seventy or older in the doorway. 'Hello, I'm John MacDonald,' the man said. Again, I was put off. Though he wore an old Harris Tweed jacket with elbow patches, it was worn in spots, and that style hadn't been in since the 1950s. But what most turned me off was his overly-long, yellow-stained fingernails. How can this guy work on people's muscles and bones with such long nails and not injure them, I wondered. My back pain suddenly surged again and I'd have gone anywhere with anyone who offered to help me right then," Bill smiled.

"What did you do to yourself?" the doctor asked, "let's see if we can work on you. Lie down and then gently roll onto your stomach."

"When I got turned over, I noticed the man's hands again, and they held strange objects, so I asked what was up," said Bill.

"I'm not going to do a spinal adjustment today," Dr. MacDonald said, "but I am going to use some magnets on your muscles." He then told Bill how, years before, he had almost lost his life, but had been given magnet therapy by another doctor and was healed so much that he decided to become a practitioner himself.

"I now use these five-inch-long bar magnets wrapped with adhesive tape, which allows me to hold onto them better," the therapist said. MacDonald also told Bill that he was fifty-six,, though Bill thought the therapist seemed to have aged badly. For forty minutes MacDonald continued his gentle treatment, and by the time Bill rose to his feet, he felt much better.

With the admonition to do no more physical work that day, the doctor released Bill after he had paid a small fee. "I think it was $25," Bill recollected, "and I told him that I needed a receipt for my insurance plan reimbursement. Dr. MacDonald went into his office, which I could see was messier than his waiting room. From somewhere in the stacks of papers on his desk, the chiropractor found an Empire Plan insurance form and filled it in.

"When I returned home I lay on the floor with my feet elevated, as the doctor had ordered. When it came to be bedtime, I had no pain at all. Next morning I felt brand new and, despite MacDonald's order, I hefted my hammer and pry bar, and felt so good that I ignored his orders and rebuilt the deck, then we left for our home near Albany.

"Two weeks later, we returned to Pulaski and, after finishing a few small jobs, I felt a small back twinge and called Dr. MacDonald for an appointment. Instead, I got a phone company recording that it was no longer a working number, so I hopped in the car and drove down to the office. The interior lights weren't on and I quickly spotted a weathered real estate 'for sale' sign from the Bognacki firm. I tried the door and it was locked. I looked inside the waiting room window and could see the interior was completely empty.

"Thinking that Dr. MacDonald had moved, I called Bognacki to find the new address," Bill told me. "Bognacki was puzzled. 'Why that building has been for sale for five years! There is no Dr. MacDonald there now; he's dead!'"

"No, wait a minute," I said to Bognacki, "this is Doctor John MacDonald. Maybe you're confused."

"The real estate man was nonplused and told me that that was the man he was talking about. 'You can see how old the sign on the building is,' he told me, 'I nailed it on there five years ago when we listed the place. Nobody has even rented the building since then.'"

Bill is a bright guy but just couldn't figure it out. An employee of the New York State Education Department at the time, he had friends in the licensing division, so on Monday, he consulted them. The staff member searched the chiropractic files and returned to report that MacDonald had been dropped from the department's listings because he had no professional training and had never been granted a license. "Besides," the clerk told him, "he's been dead for five years, anyway. Why did you want to know?" Bill mumbled an excuse and returned to his job as Director of Training in another building.

"My insurance company paid the bill, I'm certain," he told me, "though I have misplaced the old reimbursement forms that I kept after that issue. I know what I experienced and I know I met the man in his office, that he healed me and that I'm okay today, when I should have been in the emergency room that morning," Bill said. "Ever since then, I have tried to comprehend it all. What I know for sure is that I prayed really hard for someone to help me feel even a little bit better that first day as we drove down to Bridge Street. All I can figure is that my desperate need drew someone from the spirit world who should never have been in that old office. My prayers were answered, but who would believe me?"

I told Bill that I did believe him, that truth is often stranger than fiction, so we both went for some coffee therapy while trying unsuccessfully to think of alternate explanations.

Malvina and Others

St. Lawrence State Hospital

The Ogdensburg State Asylum for the Insane was created near the banks of the St. Lawrence River in 1887, but state authorities quickly changed the name and re-christened the facility as the St. Lawrence State Hospital, which name it retained until the late 1970s, when it became the St. Lawrence Psychiatric Center. In 1982, a major section of the institution was turned over to the State Department of Corrections for renovation and use as a medium-security prison. Though the living psychiatric patients were moved, some of those who had died in the hospital appear to have stayed put.

"I first worked for State Mental Health at the Rockland State Hospital," Bill Norman told me, "and then, when I was in my 40s, I took courses to continue in state service as a corrections officer. So, that makes me one of the few COs still alive who have worked under both departments. And that is why I think I know some things that the newer officers don't know—or don't want to know.

"When I began working there in 1968, I'd often hear stories from older officers about events that occurred 'down back,' in some of the older parts of the facility. One of those tales, one that continues to be told to the new officers, is that of Malvina Lemaurier. Long before I started work here, in what we call the 'Quiet Rec' area today, there was a female psychiatric patient named Malvina. She was dead and gone, well pretty much gone," he smiled, "when I started my employment.

"Before she died, the old timers often saw her hunkering down along the hallway wall there, just watching other patients go by. All of a sudden, though, she'd lurch to her feet and grab a passerby. Sometimes, I think, she'd ask for a cigarette, but other times she'd just grab at them. So, after she had died, I wasn't too surprised to feel a tug on my sleeve one day as I walked there during my early hospital days. Nowadays, however," he grinned, "there is the occasional CO or inmate strolling through that apparently empty spot, when they'll suddenly jump aside as if somebody just groped them. One old timer CO once believed he'd heard a female voice there ask, 'Do you have a light?'"

Ogdensburg Correctional Facility

Bill's story is perhaps the most commonly repeated tale at Ogdensburg Correctional Facility, even as a joke, though it usually happens to "some other guy" if you ask today's corrections officers. In a profession where "being in control" is important, not too many COs want to admit to an inmate that they can't manage. Malvina, who is said to have died in her sleep, just may not be ready to sign herself out yet.

As readers of ghost stories know, most ghostly incidents seem to occur at times when things are quiet and not much human energy is being expended—at night, usually. Ghostly energies (or voices, if they speak) are subtle, but the spirits are not respecters of office or station in life. It should not be surprising, then, that in the last two decades there has been a variety of strange events in the Flower Building.

One officer has twice caught movements in the Gym out of the corner of his eye, though nobody is there when he directs his attention that way. He also has heard talking in the 115 Corridor and, thinking once that the sound came from outside, he looked out the windows, but nobody was there. A few days later, outside those same windows, he heard the indistinguishable voices again, but this time, they seemed to emanate from inside. As he told me this he laughed, remembering being called to come to a certain place with a fellow officer, as a lieutenant wanted to meet with the pair. When the two men got there, the lieutenant was late, although when he appeared, he asked the two officers why they had been at the attic window waving at him. Both vehemently denied doing so, yet the lieutenant was sure of what he'd seen. Who would have enough free time to go into a hot attic just to pull a prank on the man?

That officer told of a recent (late 2006) incident where a lady wearing a white hospital gown was seen sitting on a bench in the 115 Corridor. A porter (inmate) was astounded to see the woman alone and unconcerned, sitting among male inmates. CO Jim told me that the inmate porter swore that he would never work on that corridor again and instead would go to the 'Box' (punishment) if ever ordered to work there again. A search of the area turned up no one matching the lady's description; after all, OCF is an all-male facility.

Another incident involved levitating coffee cups in a sergeant's office in the front upstairs of the Flower Building. "This happened to me twice in the same week," Jim told me. "The first time, I saw a cup levitate off the stack of cups and remain in the air for a few seconds. I then grabbed it and put the cup back down on the stack. The other sergeant said, 'Hey, neat trick!' The second time, another sergeant saw it happen just as it had before, "but that time, two other sergeants were witnesses."

I was told that an arsenal officer surveys the grounds all night long via his bank of television cameras. On some nights he will see faces peering out of closed office building windows. Another officer has been disturbed, upon entering the sleeping section of the Temporary Housing Unit, to hear bedsprings moving—but this comes on nights when there are no inmates there. I asked Bill Norman if he ever found himself whistling a tune as he made his rounds at night. "You bet!" he said with a smile.

CO Dan Clark gave me an escorted tour of the facility in the early summer of 2007. Probably Dan is no more sensitive than the average officer, but he is straightforward and feels the need to talk about the unexplained occurrences on his shifts in the past twenty years. "There is a small foyer just off the old gym area, right at the stair top where I often feel a 'something' but have never been able to see it," he told me. "Here is the Parole Draft Area," he told me as we walked through the yard, "and there is a history of strange events here too." The PDA is a separate building traditionally used for signing new inmates into the facility and completing the official paperwork for others to leave. "Look back there," he told me as he gestured out the window to an old no-longer-used brick building from the early State Hospital days. "See that window upstairs, near the end—a porter working in this room once saw a man looking out with his face pressed against the window. The porter just stood here with his jaw hanging until the CO in charge glanced at him and got a description. Of course that building has long been closed, and is now used just for storage."

For just a moment I quieted myself, seeking some scenes from yesteryear, and perhaps a clue as to whether the PDA office might still retain a spirit or two. I sensed the energy of a 50ish, partially bald and stooped man named Charlie. If he was real, he was thinking of his mother at the time and savoring the light duty that he had earned. To my left, where counters and shelving are today, there may once have been a couch.

"Let's see the cellar," said Dan, escorting me through several locked doors, down steps, and to the earthen floored basement. Many items are stored there, but the space is no longer used for patients or inmates. Endless miles of steam pipes and electrical conduits run through tunnels beneath the yard to other buildings. I was rather surprised then, in one room, to think I saw a very stylish, slim, black-haired woman in what was once called a "sack dress." Outlandish as she seemed in that cellar, which was quite well lit, I told Dan of my impression, as if the vision was of an old-time "flapper girl" from the 1920s.

He was silent a while, then his face lit up. "You know, there is the story passed down from the old Psychiatric Center days of a professional model from New York City being committed here. According to the story, she was involved indirectly in a murder case in New York City in 1919, then unsuccessfully attempted suicide in 1922. I believe it was Audrey Munson, a famous sculptors' model who died here ten years ago at age 105," Dan said, referring to my ghost lady.

Though I had never heard of Audrey, remembering the pretty face, I began researching her. The 1919 incident may have triggered a psychosis that helped trigger her later suicide attempt, as she then retreated to her family home in Mexico, New York. Soon after, she became delusional and was committed to the state hospital at Ogdensburg. Records show that by the time she reached Ogdensburg she was never able to speak coherently again. "Might be her," Dan concluded.

I never know how seriously to take my mini-visions, but it was interesting that the gorgeous lady fit into the prison's lore. One other factor that I discovered is that Audrey Munson was buried in an unmarked grave just

Audrey Munson

271

outside Mexico, where the historical society and several downstate authors are now attempting to finance a gravestone so that Audrey's spirit can finally be at rest. Lack of a memorial marker or gravestone can sometimes cause a spirit to remain earthbound and roaming, not able to convince themselves that they died.

In one room of the prison school building's second floor, near the Sergeant's Office, Dan showed me around; there was no staff there. I was just turning to leave that room when all of a sudden, there was a "someone" there, standing with his back to the window. In my mind, I noted first the man's black hair and short black beard, and their contrast with his white physician's coat. He might also have had a stethoscope around his neck. "Who or what are you?" I silently asked. "I'm here to make sure they all get their shots," was the telepathic response. Was he a doctor from some long-ago inoculation clinic? Dan, my guide, was totally unaware of my experience until I told him as we walked away. He gave me a strange look, but I think he believed it was possible.

Later, outdoors, I remembered a similar haunted counseling building that I had toured at Mt. McGregor Correctional Facility in Wilton, N.Y. when we passed the Activities Building. I asked my escort if, after being locked for the night, there were ever any strange events or noises in there. He smiled and responded, "One of the roundsmen (roving nighttime security men) has heard an interior door slam, though it's certain that the building was locked and unoccupied at the time." Other roundsmen encounter unique enigmas also.

Outside a Sergeant's office, near the medical office, which is kept locked, Corrections Officer Joe told me he once found all the interior lights turned on after the staff person departed and locked up for the day. Another Sergeant found a television turned on in a secured classroom. He turned it off and swung around to leave the room, only to hear the TV turn on again behind him. Undaunted, the officer simply unplugged the set and left, locking the room behind him. It stayed off that time. When I checked back with Dan in late December 2007, he reported several recent instances in which door handles had been suddenly yanked out of officers' hands, though no inmate or officer was nearby.

Bill Norman seems to have had the greatest number of spirit contacts among the still-living corrections staff. He told of his first work experiences at the old Psychiatric Center's Ward 38. "I was really beat when I came on duty one night and I'm sure I nodded off at my desk during that shift. Suddenly, I snapped awake, aware that I heard steps right next to me. I looked around and found the door from the stairs opening, then shutting. I jumped up, looked down the stairs, found nothing, so I looked into the ward. Nobody was there and nothing was moving," he told me. "This happened to two other older guys about that time, too. But I had actually seen the doorknob turn!

"Walking the dark hallway in the Flower Building one night, headed toward the front of the building, I felt someone brush past me, though it was clear that nobody else was there. But that is just one more of the experiences I encountered when I first came to work at the Psychiatric Center," Bill continued. "Once, when I was on the female side in Ward 34, I stopped to get a cup of coffee and heard walking in the upstairs. There wasn't supposed to be any person or activity up there, so I hurried up. That room hadn't been used for a long time and there was a thick coating of dust all over everything, and especially on the floor. Every light was turned on at the set of switches on the other side of the room, yet, there were no footprints in the dust between me and those switches. I just wrote it off as another one of 'those things.'

"Dick Paradise worked with me in Ward 39 once, and during the night, just after I went downstairs to get a cup of coffee, I found Dick running downstairs right after me. He was all excited and told me of a 'cloud of smoke' suddenly appearing in the middle of the ward. I went up and checked, but found nothing. Then, it occurred to me that John H., one of the patients, was regularly reporting being bothered at night by someone or something that he couldn't see there. He was delusional, however, so I never knew how seriously to take it. But nobody, patients or staff, could see anything physical there to deal with in any case!"

Bill said that he eventually chose to switch to the new Corrections Department before the Psychiatric Center closed. "So, after training, I was sent to Sing Sing and then to Fishkill Corrections Facility to work. If I thought the ghosts were just in Ogdensburg, however, I had another thought coming. But I'll tell you about those places for your next book," he laughed.

All the present-day corrections officers must be present for a line-up at the beginning of each shift, when specific orders and notices are provided for the officers coming on duty. Sometimes, anomalies reported by the outgoing shift are passed on, many times creating a humorous situation and joshing of co-workers for what seem to be outlandish stories. Corrections officers are in positions of control—they have to be if the institution is to run smoothly and safely. But who can control Malvina if they can't see her? And what officer wants to tell his buddies about invisible patients or doctors or Broadway models? And all in a prison?

One For the Books

Phoenicia Library

In northwest Ulster County on Route 28 is found one of the nicest of Catskill Mountain hamlets, Phoenicia. One of several small mountain settlements in the county, Phoenicia is a latecomer, when compared with the older, eastern settlements of the county along the Hudson River, which date from the 1600s. It was abundant timber that brought the first workmen into the hills and mountains and there once were many sawmills located here. Later visitors, however, discovered the natural beauty in the Town of Shandaken and especially the fast-flowing streams that today make Phoenicia a magnet for kayaking and tubing fanatics.

Flowing a bit more slowly and less distinctly is an evanescent energy in the upstairs of the Phoenicia Library. For quite a few years, visitors have remarked on the sudden cold spots and strange feelings that assail them as they work on the upstairs computers in the old building. A friend told me about the library and that a group of ghost hunters had done a study of the place. I had to go and see and hear for myself.

I met with two old timers, Lonnie Gale and John Breithaupt, who have the longest memories of the community. They told me that a Saugerties druggist named Van Buskirk opened a pharmacy there in the 1880s in a building that probably already existed, though the builder is unknown today. Van Buskirk's daughter, Jenny, married H. Lee Breithaupt, John's father, and the place became H. Lee Breithaupt and Brother Funeral Home starting in 1902 and lasting until 1947. "The upstairs was a display area for coffins, while the first floor contained our office and a viewing room. My brother and I grew up in the business in that building. Then, after Dad's death in 1947," John said, "the building was vacant for some years before my mother sold it for use as a library." So that was the pedigree—just three prior owners before the library days. In checking up on ghost tales, we always want to know what has happened at the site before the stories came to be known. Lonnie and John both told me that they never heard about ghost presences there before the more recent ghost flap.

The current sighting story consists of this: A library patron went to the upstairs bathroom in 2005. As he climbed the stairs, the young man noticed movement to his immediate left—a figure emerging from the bathroom, who stopped, tipped his hat to the patron, then suddenly disappeared. No one had ever before sighted such a phenomenon there, and it bore investigating. A local investigative group offered to visit the library after hours, bringing recorders and cameras. They ended up with an image on their infrared video recorder. The filmy figure seemed to move across the upper large room, and through an area where the participants felt a sudden abnormal chill. Energy also registered at the stair top, where the young patron had first spotted the ghostly man who vanished.

"I have their video on our computer," library volunteer Molly Kilb, said, and she attempted to turn the machine on. It wouldn't turn on, though it had been operative earlier in the day. We checked all the plugs and connectors, but the computer screen remained dark. My new friend apologized and said she would need to have someone look at the device. Later, I discovered that the machine had somehow "cooked," and the library had to replace it. Did the Library Ghost want to continue hiding from me?

Downstairs, on another day, a woman patron waited patiently at the checkout desk to have her book stamped, wondering why the man seated in the swivel chair behind the counter didn't stand, step forward, and help her. Suddenly, the seated figure vanished, making the unsuspecting patron an instant believer. To date, none of the staff can identify who the spectral man might be; certainly not Molly, who also told me that little things are found moved when she opens the library in the morning. As the building has been locked at night, who might do the moving?

So, my next stop was the group known as East Coast Paranormal Society. I spoke with Buffy, the organization's leader, and she reaffirmed Molly's stories, noting that much of the disruptive energy focuses in the upstairs, in the computer area. "We often hear tales of computer malfunctions which cannot be explained," she told me. "Several individuals working at their monitors have told me of hearing footsteps ascending the stairs to their left, but sometimes no one appears. When we did our investigation in the spring of 2005, I tried to photograph a particular area upstairs and my camera briefly registered a date, maybe in 2020, then the screen went blank and the camera has been inoperable ever since!" She also told me that flashlight and camera batteries drain very quickly in the upstairs.

I sure wish I could report to readers that we have solved this riddle, but I cannot do so at this time. After researching the matter, we know previous owners and some former employees. None of them match the courteous apparition. There seems to be no known connection to the residual energies in the building's upstairs. Libraries are centers for community research and the small community is fortunate to have an active library with so many programs for children and adults alike. What the unseen patron is seeking remains unknown. He must have his own "program."

Projection

When I moved to Chestertown in the winter of 2005, I was surprised to see a movie theater. Our hamlet only has a population of perhaps 1,800 people, so it was amazing to find an old building where movies are shown all summer long. In the days of large corporate movie chains, most small town movie theaters have been driven out of business.

I met Laura Pearsall, who rents a small business block which once housed the old A&P Supermarket. The main attraction in the building, however, is the Carol Theater, which has been off and on in business since the early 1930s. In the old days, during its incarnation as the Chester Theater, movies were shown on Wednesday and Saturday nights, but today's main summertime patrons are children from local summer camps.

Laura invited me and my intuitive sidekick, Susan, to visit the old building in November 2006, to see what we might "pick up." Susan never knows where we are headed until we arrive, and she was thrilled to enter an old theater, as we had never explored a place of entertainment before. We had hardly entered the building than Laura escorted Susan upstairs to investigate the projection booth and other parts of the second floor rooms. I chatted with Laura's friend, Leana, as we wandered into the main auditorium. The interior décor, though aged, was almost a perfect replica of the old Starr Theater in Corinth, where I spent many hours during my childhood, so it was like "coming home."

Immediately, I had to break off my conversation with Leana, because I sensed something upstairs; not current activity, but what I term a "house memory," some undertaking in the past. My mind centered on the interior of the projection booth, where a man worked at a large movie projector. Appearing to be active in the late 1920s or early 1930s, he was thin, quite reminiscent of Fred Astaire, and dressed in a black vest and slacks and wearing a white shirt. As he worked, I sensed the man's mix of frustration and anxiety regarding his income and expenses. He seemed a dedicated, hard worker, but not the owner of the establishment. Later that day, when I visited the projection booth, I also felt that a woman used to sit in a folding chair behind him on some evenings, waiting for the last show to end, so that she and he could go out on the town.

I returned downstairs and found Susan and Laura walking the length of the stage in front of the large movie screen. Susan kept stopping at a certain spot, so I knew she was sensing something or someone. Later, she told me that her hands had become icy cold as soon as she entered the unheated theater, and then they suddenly warmed again at one place, two-thirds of the way across the stage. Laura also sensed the sudden warmth. My thought was that there was still a residue of some old-time dramatic production taking place there. I wondered if there had been vaudeville performances in the building at one time. Later, Laura showed me an old advertisement for a local Miss America tryout held in the late 1940s at the Chester Theater, and there seemed to be good evidence for many local dramatic productions having taken place upon the stage.

Susan was now ready to share with us the results of her building tour. "In the woman's bathroom here on the first floor, where I walked as soon as we entered the auditorium, and before going up onto the stage, I sensed a small girl, about eight years old, who appeared to be hiding beneath the lavatory. She used to sneak into films, it seems, and would hide out in the bathroom, fearful of getting caught. I get the information that the girl died young because of some sickness. I felt coughing and chest pain, some kind of respiratory infection, maybe pneumonia. Later, after walking the stage, I wondered if the little girl's spirit had followed us up there, which might account for the stationary warm spot."

"Isn't that fascinating," Laura exclaimed, "this particular lavatory dripped and dripped and, no matter what the plumber did to correct it, the dripping continued. So, one day in 2004, I walked into this rest room and asked whoever was here to please not make the faucet drip any more, and since then, the dripping has stopped. I wonder if that leak might have been connected to the girl's spirit. My hands also become icy cold many times when I enter this bathroom." I reminded her that spirits seem to love lavatories, bath tubs, showers, and sinks, and appear to enjoy announcing their presence by making water run. Of course, there are few people still alive in the community who could verify the existence of such a child in the building's history.

Laura told us that many times she sensed a child running inside the theater, but no one was ever visible. Susan sensed the need to take a series of photos in the right seating area of the theater because of the energy she felt there. "I have felt that too," Laura added, "and I roped off that section, so patrons don't sit there any longer." When I researched the theater's history later, I learned from an article written by Andy Campanaro (son of a former owner) that that area was the "necking section" for high school kids attending the movies. It seems that the teens favored that section because it was darker there. I then wondered if the passions of the late 1940s remained as a palpable energy that resounds even today. Susan later told me that her camera had recorded numerous orbs of energy there, as Laura's camera had, though there were no energies photographed in the center or left seating areas. Well, I guess the Bible says that love is eternal.

"When I entered the upstairs hallway near the projection booth, I immediately felt a heavy energy and was mentally told it was that of a prominent man in town," Susan continued. "I felt sadness, tears and a weight on my shoulders. Then, as Laura and I talked, the energy suddenly lifted, as if the spirit understood that we had compassion for his situation." I wondered if that was my projectionist. Downstairs again, as Susan and Laura once more toured the right seating section, Sue saw the image of an older man in profile, almost as an old-fashioned shadow portrait. She related that, prior to visiting the theater, or even knowing she was going to a theater, she had (in a meditative state) seen this portrait. Laura then told us that she had taken photos in that section and had found the print showed several large orbs of light at that spot.

Whose energy could remain there, at least on occasion? I spoke with local resident June Maxam, whose Uncle Les used to be the projectionist there for many years. "The man you visualized in the booth might well have been him," she said, "and the lady who waited for him to finish the night's work might well have been one of his occasional girlfriends," she smiled. There were several owners in the days when the business was known as The Chester Theater. A later owner changed its marquee to The Carol, after his wife's name.

Old records of the building show that it was built about 1930 by a local businessman known as Pop Wertime, a man who was a hands-on operator, often taking or selling tickets. "He had a soft heart," an old news article said, "and sometimes let children into the movies even if they didn't have the full twenty-five cents admission." Pop owned many of the buildings around the

Four Corners at one time, so the weight of business matters might well have burdened him, especially as the theater costs rose above its income. Of all the previous owners, it seems that Pop had the deepest emotional investment in the building before he sold to Andy Campanaro, Sr.

By 1954, Campanaro, also, could no longer make enough money to pay his expenses and closed the theater, and thus the auditorium sat for years, remembering the good times had by young and old alike. "I enjoy this old theater," Laura told me, "and I'm thinking of extending my lease into a purchase. And though I may modernize some parts of the operation, I won't be in any hurry to chase out the former owners and workers whose hearts and minds have stayed here," she laughed.

As if to emphasize those former workers, owners or patrons remaining there as spirits or house memories, Susan returned to the theater in the summer of 2007 with some friends, seeking electronic evidence of the holdovers. "We got one strong spike on the EMF meter and some more energy in the area behind the screen," she wrote me. She also sent photographs taken by her team which show numerous orbs of light in different parts of the auditorium. So, the old timers are in no hurry to move on. One wishes he could just see the entertainment that these spirits must still be viewing.

Casting Call

From time to time, when I get a new story lead, I have to consider a number of factors in deciding whether or not someone's experience is truly ghostly, or is an event spurred more by a unique combination of environmental factors. Here is one of those tales that had me on a fence for quite a time.

"I've always had some extra sensitivity," Pieter Gaskin told me. "But I certainly wasn't the only worker to have those strange experiences when I worked at the Fishercast Company on Fisher Road in Watertown."

Pieter came to Watertown in the 1990s and began work as a "tumbler" of zinc castings at the thriving plant. The company sold these metal parts to auto supply corporations such as AC Delco and General Motors, and all production was expected to be without flaws. "In the casting business there are often extrusions of cooled metal that need trimming before the part is finished, approved, and boxed," Pieter said. "So, all parts coming off the line had to be carefully inspected. One thing I want to talk about here is the lighting at that work station. It was bright and without shadows, so we workers could examine the pieces fully and didn't miss any flaws. Lighting is an important element of what I'm going to tell you.

"Also," he said, "I have to tell you that workers on the line sometimes played practical jokes on one another to relieve boredom that arose from doing just one thing for hours. I understood that from the beginning, so when I tell you what I experienced at work, I'm also trying to figure whether those experiences could have been caused by any of the elements in our work atmosphere. I took all them into consideration when I first became aware of a strange situation, to be sure that nobody was playing tricks on me. Here it is: one day I saw a dark shadow move through the air in the middle of our inspection area. Because there was no single bright light, it would be impossible to cast such a dark shadow. Also, shadows have to be cast on a surface; there is nothing solid in mid-air where a shadow can register! Then, a few days later, I experienced the phenomenon again. The movement usually began just to the side of my field of vision. I really doubted myself until I heard other workers comment on the situation. So they could see the dark shadows too!

"It also began to occur to me that, from day one of my employment there, I had felt uncomfortable in the plant, though there was no logical reason why that should be so. I also noted an 'up-tightness' in many of my co-workers, as they frequently seemed irritated or uncomfortable. From time to time I'd look up and find one of the others staring at me, but why? I did my work and did it well. Did I somehow threaten them? Nobody ever said. We had some distinct negative personalities in my section," he continued, "and, a year before I began work there, one of them was arrested for a murder outside the workplace. Maybe management should have seen that one coming, as the man often talked to his machine! Another of the guys in the shipping department, young and relatively healthy, committed suicide at his home. Were these events somehow work-related?"

Fishercast had moved from a location near the airport to Fisher Road from near the airport some years before. Then, in May 1994, a fire in one section destroyed the new facility, causing the zinc casting and inspections part of the operation to be moved down the road to another building just before Pieter's employment began. Was that it? Was there an ambient energy in that second building—some negative force left over from previous pre-fire occupants? He told me, however, that he experienced discomfort at both sites where he worked. As Pieter continued on the job, he heard more and more co-workers comment on the apparent taunting by what were known as "The Shadow People."

"From time to time, these beings seemed to come up behind people," he remembers. "I don't know whether or not they wanted to touch us; maybe they had some malicious intent. My co-workers Kathy, Patty, and John B. all saw the figures, and felt the beings were trying to sneak up on them. Some other employees worked with pretty caustic chemicals (such as trichlorethylene) there, and didn't want to be distracted, because serious injuries might result if we didn't give our full attention to the task. There was a lot of cancer and strange ailments among my co-workers during my period of employment. Some of the workers developed mental problems, and I often wondered if the chemical atmosphere might have caused or worsened already-existing conditions in them.

"The parts business underwent changes, and I was laid off in 2001 just before Fishercast closed the plant and moved away. There is another company in there now," he concluded. We talked about energy becoming visible and almost tangible at times, as Pieter and I agreed it can happen under the right circumstances. Additionally, he felt that management seemed to create an adversarial atmosphere among the workers at the plant. We wondered if self-protectiveness, selfishness or fear might have drawn entities who shared these tendencies from the spirit world. Not all spirits go to a happy place in the world of spirit until they recognize and work through their earthly flaws, often shortcomings of belief and motivation.

When I asked Pieter about the history of that site—did he know of any historical battles fought there?—he reflected, then remembered a strange event. "On the second shift one night, I stood looking out the back doors, past the loading dock, toward a large field filled with grass and scrub brush. Maybe I was a bit tired, but I suddenly wondered how we would defend this place if we were attacked. In my mind's eye I could see soldiers running across that field and taking cover. Nevertheless, I felt we would be overrun. Strange, isn't it? Where could that scenario have come from? Was it part of that location's history, or something from some past lifetime?"

Strange Stuff

When she was in high school, Deborah took a test to discover if she had extra-sensory perception. She scored quite highly, so maybe that helps explain her discernment of "other world" which is never far away from our daily lives. Though she lives in Greece, New York, today, she married and lived for a number of years on Veness Avenue in the city of Rochester.

"My son, Joshua, was only four months old when I put him to sleep in his crib one day. I turned and went to the kitchen," she told me, "only to be startled by seeing a baby running from one bedroom to the other! The baby and I were the only two people in the house—I know that for sure—so I hurried to his bedroom only to find him fully asleep. And, besides, how could a four-month-old, who couldn't even walk, run?"

She told me that he was always a bit sensitive, and Deborah often saw her baby looking at a point in space and laughing excitedly, almost as if an invisible someone was making faces at him. This behavior is fairly common, that infants can see the spirits of the departed, perhaps a deceased loving relative or former tenant. Such spirits or ghosts, if highly motivated, can take great joy from newborns and dote on them.

Joshua has been as sensitive to this other plane of existence as Deborah was in her teen years. Now eighteen, with his parents divorced, Joshua spends some time with his father, and has lived in two different dwellings over the years. In both buildings, the boy has observed strange events, such as the time that a mirror didn't just fall from its position above a vanity, it flew across the room and shattered against an opposite wall.

Josh suspects that his dad's favorite mounted deer head hasn't simply fallen twice from its position on a wall, but has had "some help." On one occasion, the boy and his father were sitting in the room when the deer head trophy lifted upward on its hanging brackets before falling. Strangely, Deborah told me, the antlers have never broken in these tumbles, and one wonders if the spirit also did some "cushioning."

Light bulbs have mysteriously shattered, with no attributable cause, at his dad's house, and at Deborah's present house there have also been strange images in photographs. Lights seem to show up where they didn't exist when the photos were taken; are these energies? And if so, are they ghostly orb manifestations or are they ambient energies that are somehow energized by Josh's bio-electric field. As readers know, all of us are essentially energy, but certain gifted people can project (knowingly or not) their energy. This phenomenon is known as PK, or psychokinetic energy. Life energy in adolescents can often scare the daylights out of teens, as they don't understand that such forces can erupt spontaneously, often triggered by their emotional or hormonal upsets. Interested readers should seek to know more about Uri Geller, the Israeli phenomenon, or the now-deceased Dr. Alexander Tanous from Portland, Maine.

In her home, both Deborah and Joshua have seen lights over their dogs, causing wonder if these are canine energies or spirits surrounding the animals. Recalling an incident on a 2008 trip to Georgia, Josh said, "I saw a blob of matter—that's the only way I can describe it—in front of the windshield. It was light and bright, yet transparent, and looked almost like a dress trailing behind a woman." It seems that Josh has inherited his mother's gift for sensitivity to other states of being.

"Now, in the machine shop where I work on Lincoln Avenue in Rochester, there are strange things, too. Originally, I was told, bomb fuses were assembled in those cellar rooms during World War II," Deborah said, "because the walls are specially insulated to prevent x-rays or other energies penetrating the rooms. There is a reflective ceiling and, occasionally, when I'm working, my attention will be distracted by movement in that overhead reflection. I can see myself working from above, but there will be figures either standing or moving behind me, and I know for certain that nobody living is there! It's almost as if an invisible shift supervisor is checking my work quality. Also, on occasion, I'll catch a reflection of moving figures in the window panes, but nobody is there to move." The fact that this workspace is specially insulated seems to rule out exterior energies or forces manifesting in the shop.

Another part of her building was once a perfume factory and the pleasant odors still linger, but it seems that the former workers or their problems (which they either brought to work or found there) have also stayed on. "The building superintendent once told me that that part of the building is so active, spirit or energy-wise, that he doesn't even like to go there," she frowned.

On many occasions, new employees will be startled by those semi-people who appear in the fluorescent lighting, only to just as quickly disappear. Deborah suspects that dedicated workers from the old bomb factory, or from the Kodak operations that later took place there, must continue on, unmindful of the passage of time or the changing functions of the building. "It would be nice if they'd help out," she smiled, "instead of just watching!"

Behind the Curtain

The small town of Oswego sits quietly on southern shore of Lake Ontario where the Oswego River, flowing north into the lake, divides the town east from west. On a rise just east of the harbor, is the historic Fort Ontario. A wooden fort was built here by the British in 1755 and was later constructed in stone. After the Revolutionary War, the fortress was garrisoned by the U.S. Army from 1783 until the end of World War II. After the war the barracks and some of the 124 outbuildings housed European Holocaust survivors.

One of these structures, made of brick in 1903, was used as a commissary and Quartermaster's office while the fort was a military post, but then was abandoned for many years. In 1964 the structure was reborn as an auditorium and is now The Civic Arts Center, home to The Art Association of Oswego and the Oswego Players Inc. The Frances Marion Brown Theater is the subject of this story.

During the time the building was unused after the war, vagrants had a small "hobo jungle" camp in the nearby rail yard, and sometimes used the building as a refuge, especially during the cold winters. One of those vagabonds, (a man of mixed Indian heritage, and possibly a seasonal construction worker) hauled a discarded mattress into the crawl space beneath the first floor, present-day kitchen, where he kept his meager belongings. "I've been told that the old mattress is still down there," Inez Parker, the Players' long-time President told me. "That tramp froze to death during one particularly cold winter, and many think he is among the spirits that occasionally are experienced here."

"I remember my father-in-law, Dick Johnson, telling about the horrible smell there before the man's body was removed in the springtime," said Wayne Mosher, another durable member of the company. "Well, I guess most theaters have a ghost somehow involved with them, right?" he smiled.

Another theater company member, Larry Rose, tells of being alone in the building's cellar on various occasions, constructing a set for *Jekyll and Hyde*, and walking through icy cold spots, suggesting the presence of a spirit entity. "It's not the extremely scary phenomena that are shown in films or on television, but there definitely is a paranormal flavor to this place. I remember being in the building on a muggy summer night a few years ago, and I clearly recall that there was no breeze or other air movement in the theater itself, yet the stage curtains were flapping back and forth as if there was a strong wind. At the time, we were staging *Harvey*, and sometimes showed his passage across the stage in that fashion, but there was no play and no other production staff on stage with me that night!

Wayne Mosher and Inez talked about another issue: the strange events that occur whenever an Agatha Christie play is being performed. She told of the time when *Ten Little Indians* was playing, and part of the set was a fireplace display of ten small Indian figures. Christie fans likely know that, in the play, as one of the stage characters dies, an Indian is found fallen on the mantelpiece. "One night," she told me, "during performance, one of the figures kept falling, even before a murder took place. There was no logical reason why it should fall, and I worried that it would spoil the special effect for the play. It only happened once, but it caused me to wonder if 'the Indian' might be a residue of the man who died long ago in the crawl space."

"On other occasions," Larry said, "when putting up a production, and when I was constructing sets, I would discover that my tape measure or hammer had either disappeared or had strangely moved to backstage areas that I hadn't been working in. During those work stints, I sometimes had the uncanny sensation of being watched, or the hair on my neck would suddenly rise. Usually, that was enough prompting for me to leave off work for the night and go home," he grinned.

"Nona Turano, a deceased former member of our company, who was a sensitive and spiritual lady, had her run-ins too," Wayne told me. "As we sat talking backstage one night, Nona suddenly stiffened and related seeing the shadow of a tall, thin person cross the wall. As she remarked about it, Larry commented that he heard the ancient drum roll of 'the muster' being beaten outside near the fort. He didn't see her vision and she didn't hear his drums, but isn't it curious that it happened in the same instant?"

Inez then laughed ironically and told me, "Poor Nona—she had another experience that hurt. She was onstage, rehearsing one day. No one else was even close to her, when suddenly, we saw her arms flail outward, as if she was attempting to maintain her balance. It didn't work, however, and she tumbled off the stage, landing on her hands on the floor below. We discovered that her wrist was broken, and I drove her to the hospital. All the way there, Nona kept telling how an invisible force had pushed her from behind. But that is our only physical casualty so far."

Larry then added, "Several years ago, Nona, her brother, and I were building a set one night. All at once we heard the unmistakable sound of a pipe organ being tuned. First one note, then its flat or sharp echoed through the building. But we have no organ. Nona's brother, by coincidence, was an organ builder in a nearby city and was certain what he was hearing. I myself know many military bugle calls and drum cadences, and it seemed to me to be the 'Retreat' melody, but played on an organ. All we could ever figure was that wind must be blowing across some pipe or opening in the building, so we settled for that as the explanation, though there was no wind that night." He laughed.

"This is such a fascinating place," Wayne reminisced. "First, there is the old French and Indian War fort, there are old buildings that had many uses, both civilian and military. Then, over where the old hobo jungle was located, we now have the new Border Patrol station. I sometimes speculate as to whether or not any of these phenomena might come from this modern intrusion into their old space. Surely, the vagrants must have left some artifacts in the soil there, but the government built over the site regardless of our protests.

"The good news is that we have a nice 120-seat theater and dedicated, talented Oswego citizens come together to exhibit their artistry. Our group, the Oswego Players, has grown with the city, and we offer a place for sensitive and gifted actors and actresses to gather. The big question is, who gathers with us?"

CHAPTER 11

CHILDREN AND GHOSTS

CHARLOTTE'S HOUSE
CHECKING ON BABIES
UNTOUCHABLE PEOPLE

Charlotte's House

Charlotte Johnson told me that her son, Bill, and his new wife, Sue, rented an old house on Johnson Hill Road east of Hoosick Falls, New York, in 1975. Repairs were needed, and Bill was able to do them for credit against his monthly rent. Not long afterward, Sue found she was pregnant, and their first child, Matthew, was born in June 1978.

After the new mother and baby returned home from the hospital, activity in the old house began to pick up. Baby Matthew seemed to have an invisible babysitter. Lying in his crib, he often looked intently at someone or something the rest of the family could not see. "When he'd cry, we'd hear a soft voice humming to him in his bedroom. When we went upstairs, no one else but Matthew was there," said Charlotte. One day, Sue went downstairs to heat Matthew's bottle. She looked for the small warming pan to put on the stove, but it was nowhere to be found. "Maybe I mistakenly threw it out with the garbage," Sue mused. She used a new pan for heating the bottle. Several days later, Sue found the old pan sitting in the sink as if it had always been in that spot.

Bill and Sue carpeted the screened-in front porch so that Matthew could have a sheltered play area. When he was one year old, the baby played there with his invisible friend, and Sue often saw him handing his toys to an invisible "someone." Several times she saw him rolling around on his back and laughing heartily, as if he were being tickled by someone. The boy grabbed at his ribs while laughing, as if to protect himself from the phantom tickler, but he clearly enjoyed the companionship.

Charlotte and her husband loved the old house and often explored it. In the attic, they found photos of children who'd lived there long ago. There was a sealed room that they opened, and inside they found baby furniture. They wondered if some tragedy had befallen the house's former children, creating the vacancy that led to their rental. Grandma Charlotte often babysat for little Matthew, and one warm night, when all the doors were open, she heard the sound of a breeze and saw the living room shades blowing, though the air was very still outside. The smell of lilacs permeated the room, though the lilac bushes had finished blooming several months before.

In September 1979, the young family had to move, as Bill had taken a new job in Texas. It had been a happy home for them all. Then, in the early 1980s, the house burned, and with it, a host of memories from long before the Johnsons lived there. Today, a new house sits on the old foundation. One wonders whether the new family will encounter the ghost babysitter.

Charlotte also passed a few years ago, leaving the living to contend with their mysteries, while she has gone on to explore The Greatest of Mysteries.

Checking on Babies

Cheryl was a divorcee when she met Rick. It was love at first sight, and the product of their love was a healthy set of twin boys. Their residence was a brand new mobile home, a fact which becomes important in attempting to identify the ghost who visited their home in Dover Plains that year.

Within six months of the babies' birth, both Cheryl and her adult daughter, Dawn, noticed the infants were often distracted. "Sometimes, they would giggle and stare bright-eyed at something or someone that none of the rest of us could see, as if the babies were reflecting a smile given to them by an angel or spirit. In any case, they seemed so happy, tucked away in one crib."

Dawn remembers spending a night at her mother's home and being awakened by the infants' cries. Okay, the kids need their bottles, so I'll do it, she thought, and rose from her bed. "I went through to the kitchen, from which I could look down the short hallway past Mom's bedroom and the babies' room. I could see a woman looking in on the little ones and figured that Mom had awakened, so I told her that I was getting the bottles warmed. 'Boy, those kids have lungs!' I muttered.

"When the bottles were filled and warmed, I took them to the babies, noting that Mom had left the hall, and I could hear quiet snores from her and Rick's room. Boy, she got back to sleep quickly, I thought," and Dawn headed back to bed.

In the morning, she chatted with her mother about the incident, but her mother steadfastly said that she hadn't awakened all night. So, who was it at the babies' bedroom door? "It looked like you, Mom. Five feet and three inches tall, certainly a woman. And if not you, then who?" she asked.

Neither one was afraid of the word "ghosts," but whose spirit might have been responding to the youngsters' distress?

"Here is the only solution that we could find," Dawn concluded. "It must have been Rick's mother, who had died. He was a twin, and it is likely that his mother found an affinity with a son who also had twins. It only happened once, as far as we can tell. I was pregnant at that time too, so maybe my hormonal energies were such that my e.s.p. was enhanced, allowing me to see the woman.

"Mom, herself, was quite psychic and has seen the spirits of dead people ever since she grew up in Peekskill."

Like parent, like child, I summarized. "Your mom has quite a psychic ability and so do you. Rick's mother had a love for twins and just once popped into this realm, sharing her son's joy at fathering twins."

The more such stories I accumulate, the less I'm doubtful of St. Paul's words, "Love is eternal."

Untouchable People

Just west of the crossroads, at 630 West Dryden Road, in the Tompkins County village of Freeville, New York, is the home of Mac Lewis, a retired Navy veteran and professor, and his wife, Carol. "It's not an old home, as you can see," he told me, "so maybe the ghosts, if that's what they are, never lived here." I think he is correct, as the energies seem to be associated with art objects or items related to deceased family members. It may bear repeating once more that spirits can visit us by drawing on faint energies present on objects that they made or owned during life. Are you an antique collector? Sometimes spirits can appear when you "open a channel" by thinking of them or praying for them.

"Many times when I'm alone in my bedroom, seated on my bed," he said, "I can feel some weighty energy or person sitting down with me, as the bed will suddenly depress, as it did when my wife comes to bed. When I turn, you understand, there is never anyone to see." We talked for a while about this fairly common phenomenon. Loved ones like to drop in on us, just to say hello or communicate their love or concern for us.

"What is it about the bedroom that they would want to visit you there?" I asked him.

"In that room I have a life-sized portrait of my mother. Oh yes, and I also have a container of her ashes," he added with a grin. "Think that might do it?" I readily agreed.

"My chief ghost spotter is my granddaughter, Jasmyn, who visits occasionally from Japan where she lives with her mother right now," Mac said, "but when she was five, she told me about seeing a woman in a pink dress in our dining room. 'The lady just stands there,' she told me, perhaps concerned that the figure didn't move. In her portrait, my mother wears a pink dress. Thus, when I try to evaluate the girls' vision I have to consider that Jasmyn has seen that picture, but why would she view the woman in the dining room and not on the wall?"

Jasmyn's father, Nigel, joined Mac, his wife Carol, and me and added some more lore to the unfolding tale. "When she was younger, my daughter often told her mother and me about people that she could see and talk to. Many times she called them 'untouchable people' maybe because they had no tangible body. On one occasion, here in Freeville, I asked her if she could provide us with details of the people she saw, as we couldn't see them. Jasmyn told us of seeing a man with 'no hair and who is pudgy,' and a few more details. She was providing a very accurate description of my grandfather, George," Nigel said, "though why he was here, I'll never know. That is the same description that my friend, Eric, provided to us regarding a male figure that he saw upstairs in this house."

"Jasmyn likely saw that man or another one when she was watching television with Eric in an upstairs room a few years ago," Mac continued. "The man and his father, who was my friend, had come to visit. Jasmyn and Eric were watching a TV program when the being showed up to look around."

We talked about Mac's other experiences. He told me of being a psychically receptive individual in his youth, even while in the U.S. Navy, from which he retired in July 1946. "Even as a youngster, I had a kind of knowing. When I was twelve, I suddenly knew when my Aunt Mary was going to die. After the Navy, I found my way out west, to Billings, Montana, where I worked as a piano teacher for over five years. A local piano teacher was going overseas for a year and offered to rent me her house with a large studio. It seemed ideal and could accommodate sixty students, so I rented there. My first experience was seeing my Pekinese bark at an open paper bag or cardboard box. I kept telling him that nothing was inside, but maybe he could see things that I couldn't," he smiled.

"That house on Park Place had a lot of sounds that I couldn't account for," he continued. "Regularly, I'd hear footsteps walking in the living room and hallway, then into another room. Of course, you know that I never saw anybody doing the walking, but the sounds of it sure were present. Some of my friends used to be entertained by that event—they would come to visit and just listen to the unexplainable sounds. The steps were heavy enough that I assumed it was a man. That house had been built around 1937, so it wasn't that old at the time I lived there. I never knew much about its history, as the owners were in France."

Sensitivity to that other world seems to have been with Mac all his life, perhaps inherited from his mother. "She always knew when I was in trouble," he laughed. "Once when I was driving from Billings to Cody, Wyoming, I nearly had an accident. Next time I spoke with her on the phone, she told me all the details; she didn't ask, she told me. That wasn't the only time, either, because I almost was hit by a truck while touring in England. When I returned home, she told me about that one too. When I returned to Freeville I applied for an open position at Ithaca College, and have been here since.

"Aunt Mary, my mother's sister, came to me on a Ouija board once when I was in the Navy in Puerto Rico, and I was engaged to Irene, a redhead who lived in the U.S. 'Don't marry the redheaded girl, Irene,' the board spelled out. And that message really got my attention," he chuckled, "because I didn't marry her.

"Now, Jasmyn is showing me some new dimensions to psychic ability and ghosts," he added. "On a recent visit from Japan she saw untouchable people at the dinner table, and also spotted a little girl in the doorway of the bedroom where she and her father slept.

"I have one other issue, and it is a mystery, though I don't know if a ghost or helping spirit is the force behind it. I wear a headgear that has straps that often get mixed up, so it was uncomfortable when I tried to use it for my oxygen mask. The first night I wore it, my wife had to untangle it for me. Since then, however, there have been three or four occurrences when I've put it on, leaving the straps crossed, so it goes on a little tighter than usual, but in the morning everything is okay—the straps are placed correctly. How does it get untangled while I'm sleeping?" Who or what serves as his nightly assistant, helping him to get a comfortable good night's sleep?

Now retired from his music department professorship at Ithaca College, Mac looks back on a life filled with not-unpleasant contacts with those who have gone before him. And there are still future visits from Jasmyn to look forward to. What will she see next?

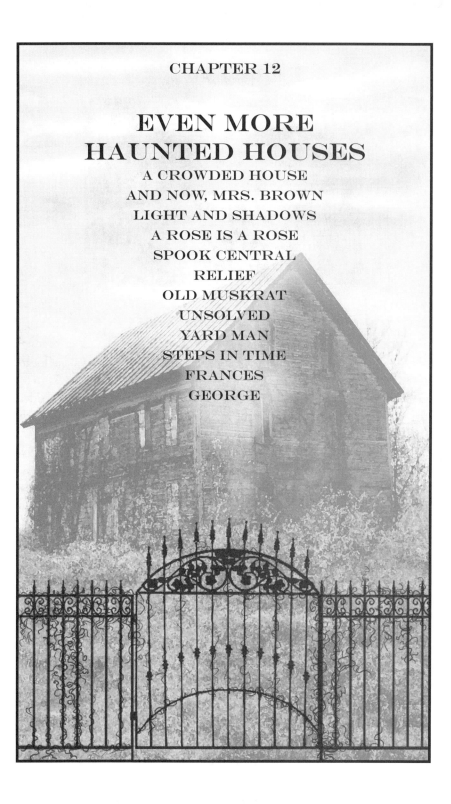

CHAPTER 12

EVEN MORE
HAUNTED HOUSES

A CROWDED HOUSE
AND NOW, MRS. BROWN
LIGHT AND SHADOWS
A ROSE IS A ROSE
SPOOK CENTRAL
RELIEF
OLD MUSKRAT
UNSOLVED
YARD MAN
STEPS IN TIME
FRANCES
GEORGE

A Crowded House

Silver Creek, Vince's

Silver Creek, New York is a nice Chautauqua County village located on the eastern shore of Lake Erie, not too far south of Buffalo. It was once a busy port for lake transport, but no longer. Vince Tampio, a longtime resident, might favor transporting some of the invisible residents of his home to another plane, if he could only be sure who they are.

"I live in an old 1896 home built by the Kofoed brothers, immigrant Dutch carpenters, who were meticulous in their work. For a long time after the first early-1800s house burned in 1863, this lot was empty until the Dickinsons built the present house," Vince told me. They were a prosperous local family involved in building dining cars (or railroad passenger-car-shaped diners) for many other small American towns.

"When I purchased the home in 1971, it was a time of curious circumstances. Widow Florice Robson, a Dickinson descendant, was still broken-hearted over her husband, John's, death three years earlier, and could no longer continue to live there alone. She was also grieving the death of her mother who had lived in my house until her death in the living room here. She also was sorrowing for her brother, shell-shocked in World War II, and then confined to a state mental facility. Yet, she couldn't bring herself to sell off the family's personal possessions, so my wife, Carmella, and I agreed to buy the furnished house.

"I think Flo enjoyed the prospect that a new, young family would keep the house active. I wonder if she knew how active the place was, though, as, at the closing, she assured us that 'there is nothing really wrong with the house.' At the time, I didn't know what she meant. Now, after thirty-five years, I sure do."

Tampio, who has held a number of important positions in the village, including the office of mayor and hospital board member, is a serious and talented man. He has written down almost every strange incident that has occurred since his purchase, a record that is so detailed that the average citizen of the village might find difficult to believe these events all have taken place to one family in one house. For those who understand that living isn't over when the funeral concludes, these events offer hope for the prospect of life beyond the grave. For the scientifically-inclined readers, there will be a great amount of head-scratching; if only they told us in high school that such things could happen to some citizens.

The most common phenomenon for this talented photographer is the appearance of orbs on his photos, with some prints showing hundreds of small dots that likely aren't bits of dust or water vapor droplets. "Some rooms, such as an upstairs bedroom, almost always show two or three orbs, and at times, I think they know when I'm photographing them," Vince told me. "After over three decades of strange noises and events, I many times now take a photo in the direction of any unexplained sound, and almost always, I get orbs on the camera screen." Even Vince's grandchildren, when they visit, make a game of catching orb images on their cameras at Grandpa's. The children sometimes have caught a man's face in the reflection on a mirror in the cellar in recent years. The mirrored box was in the home when Mrs. Robson sold the house to the Tampios. One wonders whose energy may still reside in the old looking glass.

"Recently," Vince told me, "while I sat in my recliner in the living room, I heard six distinct taps behind my chair. Without swiveling, I grabbed my ever-present camera and fired off a few shots over my head to the area behind me. The resulting image was a black cloud. Here, I'll show you," he said.

"At Christmas time in 1972, my children gathered in our music room to decorate a large tree that I'd put up. Happy at their installation of lights and tinsel, they went outside to play. I sat, enjoying their artistry from my chair in the next room, when I noticed the angel from the top was suddenly displaced several feet from the top. There was no explainable way for that to happen, so I went to investigate, just in time to see the tree begin shaking violently. The tinsel was flung outward, so strong was the movement. I called Carmella to come look, asking her what she saw. She agreed with me that the tree indeed was in motion. Gathering his wits, Vince got his step ladder and replaced the angel on the tree top. All the tree motion stopped. At first, the family couldn't conceive that these activities might be ghost-induced.

"I watch quite a bit of late night television," Vincent continued in our interview, "and once noted that a stack of newspapers on a nearby chair were crackling and compressing, as if someone had just sat on them. I watched the pile and it remained still until the program finished. Then, as if someone invisible was saying, 'That was a pretty good show,' the stack of papers faintly rustled again and resumed its normal height. Who or what was that? I asked myself," he said with a smile.

"The first strange event here, however, involved a flying record. My daughter, Ann, had bought a new hit musical record and enjoyed playing it over and over upstairs in her bedroom. She suddenly emerged in the downstairs living room with a funny look on her face, telling me that the record had been on her cedar chest, when it suddenly levitated, hovered in the air for a moment, then dropped to the floor, though it was unbroken. Facetiously, not wanting to think too deeply about the cause, I said that maybe the ghost was tired of the same old song," he laughed. After a while, he began to wonder just who the ghost or ghosts were. Soon afterward, she told of seeing an unknown man wearing a v-neck sweater in the house, followed by a sudden cold chill. She fled the house and sat on our back porch until her mom and I returned home." When I interviewed Ann, she affirmed the activity and said that other strange events happened to her brother Joe and in his bedroom.

"I had a party here for all my friends, and one of them came downstairs from the upstairs bathroom, and she was quite shaken. After closing the room's door, she heard a voice ordering her out of there. She was quite shaken up. No one else was up there to fake such a voice. I also had my bedroom door slam open once in a while, and occasionally heard a boom from up in the attic, sometimes followed by footsteps." I asked if she hadn't been scared, which she probably was at first, but Ann, like the rest of the family, just shrugged it off. It was just another kind of normal, growing up in the house.

Vince then added, "I was in the upstairs bathroom shortly after the record event, and heard a girl's voice talking to the dog out in the hall; it sounded as if she were playing with him. Then I realized that neither of my girls was home, and at that minute I heard the dog skedaddle past the door and toward the other end of the hall. As I finished in the bathroom, the phone rang, and it was the neighbor boy informing me that our dog was out on the front roof. I couldn't believe it, but went to check. Sure enough, the poor wide-eyed pooch was shivering out there, having burst his way through a bedroom window screen. What could have scared him enough to create that result? And I was certain that the girl I heard wasn't Ann. From time to time, I'll see our dog or the dogs of visitors suddenly back out of a room, sometimes with their fur raised.

"When our son Joe was younger, he worked in a bakery, so he was up early in the morning to go to work. He heard a noise in the upstairs hallway and went to see what caused it. Joe spotted a filmy female figure. At first, he thought it might be a robber, but he bravely went to confront the being. All at once, it vanished. Our daughter ran into the same phenomenon too.

I interviewed Joe, who laughed as he remembered the footsteps in the attic, the doors that occasionally slammed themselves, and the occasion when someone or something knocked on the outside of his second floor bedroom window. "When I ran into the ghost lady again, outside my bedroom, I turned on the bedroom light and opened the door fully to let the brightness fall on her. She vanished." He also laughed while remembering the times his bedroom door would audibly unlatch itself. If he didn't immediately sit up and pay attention to the unlocking, the door would open fully, then slam, he said. "It was as if someone was trying to get me to acknowledge their presence. These events were much more common around the Christmas holidays. I wish we knew what that season had meant to the former residents of our house," he concluded.

"Though I have kept a record of each one, there are just too many incidents of noises or footsteps in the house that we just can't account for," Vince told me. "Things have also disappeared, such as the time a $20 bill vanished from a bedroom dresser top, only to reappear in the same spot three weeks later. Where do these things go when they vanish? And who returns them?" he asked.

"Our son came to visit with some friends, and the woman, Kathy, is pretty sensitive, maybe psychic. As we sat chatting, her chair offered her a view of the fireplace about fifteen feet away in the other room. I noticed her staring in there for quite a while, though she said nothing. Later, she told my son, Mike, that she had seen what appeared to be a uniformed man, possibly in Civil War dress, in front of the fireplace. Mike later related that to me. That war was going on when the first house here burned, so the vision might be some history replaying itself, though we were never able to learn whether or not anyone had died in the blaze," Vince said soberly. Why would a soldier keep returning to the shores of Lake Erie, when there were "distant shores" that should seem more appealing?

The Tampios also had the experience of a missing TV remote control, which remained lost or vanished for three days before reappearing in its rightful place when they returned from an evening out. Joe then remembered the night that he and his buddies turned off all the house lights and went out for pizza and wings. Entering the car, he was amazed to look back at the house and see the attic and porch lights on. He got out, entered the house, and turned them off. Back in the car and ready to go, he then spotted the basement light on, and returned inside to shut it off. Back outside and about to finally leave, he noted the attic, basement and porch lights all were turned on. "We just peeled out of there," he told me. "I was up against something I just couldn't understand. When we returned home, all the house lights were out!"

"Some of our family members went down the road to the Lily Dale Assembly to visit the spiritualists and psychics there, thinking perhaps they could give us some explanation for the strange goings-on in our house," Vince continued. "One of those psychics told us that there were at least two spirits in our house. One was a carpenter, so we wonder if it might be one of the Kofoeds, who built the present house back in 1896. If so, is he still admiring his handi-work, or is he still trying to get some board perfectly level? The seer also told my family that the other entity here is a little girl, though they couldn't identify her. Might she have died in the fire or at another time when infant mortality was higher?

"Some local residents believe that our property might have been part of the old village cemetery, the graves of which are supposed to have all been transferred to Glendale Cemetery. I searched the Chautauqua County cemetery records on the Internet, which seems to bear out that suspicion. We heard that bones were once excavated from our back yard. I guess that's all it takes to keep a spirit here on earth." He showed me a photo that he'd taken in the back yard, which showed a female figure like a rag doll or straw doll draped over the top of the swing set. Kind of witch-like, I thought. Vince was as puzzled by it all as I was. Sometimes, one can't even venture a guess as to who or why.

Vince told me that, across the street there used to be a stagecoach stop, so for a period of the village's history, all those entering or leaving by highway would have had to come to that building. "It's strange, but I've had decades to try making sense of it all. Why does it seem that there is also an increase in spirit activity in this house when there are deaths in the village? There are multitudes of orbs that appear in the photos that I take in my living room," he noted, showing me many such pictures. "Flo's mother died on a couch right there where mine stands today. Do those good souls have to leave town through my house now, because the stagecoach isn't running any more?" He smiled at the thought. "Is this the new waiting room?" he asked. I looked again to see if he was smiling, but I couldn't be sure.

"The most recent event here was the chiming of our Seth Thomas mantle clock, which rang ten times in the middle of the night, yet we hadn't wound that clock in years. How did that happen?"

The Tampio house is one of the most attractive in Silver Creek, beautifully furnished in much of the former Dickinson family's furniture. I told Vince that antique furniture or belongings often harbor the spirit energy of the departed. He didn't seem very thrilled at that prospect, yet, his family carries on normally. As with most people who host active ghosts, they've grown used to the antics of those unseen citizens of the village. I wouldn't say bored, but just used to it all.

And Now, Mrs. Brown

"When I was a little girl growing up in Brooklyn, I just knew things," Donna Merrill told me. "Sometimes I made predictions that came true, which made my family very nervous and they begged me to stop. Well, I was a good kid, or at least I tried to be, so I did stop. But a person can't repress a talent like that forever—sooner or later it will emerge again," she grinned.

"As a young housewife during the 1980s, I lived at 1729 E. 48th Street, off Avenue N, and, one day, heard wood crackling in our apartment. Must be a squirrel or small animal has gotten in, I concluded. An exterminator was called and he did his thing, though he never turned up a squirrel, living or dead. Afterward, at times, our living room turned icy cold during the summertime. I checked our thermostat and it registered about thirty degrees, though we had no air conditioning. I called two neighbors over, and they attested to the very cold air. While I was trying to figure that out, I occasionally saw objects fly across the room and could hear the television set volume going up and down. This surely is not a normal situation, but I was able to rationalize it all until the day I walked into our spare room and a big desk moved across the floor right at me! Now I knew something big was going on—but what?

"From her bedroom I heard my three-year-old calling me to come look—her toys were moving. I got in there quickly, in time to see the toys moving around the floor all by themselves. I suggested that she not play with them any more, but I didn't have a clue as to exactly what was going on. Just then, my daughter shrieked, 'Oh look! A big red man!' I couldn't see anything, but I knew she was very frightened, so we went downstairs. What was all of this stuff? I was raised Catholic but none of this was explained in our Catechism, so I called our priest and he came to give us a house blessing. Some neighborhood

Hari Krishnas heard of my problem and volunteered to dance around my house until the phenomenon ceased, but I politely declined. Amateur parapsychology groups wanted to come and investigate, but I wanted someone to tell me precisely what was taking place."

She telephoned Duke University in Durham, North Carolina, home of Dr. Joseph B. Rhine's famous parapsychology lab, and begged for advice. The staff suggested that she contact the American Society for Psychical Research at 5 West 73rd Street in Manhattan, an organization of reputable scientists who would be able to evaluate her situation and offer solutions. "They came and, after an interview, looked at one another and decided I was a medium who could channel psychic energy. 'What is the status of your marriage?' one of them asked me. Even though I wondered what the heck that had to do with flying objects and TV set volumes, I confessed that the marriage was in terrible shape. My husband was addicted to drugs and, many times, was not the same guy from one day to the next. I felt helpless to control our home and protect my little girl. Because of my conflicted feelings, I often lulled myself to sleep at night by fondly remembering a former boyfriend named Mike. Maybe that made him too real in my mind, with the strange results.

"'So, your psychic energy is shooting out all over the place and moving things,' one expert said to me. 'We call that poltergeist phenomenon.' I had heard that word, but me? I was just a Brooklyn housewife trying to raise my little girl. Then, walking through the house, one of their experts, who I think was a psychic, said, 'This poltergeist guy wants you to come with him, and he says his name is Mike.' At the same time, she reached up onto a shelf and took down a scarf that had been given to me by Mike, who said it was his dad's when he offered it. Since the poltergeist phenomenon started, it had begun to deteriorate, I told the researcher. These investigators wanted to take the scarf to their lab for testing, and I agreed.

"What was this? It sounded like I had wandered onto a movie set for some horror movie; this couldn't be real life. Then these experts asked me about my psychic abilities, and after I described my childhood, they told me I had to start developing and using my abilities so that my frustrations didn't wreck the house."

As weeks went by, and as she began divorce proceedings against her husband, who was increasingly abusive, the ASPR people came again. They explained how the mind can exert force upon physical objects. "I had to learn to discipline my mind and my abilities, they said. By holding onto the memory of my dead friend Mike, I had opened up a channel by which he could attach his spirit energy to me, they said." Donna's demeanor was partly serious and partly humorous as we chatted. The whole incident that lasted several years was almost laughable in retrospect, she told me. "How and where could I develop my ability?

"The last straw, the one which finally moved me to begin my studies, was my daughter's urgent cry to come upstairs one day. I ran up to her bedroom and saw the child sitting there with a few strands of her hair held straight up, as if in the grasp of an unseen hand. That was it! 'Let go of my girl,' I screamed, 'By the power of the Holy Spirit, get out of here!' The hair dropped down as if it had just been released, and Mike, or whoever it was, apparently left."

The compelling need to find peace in her home led Donna to Kingsborough Community College, where she took courses with Dr. Philip Stander. She came to understand psychokinesis (PK)—where the mind can move material objects. Then she was contacted by Reuben Stone, who wrote of her case in *Poltergeists and the Paranormal*, a book written by him and Dr. Stander in 1993. By then, she had moved with her daughter to Nyack, and began a psychic assistance service based on her studies, to aid those who had native psychic ability. Donna began doing psychic readings, naming her business Mind Over Matter, because she had learned that the mind really could control matter and bring good things into one's life.

She occasionally taught courses and counseled those beset by ghosts and spirits, as stories of her abilities and services spread through the community by word of mouth. Then she met David, a man who had been studying mysticism for several years, and she knew she had found the first peaceful, spiritual partner of her life.

Shortly afterward, they purchased a house in Ithaca, New York. "The former owner of our home was a Mrs. Brown, who had died there a short time before we bought the house," she told me. "It is a pleasant place and I was encouraged to make that my base for helping people. Before my husband and I moved in, we had painters repaint the walls, and we'd come up from Nyack to inspect on weekends. One Friday night we got there to find all the lights in the house turned on and all the doors unlocked. Had some disaster taken place? I wondered. I called the head of the painting crew who told me, 'Well, we had a problem, things were flying around inside the house and the cellar door kept opening and closing. My guys ran out like their lives were in danger. They were scared, but I'm not,' he added.

"'So you will come back and finish the job?' I asked. 'Not unless you stop that crazy stuff,' he responded. So, I went inside and told Mrs. Brown to knock it off, as I was certain it was her. Over the next few years, Mrs. Brown created noises; when we were downstairs, we could hear footsteps upstairs. When doors opened or closed for no apparent reason, it didn't bother us because we knew Mrs. Brown was a ghost and not a poltergeist," she told me.

In 2007, David became a Catholic and they now attend church and do community work as often as possible. One night, he and she were in bed when they both were tugged by something invisible. "Get out of here," she told the spirit, but she wasn't so sure it had left, so she contacted a Franciscan friar who was supposed to know about ghosts. "Yep, you got a demon," the man said. A demon! Now what does one do with that? "No problem," the friar responded. "You have to say a rosary and you have to do it every day—they can't stand that, and they'll have to leave."

"I told him that saying rosaries takes a lot of time, but once we got into it, I found it was a peaceful experience and took only fifteen minutes out of my busy days," she recalled. "So we kept it up, day after day, and one day, whatever troublesome being it was, it stopped. That left us with just Mrs. Brown, and she's much easier to get along with. At various times, when I hear footsteps in the house, I check it out, but I never discover a break-in. So, I just say good-night to her and go off to bed. I told her she is welcome to stay but she has to be quiet when I'm sleeping. In her mind, it's still her house, so this arrangement seems to work pretty well," Donna chuckled.

Meanwhile, Donna continues to do her unpublicized counseling with people who never learned about their soul powers or psychic abilities. "Just tell the people they can call Mind over Matter at (607) 272-6604. If people want to find me badly enough, they will," she concluded. I guessed that was true of the spirits also.

Light and Shadows

Hyde Park, in Dutchess County, is one of the more beautiful towns in the state, and much history has taken place here. The Roosevelts, Vanderbilts, Bards, Dinsmores and many other notables have counted themselves citizens of this historic area. Though I'm a less illustrious former resident, I did my student teaching at Roosevelt High School there in 1958. Perhaps a few other, even less renowned individuals loved their tenure in the town so much that they still refuse to depart. And a prime location for such activity might be a house on Violet Avenue, or Route 9G.

"I bought this house in July 2000," Ann told me, "but I didn't un-derstand how sensitive I was, or had become by that time. One morning I was working in the basement, while my seven-year-old daughter played outside.

Suddenly, I gave out a big 'Achoo!'and almost instantly, from elsewhere in the cellar, I heard a male voice matter-of-factly respond, 'God bless you.' Now, that didn't scare me, but I was startled. There was no one else in the house—I was certain of that. How could such a thing happen unless I imagined it? Maybe, I told myself, it was a noise out on 9G, perhaps a sound similar to the human voice and made by a passing truck or car. The more I pondered the impossibility of a voice without a body speaking to me, the more I assured myself that it was some trick of acoustics, so I relaxed.

"But, within a year, I had a second experience. Dozing on my daughter's bed, I came up almost to full wakefulness realizing I wasn't alone. I opened my eyes to see an impossible sight: at the foot of my bed stood a male figure in jeans and a denim shirt, holding out his hands to me. Who was he and what did he want? This time I was scared and yelled, but of course, no one else was home and I couldn't be heard. What most frightened me was that I seemed paralyzed. Soon, he vanished and there I was with the remainder of my fears. This just couldn't happen, but it had!"

As with many readers, especially those of you who have had similar experiences, Ann reluctantly had to consider that she had a ghost. But how could that be? This wasn't some old Victorian mansion with broken windows, hanging shutters and bats in the attic. Instead, she knew for certain that the house was built in 1957—a building almost indistinguishable from neighboring houses. What could be so special about this place? Her neighbors had never spoken of neighborhood ghosts.

Many of you who have awakened to similar visions (after a quick sanity self-test) recognize that something strange has happened, an event that will make the rest of your life different, if only in your beliefs. What Ann might not have known, not being a fan of ghosts at the time, is that the vision/paralysis experience is quite common.

When we are in deep sleep, in the state where dreams are born and resolve themselves, our body makes a natural paralytic chemical so that we don't act out the dream (running, punching, etc.) while asleep. Sometimes, if our unconscious mind is stimulated by a sound (or foreign energy field in this case) it can snap into full wakefulness (still under the influence of the endorphins) and see either a dream figure or ghost. Our terror increases if we cannot snap back to our fully awake "beta state" of consciousness—we feel totally vulnerable and at the mercy of the being. Many times, as we will see, Ann has experienced many paranormal experiences since that first "Achoo!" and usually when she is relaxed and open to inspiration, in a state that dream doctors or physicians know as "an alpha state," when the brain's electrical activity can be seen to change its frequency of activity.

"Relaxing on my living room couch a few months later, I spotted a grey/black mist slowly pass by me," Ann continued. "I know I was conscious because I was watching a program on television. As the event took place, I wondered why I wasn't scared, but only curious. Part of my mind knew that this didn't happen every afternoon, yet I felt that, unique as the experience was, it didn't rattle me. That was the first of two such experiences, and as I tried to figure out what was happening, I concluded that it might be an angel or perhaps a previous dweller who had died in the house. So, why should I be afraid of a cloud of mist? The second time, I saw a black mist move quickly from the front door and through my living room into the kitchen, which was empty in the next minute when I went to look."

She told me of another occasion which might have frightened a less-philosophical person. Lying on her bed on another afternoon, waiting for her daughter's return from school, she heard heavy breathing coming from the room's doorway. Still, she could clearly see that no one, physically anyway, was there. A short time later came a humorous event, with Ann asleep on her living room couch. Suddenly, near or behind the couch, a harmonica began to play. Nobody in the family even owned such an instrument, much less was able to play it. "I can't quite remember what the tune was," she recalls, "but it was nice. How can music come from a nowhere and not a something?" she asked. Of course, I don't know the answer to that one, either, unless the sound is a bit of the house's history replaying itself. It became clear to us both during the interview that Ann needed to discover much more about the history of the house—who its former occupants were, and if any of them were musically inclined.

This story is interesting for several reasons. The first aspect involves brain activity, which all readers should understand. On its way down into the "theta state," or even-deeper "delta state," as we enter sleep, the brain moves first from the waking beta state, down into alpha. All that is necessary for that switch to occur is for us to relax, as in meditation; shut off all sights, sounds, tastes, smells and physical discomfort. Most eastern religions recommend this process as a quiet means of connecting with our soul's mind. In alpha brain activity we all have a certain amount of daydream or psychic ability, if only gaining insights into our relationships with others. Many researchers say that is also the place where we become more inventive or creative. Turning this section of our semi-consciousness into an idea factory is sanctioned by many of the Fortune

500 corporations, as a way to become inspired, "out of the box" of traditional approaches to problems.

An even slower brain wave frequency denotes our movement down into theta rhythms. Much greater Sixth Sense activity occurs here, mining our subconscious memory. In theta state we are much more creative, and flurries of our innate genius begin to occur. Finally, in our deepest levels of sleep and dream activity, when the brain is functioning at less than four cycles per second, comes delta level activity. We are paralyzed here by endorphins (natural opiates), and are physically unable to respond to life in a conscious manner. Likely, then, Ann gets down to alpha or theta levels quickly, and this can be associated with a developing psychic ability, whether or not she chooses to use the ability.

Secondly, this case points up a sometimes-easy technique to be used if you hope to identify the ghost's identity. Many times, that is my first clue as to who it is that might still be hanging on. Many deceased individuals leave records of their trials and tribulations in data files, and these discomforts are many times a cause for hauntings.

Ann has a deed for her July 2000 purchase of the house. In N.Y. State, all deeds have a process for recording. When you buy a house, the deed is filed and recorded at the county clerk's office. Its place of storage is printed on the front of deed at the time of recording. Your house's deed will begin with the fact that you bought the house on such and such a date and who you bought it from. Clue number one: follow that information, then. The deed further states that this is the same piece of property conveyed by an earlier owner to the person that you purchased from, and in what book of records (even giving page number) that deed can be found. Keeping up this search, with any luck you can retrieve the entire history of your building or property, all the way back to the original land conveyance from government to a long-ago first owner.

"I have had other paranormal experiences here," she told me. "One day when I'm sure I was awake, I spotted a red and white 1950s model car in our driveway—certainly not anything our family owns. Even more puzzling, looking farther out, I could see Route 9G/Violet Avenue was unpaved." Sometimes, such clues in an investigation can suggest that time period from which the ghost entities came and what family owned that car, if indeed it ever was real.

Research showed me that that street received its first hard coating (water borne macadam, a mix of stone and dust) in 1904 on some sections, but all parts of the road were finished by 1907. Was that the period she spied? If so, why was a '50s car there? The State Department of Transportation told me the road was re-worked and twin layers of nine-inch concrete were installed in

1931. More questions still have to be answered to understand just this small part of the larger phenomenon.

"Another time when I was upstairs, I heard a sound and looked down the stairs. Just briefly, there were two guys who appeared to be in their twenties. One look up at me directly, put his hand on the wall, and said, 'Nice wall!' then they vanished. Was he a long-ago resident of the house? Possibly one of the builders? Was he revisiting my home from some place in the world of spirit? Also, maybe he isn't dead. I've heard strange cases of people being alive somewhere else and yet appearing in far-off locations (bi-locating). Is that possible?"

I assured her that it was. My old friend, Dr. Alexander Tanous from Portland, Maine, was a bi-locator, which often drove his friends to distraction. They'd know he was in New York City, all wired up in a lab experiment, yet he'd visit a friend in Maine and actually have conversations with them before suddenly disappearing.

"I have recorded a strange banging sound," Ann told me, "and just recently, when I was doing my laundry, I heard a strange, muffled, almost as if recorded voice, say, 'Hello!' Of course, there was nobody else present. My daughter, now fifteen, has heard sounds and has seen orbs in her bedroom, leading me to think it's not just some activity inside me."

Either the spirit activity is increasing or Ann is rapidly developing her psychic sensitivity, which all people have, though only a few choose to develop it safely and selflessly, or maybe both are occurring simultaneously.

A Rose is a Rose

There is much more to a human being than a physical body. Ghosts are a non-physical, energy remnant of the person whose body has died. Spirits are just as "real" as any other energy accumulation (i.e. magnetic or force fields), but the elements of a spirit remain together until the work of that entity is finished. As readers well know, ghosts "hang around" until the last remaining conflicts of the finished earth life have been emotionally and spiritually cast off. In theory, at least, all of us should be able to experience ghosts of the deceased. However, some of us are "tuned" more to experience sounds, smells or subtle touches, and only some people can see the spirit inhabitants of our world. And still others are trained to fear and blot out the subtle advances of spirits.

Many, or most, as some would argue, human beings have a difficult enough time just managing the physical, emotional and spiritual affairs of their lives, and would experience an overload if confronted with too much of the spirit world. Such sensitive people first need to overcome a tendency to fear the unknown. But some of us, I maintain, especially those who profess belief in a transcendent destiny for humankind, should consider assisting the struggling spirits as a part of our religious or spiritual ministry. These beings were once as hopeful, loving, and energetic as we, the living, are now. Do you recall the old New England epitaph?

> *Remember friend, as you pass by,*
> *that as you are, so once was I.*
> *As I am now, so shall you be,*
> *Repent your sins and follow me.*

Most of the stories in this book come from first-timers: men, women and children who have caught their first glimpse of the earth's former residents. For some, it was a life-changing episode; for others, an occasion of dread, fear and ultimately, the urge to repress the phenomena. Here is a typical story that became an experience of curiosity and ultimate re-affirmation of the human condition by a friend of mine named Faye.

Following some early adulthood experiences with ghosts in Buffalo, this Capital District resident came to know and work with a noted psychic and healer, a man who helped her to develop her native intuitive powers so that she might experience more of the world of energy. He taught her not to fear, but instead to lend a helping hand to the spirit entities when and where she could.

"I moved into my present Schenectady home," she told me, "shortly after I began working with Sam, and I found myself developing new insights, now able to sense things I never dreamed of before. I love assembling jig-saw puzzles, and one night I sat working into the wee hours of the morning, dealing with some of the puzzle's physical mysteries. I was trying to see 'the whole, big picture,' I guess, and I didn't understand how big that would become. Maybe it was 3:00 a.m. when I suddenly was overcome with sadness, and it got to the point where I just broke down and sobbed, unable to finish my puzzle. There seemed to be no logical reason for that outburst of emotion."

At the time, Faye was working with not only her mentor, Sam Lentine, but also a sensitive couple named Joe and Judy. "When I told Sam about the overwhelming sadness that came to me in the night, he suggested that I might be taking on the emotions of a spirit or ghost in the house. So, I asked Joe, Judy and another student to visit my house, to see what they'd pick up. At that time, my sixth sense or 'third eye' only allowed me to 'see' clearly at times, but that night, things really changed."

Each person has a spirit guide, though some prefer to use the term "guardian angel," whose purpose is to keep the individual on an unselfish and safe path, though all of us have free will and can tune out that guide if we desire to do so. "As the four of us talked," Faye continued, "I suddenly began to see the guides accompanying us all. And as the group talked about spirit entities, suddenly I saw her! A woman in '40s style dress began to enter the room, then she abruptly stopped, and an expression of absolute horror came to her face. I heard her exclaim, 'They're ghosts!' as she spotted our spirit guides. Evidently, the woman had no idea that she too had passed.

"Since that time, I've learned that one of the guides I saw works on what I call rescues of those in spirit," Faye continued. "During my vision of the '40s woman, I saw this guide put an arm around her as the other guides gathered lovingly around, and then the entire scene faded. How beautiful, I thought, if all of us pass over fully in a way like this. There is always someone to greet and aid us, if we only accept that only this part of our eternal life has ended," she said. Apparently, none of us can die alone.

"The members of our group later commented that there had just been the spirit of a much older woman present, and that they felt she had once lived in the house. They also said they got the information that she was somehow connected with the word 'rose,' maybe as a personal name or as a florist or gardener," said Faye.

The following day, Faye felt impelled to verify the vision and struck up a conversation with a next-door neighbor, a woman named Rosé. "I asked her if she had known any of my house's previous residents. She said yes, and told me a bit about the people I'd bought from, and then the previous owners. In that family was an older woman who loved her flowers and always worried about them, whether they'd be healthy or killed by an early frost. She spent hours cultivating and spraying them, especially the roses by the garage. After my neighbor told me this, I never again experienced the woman's spirit in my house. Isn't it nice," Faye exclaimed, "that we can continue to help one another up the ladder of life?"

Spook Central

Spook Central

In 1870, James Cragg built a beautiful house in the Second Empire style at 4138 Lake Road in the Wayne County village of Pultneyville. Not many records survive relating to his ownership, except that he willed the building to his daughter, and that she sold it to Jennie Stell in 1929. Mrs. Stell hoped to operate a boarding house there, but the Depression came and times were uncertain. Mrs. Stell's rental income never exceeded her costs so, in less than ten years, the bank foreclosed on the property.

The new owners were Mr. and Mrs. Francis D'Amanda, who were able to assume the Stell debt. In October of 1939, Jennie Stell wrote a bitter letter to the new owners, which seemed to indicate her desire to haunt the structure after her death. "When you awake in the morning," she wrote, "and see the sunshine, you and Mrs. D'Amanda will know that my living spirit is there and that you got it [the house] by taking it, and in no other way."

In 1994, student Rebekah Porray interviewed the present owners, John and Kathy D'Amanda, who retain John's parents' suspicion that the invisible house guest is Mrs. Stell. The D'Amandas did not become aware of this presence, however, until after their children were born. Rebekah wrote, "Since then, they have had many guests stay in the rooms on the third floor. Many times the guests have come down in the morning and asked if the house was haunted." John and Kathy asked their guests why they would ask such a question, and received many variations on the same response. The heavy sleigh bed in one room seems to move or vibrate. Yet, if the guests stay several nights, the phenomenon usually ceases by the third night, as if the ghost simply wants the new people to understand that she is still in charge.

The house gained its curious informal name, "Spook Central," from construction men who were hired in the 1970s to renovate parts of the house. One of the men fell from a ladder on his first day at work and refused to return. Three of the repairmen had flat tires either on the way to work there or in the driveway. Another of the workers got paint sprayed in his face as he walked past a can of spray paint, though, needless to say, there was no other human presence near the can at the time. Another workman, laboring in the downstairs, heard a woman's footfalls upstairs all day long and assumed that Kathy was roaming around, but at day's end, the man discovered that he was the only living person in the house.

It appears that Jennie, if indeed it is her, is drawn to the nursery. When the D'Amandas' son, James, was a baby, he was afraid of old women with wrinkles and white hair. John and Kathy told Rebekah that many times at night, they'd check on little James, only to find him awake and watchful, and they felt a strong presence in the room, though no one was visible.

John and Kathy once went out for the evening, leaving little James asleep in his crib, watched over by a babysitter. When they returned, the girl was frantic because, on the baby's crib monitor, she had heard the infant crying and then suddenly hushed by a woman's voice saying, "Oh, it's all right, it's all right." The teenager had rushed to the nursery but found nobody except baby James. In the end, the D'Amandas rationalized that the sounds surely came from an electrical malfunction on the monitor, perhaps a sound emanating from a neighbor's house.

Ghost story aficionados understand that bitterness or an urge for revenge can often cause a discarnate being to remain trapped on the earth plane to interact with the living until they find release. It seems that Jennie wanted to retain her presence as mistress of the house and has given Kathy D'Amanda a run for her money in that capacity.

Relief

"As I sit writing this, I still can't help but think I am the crazy one!" Patricia wrote. She thanked me for aiding her in believing she hadn't lost her mind. Like many modern people, she had come to dismiss folktales of ghosts and spirits and many of the other phenomena that disbelievers stir into the mix. She and her husband were 21st century people who leaned on what science could prove and explain. However, ghosts don't always fit into an explainable category, and they are rational only if one knows their stories.

Patricia's family lives in a Stafford, New York, house that dates from the 1830s, a time when the railroad was just establishing a commercial link westward to Buffalo and eastward to Rochester. Pat and her husband, Bob, moved into the old structure in September 1992, and it seemed the perfect place to settle and raise a family, she said.

A month later, they recognized they were not alone. Sounds of digging came from the basement, and at first puzzled, then alarmed, they worried if there had been a break-in. Figuring that there had to be a rational explanation, each time the sounds occurred, they cautiously went downstairs to investigate but never found anything amiss. "Those sounds happened twice the first night and have occasionally reoccurred. But then came a series of other experiences that seem almost cyclical in nature.

"We have lights that turn off and then on again, many times when it is inconvenient for us. We hear footsteps on the stairs, but no physical person ever shows up. Food turns up missing at times. The automatic garage-door opener raises and lowers the door without our prompting. From time to time, in the living room, we hear deep voices speaking, though it's hard to decipher what they are saying. And, of course," she said with wide eyes, "there is nobody there to make those sounds, anyway!"

On occasion, several of her son Liam's toys begin to move and make noise without any apparent cause. "Even removing the batteries many times doesn't stop them, and the only way to get silence is to stuff them into a hamper with the dirty clothes." She is sure the eight-year-old hears and sees more than he lets on, but she is particularly puzzled by his statements (made when he was five) that he had a new friend, a boy who is black. Acknowledging that many children have imaginary playmates, Patricia is not certain that the stranger really is entirely imaginary, though Liam gives few explanations about his relationship to this invisible friend.

The episodes continue on an irregular basis. Patricia says that the family can go for weeks or even months with no problems, but then comes a voice, a sound, or a disappearing object.

It seems clear that the digging sounds and perhaps even the voices are a residue of former owners. I recommended that the family do a more intensive search of the property deeds as to prior owners and see, if possible, what traumas those people endured. Likely, such unresolved frustrations have kept that former resident tied to the structure, perhaps still trying to resolve an issue.

With a proliferation of television "ghost-search programs," more and more Americans are coming to see that energies (as a form of matter that cannot, according to science, be created or destroyed) can and do linger. And consciousness of former lives can be retained in that energy, seeking peace and resolution to the difficulties that all humans experience. Someone should tell our young people that this is true, so that in adulthood they need not be surprised or fearful when this "other world" intrudes.

Old Muskrat?

"My Uncle Ronald once told me of Muskrat Robare, a murderer from long ago, who had lived in our old house on Grove Street in Keeseville, New York. It was said that Muskrat had killed many people and that some of those bodies were likely secreted under the house, the chicken coop, or somewhere else on the property." Thus did Thomas Pray introduce a Halloween story in his October 2006 column, "Growing Up On Grove," in the *Lake Champlain Weekly*.

As with many of us, in childhood Tom found the dark recesses of his old house to be mysterious, even terrifying at times. He believes that 1967, when he was thirteen, was one of the scariest years of his life. Part of a former upstairs apartment, his bedroom faced an unused room, whose locked door's doorknob often jiggled and rattled in the night, especially when he was in the house alone. Even on windless nights he'd hear the rattle, which would then stop, to be replaced by the sound of retreating footsteps within the unused room. By day, his bedroom was cozy and warm—a great place to work on model airplanes, ships and monster figurines.

His collection of the latter on one shelf included The Hunchback of Notre Dame, the Werewolf, Godzilla, Frankenstein's Monster, Dr. Jekyll and Mr. Hyde, and the Creature from the Black Lagoon. On the shelf below, he had statues of baseball heroes. By day, everything sat unmoving, but in the night the figures moved, so that in the morning all the figures and models seemed reoriented, often pointing at him.

Darkness, because it lacks specifics to focus on, is often a creative time for the brain and its imaginative powers, but Tom couldn't argue that he imagined the moved figures. Every morning they were moved. The remnant energy of old Muskrat's murders, it seemed to Tom, might easily move up the common stairway from the dark, dank cellar, past the first floor, and to the second story where he slept. On certain windless nights, there was occasionally the sound of moaning, but only if his parents were out. His father's reassurances of a house making "shifting noises" didn't seem logical for a building dating from the late 1800s. And his mother's explanations of mice moving didn't cut it for Tom either. He did his best, as many of us do when first confronted with strange nocturnal sounds, to find a rational explanation.

On his nights alone, he always checked beneath the bed to be sure there was nothing capable of movement or noisemaking there. Then, once the lights were out, there would first come the scratching sounds in that locked and empty room, then the rattling doorknob, and finally the retreating slow footsteps inside the empty room. By daylight, trying to rationalize it all, time and again, he checked off the logical potential causes, such as passing trucks, strong winds, B-52s from Plattsburgh Air Force Base to the north, or hot water pipes. By night, the lad found himself unable to muster the courage to jump out of bed, seize the doorknob, turn it, and confront once and for all whatever monster lurked there. No, it seemed the better part of valor was to dig in and submerge himself in the blankets, covering his head in the bargain.

In the morning, one or both of the baseball players and several of the monster models were turned to face his bed. It was all imagination, he tried to convince himself, but that only worked until "that night." One evening, having been away for several hours, he decided to reenter the house via the back shed roof, then into his bedroom window. "There, standing in the shadows of my room was a dark figure. It stood near my dresser, seeming to float there. Finally, it drifted toward the locked door and faded from sight. It took me quite some time to convince myself it was only the lighting, and not a ghost. Looking back on that experience, I now know that it made me less afraid. There was now a 'something,' and my mind no longer insisted on making it worse. If the figure was real, it was only a shadow. And if it was my imagination, then that's all it was."

Fortunately for Tom, later in the year he discovered girls, who took his mind off the non-physical world all the way through to high school graduation. At about the same time, he moved his bedroom to the ground floor, so he was no longer near that uninhabited upstairs room. Later Tom married, moved to a new house in Peru, and became involved in a writing career. However, he now wonders why the bathroom doorknob in his present home rattles at night.

Allan S. Everest's book, *Rum Across the Border*, tells the story of Charles Robare, who earned his nickname by swimming away from federal officers pursuing him during his bootlegger days. After that escape, Robare is said to have always worn a muskrat hat. Never caught running rum, Robare was convicted of running a still, however, and went to federal prison in Atlanta, Georgia. Upon his release he was convicted of auto theft. The reputation of being a murderer was earned when Robare murdered Yale Morris with a pickaxe. Awaiting trial in jail, Muskrat hanged himself, thus cheating the state's hangman. Such was the reputation that must have inspired Tom as a child.

Unsolved

The Germond House

"I grew up in Stanfordville in Dutchess County," Micki Chapman told me. "One of the horror stories that all us children heard was that of the Germond family just outside the village, who had all been murdered by a mysterious man who got away, so the case was never solved. I was always too scared of even seeing the place, so I never went. When I actually did enter the house, it was years later and I didn't know at first where I had been."

She referred to a famous case from Thanksgiving time in 1930, when a neighbor discovered the bodies of James and Mabel Germond and their two children, Bernice, eighteen and Raymond, ten, horribly murdered. Prior to death, all had been slashed by their murderer and State Police determined that the weapon had been a butcher knife. The father and son's bodies had been dragged into the wagon shed and dropped there; the mother and daughter were discovered dead in the house. A mysterious stranger, a vagrant identified as Florentine Chase, had been seen in the area before the murder and immediately went missing. It was discovered that an unsuspecting neighbor had driven Chase to the railroad station in Poughkeepsie, and a Hudson Valley manhunt ensued. All other suspects were cleared, however, and because Chase was never found, no one was ever brought to justice for the foul deed.

The murder victims were interred in the Stanfordville Cemetery and, after the murder investigation concluded, the old Shaker style farmhouse, which had been owned by the Germonds since 1898, sat for a while boarded up and abandoned. Over the next seven decades, tenants attempted to live there, but quickly moved out, creating the legend of unquiet ghosts. When I met Micki Chapman, I discovered information from this period in which people came and went.

"Eventually, in my role as a house cleaner, I got a chance to enter the old house," she told me. "I worked for a small company of women who were hired to clean houses in between owners, or after special problems such as a flood or fire. It was just another job that day, and I didn't pay particular attention to the exact address. What struck me from the outset, however, was that I became very uneasy and felt closed-in when I first entered the house.

"The second day, when we went to finish our work, I entered apprehensively. Soon, working upstairs, I was rewarded by a strong pull on my ponytail as I worked on my hands and knees on the rug. Startled, as nobody was nearby, I stood, and was immediately engulfed in a very cold air. Realizing what I was experiencing, I ran outdoors to our truck to get my camera. Maybe I could capture a ghost on film, I thought."

She had been working in the master bedroom and now had to clean in the master bathroom, which had an old tub, perhaps the one that the Germonds had bathed in. "There was a new shower, however, with a glass wall and, as there seemed to be a stain of some sort on the glass, I wiped it clean. Suddenly, there emerged a pattern of three fingers drawn across the area that I had just wiped. I cleaned the image off, but it emerged again within a minute. I did that activity one more time, then realized this was something supernatural. Suspecting there was a ghost there, maybe even one of the Germond family's spirits, I announced to the room that we were leaving soon, which we did. Once in the truck, we sped away, and a short time later, I left the company. So, that was my experience with that house in 2006," she told me.

When I visited Stanfordville, I learned that the old house had new owners who had moved to the area, and when I saw the house, I was struck as to how beautifully it had been restored. The main house and outbuildings looked like a picture postcard advertisement for rural Dutchess County; something that a reader might find in *Good Housekeeping*. The present owners were away, and the women who were working inside, as cleaners and maintenance workers, were courteous but not very forthcoming, except to tell me that phenomena still take place, though the pair just walk around the events.

I also located several previous occupants or owners of the place, but none wanted to talk on the record about their experiences. I did find an on-line interview with Karen Staats, one of the previous owners. When interviewed by columnist Frances Sandiford in 2002, Mrs. Staats stated that she had no fear of ghosts, but was puzzled that her dogs acted in very strange ways at various times. Most often, they would scratch and dig at a certain spot on the dining room floor, a place where the Germond women's bodies were allegedly found.

I never pry into matters that people consider too frightening or private to discuss, but seek to be open and understanding to their experiences when they tell them. So, unable to gain much more information on the matter, I have done this brief write-up, perhaps more as evidence that acts of violence and sudden death do remain in time and space, reverberating for decades or even centuries at the place of trauma. Many of the ghosts that people experience are the remnants of once living individuals; in this case, a happy family gathered for celebration, but viciously sent into the spirit world against their wishes.

Yard Man

The school year had just concluded in June 2007 when I received a well-written e-mail from Amanda. She and her father believed they had a ghost in the house, she wrote. There was no indication of Amanda's age, so I was somewhat surprised to note that she was eleven when we began corresponding. I always like to talk to youngsters and teens about their experiences, as many are either afraid or worried what their peers might say if the story gets out.

In any case, I found Amanda bright and well-spoken and she told me this story, which is fairly common in the world of spirits. "My parents bought our house on Ridge Road in Delmar in 1998, when I was two," she told me. "There was no indication of any presence until late in 2006, when I stood in the upstairs bathroom one day, washing my hands. When I glanced out the window into the back yard, I was startled to see a dark figure that looked like a man moving across our lawn. The odd thing is that he didn't go all the way to the ground, being visible only from the waist up. Then, just before he disappeared behind our shed, I noted that he had red eyes. That all left me both curious about his identity, but also with a good case of goose bumps."

At her parochial school in Albany, ghosts aren't part of the curriculum, and Amanda struggled with her own disbelief before finally sharing the vision with her parents. They asked her for a description of the figure and, in the end, wrote it off to imagination. "I thought well, maybe they were right," she concluded. "But, two weeks later, I changed my opinion very quickly. My second floor bedroom has an attic entry at the back of the clothes closet, and upstairs over that door I clearly heard heavy footsteps at one a.m. I knew nobody would be up there at that hour, and shot out of my bed and into my parents' bedroom, where I woke them up and related my experience." Most parents try to be rational, and there was no logical explanation for this phenomenon, so Larry and Molly told their daughter that, in all likelihood, it was a dream. Mumbling to herself, Amanda returned to her bed, but not to sleep. She kept waiting for the walking to begin again, but it didn't.

November came and the air outdoors was cold, so all the windows were shut. Thanksgiving was coming soon and Amanda sat talking to her father in his bedroom as he picked out his outfit for the next day. "Suddenly the room seemed filled with an intense cold," she told me, "and the hair on the back of my neck stood up straight. Though I scurried around checking for an open window, I didn't find any. I returned to tell Dad what had happened and to ask him if he had felt the cold, but he hadn't. How could I feel almost frozen and he hadn't experienced it? That really puzzled Dad and he didn't know what to make of it, but it made me nervous. The next day in school, I shared my story with some close friends, who just didn't know how to react. They told me they were never coming to my house for a visit!" As with many experiences, it can be a lonely feeling if others in the house don't pick up the sounds, smells or sights. Amanda wondered why her parents weren't experiencing the events that she had.

Finally, in February 2007, she got the confirmation that she sought. On a Saturday morning, Larry filled the coffee maker with water and coffee grounds and the brew began. Suddenly, with both Amanda and her father watching the timer, it reverted to a display of the time two hours before. As they stared in amazement, the timer then sped forward to a time 5 hours in the future. By now her father was intrigued—a no-nonsense guy, Larry knew what he'd seen, and he also knew there wasn't any easy explanation for the malfunction. Molly, Amanda's mother, now had to contend with two family members tuned to some other reality, when she had had no experiences at all. Larry told her what happened and Molly raised her eyebrows until Amanda exclaimed, "Mom, it's the truth!" They went to the kitchen and found the clock mechanism restored to the regular time, and that timer has behaved itself ever since.

As Amanda and I talked about these experiences, it became clear to us both that somebody in spirit was attempting to get the family's attention. Many times, because youngsters are more "open," the entities will try to contact them first. "Was that the end of it, then?" I asked the girl. "No way," she replied. "Not long after that, I was in the bathroom taking a shower when I saw a dark hand approaching on the other side of the plastic shower curtain. Suddenly, the entire curtain swung out horizontally into the bathroom, but I could see that there was nobody there," she told me with big eyes. "I screamed and Mom came running, but all she could tell me was to get out of there fast. She didn't have to tell me twice! So then, I told Mom about seeing that figure in the back yard the previous summer, but how could she explain that too?"

Finally, the school year ended in late June and Amanda sat relaxing and reading a book on the porch. All at once, she felt impelled to stand and look into the house through the screen door. "At the top of the stairs, I spotted a dark figure with what seemed like amber or yellow eyes, and then it vanished. All I could do was to tell Dad, but what could he do about a disappeared spirit?"

Here is where we are right now. The family bought the house when Amanda was two and she has grown up there. The building is about eighty years old, as are many of the homes on Ridge Road. As a former history teacher and present-day investigator, I advised Amanda that it was time to begin investigation. "First, ask your mom and dad to show you the deed to the property; that will provide the names of the most recent owners before your parents. Then (as I would do) visit or phone the village historian, and ask that person if those previous owners are known. Ask the old-timer neighbors if they knew the family and whether or not there was any calamity during their ownership of the property...maybe something in that back yard? When we get some results on that quest, we may need to visit the County Clerk's office and find who those previous owners bought from and whether or not anyone alive today knows of troubles in that family. Discovering the history of a ghost is not much different from doing archaeology, you just dig away one layer after another. If you're lucky, you find why some being's consciousness is still hanging around.

"The good result of doing this work," I told her, "is that you're learning to be a researcher, which will help in high school and college. And, if your sixth grade teacher gives you a report to do next year, you'll have one all ready!"

Steps in Time

By now, reader, you know that what we cling to in life, whether it is our possessions, our name and reputation, or some deep need or addiction, these can, in the end, be like an anchor weighing down our spirit once it is freed from our flesh body. Such profound concerns or preoccupations, when our soul seeks to ascend into a heaven after death, become a burden blocking our onward movement. These dependencies aren't often calamitous, however, as they only delay our eventual passage into The Everlasting Light. Sounds, smells, sights, or other sensations that are experienced as ghosts are not often malefic or turbulent, but are simply our experience of those trapped or idling in between the planes of existence. The fortunate people are those who can witness, and then assist, the departure or liberation of another's soul.

McHarrie Street in Baldwinsville, New York was named for early set-tler, John McHarrie, a 1790s farmer who used to move his crops to market by boat, through the rapids on the Seneca River. Today, McHarrie street is a quiet thoroughfare.

Another John, a youngster, and his family moved from Syracuse to Baldwinsville in 1960, when his dad purchased a house on McHarrie Street house from a former navy buddy, Captain John Carbone. The Captain and his Filipino-born wife, Tarcellia, were moving to a new duty station, and for Tarcel-lia it was an unwelcome move. She had been born into the troubled Philippine Islands, probably near the navy base at Subic Bay, just as Asia was about to plunge into World War II. When she reached teen age, the Imperial Japanese Army invaded and reduced the countryside and its people to starvation, bru-tality and even-worse poverty. After the American liberation of the islands in 1944, petite young Tarcellia caught the eye of U.S. Navy Capt. Carbone and the couple was soon married, with Carbone promising her a nice home of her own in America. In the post-war period they came to Baldwinsville, and she became mistress of her first secure home on McHarrie Street.

It was with great anguish, then, that she too quickly had to relinquish that home, of which she had been the proud mistress, and move to another Navy base far away. Her only consolation was that young John's family, friends of the Carbones, would now own and live in her beloved house. As Tarcellia was a meticulous housekeeper, she was somewhat mollified that young John's mother promised to keep the house spic and span. It was with sadness that young John's family learned of Mrs. Carbone's passing just three years later.

As a youth, John was astounded, shortly afterward, to hear quick foot-steps walking across the basement floor. He knew Mrs. Carbone and remem-bered the quick gait with which she moved, and especially the click, click sound of the wooden heels on her shoes, footwear that she always wore. But then the sound stopped for a few months, so John was puzzled and attributed the sound to his active imagination. Then, three months later, the sounds resumed, always quick and deliberate, as he remembered her pacing while alive. He had to share this experience with his mother, who lovingly rubbed his head and told the boy that it was only imagination.

Not long afterward, however, while seated at the kitchen table with his mother, John heard the sound once more and urged his mother to listen. Then, she heard it too. Again and again, the two of them could hear Tarcellia, though they were never frightened. It was as if these sounds were only an echo of former events. It even became a joke between the two, though they didn't dare share it with John's father, as he was a no-nonsense guy. There was no other ghostly activity however, just the footsteps, as if Mrs. Carbone would arrive at irregular intervals to inspect her old home; perhaps she was unable to do otherwise in spirit.

Sometime later, around 10:00 p.m., as John lay on his bed ready to doze off, everyone in the family heard her. Mom and Dad in their bedroom were roused by a new dimension of Tarcellia's striding—this time she was heard coming up the stairs to the second floor! "It was the first and last time that happened," a much older John told me in 2007. "I heard my father bound out of bed, fling open the bedroom door and roar, 'Who the hell's in here?'" The boy emerged from his bedroom to see his father standing in his skivvies at the stair top, almost shaking with a mixture of anger and fear. All the man could do was utter a few more "Get the hell outta here!" warnings," and then return to bed. "That was the last we ever heard of Mrs. Carbone," a smiling John told me. "It was never discussed in our house again."

John's dad died while the young man was in college, and not long afterward, his mother became terminally ill. John returned home to care for and reminisce with his mother, and in a lucid moment, she remembered her husband one day saying, "When I die, I'm going to take those trees with me," referring to two pine trees that he had planted near the front sidewalk in 1961. By 1973, the trees had grown to almost twelve feet in height. Now, as his mother lay near death, she smiled and remembered, "John, just after your dad died, one night I heard a tremendous roar, as if a tornado had hit the Syracuse area. When I awoke the next morning, there were those two pines on the ground, almost as if a giant hand had simply pulled them straight up from the ground. There was little mess of dirt or broken branches on the ground, just two drying-out trees." His mom smiled again, as if savoring the incident; "The old man did just what he said he was going to do!"

That was pretty much the end of the Mrs. Carbone story. She had gone to her rest, as had John's father and mother. The house was sold after the mother's death and John moved on to his professional life. "One postscript to all this," he remembers, "is that I returned to Baldwinsville one day and visited the old neighborhood. The old house on McHarrie Street looked great; the new owners had fixed it up nicely," so he risked stopping his car, getting out and knocking on their door. "They were very gracious and allowed me to explore the house again, a home they had lovingly cared for. Memories of happiness and sadness came to me and, in the end, I felt rejuvenated by the visit with memories of my past. Just as I bid them goodbye, the wife commented that there was a lot of psychic energy in the house, which took me by surprise.

"'Yes, there certainly is,' I replied slowly, wondering where she was going with this conversation. Then, emboldened by my reply, and with a curious look on her face, the woman asked, 'Did you ever hear someone walking around in the basement when you lived here?' Smiling, I told them the whole story of Mrs. Carbone and my family's experiences with her footsteps and their eyes lit up when I mentioned those distinctive wooden shoes that she always wore. I departed and assured them that Tarcellia Carbone would have loved what they had done with the place. All three of us agreed that Mrs. Carbone just came in from time to time to have a look around."

In the McHarrie tradition, Mrs. Carbone had found her way around the rapids between this world and the next, and now has apparently sailed peacefully onward upon the River of Life.

Frances

In 1982, David Preston moved his family into an old house at 1136 Dix Avenue in Hudson Falls, New York. Little Kimberly was just five at the time, but told her parents almost immediately that she sensed an unseen individual in the house.

There was much fixing up to be done in their new home, and one of the earliest items to be replaced was the old wooden front door. A nice, new wooden door was installed, but strange phenomena began soon afterward. Family members sitting in the living room began to hear the doorknob twisting and turning. Sometimes it rattled and kept up the movement for as long as twenty seconds before becoming still again.

"One of the first strange events, beside the doorknob, was when Kim, who was then eight, got out my old transistor radio that she'd brought from our former house," David said. "She played with it before going to bed. Then, in the middle of the night, the radio began blaring away and woke us all up. I went in and turned it off. What made it suddenly turn on? I wondered. The next morning I went in to examine it. I took the radio out of its leather carrying case and opened the battery hatch—there were no batteries inside! How had it made all that noise?"

As she grew into a teenager, Kim was allowed to stay home without a babysitter when her parents went out. "I stayed up late one night when, all of a sudden, the front doorknob started turning and twisting, though the door didn't open," she told me. "This activity kept up from 10:30 p.m. until after 2 a.m., when it suddenly stopped. That was the longest episode we'd ever had.

When I got up the next morning, I discovered that I'd left my keys in the outside door lock, and I wondered if the ghost was trying to warn me.

"In 2001, I had my first sighting of the ghost woman. We had a new puppy at that time, and he was anxious to go out for an evening walk just before bedtime, so I took him outside. Then I came back and prepared for bed. As I was walking down the hallway, all at once, there she was. I looked at her, walked past her, and went into my bedroom. Suddenly it hit me—what did I see? I went back out and turned on the hall light, but nobody was there. I recalled that she had been short, almost tiny, wore a long white gown, and had her hair done up. She sure wasn't a relative, so I was pretty certain she went with the house.

"Not too long afterward, in the winter of 2002, I stood at the kitchen sink washing dishes and again got that eerie feeling of not being alone. I turned toward the doorway, and there she was again, dressed almost as I'd seen her the first time, except that this time she definitely wore a dress and not a nightgown. Our eyes met and she quickly dissolved in mid-air. After that, on several occasions, I felt someone sit on my bed, though nobody was visible. It didn't scare me, as I understood the old lady was just curious about the new occupants of the house."

Kim, who works with genealogy and is an expert at research, went to the Washington County Courthouse and Village Clerk's office to research the property. She discovered that a former owner of the property, a Frances Tefft, had died there in 1929. Frances, Kim discovered, had been well-educated and was a preceptress at the old Union School in Sandy Hill. In 1877, Frances left to serve as co-owner and principal at the Glens Falls Academy. Eleven years later she returned to Union School as the principal and was instrumental in the building of a new high school in 1892. Research shows that she lived in a now-demolished house on what became the Preston's Dix Avenue property. Their house, which replaces Frances', dates from the 1950s. "I found her obituary in the local papers, and she looked like the woman I'd seen twice," Kim said.

"I saw her, too," said David, "though my wife only saw the doorknob moving, and never saw the woman. I also saw a man pass through the house once, and I discovered that a man in the family of the previous owners of our house died in the room that Kim now occupies. One of the stranger experiences that I had was hearing the puppy barking away one night. I yelled to him to quiet down. Kim was out, so I was surprised a minute later to hear a woman's voice telling the puppy to be quiet. He obeyed. The next morning, I mentioned to Kim that she had gotten in early and quieted the dog, but she denied it, saying that she had returned late, and the dog was already asleep." One can only guess that it was Frances who had charmed the animal.

"I think she kept an eye on us while we lived there," Kim said. "One night I scrambled some eggs. Leaving the pan and spatula on the stove, I took my food into the living room to eat. I had barely reached the living room when I heard a noise in the kitchen. I quickly went back, turned on the light, and found that the spatula had moved out of the frying pan, across the room, and had landed in the chair where I normally sat. I wasn't quite sure how to interpret that, but I figured maybe it was a message from Frances to clean up after myself. Now, I always clean up my pans after cooking and before I sit down to eat. Since she was in education, maybe it's hard for her to let go of teaching people new habits.

"I went to a pet shelter in Corinth one day, taking the puppy with me. Maybe, I reasoned, there is something or someone else beside Frances who is making the dog bark so much at night. The shelter had a fundraiser that offered a pet psychic who would converse with our pets for a fee, which was then donated to the shelter. The seer told me that he saw the dog being disturbed by the flow of spirit people through our house, most of them from an earlier time in history. Almost all were women dressed in the old styles. My research confirmed that, as Frances had been quite active socially and politically, she often hosted teas in the old house that predated ours. The psychic gentleman specifically mentioned one short woman in a white dress—that was Frances. I later learned that she died in 1929 and was buried in Union Cemetery in Hudson Falls."

"The time I saw her first," David continued, "I awoke one morning before dawn and saw a woman in a white dress kneeling alongside the bed on my wife's side. When the ghost caught me watching her, she stood and went out the door into the hall. I got up to follow her, but the hallway was empty. Another time, I sat on the edge of the bed in a pitch-black bedroom. I had just reached down to pull off my socks, when I looked up to see the lady, right in front of me, watching. I rose as if to touch her, but she backed away, seeming to avoid my touch, and then faded out.

"One thing that I never got used to," he said, "was what happened to my pocket change. Often before going to bed, I'd take the coins and my money clip out of my pocket and place them on top of the TV. Yet, about a dozen times over the years, I'd find these items on the hutch when I got up in the morning. We just couldn't figure out how it happened or what it meant.

"On another occasion, as we sat watching TV at night, we suddenly heard a big bang. I went to the front door and found that it had apparently blown all the way open, striking a wall. Must be the wind outside, I thought, but when I looked, the outside glass storm door was tightly closed. There was no way a breeze could have gotten through it to slam the door open that forcibly. So what or who was it—Frances? And, if so, what was her message?

"A few years later, in June 2003, we had a chance to move into a more spacious house and put our old home up for sale. When the bank appraiser came to take exterior photos and do an inspection, one photo clearly shows a woman in the window looking out intently at us. It wasn't my wife, as she was working in the backyard. It wasn't Kim because she was away working, and I was standing outside with the man when he took the photos. Not wanting to withhold any of our experience from the purchasers, I later showed the photo to both the real estate agent and the new buyers, but they declined to be impressed—they didn't believe in such things."

Interviewing the Prestons was a fascinating opportunity for me. They had more than their share of spectral experiences, yet they were not overly concerned and definitely not afraid. Kim related another experience to me that reaffirms her belief in life after death. One Memorial Day she went to the Catholic cemetery on Burgoyne Avenue to visit the grave of her best friend's mother. All at once, she felt the sensation of someone coming up behind her and then gently placing a hand on her shoulder. "Of course, nobody was there when I turned, but I have felt her several times since, almost as a friend who cares for me as much in death as she did in life. It's a nice feeling."

I asked Kim what she thought about all these varied experiences with the world beyond. She answered, "I think they're interesting, though I believed in life after death even before I saw Frances for the first time. It's nice that I now have the evidence that life continues after death." I couldn't have been any more concise myself.

George

Many people prefer to put a name on their ghost, maybe because it makes the being seem more of a personality and therefore less scary. I have found that George seems to be a most common appellation, even when the guy's name likely was George. Here is a neat experience from East Syracuse.

"In the year 2000, I'd had a breakup with my boyfriend, Chris," Leslie Mitchell told me, "and I moved out, renting an older house on Route 298. The landlords, an older couple, seemed nice enough and lived right next door. It seems that my house actually had been a section of their home long ago, but the two parts of the building were now separate. In any case, the house was big enough for my daughter, Lauren, who was 11 at the time, and me. We thought we were settling in to a quieter existence.

"One day, I noticed a new woman next door and went over to meet her. It turned out that she was the daughter of the family, and she said she had moved home because her mother had been diagnosed with cancer. The two of us conversed from time to time, and one day I confided to her that I thought I was 'losing it,' because things that I'd placed in a certain spot sometimes disappeared or were later found elsewhere. It wasn't like someone stole them, but it was irritating to not find some object when I needed it. My new neighbor smiled and told me that the house once had a ghost. Hmmm, I thought to myself, is she serious?"

The neighbor recounted a situation when she was younger, having heard her parents discussing the matter. It seems that, in the 1940s, a previous tenant had been a man named George, who lived there with his wife and daughter. During World War II, he worked long, hard hours at the old Mattydale Bomber Base (now Syracuse Hancock International Airport), and he was broken-hearted when his wife told him she wanted a divorce. After his wife and child departed, George moped around, inconsolable. The new neighbor told Leslie that George had died there. "Too bad, I, hope he had gotten over it," Leslie said.

"But wait, there's more," the neighbor continued. "In the 1960s, a new family consisting of parents and a girl lived in your place. From time to time, the child told her mother of playing with her special friend, an older man who wore blue overalls. Fearing for the girl's mental well-being, the parents took her to a counselor, where it was determined that the little girl was seeing something, as she had no reason to lie, and that she seemed happy to have a surrogate grandfather. Doing some checking, the parents discovered from neighbors that George, in his work at the airport did wear blue overalls! So, my parents decided they needed to have George's ghost exorcised if they hoped to ever rent the house again. An exorcist was called and did the ceremony, and we figured it was all over," the neighbor said. Leslie crossed her fingers behind her back and went home.

Rather than ending the matter, however, things began to escalate. Many nights, Leslie was startled awake by a boom, though she could find no cause when she walked through the house. In the mornings, Lauren said she had not heard such a sound and, apparently, never did during the Mitchell family's one-year time there. "I kept trying to assign some common explanation to the sound," Leslie continued. "Maybe it was a sonic boom from over at the airport. Or maybe a backfire from a tractor-trailer out on 298 or on Route 41. We had a big old furnace downstairs, so I also considered that as a possible cause, but I could never be sure. Meantime, the occasional disappearances continued in the house, and once in a while came the nocturnal sound of an explosion. I wasn't happy with losing sleep, as I had to be at work early in the morning.

"One night, when I returned from work, I had a phone message from Chris, my old boyfriend, wanting to know if Lauren and I were okay, as he'd had a troubling dream about us not being safe. I called and reassured him and hung up, but that night came another boom," she winced. When Leslie explored the house the next morning, she found her old childhood toy box had moved across the nearby room, so that it now blocked a closet door. "It was a heavy box," she told me, "not something that would jiggle itself across the floor because of rumbling traffic outside. That experience made me really curious."

In any case, maybe from the concern shown by Chris's dream, Leslie and her beau decided to make up and she began to pack, preparing to move back with Chris. "I left for work one morning, having given my notice to the landlords, while Lauren was showering around 7 a.m., readying to catch the school bus. A few hours later she called me at work, to tell me that a friend had driven her to school. It seems she had been in the shower and had heard lots of banging outside the bathroom; it sounded as if someone were slamming the kitchen cabinets. She called out for me, but of course, I wasn't there to answer.

"Lauren, with hair still wet from the shower, frantically called her friend to pick her up, as she didn't want to wait alone any longer. Now from the safety of the school she was telling me the story. I felt it was time to talk to my neighbor once more; apparently, the exorcism of George hadn't worked. When I went next door, I explained to the neighbor's daughter that I'd patched up my romantic life and that was the reason I hadn't renewed my lease. But I also told her that George was back—big time. When I mentioned the booms, the lady got a funny look on her face. 'I did tell you,' she said, 'that George had shot himself, didn't I?' she asked innocently.

"So, ever since, I've marveled at those who see ghosts, because Lauren and I heard one, and are sure we now know who he was. It's kind of sad," she said during our interview, "isn't it? Here was a hard-working guy who lost his family through divorce, and he killed himself in despondency. As a ghost, he hung around until another nice little girl came to live there in the 1960s—someone to befriend before she and her family moved away. Then, of course, he tried to get Lauren's and my attention. He sure was a success," she laughed.

CHAPTER 13

DEAR FRIENDS

IT'S ALL OKAY
REACHING OUT
TAKING LEAVE
CLARENCE
NANCY AND HELEN
THE BEDROOM
TOUCHED

It's All Okay

Whenever I finish an interview, I ask my informants whether or not they will permit the use of their full name and/or street address. As you might expect, and as you discover in this book, many people are content to give just first names in the story. Others are willing to permit only the name of their street location to be used, though not the precise house number. Other people, for understandable reasons, seek greater anonymity. I like this story, both for its content and for the willingness of this couple to fully disclose their experiences. Though James and Denise Strait from the Chemung County town of Horseheads, New York, who are my sources, were willing to give their home phone number also, I declined to include that information. Nevertheless, they are a sincere couple, knowing what they experienced and, finding the events to be a promise of continued life, are willing to help others find a greater faith that life does go onward.

"In the 1980s my brother bought this large duplex house," James told me, "and it is quite large, with almost five thousand feet of living space. Over the course of years, Denise and I have lived on both sides as tenants. My brother's wife, Marilyn, died here of an embolism and toxemia in May 1992. It was very sad, but what has stayed with me over the years is Marilyn's revelation of having a dream a week before her death. In that dream, she felt she had been shot in the head, and told me about it the next day. And, of course, the brain embolism must have felt like just that—an explosive shot—when it occurred. She appeared to me in a dream thirteen years ago, clothed in her wedding dress, and telling me that everything is now fine. I believe that was a genuine contact with her spirit," he told me.

A Navy man at the time, James married Denise, his sweetheart from Long Island, and they moved into the duplex where, on her first night in the new home, Denise had a vivid dream. "A woman that I didn't know approached me and told me, 'It's all okay.' I took comfort from that when I awoke," she said, "but I didn't know if she was real or just some dream figure. Some months later, looking through a family album, I spotted her—it was Marilyn. How loving that was, to greet me as a new family member!"

In 1999, Denise became pregnant and, in her seventh month, was making preparations for the coming birth. She and James installed a monitoring system in order to hear any sounds from the baby's room after she was born. "But as soon as we turned the system on in our bedroom, we could hear footsteps, someone giggling and drawers opening and closing somewhere in the house. I investigated the whole building," he said, "but as you might guess, there was no one here but Denise and me.

"Three years later, I entered our kitchen, which I had just painted, and found all the cupboard doors open, though I'm sure they were latched at bedtime the previous night. It suddenly struck me that Marilyn had 'a thing' about keeping doors and cabinets closed and latched. Could it be? I asked myself, might Marilyn still be here? Then for a while there was nothing new or strange.

"Nevertheless, the concept of Marilyn remaining here opened up an old memory for me," he said. "Marilyn had always complained about the design, construction, and safety of the house's back porch. On the day of her funeral, I was in a group of mourners seated in a room on the north end of the house, when a big bang could be heard. When we got up to investigate, the old porch (on the opposite end of the house from where we were sitting) had fallen and was a shambles. It was a clear day and there was no wind—how could it happen?" Then James smiled. "You know, Marilyn did get what she wanted.

"Two years later, a similar thing happened in March of 1994. My dad died and quite a way from there, in Watkins Glen, where my mother lived, her awning simply tore apart on a clear day. I often wondered if this was a sign, just as the porch had been, that Dad's spirit was still there, despite his burial.

"In 2006 I re-carpeted our living room, stairs and hallway, and wanted to show friends how it had been, so I took before and after photos. In both sets of pictures there were orbs, and people believe this is the energy of spirits in the house," he said. We talked about orbs, as they are common in haunted sites during this age of digital photography. Still, if those pictures were a registry of spirit activity, whose was it?

"One of the ongoing strange things here is the sound of small footsteps under our bed. It might sound as if someone is walking quietly or is a very small person, but I assure you," he laughed again, "there is nobody that tiny in our house. Another oddity, from time to time, we will feel something quite light suddenly land on our bed, almost as if it was a small animal. This causes me to think of a cat that I had years ago, which died in the cellar—might its ghost still remain here?" We talked for a while about pet ghosts, and how common it is for pet owners to receive visits from deceased cats or dogs, even birds (see Ghost Birds story in the chapter on animal ghosts in this book).

But then I shared with him the story of my friend John's death in a deserted building in Saratoga Springs in 2005. I hadn't heard from John in over a month, and he'd always been a frequent caller. I phoned the Saratoga Springs police to see if he was a missing person, only to be told by the lieutenant that John had been found dead two weeks before. That night (and I don't know why this didn't happen on the night of his death) I felt what seemed to be a small animal, such as a guinea pig or kitten, slowly crawling up my blankets from the foot of the bed. Maybe this is the blanket shifting, I told myself, but the movements were coming in a straight line, already having traveled almost four feet before I caught on. I spoke aloud to John; certainly it must have been him. I said that I was happy he'd finally gotten to see my new home, but he couldn't stay. "You've died, John, and now you are free. Turn around and see the beautiful white light (John was quite aesthetic) and walk into that. That's what you're really looking for." The movement stopped right there and never resumed, not then nor since.

James found that story interesting in the light of his own experiences. He told me of their cat and small Doberman who often seem to watch something walk down their stairs. Another mystery is the activity associated with their security camera outdoors. There is a sound pickup on it, so that intruders can be both spotted and heard. "This one, though," he grinned, "plays Christmas carols around the holidays! There has to be a radio receiver in order for that to happen," he told me, "and there is none. For the first time, though, this didn't happen during Christmas 2007."

The Straits seem to live in a "busy zone" of experiences and James then touched on a potentially scary one. His family lives on one side of the building and, in May 2007, a tenant on the other side tried to burn the place down. "The woman threw a lighted, liquid candle on the wall, but it didn't burn at all. Instead, the fiery material crossed the floor to an opposite wall, that wasn't as flammable. We caught it quickly and not too much damage was done. But, why hadn't the first wall burned? Do you think it's because there were two crucifixes there?" He gave a big grin.

Denise added that there certainly are spirits there, and an ordinary person might fear for their little girl, but not the Straits. "When she was small, Kaarina had a toy telephone, and one day she told me that someone wanted to talk to me on the phone. Playing along, I asked who it was. 'Gamma Doane,' she replied in her childish voice. At first, the name didn't register with me—could it have been an imaginary playmate? I asked her who that was, and my daughter replied, 'It's your mother! She is the one who comes to visit me in my bedroom.' How could she have known? My mother's name was Joan, but Kaarina never knew her. Yet, if she was being truthful, my mother was her companion at bedtime. This went on for a few years during which I'd often hear others' voices in her bedroom, though I never discovered any intruder.

"My daughter also spoke of a Katie or Katherine who had died in the house years before. We don't know of any such person, or of a child's death here, but that might take a lot of research, too. We look at the big picture of all this," Denise told me, "but nobody is being hurt. Our daughter isn't acting up because of these 'friends'' visits. In fact, these beings seem to surround her in love. James and I don't encourage her, but we don't discourage her either. We truly believe there are spirits here, but they are the spirits of loving people. So, we have nothing that we'd want to hide. Yes, please use our name and tell people that we live at 1978 Grand Central Avenue in Horseheads. We'd like to share with parents that love goes on past the body's death," she concluded.

So, with this story, I'm doing just that. Perhaps not all ghosts or spirits are that friendly, but it seems to run against the Law of Love to be frightened of those dear ones who return to us in friendship and comfort.

Reaching Out

Ghost experiences, we are taught by the commercial media, are scary and demonic and to be avoided. Except, perhaps, when those media can profit from our attendance at the cinema or at sponsored television programs. Then death, the more ghastly the better, is good—for their cash registers. "Can't ghost appearances be good?" people occasionally ask me. I tell them that the answer is yes; ghost appearances (whether seen, heard, smelled, dreamed of, or felt) can sometimes heal our pain.

When my father died in 1975, we were not on the best of terms. I had not been ready for his death, so I had some inner turmoil that led me to work with a psychotherapist in order to surface all my sorrows and gain closure. Twelve years later, Dad appeared in a very vivid dream, put his arms around me and said simply, "I'm sorry." That is all that was needed for my healing. I don't often speak of this incident when I'm out storytelling, but I did tell it to an audience in Lake George, New York, when I spoke there in the summer of 2006.

After the program an attendee came forward and related a similar story from his own experience and I asked him to share it with me (and you) in writing. Here it is.

Rick Wakefield grew up in Oxford, (in Chenango County) during the 1960s and early 1970s. It was a time when rebellion against the established order was stimulated in popular song and films, "so my dad and I never saw eye to eye, which led me to enlist in the military at the end of my senior year in high school," he told me. During his years away from the central New York canal and mining town, Rick gained a new appreciation for his personal uniqueness and the estrangement from his father abated somewhat. Their relationship was still not as solid as they both would have liked, however, when Leon Wakefield died in 1981 at the age of 66. "He may have been ready to go anyway," Rick said, "because he'd had a leg amputated and suffered from severe medical problems.

"Four years later I moved to New Jersey and was troubled by the end of my marriage and an impending divorce. It was on a Friday evening around 8 p.m. that my sister called, and it was nice to hear her voice. We chatted about normal, ordinary things, then hung up. I prepared to get dressed for an evening out and, for a moment, sat on the edge of my bed. Suddenly, a strange feeling came over me, and it's a sensation very difficult to explain to others who have not experienced something similar. It was an event of almost depression—of lost hope. I didn't know where it came from and sat stunned.

"Then, all of a sudden, a warm feeling surged through me—a very calming energy that hadn't been there a few seconds earlier. I was almost a spectator, witnessing the sudden surge from desolation to warmth and new hope. I asked my inner mind what it was all about and I received an immediate response that Dad was there with me, offering healing at this time of turmoil in my life. Immediately, I could smell his after-shave lotion. You know, a familiar smell can cut through time, instantly linking a person with a loved one, whether alive or not. I could feel him urging me to move on with my life and find new happiness. I think this sensation may only have lasted a few seconds in real time, but it seemed hours long to my emotions—a very powerful and lasting experience that still buoys me up today," he concluded.

These events were so powerful that, over the years since, he never related them to any other person, not even to his new wife. Then, in Lake George, hearing my own revelations, he knew that such things could be talked about, and the sharing might even heal others who silently carried such burdens of doubt. Did it happen? How can it happen that a dead father reaches out to his struggling son? Many others in our country hold such experiences as private doubts.

"But I wasn't finished with such things," he continued. "In 2002, my older brother, Gary, who lived in Norwich, New York, was struggling with cancer while still wrestling with medical problems resulting from a car accident in the 1970s. We often didn't see one another, as my job kept me moving all over the East Coast, but we did talk on the phone at least once a week. We both hoped that chemotherapy would resolve his health problems.

"Then, my schedule called for me to go to Syracuse for a business meeting, a trip that I'd usually make straight from home in New Jersey to Syracuse via the N.Y. State Thruway. It was always the fastest route and would avoid the slower traffic of central New York State's little towns and villages. At the last minute before leaving home, however, I decided to go up through Binghamton, then onto Route 12 and into Norwich to see Gary. My wife wondered at the sudden inspiration, as it was time to leave and because I never deviate from my official travel plan. But, I did go to Norwich and took Gary and his wife out for dinner. He looked horrible but was in good spirits as we sat in the restaurant chatting about old times and catching up on the little details of our lives, as we hadn't seen one another in two years. According to his doctors, Gary had fought and won the hard battle against his unusual form of cancer, and he told me of his plans for a vacation with his wife and two daughters. We both felt happy as I pulled out, headed to Syracuse."

Rick went to his Syracuse business meeting, then drove directly back to his home in New Jersey. A week later, as he sat in a business meeting in Edison, he had an emergency call from his wife at home. "There's no easy way to tell you this, honey, but your brother has just died." As he had two brothers, Gary couldn't imagine which one had passed away and asked his wife which one had died; she responded that it was Gary. "I sat stunned. I'd just visited him! Sure, he looked bad, but the reports from the doctors were good, and my brother had been planning a long-delayed vacation. But death is so final that I couldn't quibble with the truth. All the way home, however, I pondered the past few weeks. I hadn't seen Gary in two years, but it was almost as if someone pushed me to go visit this brother who would soon die. I had, for the only time in my life, departed from my travel plans—and we'd had such a good time. Call it fate or luck if you want, but I know some presence moved me to a last good time with my brother. Do you think Dad was that force?"

This was a powerful story for me to hear and read. It was so similar to my own experience, and to events in others' lives that I've heard in the past few years. While body death is certain for us all, our spirit and consciousness do survive. How wonderful that love does also.

Taking Leave

When she was fourteen and living in West Babylon, Janice had a loss and then received a gift to compensate for it. "In January 1962," she told me, "my dad died, and that was a terrible loss. I missed him terribly but had to accept what was inevitable. Summer came that year, hot and muggy, and I didn't have the routine of school to keep my life orderly. The strongest memory that I have of that summer of 1962, however, is of the night that Dad returned.

"We had no air conditioning in our house, and I remember tossing and turning that summer night, trying to get comfortable enough to drop off to sleep," she said, "when suddenly, a bright sphere of light came into my bedroom from some place. In that ball of light I could see my father's face. His hand reached out and affectionately stroked my hair. It couldn't be! But it was! Dad had come back and showed his love for me, saying that he would return soon. All at once, there was a second orb of illumination, and within that light I could see an angel. I overheard the winged creature telling my Dad that he had to go now.

"Then, quickly, the light was gone and I was alone with a jumble of thoughts in my bedroom. How soon was 'soon?' Tomorrow? Next week? For quite some period of time, I waited expectantly, but he didn't show up. Eventually, I chose to think of it as a nice dream, though I knew that I had been touched."

Years went by, and Janice finished high school and later married. Two decades of domestic life passed in their Bayshore home. Then, in 2005, her husband, affectionately known as "Bunkie" suddenly became ill and was hospitalized. He didn't survive the surgery and suddenly she was a widow. "I wasn't prepared to live all alone, and often cried myself to sleep," she said. "I remember the night some months later, when I lay there half-asleep, and suddenly a big strong arm reached across my body and pulled me backward to cuddle in the spot that used to be Bunkie's part of the bed. It was so nice to feel him again, as if he'd never left. How could it be real? You know how it is?" she asked, "You are all alone and not sure whether it is real or a dream, but I knew I was awake! Of course, there was no one to see when I finally got up the courage to turn over and look, but it had been a wonderful reverie of good times now passed."

In the morning she began pondering all the events of the past year, such as the flitting dark shadows that she occasionally had spotted from the corner of her eye, when Bunkie first became ill and used to lie on the couch. What were they, she wondered, and what was causing them? She also recalled the day that their dog had gone into the living room and walked over to Bunkie, perhaps sniffing him or staring at her owner. "Suddenly that dog shot out into the kitchen and cowered under a chair. I was flabbergasted—she'd never done that before or after. What alarmed her? Only in retrospect did I suspect that, somehow, the dog had discovered that she was going to lose her master, though that fact was kept from the humans in the house. Now, it made some kind of sense, Bunkie was preparing to take his leave of his family, even if we weren't aware of it. His inner illness was winning the battle over health and survival. I wonder if other families have such warnings?" she asked.

Two years after her husband's death, Janice's younger sister, Linda, died, and Janice once again felt grief and deep loss for this sister and close friend. "I remember again lying in bed, but this time with the bedside television turned on low, and with the brightness turned down. For a moment I closed my eyes, which were becoming heavy. Suddenly the light level in the room shot up and, startled, I roused myself to look around. My bedroom was filled with a swirling bright mist. I knew, almost certainly, that Linda had come to visit me. 'Is that you, Linda?' I asked out loud. 'Are you close by?' I asked again. Suddenly I was enveloped in a chill and the presence of another being, though I could see no one."

We talked for a while about this experience which so many people around the world experience. When skeptics say that we are left alone by the death of a loved one, does that ring true when so many of us have such visitations? I asked if she felt she was sensitive or perhaps psychic.

"Well, I don't know," she responded, but so many things from earlier in life make sense now. After my father died in 1962, my mother remarried and I liked my step-dad too. He used to sit out in the garage and drink beer and sit there burping. We thought that was funny, but after his death, we'd occasionally smell the strong scent of beer—you know, that malty smell? And, I needn't tell you that nobody was drinking beer in the house at such times. Also, we'd often smell my grandmother's perfume after her passing. I knew for sure that it was her because I used to hate that scent, and now it was back in the house, if only temporarily."

When loved ones take their leave and depart from sight in our lives, it doesn't mean that we are no longer enfolded in their love. In fact, this is a major reason why I love to interview people and then can share with you that love is eternal. We can never leave who or what we love, at least not for long. We all will meet them again—soon.

Clarence

Clarence Getz, a longtime engineering model maker for General Electric Co. in Syracuse, died in Oswego in August 1987. He had a beautiful funeral with soaring choral music. "Even during the funeral mass, I knew this wasn't going to be an ordinary death," said his son, Bill. "I hadn't been an active Catholic since high school, and during the service, as the Communion service approached, I wondered if I should or could receive the sacrament. As I pondered this I heard, inside my head, 'Come—have supper with me.' It sounded like my dad's voice, so I did receive Communion, though later I wondered if my father's voice really hadn't been my heavenly father's voice." By early October, when the trials and tribulations of Clarence's passing subsided, and she had a chance to look at the realities in her life, his widow, Evelyn, became alarmed.

Clarence's GE pension benefits ceased and his Social Security check stopped. The proceeds of his small life insurance policy had gone for funeral expenses, and her own Social Security allotment was not much more than six hundred dollars per month. How was she going to keep her house and live even a subsistence life? She did own some GE stock, but it had recently plummeted in value, and she was despondent. Her son, Bill, had told her that GE was a good stock and it was bound to rise again, but would that occur quickly enough to forestall losing her house? She kicked back in her recliner chair to brood.

Suddenly, just eight feet in front of her, there stood Clarence. Not a wispy ghost or transparent apparition, but a solid man! Before she could react, he said to her, "Evelyn, quit worrying, everything is going to be okay. Go into the bedroom and get the strongbox that I keep under the chair." As she lowered the footrest and stood, she wasn't really surprised to see her mate. She was intuitive and had always known when her children were hurt or in trouble, but what could Clarence show her that she didn't already know? She reached under the chair and brought forth the metal strongbox. It was locked, and only Clarence had known the key's location.

Evelyn brought the box to the living room where Clarence waited. "I can't find the key," she complained to him.

"Turn the box over," her mate instructed. She turned the box upside down, and there, taped to its bottom, was the key. Evelyn opened the container and, found thirty thousand dollars in matured savings bonds inside! She never realized that he had bought them and put them away. She looked up to thank him, but Clarence had vanished.

Evelyn Getz cashed the bonds and put the proceeds into long-term H bonds, which supplemented her income until she died ten years later. Clarence had always promised her that she'd be stable financially—how could she have doubted him?

Evelyn worked through her grief and became socially active again, traveling a bit, visiting old friends and attending spiritual group study. In 1996, however, she developed uterine bleeding. She scheduled an exam with her doctor. Anxious during the night before the appointment, she awoke to find Clarence looking at her. "Evelyn," he said, "you won't die of cancer, so don't worry." Then he vanished.

The next morning, she told the doctor that she had known for years that she had a benign tumor and felt that the growth was now bleeding and was likely cancerous. The physician ordered a CAT scan and, shortly thereafter, returned with the results. The image showed no tumor of any kind! He found a simple cause for the bleeding: her blood thinner needed regulation, but she did not need an operation. Cancer never claimed her.

Death waited for nearly two years more—a period filled with happiness. On Christmas Day 1997, she announced she was tired after lunch and took a nap. Next to her was a photo of Clarence and the rosary beads that he had always cherished. At 2 a.m. the next morning, she drew a slow last breath and joined Clarence, who had become her guardian angel. It was a wonderful life.

Nancy and Helen

Nancy Kraeger was a sensitive and talented lady, adept at helping others with her Tarot card readings. She also had a number of special experiences with the world of spirit, and she expected to inhabit that realm sooner than later. A resident of Remsen, New York, she was treasured by all who knew her. Nevertheless, she knew she could not beat the cancer that was slowly sapping her life energy.

One day in the early autumn of 2005, her friend Russ from Barneveld dropped by with a gift of apples, and found Nancy chatting with a woman friend. As hostess, Nancy introduced Russ as another sensitive person who often saw ghosts. The visitor expressed a desire to see a ghost one day, but Russ told her it was improbable, as only certain sensitive people see these entities. Undaunted, the woman smiled and turned to Nancy. "Nancy, I would like to see you when you finally pass. I hope that's not offensive to you." Nancy just smiled and cast a glance at Russ.

As the weeks passed, Nancy became weaker, and it came as a surprise to Russ when he awakened on the night of November 20th to the sound of someone rapping on his front door. When his dreamself opened the portal, there stood Nancy smiling. Not a substantial body, but a wispy, semi-transparent self. "Hi, Russ. I just wanted you to know I made it," she declared. Puzzled, Russ asked her what she meant by that statement, but Nancy told him she had to leave.

Turning toward the north, where her house was located, Nancy's spirit body began to transform. "She became blurred and then flitted into the shape of an orb of light and instantly flashed out of sight," Russ remembers. He told me that he then sank into a deep sleep. In the morning, he recalled every vivid detail of the experience, which seemed more of a lived experience than a dream to him. At work, he puzzled for hours about her words, "I made it." What had she made?

When he returned home that evening, he noted the blinking message light on his telephone answering machine. The message was from Nancy's cousin, Jean, informing him that Nancy had died early that morning.

At the funeral, Russ spent several hours talking with Nancy's friends, and as he passed through the receiving line, Arlene, Nancy's daughter-in-law, said, "You know, Russ, if Nancy's spirit gets in touch with any of us, it will be you because you are so sensitive. You will let us know, won't you?" Too many people were listening, and Russ didn't feel he could share his experience there in the line, but in the morning, he called Arlene and related his dream experience.

Arlene, in turn, shared her experience, telling Russ about a book falling out of the bookcase after the funeral at Nancy's house. Arlene is of Italian heritage and shared that, in her family, such unexplained events following a funeral are always thought to be a communication from the deceased, essentially saying what Nancy verbally conveyed to Russ in the dream.

And Russ then remembered some of the last words that Nancy had spoken to him before her death: "After I die, Russ, I will be around, but I don't know where I will be going." Now, it all seemed clear that she had reached her destination and was happy to share the news with family and friends.

***

So many times, vivid dream apparitions of a deceased individual are a verifiable form of communication. This reminds me of my own experience in 1957, one of the first paranormal experiences that I can recall.

I was a sophomore at the State University of New York in Albany and lived in Sayles Hall on Partridge Street. Herb, my meticulous roommate, was very unhappy one spring morning when I awoke quite early screaming, "Who are you? Come back, come back!"

"David, it's only 5:30, go back to bed, will you?" Herb groaned.

But I was so agitated. I had awakened from a dream in which a lady in black, wearing a veiled hat, was rapidly receding into the background and vigorously waving her hands. Because of the veil, I couldn't recognize her, and I was terribly afraid, so I awoke yelling at her. I had an 8 a.m. class and was too worked up to return to bed. Herb rolled over, mumbling to himself, and I dressed and went downstairs to breakfast.

Then, grabbing up my notebooks, I prepared to walk the several blocks to campus. As I left the dorm, I heard the door open behind me and Stu, a fellow student, called me back. "Pitkin, there's a phone call for you." I wondered who would call me at 7:30 in the morning. It was my mother, saying, "I don't know what you have planned for this weekend, but Aunt Helen Phalen died at 5:30 this morning, and her funeral will be on Saturday. It would be nice if you could come home for it."

What answer could I give? That I had just fearfully said goodbye to Aunt Helen? She was an Irish widow who dressed in black, and, as did many of the elderly Irish women in Corinth, she wore a black hat with a veil across the brim. Instantly, I knew the identity of the dream figure, but I had no previous experience with the dead or ghosts, and chose to keep the matter to myself for a few years, simply chalking it all up to "coincidence."

As do many experiencers, I have often wondered why Aunt Helen appeared to me, in my dream. She was my great-aunt, my mother's aunt, and I really liked her, but I surely wasn't the closest family member to her. Why me? Years later, a clairvoyant friend told me, "It's because you were 'open,' and sensitive to that realm. Most of your family members were probably pretty down-to-earth, and likely wouldn't have remembered to value the experience." Well, I sure valued it once I understood what it meant, and have pondered my relationship with Aunt Helen ever since.

At my storytelling and lectures, many people approach me saying that they so wish they could see a ghost. And I tell them to pay more attention to their dreams. I truly believe that dream contacts are the equivalent of hearing the loved one's voice or seeing their shape or even feeling their loving touch. We can experience ghosts with all of the five senses, though I can't say I've ever tasted one! But then, how would I know?

The Bedroom

There is an old farmhouse on Burke-Delosh Road outside North Lawrence, New York, that one family member called "a screwy place to live." The events that have taken place there seem more rooted in the past than related to the present residents or their activities.

"My parents bought the house in 1953," Jackie Moody told me, "and it was in pretty rough shape. There was no electricity or running water and, for a family of eight, that was sure inconvenient, so my parents began the work of modernizing the downstairs soon after we moved in. There was one room, especially, on the first floor, that none of us liked, especially after we learned that the previous owners, the Hurleys, held wakes for their deceased family members in there. It was always cold inside, though we couldn't see any ghostly presence. We children later concluded that at least one of those deceased had remained in the house. I think my Mom agreed with us kids, though my father refused to believe."

Jackie told me of hearing stories from neighbors and kids at school that the Hurleys had been involved in bootlegging. One of the major areas for rumrunning in the United States had been the northern counties of Clinton, St. Lawrence, Franklin and Essex, with illegal booze brought over the border from Canada between 1919 and 1933. After World War I, many American farmers experienced a depression, ten years before the national economy went into the tank.

When the Volstead Act was passed, prohibiting the transportation and sale of alcohol, northern New York State's struggling farmers realized that they could make a better living transporting and reselling whiskey, beer, and rum to those who sent the booze farther south to the big cities. All one had to do was know the backwoods roads and trails that touched Canada's border; the Feds were too few in number to catch them all. Many poor Irish and French-Canadian immigrants kept their families fed and bills paid by this method.

"I remember being alone in the house when I was ten," Jackie said, "and all of a sudden, there was a black shadow standing in a closet. I was absolutely petrified, because I knew it couldn't be a living person. Then, a short time later, I heard footsteps upstairs, and again, I was certain that nobody was there. That section of the Burke-Delosh Road was not very populated and I was scared. That upstairs part of the house never got finished," she said, "and even today it is used just for storage."

Her brother, Leo, died in 2004, and the strange activity seemed to follow the mourners to the funeral home, where the lights flickered throughout the wake. At home, for another day after the funeral, their lights flickered too. "By then, having grown up in a haunted house, I simply figured Leo was saying goodbye or letting us know that he had made it to the other side. Why do I suspect that?" she asked rhetorically. "I have my brother's lamp in my present home, and now my lights flicker or go out when there is no outage in the neighborhood!"

Family members who still live in the old house aren't inclined to attribute these events to ghosts, preferring a more down-to-earth explanation, but ghost fans will see the connection.

Who might the phantom walker have been? Who or what might have been the identity of the dark, shadowy form in the closet? As with all old farms, there is often a history of injuries, especially for those who did plowing, haying or working with animals. Might an old-time farmer have died of injuries on the property, yet still remain there to "finish chores"?

Likewise, it is known that there was an increase in violence in the North Country as FBI and State Police efforts to suppress rumrunning more and more involved firearms. In Prohibition's early days, it was more a rural catch-me-if-you-can game played by the locals, but New York State's government was sometimes ambivalent in enforcing the laws. With the introduction of the "tommy gun" in federal law enforcement, it was easier for the FBI to stop a speeding, alcohol-filled car careening down an unlit back road. Might a prior resident of the house have been gunned down by the police or some competitor? Such dark night, roadside encounters are today almost impossible to document, as over eight decades have passed. Most police records from that period are usually inaccessible. Might one of the bootleggers have tried to "short-weight" his buyer and been punished fatally for it? These things were known to happen. And we know that sudden or violent deaths can often lead to the lingering presence of a spirit, still unready to cross the Great Highway to Heaven.

Touched

After she and her husband separated, Margaret Mary Lynch raised five children alone and life was often a struggle, just to put food on the table and to raise respectable youngsters. By early 1992, when she was sixty-four, however, her loving heart began to fail. By November, she knew that the end was near when a coronary arrest placed her in Bellevue Hospital in Manhattan. She slipped peacefully into a coma and died a few days later.

This is the background to an amazing story supplied to me by Bill Lynch, a New York City teacher. "At the time of my mother's death I lived on the sixth floor of an old building on W. 13th Street," he told me. With friends, he had been partying one night in 1992, and slowly made his way home. Suddenly, he was attacked by a wild-eyed stranger who slashed at him with a straight-edged razor. "I managed to fight off my attacker, punching the guy in the face and breaking his nose before he fled. Only later, as I passed a shop mirror, did I see my bleeding face reflected, my clothes covered with blood.

"With a friend, I got to St. Vincent's Hospital, just two blocks away. In the ER, my shock began to dissipate and I felt the pain while the surgeon took over one hundred and seventy stitches. Tired from a long night's work, the man blurted out, 'This young man's face is so badly cut up, he's disfigured for life. His face will never look normal again, unless he has plastic surgery, and even then, he'll never be the same.' That prospect numbed me so that, as I looked in a mirror on the way out, I could see my facial damage," Bill remembers.

His pain dulled by sedatives given in the hospital, Bill lapsed into a fitful sleep at home. A dream image showed him one of his mother's white Persian kittens lying wounded on a curb, with blood on its leg. As a dream person, Bill reached out to pick up and comfort the animal, but the cat suddenly struck out and raked his face with its claws. And, as it did so, the cat morphed into his human assailant.

"I jumped out of bed, sitting bolt upright, and suddenly realized I wasn't alone in my dark bedroom. My mother, dressed in her favorite blue dress and silver necklace, stood before me, looking with tender concern and sadness. I knew I was not dreaming, and yet there she was. I vaguely remembered her funeral during the previous November. 'Mom, Mom,' I struggled to say. She never said a word, but just reached out her hand and I felt her touch my face. My worst scars were on the right side of my head, but she touched only the biggest of these, and not the smaller ones around my eyebrows or on the back of my head. Her touch was warm and comforting. Once more, I uttered, 'Mom!' and then, exhausted, I fell back asleep.

"Early the next morning, I awoke from a dreamless sleep," he continued, "and I remembered every detail of Mom's visit, and I knew the event hadn't been a dream. Rushing to the bathroom mirror, I could see the great damage to my face, punctuated by countless stitches. None of the attack had been a dream, I concluded, so my mother's appearance must have been wishful thinking on my part. The next two weeks were dreadful, and I got larger sunglasses to wear, hoping to cover the scars all around my eyes. When I got to work at the temp agency, I explained my previous day's absence to my supervisor. Several women standing nearby screamed when they saw my face. Then I realized that the ER doctor was right—I would be disfigured for life."

Bill had no health insurance and no stable job. He knew that any contemplation of plastic surgery would be a fantasy, always beyond his financial grasp. He told me that, though he tried to avoid looking at his face, he groaned that it resembled one of Picasso's later abstract paintings. Two weeks later, as instructed by the doctor, he returned to St. Vincent's to have his stitches removed and asked the doctor what he could do for his red scars. Only aloe vera lotion could be recommended. "But this new doctor, not the man who had stitched me up in the emergency room, re-read the surgeon's report from my initial visit.

He frowned and called over some of the staff who had been on duty on the morning I had come in wounded.

"This new doctor was irritated that the first ER doctor had labeled me as 'disfigured for life,' and, as he peered closely at my face, exclaimed that it was irresponsible that the treating surgeon had given me such a scare with his prognosis. Either that doctor was totally mistaken or my face had shown such rapid healing as to be remarkable, this second physician concluded. They provided me with a mirror, and I could see that the worst scars had healed at an incredibly fast rate. So, I concluded, maybe the aloe vera was very effective, or else the man who stitched me up had been horribly wrong.

"That could not explain, however, why the lesser scars remained around the eyebrows and on the back of my head. These were totally visible and had not been as severe as the savage cuts that a doctor had deemed would disfigure me for life, and which I had treated with lotion. By the end of summer, my face, at least most of it, was totally healed. Today people look at me and say they cannot believe I ever suffered more than a few nicks. It has been sixteen years now, and the scars on the back have largely faded, but are still there, yet those were nowhere as deep as the ones on the front of my face."

Was this a miracle of a mother reaching out beyond the grave to heal her afflicted son? I certainly would want to believe it was, knowing the healing power of love. Bill is very humble about the matter, recounting the horrific events in a calm, matter-of-fact style.

So many contacts with the deceased take place in solitude and quiet, often in the dark, when surrounding energies are low, so a skeptic probably would not be inclined to honor Bill's story. He notes that his friends, however, will testify to the dramatic change that he underwent in just two weeks.

"I prefer to think that Love is stronger than Death," Bill concludes. "In my extreme pain, I believe my mother interceded for me in a special way, in what we call The Communion of Saints." He smiled a bit while reflecting, then added ruefully, "Of course, that was the very last time that I ever went out clubbing!"

NEW YORK STATE GHOSTS

CHAPTER 14

MOVED OBJECTS
JULIUS
NEIGHBORHOOD GHOSTS
THE RING

Julius

"I don't know why our ghost got his name, but I do remember why we use the name—my aunt used the name when we had an early experience with him at Grandma's house in the Wyoming County hamlet of Perry, New York," Tammy told me. "Grandma and Grandpa had bought the house in 1945 and I don't recall any rumors about ghosts or strange goings-on until 1982 or 1983, when I was involved in the first odd episode. My grandmother is very traditional and changed her drapes from 'winter curtains' to 'summer curtains' and then back when the seasons changed. I had helped her take down the winter curtains that year and put them in a closet that she called 'the clothes press.' A short time later, when she went to that closet, the folded curtains were gone. It was true, neither she nor I had touched them, but they were gone. And they stayed gone for almost four months," she grinned. "Then, one day, she opened that clothes press and let out a yell and I came running. She had found them again, just like that, folded and on top of the pile."

When one similar strange event took place at Grandma's, her aunt referred to the mischief-making spirit as "Julius," though neither Tammy nor the aunt can remember where the name came from. When Tammy revealed the series of strange events, I asked if her grandfather had ever witnessed any of them, but she noted that Grandpa had died on Halloween in 1976. To me, he sure sounded like a candidate for invisible imp, maybe just attempting to let his wife and her family know that he had survived the supposedly permanent state called death. Nevertheless, Grandpa apparently has gotten used to being called Julius.

"In late 1983, I stayed with Grandma," Tammy continued, "and slept in a bedroom upstairs. That night, I took off my glasses and rings and put them on the dresser. I might add that the bedroom door was locked, because it was a great mystery how my favorite of those rings was gone in the morning. No way, I said to myself, and searched the room. Nevertheless, my investigation was fruitless. Months went by, and I had given up hope of ever getting the ring back, even though it wasn't especially valuable, just something that I liked and loved to wear. As I entered the kitchen one day, I saw the cat playing with something on the floor—an object that made a noise when she hit it with her paw. When I bent down, I discovered that she was playing with my ring! Though one of the stones was missing, I now had it back. But where had it been?"

We talked a while about ghosts' propensity to take physical objects in order to get our attention. At least she got her ring back, I told her, because some 'stolen objects' are never returned again. Tammy returned to western New York after her first marriage ended. One Christmas, she helped Grandma store some presents for Tammy's mother—two bags and a box. Of course, those were placed in the clothes press for a few days before it was time to wrap them. Then, just as with the curtains, the presents vanished and Tammy's mother had nothing under the tree that year. Discussing the matter later, Tammy told her mother how it had all happened, even opening the closet to show where they had been hidden. But right there—on top of the other items, were Mom's presents, still in a box and bags. So, Mom's Christmas did come, if only a bit late that year.

"A few years later, I met a nice guy and we married," she continued. "Shortly after that, we visited Grandma's house and she insisted we sleep in the 'good bed,' which was hers. I don't think my husband really believed my tales of Julius, but that ended soon. We went to bed that first night but my husband didn't sleep well, he told me in the morning. 'Your grandmother came into the room during the night. At first I tried to stay asleep, but I wondered what she wanted and woke up, just in time to see the doorknob turning and the door closing. So I got up early this morning,' he told me, 'and went into the kitchen to ask Grandma what she had wanted, but she denied getting up at all,' he said mystified. It seemed that Julius must have been inspecting the new family member. "But for me," Tammy continued, "I do remember feeling a presence in our bedroom that morning before I went out into the kitchen, though nobody could be seen."

Tammy and her husband live in Springville, but Julius apparently wanted to visit their home because someone or something took her husband's keys off a lathe that stood near their front door. A key ring with all his important keys was missing and a desperate search was begun. "We looked all over, but they had vanished," Tammy smiled. "Eventually he had to go to the expense of having all new keys made. Then, returning from the hardware store, he sighed and said aloud that he wished the ghost had returned the keys so he hadn't had to go to the expense. Next day, there was the old key ring, lying on the lathe! Was Julius being playful or mean? We never figured it out."

"We knew that we had to take Julius back to Grandma's but another event took place before we could do that," Tammy added. "We have a post in the kitchen, which we have decorated with several sizes of cast iron frying pans. A friend of ours often visits and we play board games on the kitchen table, though our friend many times would bump the lower frying pans, sending them onto the floor. Eventually, we just took them down and put them in the oven when we knew he was coming to visit—except for a decorative one at the top of the post. There was no way he could hit that one because it was too high. Well, you guessed it," she said, "that top one showed up missing, and it was quite a while before we found it again. So Julius had to go back home to Grandma's."

When the couple visited Grandma's soon afterward, they told Julius to come along, and once at their destination, ordered him to stay at Grandma's house. Apparently, that worked.

Tammy revealed that she has always been curious about life's mysteries, so she was able to take Julius in stride. Since those mysterious days, though, her mother died in 1997. "Then, in late April of 2008, I had a vivid dream of my mother and woke to find a 1947 penny on my bedspread. Where did it come from? I wondered. And what should I make of the fact that 1947 was the year that Mom was born?" I noted to Tammy that many people who find mysterious coins (mainly pennies—do they come from Heaven?) believe that these are tokens from our loved ones who have died and are just "staying in touch."

For me, Tammy's grandfather is the chief mischief-maker suspect, though the incidents at Grandma's have pretty well ceased as far as Tammy knows. With a laugh, she suggests that Julius may be visiting other family members.

Neighborhood Ghosts

Some people have but a single experience with spirits, one which stays with them through the years. Then, there are other folks who live in almost constant contact. Some of those react in ways that vary from terror to toleration to amusement, even to a type of friendship. I recently met a woman from Kendall, in Orleans County, who frequently hears of such encounters from family or friends, and who lives daily with the little things that a busy house ghost might do.

Amy lives on Center Road, in a house built in the latter part of the 1800s. "The first two experiences happened as I was driving home from my job as a resident counselor at a group home in the early morning hours a few years ago. Near a house on Route 104 in the Town of Murray, I saw a figure walking directly toward my car, as if she might be strolling to her mailbox. I slowed down to verify that a person would be getting her mail at that time of night. I looked at her one more time but she had vanished! I never had had such an experience before and wondered about being too tired; or maybe I imagined it?

"Not long afterward, near the intersection of Carr and Center Roads, I had another encounter with that other world, when I'm sure I saw an angel. The figure was glowing white and startled me; I didn't think I'd ever see one," she told me.

I asked Amy if the figure had wings and looking back, now she isn't sure, but the being's appearance was striking. "Why there?" I asked her; "What is so special about that spot?"

She told me that, long ago, there was a fire which completely demolished an old dwelling at that corner. Then, she anticipated my next question by adding, "But nobody died in that blaze. Some folks around here thought the origin of the fire was suspicious, though." She added that she was never able to figure who the being might be: angel or ghost? Other than a death by fire, there wasn't much else to go on, and in the end, we had to just scratch our heads as to the spirit's or celestial being's identity, as she only saw the figure once.

"But I'll tell you another incident that my husband, Charlie, experienced. When our daughter was little, he'd take her for a walk, pushing her stroller down the road. One time, at a nearby cemetery, he paused to inspect a gravestone, as he is fascinated by genealogy and knew the family name on the marker. Charlie left the baby's stroller safely parked in an old driveway, with her sleeping inside. Walking just a few graves away he paused to read the names: parents and their child who had died in another neighborhood fire some years before. He remembered having heard about the tragedy when he first moved into his house almost thirty years ago. Suddenly, a movement caught his eye, and looking toward the stroller, he saw it rocking gently, as if moved by an unseen hand. Somehow, he figured it was a friendly ghost and spoke out loud to the unseen rocker, saying that it was a nice deed for them to do, but the rocking suddenly stopped and didn't resume." I told Amy that many ghosts just don't like to be acknowledged or seen. Some researchers theorize that there is a faint energy in the human gaze that can cause spirit figures to become unstable; maybe uncomfortable. Might the rocker have been the spirit of a bereaved parent who had lost track of their dead child, but had happily found another to comfort?

Amy told me that everyone in Kendall knows where to find Woodchuck Alley, which is a nice quiet route between Kendall Road and West Kendall Road. The town operates a wood-chipping operation there, and the spot is secluded enough that a lovers' murder-suicide took place out of public view there in 2002. Not long afterward, there was a suspicious fire at that site, though there was no apparent cause for the blaze. The event wasn't proof of any ghostly activity, yet one wonders about the connection between other town ghosts, deaths, and fire.

"We have an ongoing interaction with spirits of various kinds in our old house, too," she smiled. "The only connection between deaths and ghosts that we can find for our home is that a long-ago owner was waked in the living room before his funeral. For some reason, whenever strange events occur, we blame it on the ghost. I can't remember exactly why we began calling the ghost 'Charlie,'" she smiled again, "but that's my husband's name, of course. Things disappear from time to time. Important papers or my car keys seem to vanish for a time. I always get frustrated and demand that whoever it is should return the items, and usually, they turn up again."

Perhaps the strangest experience that the couple shares is hearing their names called from some other part of the house. Each will answer their spouse, but only to find out that that person never called out. I mentioned to Amy that this ability to hear into the spirit world, or be sensitive to voice communications is called "clairaudience" or "clear hearing." I believe that the person has some special sensitivity or psychic ability when such activities take place.

What is it in the Kendall neighborhood? Is it just coincidence that fires and ghosts somehow get together? Yet, the ghost rocker at the cemetery seems kind enough, though the house ghost seems a bit mischievous. Amy really doesn't seem to mind, and neither does her Charlie. They accept that this other dimension of life will occasionally intrude. "But they're usually well-behaved," she joked. "So we don't mind."

The Ring

Most sophisticated ghost story readers know well the numerous stories of disappearing objects. For many years this phenomenon has been attributed to mischievous ghosts. Here is a fun story that should also be instructive to those of you with mysteriously missing objects.

Pat is a native of the Keuka Lake area, where she and her husband, Bill, built a stylish log home overlooking the lake several years ago on Route 54. They had both grown up in the village, then moved away for years, but longed for the quiet beauty of the lake's east branch. During those years away from her hometown, Pat always treasured her graduation ring from Penn Yan Academy. A 14K gold ring with a black onyx stone and small gold school emblem in the stone's center, it was the same design worn by all past graduates, but it singled out those who shopped in nearby villages as "local." Her description sounded identical to the ring I got as a senior at Corinth High School, but lost just two weeks before graduation, so I was ready to hear her story.

"As I usually did at bedtime, I placed my ring on the dresser one night in 2005. It was strange, just a short while later, that the ring was no longer in its accustomed spot," she said. "So, Bill and I got immediately into the task of furniture moving—every piece in the house, but no result. It had to be somewhere, as only the two of us inhabited the house, and he had been nowhere near the dresser. I emptied every drawer in my desk and the dresser also—no sign of the ring. One of the suspects in the disappearance was our cat, Mokie; sometimes she would knock items off the dresser and play with them. We continued our search and, in desperation, finally rented a metal detector. No result. After vacuuming the entire house, we examined the place where we dumped water from our Rainbow Vacuum cleaner. Again, the ring was not there."

After her inability to find her ring in teenage, Bill (an agnostic when it comes to ghosts and other ethereal creatures) recently half-seriously told her, "If your ghosts are real, why don't you ask them to find your class ring?" With no better plan, when she went to bed that night, Pat opted to speak to the "whoever" that lived there with her.

"I stood in the bedroom and quietly said, 'If you would be so kind, do you think you might be able to help me find my class ring?' Of course, there was no response and my ring didn't suddenly manifest; I figured that," she laughed, "so I pulled up the bedcovers and went to sleep. But it was a sleep punctuated by a marvelous dream in which I discovered my vanished ring in the dresser's sock drawer. Immediately upon getting up the next morning, I dashed to the dresser and opened the drawer. Remember that I had checked and re-checked that drawer over three years, and once emptied it completely without results. My eyes fell on the ring, just sitting there in plain sight. I didn't have to fumble or search—there it was! And it was certain that Mokie hadn't opened the drawer and placed it there.

"I'm in my seventies, now," she laughed, "and that must be the strangest story I could tell you." Her experience points up the need to ask the invisibles to find or return your missing items. Maybe they are just waiting around your house in order to do a good deed, rather than scare you, as Hollywood would have it.

NEW YORK STATE GHOSTS

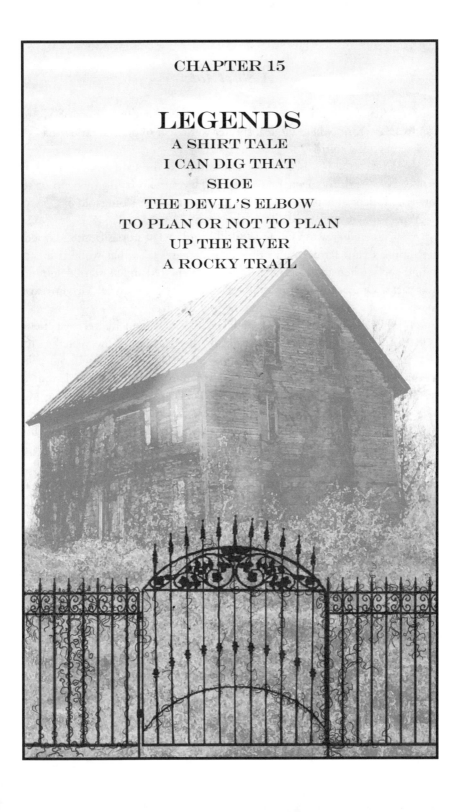

CHAPTER 15

LEGENDS
A SHIRT TALE
I CAN DIG THAT
SHOE
THE DEVIL'S ELBOW
TO PLAN OR NOT TO PLAN
UP THE RIVER
A ROCKY TRAIL

A Shirt Tale

What follows is a long-forgotten episode in the history of Warren County, New York, where the real specter was a fear of ghosts, rather than the scary activity of a spirit.

During the 1990s, I was fortunate to make the acquaintance of Schuylerville, New York, octogenarian Howard Hayes, who had grown up in the Town of Horicon. He provided several provoking stories (some told in *Ghosts of the Northeast*), and this one still tantalizes me.

"Where I grew up in the 1880s, I heard lots of stories from the woodsmen, miners, and farmers, and they had so many tales that we kids just sat around the kitchen table entranced whenever the old timers started spinning their yarns. One of my favorite storytellers was my great uncle, Melvin Hayes. I never forgot a Halloween story that he told us once.

"Halloween had arrived, and Uncle Melvin and his teenage friends hadn't yet worked out a suitable prank for the big night. One year they had taken a wagon apart and reassembled it on someone's roof—all without being caught. Another time, they tipped over a neighbor's outhouse—while the guy was inside—and tossed it in the creek. This year's prank promised to be a big one, but here it was Cabbage Night, and they just couldn't get inspired.

"The subject of the boys' discussion turned to fear and what each of them was most afraid of. Finally, they arrived at a consensus—they most feared being in a cemetery when it was pitch black out. Now, mind you, they had no streetlights or even flashlights in the rural areas back then, and if there was no bright moon, it could be really scary getting from one place to another after dark. It was agreed that each boy would sneak out of the house just before midnight, make his way to the old cemetery, and nail a personal handkerchief on the big old wooden gatepost. That would be the proof to everyone the next morning—here is a guy who is brave and not scared of the burying ground. Hopefully, the local girls would be impressed.

"Uncle Melvin did as they agreed. He heard someone else running as he left the cemetery gate, but he went straight home. In the morning, he was surprised to see Alex's mother walking up to their back door. Alex was one of his buddies who had dared to do their prank, but his mother said Alex hadn't come home, and she couldn't find him. My uncle told her the details of the prank, and they walked over to the cemetery. They were stunned to see Alex lying on the ground. There was no heartbeat and he was stone cold dead.

"Alex's shirttail had been torn badly, and a nail was found to be driven through it. After the funeral, we figured it all out. Alex had gone to the gatepost, reached in his back pocket, grabbed for his handkerchief, and, using a nail he'd brought along, fastened the cloth to the post. But when he turned to run home, something held him fast. He panicked and yelled, but the invisible creature seemed to be pulling him backward. Alex was probably out of his mind with fright, and that must have triggered a heart attack. He had a weak heart, but none of us ever knew about that. What he nailed to the post wasn't his hand-kerchief, but his own shirttail. He scared himself to death."

I Can Dig That

Ghostly energies abound wherever human beings have toiled, had accidents, experienced violence, and died. Just north of State Highway 8, east of Brant Lake, in the Adirondacks, one can see a sign reading "Graphite." There is no other explanation. Few today know of the old mining town and the hundreds of laborers who mined the world's largest deposit of graphite to make America's "lead pencils" in the late 1800s and early 1900s. Graphite, New York, once a beehive of excavating and tunneling, as well as mill activity, no longer exists because foreign sources of the mineral became cheaper, and the mines closed in 1924.

The small hamlet of Graphite, with homes, churches, a school, hotel, store, three saloons and a post office became the place to work for local young men who had tired of farming. When the mining operations ended, the houses and other buildings were left to decay in the weather. However, in and around that community a number of memorable ghost stories remained in former residents' memories.

Though the names of the people involved are no longer recalled, a few old-timers in Hague and Brant Lake remember hearing this tale. It was related to me by Howard Hayes of Schuylerville, NY, whose ancestors once farmed a tract near the old mine works.

The story goes like this: A stranger came to the Warren County mining town in the 1880s and bought a small house in or near Graphite. From the start, the man and his wife were ill at ease. Around midnight, when the house was still, the couple heard a moaning sound echoing throughout the house. The pair was unable to locate its source, so the wife invited a neighbor to come over and help discover the sound's cause. The neighbor, who visited several times, was unable to hear anything unusual and gave the wife many sidelong glances as she returned home.

The housewife then invited her sister to sit and listen with them, and the sister did, in fact, hear the moaning, which seemed to be louder than ever, though the sister ascribed the noise to the wind. Finally, the housewife could stand the emanations no longer—she left the house and told her husband to sell the place. The woman moved into another house closer to the top of Graphite Mountain, telling her husband to catch up with her soon before she went mad.

Finally, the sale of the haunted house was concluded. The new owners, smirking at the "superstition" of the former occupants, claimed for a long time that there was nothing amiss in the building. In any case, they had plans to modernize and renovate the small house and began the excavation of a cellar under the original structure. An addition would also be built above ground. The new, spacious cellar replaced a small root cellar that had been reached by descending a narrow staircase along the side of the foundation. A new set of cellar stairs was constructed, leading to a first floor door in the center of the house.

Descending to the cellar on the new stairs, the workmen then tore out the old, narrow stairway from the cobblestone cellar wall, and, lo and behold, a skull and several bones rolled from a space within the old foundation and onto the new dirt floor. Who was it? Had a long-ago resident been the victim of foul play? The new owners figured it best to simply bury the bones in a nearby cemetery, as constables and sheriffs had more important things to do than investigate a long-ago death. The owners then claimed that the sounds, if indeed there had ever been any, were now gone, and the couple apparently lived at peace for the rest of their years there.

Howard told me, however, that some years later, the original housewife came to visit the new owners, only to leave the house rapidly. She could still hear the ghostly moans and groans.

Shoe!

There are many fascinating and sometimes humorous stories of life's energy continuing following a death. A simple example comes from the farm country northeast of Watertown.

Nan Dixon, co-coordinator of the Jefferson County GenWeb genealogical Web site, remembers the story of a long-ago family member who needed to correct her thinking. She was Hannah Smith Petrie, wife of Sant Petrie, a respected farmer and businessman. Working his own large farm between Stone Mills and La Fargeville, he was not too busy to also serve the larger business community of Jefferson County. Petrie (1818-1885) was a trustee of a local bank and an officer on the board of directors of a local cheese factory. Hannah liked the prosperity of the farm and the recognition earned from Sant's position on the bank and factory boards.

Nevertheless, she was a woman of strong opinions, and she simply could not abide one of Sant's activities. In his spare time, her husband worked ignobly as a cobbler. Knowing how to work with leather served him well, however, as he could easily repair footwear and harnesses on his own farm and for his neighbors. Though Hannah welcomed the additional income resulting from Sant's making and selling of boots and shoes, she grumbled and griped that if one of the rural neighbors needed shoes and couldn't afford them, Sant would make the footwear and provide the boot or shoe free to the needy person. Day after day, she let him know his charity was foolishness, and the days of criticism extended into months and years.

Often, in the cold winter nights, Hannah fell asleep to the sounds of tapping that came from Sant's workshop at the rear of the house, as her husband stayed up late, making shoes for people who would never pay him. And, with each tap and thud, her ire grew. His generosity and "wasted time" were the only bones of contention between the couple before Sant went to his heavenly reward in 1885.

"We know he was rewarded," Nan told me, "because he had been a good neighbor to so many local people over the years. Aunt Hannah, on the other hand, continued to live in the old farmhouse for another fifteen years after her husband's death, and the family memory is that she learned repentance during that time. You see, each evening, as the kerosene lamps were lit and Hannah sat down to read and contemplate her life, she continued to hear the tap-tap-tapping sounds emanating from Sant's workshop. And she had to come to terms with the fact that her husband's generosity lived on long after he had physically died."

The old farmhouse and its memories cast in sound are gone today.

The Devil's Elbow

How long do ghosts last? That is a question that often comes up when I do storytelling. I'd guess the answer is that it all depends on why the spirit is earthbound, why the soul can't move onward, and whether or not anyone living is willing to help release that spirit into Eternity.

This little bit of philosophy was occasioned last year when I ran into accounts of a series of 20th Century "hitchhiker ghost" sightings in Tioga County. When researching some of the late professor Rod Roberts' reported anecdotes at the N.Y. State Historical Society in Cooperstown, I was referred to an unpublished thesis in the Cooperstown Graduate Program records, written in 1966 by Janson L. Cox, one of Dr. Roberts' students. To tell the truth, after reading several hundred variations on the ghostly hitchhiker, I started to doze…it all became so commonplace and almost predictable!

Nevertheless, I found a long series of such events took place at a location called The Devil's Elbow, a highway site on Route 17C along the northern shore of the Susquehanna River, and west of Owego.

***

There are quite a few places, either towns or geographic locations, by this name in the United States, at least one in Canada and one in the United Kingdom. Each one probably was named for difficulties that early settlers experienced at that spot and were possibly blamed on a malefic being. In Tioga County, in New York State's Southern Tier, the name was once commonly given to a large turn in the Susquehanna River west of Owego, though many young people no longer know the name. Nowadays, it seems that the appellation is forgotten—several locals that I queried claim never to have heard the term. But, before World War II, apparently, lots of Tioga County citizens and travelers had reason to use the name. Perhaps some long-ago pioneer encountered dangerous rapids or a flood at that spot, but today, nobody seems certain where the name originated.

Route 17C, as with many highways in New York State, once followed the river's course quite closely, and as the area is also hilly and mountainous, there were several hairpin road turns which had to be negotiated, and must have been upsetting to early motorists. Maybe one of the most upsetting events was an occasional encounter with "the White Lady," a hitchhiker ghost.

Janson Cox's 1966 research turned up many anecdotal references to the girl. Who she was seems never to have been ascertained, and when and how she died likewise remains a mystery. It seems clear that she was indeed a ghost, though there may have been several spirits whose appearances are noted in his document.

A story that Cox found stated that in 1937 two men were driving between Binghamton and Elmira when they spotted a white figure in the center of the road, clearly visible in their headlights. They screeched to a stop to avoid hitting what was clearly a young woman. A hitchhiker, she asked for a ride to an address in Binghamton, so they offered her the back seat and resumed their journey. Entering the city sometime later, one man turned to tell the girl, "It won't be long now," but she had vanished. They drove to the address anyway and knocked at the door. A woman, not of the girl's family, told them that such a girl used to live there, but had been killed in an auto accident some years before. She turned and took a photo from a nearby stand, and both men identified their vanished passenger.

A few years later, the Captain of the Endicott Police Department was traveling through the turns of Devil's Elbow, driving from Owego to Elmira. He saw a young woman in white in the road and stopped to question her, then offered her a ride to her destination. She got into the back seat and began a conversation with the officer. At one point she went silent and he turned, only to discover an empty seat. At the time, the local press assumed she was a long-ago traffic victim named Kay Sullivan, who had perished in an auto accident, and it was believed that she reappeared at Devil's Elbow on the anniversary of her death.

At another imprecise date, two young men drove the route, saw and picked up a girl in an evening dress, but she, also, soon vanished from the back seat. Driving to the address which the girl had given, they questioned a woman there, who said such events happened often after the girl's death in a collision. The two young men had a Mass said for the repose of the young woman's soul.

A truck driver driving from Owego to Elmira, a few years later, picked up a young woman wearing black clothing who had hailed his truck. The passenger wouldn't talk to her driver, however, and he became engrossed in staying on the road. When he finally looked at her again, she had vanished from the seat beside him. This was one of three such reports that preceded the Endicott Police Chief's experience, by which time the girl had changed to white again.

Prior to 1944, a traveling salesman passing through Devil's Elbow saw a girl walking in the rain and picked her up, offering his rear seat. She gave him a destination address and settled back. A few miles later, he turned to talk to her and found the seat empty. Stunned, he pulled over and closely examined the back seat; he found it completely dry. Arriving at the address, the salesman met a woman who identified herself as the girl's mother, and who said the girl had died on that road five years before.

Another imprecise (as to detail) story tells of a minister and his wife from Greene traveling toward Binghamton, though it isn't clear where they were coming from. They saw a young woman wearing an evening dress and slippers on the road and offered her a ride. She told the couple of being in an accident and gave a destination address. The girl vanished from her seat and, when the couple went to the address, a distraught mother told of losing her daughter two months earlier in an auto accident following a school dance.

The entries go on and on, with a strong similarity in the stories. One is tempted to excuse the similarity with the term "urban legend," a story told and retold, with details shaded anew with each retelling. Yet, the local press seems to have covered the stories, leaving them in journals and newspapers for Cox to find years later. His manuscript contains countless entries of a similar nature from Rochester, Syracuse, Utica, New Paltz and New York City.

The "hitchhiker ghost" seems to be the most common of ghost stories, unless one also considers "the murdered pack peddler" type. Close on the heels of these is the deceased relative (most often, a grandfather or grandmother who appears to comfort the living, often attempting to coddle or cuddle survivors, especially babies). Even if a few of these anecdotes are urban legends, readers should know that there is some historic event at the root of most such legends.

Assuming these stories are accurate in principle, if not in every last detail, why would an accident victim hang around for untold decades, reenacting the pre-death activities? One bit of angst that many victims of accidents seem to retain is the urge to let next of kin know that they have died. Should your family lose a member in a sudden death, it might be healing to address the individual's spirit, saying that you know they have died, but that they are also now safe in Greater Hands and can relax in the safety of that Being. Another case that I recently studied indicates that the traffic victim is still overcome with shame for having stepped in front of the oncoming car. Shame is a big anchor to souls—they seem unable to forgive themselves or seek forgiveness from a higher source. Ultimately, it's an ego thing.

The precise location of Devil's Elbow is hard to ascertain, as there has been road straightening on the highway, but Roxanne Yaple, a former student of mine, informs me that the spot might be found just west of Glen Mary Road. The Tioga County Historical Society (info@tiogahistory.org) sells a small book (for $4) entitled *Tioga County Ghostly Tales*, from which I have drawn some details for this story.

Before I concluded my investigations along Route 17C, I met a former Tioga County Sheriff's Deputy, who agreed that the regional place name has recently fallen into disuse. After pausing a bit, he added a bit more to the area's legend, on the condition of anonymity, of course.

"In 1981, while doing our routine patrol, my partner and I checked buildings for open doors and other security concerns," he told me. "The hamlet of Tioga Center is only a little over a mile southwest of the Devil's Elbow turns on the river. When we drove down Fifth Avenue, to the Tioga Center Elementary School, we discovered an open door. It seemed possible that some local vandals might be inside, so we entered. There were a few lights turned on in the hallways, so it wasn't dark. We discovered no one, however, nothing out of order, and finished our search by checking out the auditorium.

"We thoroughly checked that large room and even went up onto the stage, to be sure no one was hiding there. All that was on the stage was a piano, in the center, with a single overhead light shining down on it. After checking behind the piano, we figured it was all just a false alarm. Readying to leave, I drew my fingers across the piano keys, creating a little tune. Then, from the rear of the seats, there came a scream. That sure got our attention, especially after we had just adjudged the building empty. We instantly drew our guns and took cover behind the piano. Who was back there? We looked for a fleeing silhouette against the open doorway, and seeing none, we separated and edged toward the back of the room.

"But there was nobody there! How could a nobody scream like that? We did everything we could to explain to one another what had happened, but there was nothing in our training that explained a voice without a body. We really didn't want to use the word ghost, but what other explanation was there? On the way home, my partner suggested that a spirit was trying to warn me away from a career in music. I'm sure my tinkling the keys wasn't that bad," he said with a smile. Apparently, several present members of the Sheriff's Department regard the school building, mainly the older part, with some suspicion. How can disembodied voices be explained, especially on a police report?

So, there is one more story, a more modern-day episode to add to the legends along the Susquehanna River in Tioga County.

To Plan or Not to Plan

On April 7, 1958, Peter John Butterman of Fulton, N.Y., entered the State Street Elementary School in that town and shot the janitor, Fred Maude, several times. Then, stooping, he took Maude's wallet and emptied it. Hmmph! Just ten dollars. Oh well, it's better than nothing. Butterman then hurried to the Barge Canal and threw his stolen Luger pistol into the water below the Oneida Street Bridge. Before the pistol had sunk to the bottom, Fred Maude was dead.

When he didn't return home for lunch, his wife went in search of him and was horrified to find her mate in a pool of blood in the school's cellar hallway. Fulton Police knew who to look for, and within twenty-four hours, Butterman was in custody.

The community buzzed for months. Why would that twenty-year-old want to kill Fred Maude? they wondered. All the elementary school kids loved him, though he occasionally tossed eggs at certain wise guys. Maude had even befriended Butterman when the lad was a student at State Street School. Fred was a whiz with electronics and had set up a ham radio club for students after World War II. Even the local police, when their patrol cars had radio problems, would visit Fred at school and get his advice or help in making repairs. Everyone loved Fred, and there was a big crowd in support of his wife and children at the funeral. Later that day, Fred Maude was laid to rest.

Initially, Butterman was confined in the Syracuse Psychiatric Hospital, then jailed for a long term after being found guilty at his trial. Curiously, he was found dead under suspicious circumstances in a field in Syracuse forty-two years later, a victim himself, though the death was ruled accidental.

As Butterman sauntered toward a showdown at The Pearly Gates, Fred Maude's spirit continued his regular chores in the school building. Often, new custodians at the school during the 1960s through the 1990s found lights burning in a room that had been cleaned, had its lights extinguished, and doors locked. They had to do the chore of closing the room once more. Once, a school administrator looked up to see a hall door opening and closing itself, and many times, there were strange noises from the school cellar when the building was almost vacant and the custodians had left. Doors that had been secured were found strangely unlocked and/or opened.

In later years, the school ended its educational function and the building became the home for Fulton's ARC program for adult clients. A man named Ron worked as custodian there in recent years, doing the work that Fred Maude had done four decades earlier. Incidents continued to occur in the school's lower hallways after hours, and the young custodian reported sensing that someone continually walked alongside him as he swept. Interestingly, Ron had never heard of Fred Maude or his grizzly end.

So it may be that Fred is just getting in some after time overtime, or maybe he sees himself as mentor to the old school's new and ever-changing custodial staff.

Fred didn't plan to die that April day in 1958 and, thus, had to wrestle with the exigencies of his sudden departure from the flesh, if not also the job.

But there are fortunate others who see the Grim Reaper coming and make detailed preparations. The following isn't really a ghost story, but old Dr. Waters is out there somewhere, though we're not sure we know where.

Dr. Columbus Waters was a local sawbones who lived on Oneida Street in Fulton and died in 1859. Having sensed his end coming at him slowly for several years, Waters prepared for all eventualities and inserted them in his meticulously drawn will. Because most physicians of his time understood catatonic trance, Waters was suspicious that an inert body (perhaps even his own) might not actually be dead. And, as embalming was in its infancy at the time and funerals were rather impromptu affairs, Waters understood that a man might find himself below ground in a hurry, though he might not yet have had his ticket officially punched.

Determined not to be one of those living corpses, Dr. Waters bought a burial plot in Mt. Adnah Cemetery and had an elaborate mausoleum constructed upon it, just waiting for him *in extremis*. In the chamber, a simple rack was built to hold his specially moulded casket. Made of cast iron and shaped to fit his own body, the burial container had a removable lid. If Waters found himself still alive after the mausoleum was sealed, all he had to do was push up on the coffin lid, step out into the crypt, and find the matches and candle that he'd arranged to have standing by. Then, in the candle's glow, he'd retrieve the vault's key from a hook and let himself out into the world again until The Real Thing did happen. Readers might well guess that Dr. Waters, once he was buried, never came out under his own power.

A few years later, when the physician still hadn't emerged, local occultists conducted a séance in order to contact the good man's spirit. "I am very uncomfortable," the medium reported Waters as saying, "because the coffin pinches my feet." And that was the end of the message. For a communication from beyond the grave, the response left a lot to be desired philosophically.

In the 1980s, John Byard, a Fulton-area researcher of odd goings-on, sought more information on the good doctor, whose burial centennial had already passed. Byard sought out Milan Hubbard, superintendent of the Mt. Adnah Cemetery, and asked to see the doctor's mausoleum, which was precisely marked on the cemetery sketch. The two went to the appointed spot and found—nothing! No mausoleum at all, but instead, a number of smaller headstones bearing names that were not of the Waters family. Who would steal an entire mausoleum?

All Byard could turn up was a bill of sale by which the Waters family had conveyed the plot to others after the doctor's interment. But there was no mention of the removal of the mausoleum! Then, Byard mentioned the curious fact to local historian George Wise, who made it a priority to dig deeply (to coin a phrase) into the matter. Finally, George found the answer in a microfilm copy of the *Fulton Times* dated November 9, 1881. The correspondent had noted that the cemetery roadway was to undergo straightening that year, and that arrangements had been made to remove the Waters vault to another section of the cemetery, though the writer didn't specify the new location. And, apparently, the new site wasn't entered in the cemetery records. In a macabre addendum, the story writer noted, "The remains are in a remarkable state of preservation and were easily recognizable by old acquaintances."

George Wise concluded that the cemetery crew may have found it more expedient to just dig a new hole in the ground and not bother re-erecting the vault. My own thought is that the movers might easily have broken or damaged the stonework, leading to a more pedestrian location for Waters' remains until Gabriel announces that time is up.

Up the River

This old tale is a short one preserved by Elizabeth Bilobrowka, former St. Johnsville librarian, who used reputable sources in the stories she recorded for Utica television station WKTV in a series of 1955 programs.

Did the Iroquois ancestors in what is now New York State have ghosts to contend with? Because these wraiths are a human phenomenon, not limited by nationality or geography, it seems certain that they did. Nevertheless, Tom Porter, Mohawk chief, told me that Indians don't talk to or about ghosts. They are generally considered "bad medicine" in Iroquois lore.

Nevertheless, non-Indians seem to have witnessed the departed natives on at least one occasion. Bilobrowka asserts that, in the Colonial Period of our history (roughly 1614-1783), one old Mohawk remained alive in the forests west of Schenectady. The man was something of a recluse, coming into the white man's settlement only twice a year to purchase or trade for necessities.

One day, the native was fortunate to make a great catch of fish in the Mohawk River. Shortly afterward, he approached a white settler and gave the man his entire catch, giving only the briefest of presentation speeches, "Great Spirit call—Indian no need." Then, leaving the puzzled colonial scratching his head on the shore, the Indian walked to the riverbank, stepped into his canoe and paddled westward, upstream.

Children playing along the river noted that the canoe moved against the current, onward and upstream, though the lone Indian passenger sat erect, with his arms folded, in the stern. No paddle was evident, so how could the canoe move? Finally the boat vanished around the bend and the boys only told of the strange event later, over supper.

The following week, the Indian's canoe was found drifting far downstream, though there was no sight of its owner. Then, perhaps a week later, a settler who knew the Indian, was fishing among the river's islands and spotted his old acquaintance seated upon the shore of an island. Rowing toward the old-timer, the settler called out, offering the native a ride to shore. Hardly had the echo of his words died out than the Indian became transparent and faded from sight.

For many years, the librarian attested, the Indian's spirit was seen seated on that island, always with arms clasped around his knees, and staring upriver toward the Mohawk's far-away source. There have been no such reports, however, since the middle 1950s.

A Rocky Trail

Rocky Trail
Courtesy of Stewart Orcutt

I thought I'd share this odyssey with my readers as the volume concludes, if only to show that folk legends (urban legends) of ghosts and cemeteries can be so misleading, even if there seems to be great "evidence."

In 2001, while researching a story in Maine, I wandered through the old cemetery at Pinelands, a former state institution, where. I met a nice couple from Canandaigua, N.Y. We compared our reasons for searching, and when they heard that I research mystery and history, they told me of a strange cemetery in Penn Yan, a place that "everybody" in the Finger Lakes Region knew about. The details sounded appropriately weird and I made a mental note to follow up on the story of "The Lady in Stone."

A co-ed from Keuka College, among several alumnae, related the often-told tale sweetly and briefly. Long ago, there was a man who cheated on his wife and she was helpless. Eventually, she lay on her deathbed and the Romeo husband paced the room waiting for the Grim Reaper to come and free him. He

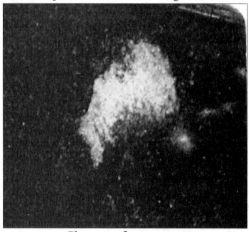

Close up of monument
Courtesy of Stewart Orcutt

told his dying spouse that he'd be glad when she was gone, but she responded that she would never go. "I'll return, you'll see!" she warned, and also told her close friends of the threat.

After the wife's funeral, the student told me, a large gravestone was placed over the woman's grave, but soon the black granite developed a strange whitish blemish and local people recognized it as the profile head-and-shoulders silhouette of the dead wife. Allegedly, the

stone has been replaced many times, yet the image kept reappearing. Was the dead woman making good on her threat?

That was a story worthy of Ripley's Believe it or Not, and I thought the trail to truth would be easy. But not so. First, "all the Keuka girls", I was told, knew the woman's identity: she was, in fact, the first female president of the college, who died in the early 1960s. And, even more, the girl told me, as the woman's face appears higher and higher on the gravestone each time it's replaced, after the next replacement, the face will reach the stone's top, whereupon Ball Hall, one of the college's oldest buildings, will collapse. Well, it sure gives the students something to look forward to.

I consulted Fran Dumas, the Penn Yan historian, on this matter, and when she finished laughing, she told me of the time in 1995 when she liked to sit quietly reading on the hill in Penn Yan's Lakeview Cemetery. "The silence would suddenly be broken by screeching brakes and a car loaded with teens would zoom up the road to stop in front of the Bishop/Gillette stone. Kids jumped out and suddenly became quiet in awe of the supernatural story of the lady's revenge. Then they laughed, screamed, touched the stone, returned to their cars and zoomed away. So many high school and college kids are absolutely certain that their version of the story is the real truth."

One Keuka College alumna told me that, during her college years, Keuka co-eds made pilgrimages to the grave and ran their hands across the whitish image. "We believed that homage would give us good marks on final exams," she said with a twinkle in her eye.

So, what's the story? Do we have a case of retribution here, divine or worldly?

Mrs. Dumas told me that she has found countless variations on the story, but here is the historical record. The woman in question is Sarah (Haines) Bishop Shove, who lived from 1832 to 1904. Her first husband was Caleb W. Bishop (1834-1895), and the only remote connection to the deceased Keuka College President, Katherine Gillette Blyley, is that they shared the Gillette family relationship, as the cemetery lot is in the name of Matilda Gillette (1859-1936), a member of the Haines family.

Sarah clearly outlived Caleb, as she married Mr. Shove later. The legend says that the stone is continually replaced by the guilty widower, but Mrs. Dumas assures me (consider the size of the pictured memorial stone, then estimate its cost, even in the early 1900s) that this is the original marker. To replace the stone in Twenty-first century dollars would require a king's ransom, I'd say. In any case, the reputed guilty husband will have long ago passed to his reward, and thus it isn't likely that any descendant would be willing to ante up for the stone's replacement. Sorry, Keuka students, Ball Hall's future seems guaranteed, and, apparently, study will still be required to pass those finals.

One variation on the story says with certitude that the stone's image is only visible at night, but please consult the photo again, taken by Stewart Orcutt, a Geneva resident—it's daytime. Others vow that the head can be seen only when the stone is wet. Stewart took this photo for me on a dry sunny day. Some assert that the cemetery is locked at night, so nobody can say for sure whether or not the stone glows in the dark, as some have said. That reputed glowing also seems apocryphal, as there is no recorded testimony to that fact, only the rumor, and there isn't any real gate. A retired engineer in the village smilingly notes that the silhouette side of the stone faces eastward, the direction in which the image will be illuminated by the rising moon.

Fran Dumas adds that "the stone is right next to the cemetery's central road, so it is very easy to find, even at night. In any case, many young people do visit the stone after dark because some have heard that it glows. Perhaps the attribution of a glowing stone seems credible because of the dark and ominous color of the stone. Mrs. Dumas adds with a smile that perhaps the scary stories do serve a purpose, as the curious stone has never been defaced or vandalized.

Wanting to get some "hard facts," I contacted Jeff Martell at Granite Industries of Vermont in Barre. Viewing the photo that I sent, Jeff puzzled aloud. "That is certainly Quincy granite," he said, "quarried near Quincy, Massachusetts. Sometimes such dark stone will have or develop what we call 'white knots,' which will appear throughout a monument, but this image is too localized for that to be true here. There is an outside chance that somebody might have used a very strong cleaner to wash the monument, but who does that—especially on polished granite? This is certainly strange!" So, to a rock man, the phenomenon is indeed strange. That the image appears to be a woman is stranger still. Yet, nobody seems to present a credible candidate as the scorned woman. Likely, somebody would have to make up a story just to fit what "everybody can see." So, in the end, it is a mystery, though there may not be any ghost there.

Young people have always been adventurous and there seems to be a human inclination to touch the ineffable, the mysterious, or that which seems to occur beyond the bounds of science. For that reason, the spate of television ghost research programs and the rapid growth of amateur spirit hunting groups is thus understandable. It seems preferable, except for the individuals that Mrs. Dumas has seen cringing at the foot of cemetery hill on Elm Street (young people afraid to confront Sarah Bishop Shove's stone in the dark) to reach out and touch a magic stone. The true magic, I've discovered, is not in what we touch outwardly, but what we touch within ourselves that is transcendental.

VOLUME TWO
NEW YORK STATE
GHOSTS

ACKNOWLEDGEMENTS
AND INDEX

Acknowledgments
Many thanks to these individuals for assisting me in story collections and research:

John Abbott
Lorrene Adams
Leslie Allen
Carrie Anderson
Judith Baldwin
Stephanie T. Bambina
Charles Barnett III
Spike Barton
Crystal Bass
Ritamary Bell
Leana Bleimiller
Blodgett Library
Joe Bonk
Laura Botka
John Breithaupt
Johnna Brennan
Lee Briggs
Frances D. Broderick
Warren Broderick
Marion Flint Brooks
Buffalo Public Library
Pat Burget
Pat Burns
John Byard
Connie Cavallo
Micki Chapman
Dan Clark
Raymond & Sue Comish
Peter & Sue Conlin
Wally Cook
Nick Conti
Fran Corey
Cheryl Ann Costa
George Coyle
Gae Crosby
Dawn DeVoe
Lynne Dolan
Tony Daou
Douglas Dean
Maureen Dempsey
Bob Dingman
Nan Dixon

John Dousmanis
Fran Dumas
Dan Fortier
Peter & Judy Foster
Cherie Freeman
Sandy Freyer
Tonya Frickey
Bill Fries
Lonnie Gale
Victoria Garlanda
Monica Gartler
Peter & Holly Gaskin
Gazel, Ed
Anita Gehrke
David Gens
David Gerling
W.G. Gerthe
William Getz
Linda Goebel
Linda Grillo
Janice Guy
Janice Hagglund
James & Carol Hill
Howard Hayes
Frank Hoenig
Donna Howay
Gary Howard
Ken & Marcy Hussey
Stana Iseman
John Jensen
Charlotte Johnson
Luigi & Victor Kapiti
Ray Karpicki
Terry Kelly
Vance Kibe
Molly Kilb
Susie K. Wilkening
Tamara King
Lois Kling
Richard Knapp
Carle Kopecky
Jeremy & Laura Kristel

Ed Lannigan
Tammy Larry
Jim LaFave
Dorothy Laselva
Rosemary Lattimer
Kathleen Lenhardt
Mac & Carol Lewis
Vin & Kathy Lombardi
Bill Lynch
Jeff Martell
June Maxam
Larry Marrish
Linda Warner-Marrish
Ashley Mazzone
Marian & Vin McCann
Gail McKenna
Donna Merrill
Lesli Mitchell
Corbie Mittlieb
Jackie Moody
Wayne Mosher
Florence Murtha
Faye Nadler
Cathy Neal
Barbara Nichols
Michael & Maeve Noonan
Christopher Nowak
Cheryl Olsen
Bill & Pat Orcutt
Stewart Orcutt
The Oswego Players
Inez Parker
Perry Paul
Laura Pearsall
Amanda Pentak
Doug Plummer
Frank Porpora
Rebekah Porray
Tom Pray
David Preston
Kim Preston
Rensselaer Cty. Hist Soc.

Pam Ribbing
Melinda Riggs
Garth Roberts
Russell Roberts
Larry Rose
Ken Rossi
Linda Roy
Peter Ruckdeschel
Gayle Ruggiero
Lauren Saltsman
Jim & Betsy Scheffel
John Shaffer
Kathy Sheaks
Amy Sheffield
Tammy Sherwood
Jessica Simpson
Diane Singer
Lloyd & Diane Smith
Frank & Ana Sporer
Deborah Stein
Tamme Stitt
James & Denise Strait
Gary Strauss
Marc Strauss
Vincent J. Tampio
Lori Thompson
Tioga County Hist. Soc.
Kevin Toomey
Steve Totten
Michael & Petra Trunkes
Lori Van Vranken
Rick Wakefield
Marc Wasserman
Fred Wickert
Maureen Wildman
Susan Wilson
George Wise
Gerri Yager
Peter Zendzian

INDEX